The Jews in the Roman World

The Jews in the Roman World

Michael Grant

Charles Scribner's Sons
New York

Contents

Contents

Maps and Plan

Acknowledgments

The author and publishers would like to thank the following for granting permission to quote from copyright sources: Cambridge University Press and Oxford University Press for the New English Bible; English Universities Press (and Penguin Books) for A. H. M. Jones, *Constantine and the Conversion of Europe*; Heinemann and Harvard University Press, the Loeb Classical Library, for Josephus, vol. i *Against Apion*, I, vol. II *Jewish War*, VI, vol. ix *Jewish Antiquities*, XVIII; Macmillan for A. H. M. Jones (ed.), *A History of Rome through the Fifth Century*, vol. II; Penguin Books for Tacitus, *Annals*, XV, *Histories*, V; Pliny, *Letters*, X; Juvenal, *Satires*, VI and XIV; Thornton and Butterworth for A. D. Nock, *St. Paul*.

Introduction

To study the Jews in the Roman world is one of the best ways of making close contact with that world, because although the ancient Romans and the Greeks have gone for ever, the Jews are still with us: in them, continuity between ancient and modern life exists for everyone to see. Numerically, taken over the whole earth, they were fewer in those days than they are now – perhaps eight million as against fourteen million today. But no less than seven of these eight million were in the Roman empire, where they constituted between six and nine per cent of the population – in the eastern provinces, the percentage was perhaps as high as twenty. Comprising, as they did, such a high proportion of the total number of inhabitants, they could scarcely fail to exercise an influence upon events; and given their highly distinctive beliefs and customs, so divergent from the Greco-Roman way of life which surrounded them, it was predictable that their relations with their neighbours would become both dramatic and explosive.

And that, indeed, is what happened. A writer on this great subject, whatever his own inadequacies, has the advantage of one of the most absorbing and exciting themes in the history of the world. For he is called upon to display the workings of the greatest multiracial empire the world has ever known, and to show how its Greek and Roman and particularly Jewish communities all kept up a continual, triangular effort to maintain their own points of view: he also has to describe how, more than once, these endeavours crashed in terrible catastrophe.

We derive our civilization, it has often been said, from Athens, Rome and Jerusalem. While the stark simplicity of this assertion has been somewhat eroded in our own times by the recognition of Byzantium's intermediary role, and by the claims of the Germanic and Celtic north, yet the old saying still contains a great deal of truth. However, it is only rarely that students of history fully pursue its implications and objectively attempt to consider the three cultures side by side with one another. For most of us, apart from specialists, are conditioned to regarding Athens (or, for the purposes of the present study, let us rather say its successor Alexandria) and Rome as secular subjects, but Jerusalem as a different sort of subject altogether, a religious concept and theme which cannot be regarded as history in quite the same way.

This attitude inevitably hampers our endeavours to discover what was going on. For when we turn to the ancient authorities for the information that we require, it becomes clear that they fail to give us the balanced picture for which we might have hoped. Pagan writers are always ignorant of the Jewish world and usually biased against it; and the biblical sources, even when seemingly historical or biographical, prove to be *primarily* concerned with another matter altogether, the demonstration of the super-natural, supra-historical, validity of their faith. There remains another Jewish historian, Josephus. Nowadays much neglected, he is a writer who deserves and demands urgent attention. But, for reasons of his own – which will emerge in the course of this story – he, too, does not rank high among historians for objectivity.

So the attempt to describe the interrelationship of Jews, Greeks and Romans presents challenging difficulties and problems, which can only be approached with great diffidence. The late Cecil Roth's remark, that the author of any general account of the Jews needs to know 'not just everything about one thing or something about everything, but everything about everything', scarcely helps to dispel that justified diffidence. Nevertheless the effort, however formidable and numerous the pitfalls which beset it, surely needs to be made. For religion is an immensely significant part of secular history: whether god-given or delusive, its beliefs and cults have guided people more powerfully than any other force. And yet in this field of ancient history, covering all-important centuries for Judaism and paganism alike, we find ourselves hindered in conducting the investigation that is needed. We are hindered, as we have seen, because our information about the vital Athens (Alexandria)–Rome–Jerusalem axis, the necessary basis of any reconstruction of that age, is so very uneven. It is essential, therefore, to try to even it out, presenting each of its elements according to just the same sort of historical criteria as the others, in the hope that the true relations between the three of them will then emerge.

This is all the harder, and yet all the more urgently needed, because of the most significant of all the developments that overtook Judaism in the Roman world. For this was the time when the Jewish religion, in addition to achieving new forms of its own that have proved durable and permanent, gave birth to the Christians: a body of Jews who, unlike the majority of their nation, believed that, in the not so very distant past, the awaited Messiah had already come to live for a time upon the earth. Within a century after the date ascribed to his death, his followers had become completely independent of world Jewry. But until that final rift occurred, they were still linked in various ways with the Jewish origina-tors of their church – so that they form a part, and some will say the most important part, of the present story. The final separation between Christians and Jews 'is coming to be seen by many scholars, both Chris-tian and Jewish, as a greater disaster by far than any subsequent schism within the Christian church itself'.[1] Whether it was a disaster or not – from the point of view of the spiritual salvation of mankind – is not my present concern. My purpose is to show, as far as I can, how this situa-tion, throughout the various dramatic stages of its development, affected the relationship between Jews, Greeks and Romans which is the subject of my book.

For the same reason, I do not in the least aspire to present a general picture of the Jewish or Christian religions at this epoch. I only seek to pinpoint those aspects of the faiths which chiefly affected their impact upon one another, and once again upon the Greeks and Romans. In order to fulfil this aim, it will be necessary to begin with a brief intro-duction referring to some of the landmarks of early Hebrew history and legendary history, for the Jews continued, through the period we are considering as well as later periods, to conduct their relations with other peoples, and indeed almost all the affairs of their lives, in un-remitting recollection of these sagas. As for the end of the story, I have concluded, apart from a brief epilogue, with the conversion of the Roman empire to Christianity, because this was the most decisive of all changes in the religious power-structure of the ancient Mediterranean world, confronting the Jews with an entirely new set of problems which superseded the themes handled in the present volume.

Terminology offers an almost hopeless problem – though it is the sort of problem which, to someone who has lived in Ireland, is not wholly unfamiliar. For example, if one says 'BC' and 'AD' one seems to some to be approaching the entire matter from too much of a Christian stand-point, whereas the Jewish terms BCE (Before the Common Era) and CE (Common Era) suggest an exclusive preoccupation with the Jewish point of view. Since one has to choose, I shall employ 'BC' and 'AD' – because it is a more common usage than the other. One is also very frequently confronted with the problem whether to spell a name in its Jewish or Greek shape, the former being employed by the Hebrew writers and the latter by Josephus, whose works, as they have come down to us, are in Greek. Here again, I have been guided merely by the reader's convenience; the multiplicity of identical or similar names in the period is already so confusing that my chief concern has been not to add to the confusion, and with this in mind I have often put both forms in the index. And should one, in presenting a Jewish name, say 'the son of' or 'ben'? I have tended to reserve 'ben' for the later period, when rabbis are customarily described by this patronymic. Again, when one speaks of the two great Jewish uprisings against the Romans, non-Jewish writers tend to call them Jewish Revolts, whereas Jews describe them by a variety of other terms; and in particular they often designate the first of them (AD 66–73) as the Roman War, or the War against the Romans. I shall tend to call them Jewish revolts or rebellions against the Romans, not because I necessarily hold a brief for Roman methods, but for the factual reason that these upheavals *were* revolts or rebellions against the occupying power: whether their leaders are best described as freedom fighters or terrorists (another controversial point), to call them rebels is a statement of fact.

But this sort of difficulty reaches its height, as Dr James Parkes recently recalled (in his book *Whose Land?*), in the question of how that land itself ought to be named. Whether we call it Israel, Judaea, the Promised Land, the Holy Land or Palestine, 'each name has a slant in favour of one hypothesis or another'.[2] Perhaps it is best to call it by different names at different stages of its history, especially as its successive geographic swellings and shrinkages affect the appropriateness of this or that designation. But I do not pretend to be consistent. At least, however, my use of one name or another – or for that matter of terms such as Torah, the Law, the Old Testament, or New Testament – does not imply any political or religious partisanship. If any picture of Jewish learning and heroism, Christian perseverance and devotion, Roman grandeur and (at many times) tolerance emerges from the book, I shall be glad, but I should not wish any one viewpoint to eclipse the other two.

Writers about the world of antiquity sometimes complain not only (as I have) of the unreliability of the ancient sources, but also of their sparse, inadequate volume and quantity. Here, however, such a complaint would be somewhat less justified than usual, since we have at our disposal not only the writings of the Greeks and Romans (in so far as these have survived) but also those of the Jews – the only one of the subject peoples of Rome who possessed, and continued to possess, a great literature of their own. For this reason, as A.H.M.Jones, that great student of Judaism within the Greco-Roman framework, pointed out, 'Palestine is almost the only district of the empire whose story we knew not from the point of view of the Roman government but from that of the subject people. From its history we can learn what the Roman empire meant to the vast majority of its inhabitants, who did not live in Italy and belong to the ruling race.'[3]

Because of this unique situation, the modern literature on every aspect of these deeply significant developments has been vast. With regard to the Jews, that wonderful people who have spanned the ages like no other, every incident of their ancient history has been the subject of a host of special studies. When one comes, moreover, to the early Christians, who against all conceivable odds proceeded to the conquest of the western world, the number of such works mounts to gigantic proportions. I have therefore felt obliged, with few and unavoidable exceptions, to limit the references in my notes to original, ancient sources, since otherwise the notes would have been twenty times as long as the book itself. With regard to studies undertaken in our own times, I have listed a few of the most essential works at the end of this volume.

I am very grateful to Mr F.G.B.Millar for showing me an unpublished lecture, to Mr J.C.T.Oates for bibliographical advice, and to Mr Julian Shuckburgh, Miss Susan Phillpott and Miss Gila Curtis, of Messrs Weidenfeld and Nicolson Ltd, for seeing this book through the press and making many valuable suggestions.

MICHAEL GRANT

Gattaiola, 1973

Part I

The Jews Before the Romans

I

Prologue: The Traditions of Israel

The nucleus of ancient Israel, and now of modern Israel too – though until 1967 the greater part of the area belonged to the kingdom of Jordan – is the broken table-land round Jerusalem, roughly corresponding with the territory known in Roman times as Judaea.[1] It is a small plateau, slightly smaller than the county of Essex and a little larger than Rhode Island: from north to south, it measures about thirty-five miles, and from east to west only about twelve or fifteen. A rocky, stony, largely waterless moorland, rising to over 3000 feet, it contains deep gorges and narrow defiles ideal for guerrilla operations. Rough scrub and thorns contend with heaps of boulders; and rain, eked out by dew, is less reliable and predictable than anywhere else in the Mediterranean – the Bible often refers to God withholding it in his displeasure. Yet there are enough fertile places to make two thirds of the region habitable.

To the west, the rounded limestone hills slope down to the Mediterranean plain, which has not played a great part in the country's history since in this region it is short of adequate harbours. To the east, the heights descend sharply to the hollow profundities of the Jordan valley and the Dead Sea, at the head of which stands torrid, tropically lush Jericho, the home of magnificent date palms. On the table-land between Mediterranean and Dead Sea, in the centre of Judaea, a projecting spur houses the city of Jerusalem, the ancient capital of Israel. But it was a strange, relatively isolated capital, recommended by no river, no major road, no convenient market for foreigners. The site of Jerusalem has often stimulated a passionate local patriotism indifferent to the world, a stubborn concentration on values that care little for the values of others.

To the north, separated by a belt of lower hills, rose the central highland of Samaria, the land of Mount Ephraim and its shrine, Gerizim. Samaria was a little larger than Judaea, more fertile and better wooded, more favourably equipped with rain and running water. The people of Samaria, more numerous than the Judaeans, lived at an observation point from which they could look down on the lowlands around them. And look down they did in every sense, for their habits and beliefs were their own, as particularistic, separate and censorious as those of their Judaean neighbours, with whom their relations were generally disastrous.

Indeed, in all these miniature lands hostile parochialisms thrived, and maintained themselves over the centuries. This was also true of the land of Galilee, which could be seen when one looked northward from Samaria across the plain of Jezreel (Esdraelon). On the east side, Galilee extended to the 'Sea' of that name (Lake Gennesaret), 680 feet below sea-level, into which the River Jordan formed itself at that point – the border between modern Israel and Syria until the Israelis annexed the adjacent strip of Gaulanitis (Golan Heights) in 1967. To the north, Upper Galilee, a series of plateaux surrounded by hills between 2000 and 4000 feet high, rose gradually into Mount Lebanon. Nearer at hand, Lower Galilee was a series of parallel ranges and valleys. This was the richest and most populous part of Israel, studded with hundreds of peasant villages, and with small but excellent stretches of cornland and attractive orchards. And above all, Galilee was covered with roads that ran everywhere: roads leading to the outside world, to Tyre and Sidon on the coast of what is now the Republic of Lebanon, and to Damascus, the chief city of inland Syria. The Galileans, there-fore, had freer intercourse with the external heathen than either the Judaeans or the Samaritans. And so the two latter peoples, disunited from one another in everything else, were united in hating the men of Galilee, whose coarse, guttural dialect they liked to mock. The Galileans, for their part, maintained a strong individuality, carrying bravery in Quixotic, seditious causes to violent and fanatical lengths.

Those are the three principal lands, Judaea, Samaria and Galilee, whose course must be followed in every attempt to reconstruct the ancient history of Israel; though the dislike their inhabitants felt for each other adds greatly to the difficulties of forming an objective impression of the course of events. To their east and south lay further territories which likewise belonged to the heritage of Israel, though they played a rather more shadowy part. To the east of Galilee, across the Jordan, Gaulanitis led into a vast stretch of crumpled and cracked lava, Trachonitis. There, agricultural colonization was attempted from time to time in order to swamp the local Arab shepherds and robbers, who in their turn were stirred to rebellion by the kingdom of the Nabataean Arabs, extending along the entire eastern and southern frontier of Israel.

To the south, Trachonitis bordered upon Israel's further Transjordanian territories of the Decapolis ('Ten Cities') and the Peraea, which comprised a fertile plain (Bashan), breezy highlands (Gilead), and steppes (Moab and Ammon). The Ten Cities were Greek, but the Peraea was inhabited mainly by Jews. Beyond it, the frontier with the Arab kingdom curled round the south of Israel, leaving the Negev and Sinai in Arab lands. Judaea's southern bastion on the border was Idumaea. It was a heritage of Edom, but that had lain further south, and its population had been displaced northwards as far as Hebron, within twenty miles of Jerusalem. In the Greek and Roman periods the inhabitants of this feudal land produced excellent soldiers, and powerful rulers of Israel. Though Arab in racial origin, the Idumaeans had by that time been converted to Judaism. But the pure-blooded Jews of Judaea claimed in antiquarian fashion that their Edomite forefathers had denied a passage to Moses,[2] and detested the Idumaeans quite as heartily as they disliked all their other neighbours.[3] Idumaea shaded from cultivation – producing vinegar but no good wines or grain – into half-desert, and to the east it descended into the Dead Sea Wilderness, a region of deep canyons and inaccessible, moistureless caves which will have its part to play in the present story because of the religious sects favouring this desolate region.

This, then, was Israel, measuring a hundred and fifty miles by less than seventy-five. If you came to it from the Mediterranean sea, it presented four successive strips or belts. First came the coastal plain, terminated at the north by Mount Carmel. Then rose the western highlands of Galilee, Samaria, Judaea and Idumaea, broken by the plain of Jezreel between Galilee and Samaria. Next came the Jordan valley, widening into the Sea of Galilee and the Dead Sea. And finally, in the background, could be seen the loftier regions across the Jordan.

Israel was not normally a grain-exporting country; for the most part it could only provide for itself, if that. Nor was it equipped, either by its natural position or resources, to create a great empire, though it had achieved this for a brief moment in the tenth century BC, under David and Solomon. For the most part the country was a pawn, the meeting place and battlefield of empires, an area of perpetual conflict. Before the Greeks and Romans came on the scene it had been, above all, the battlefield between the two great imperial powers of the near east, the Egyptians on the one hand and on the other the Assyrians, Babylonians and Persians, the successive lords of Mesopotamia, the land of the Tigris and Euphrates: as we shall see in the present story, these two regions were still exercising a powerful effect on Jewish history in the Greco-Roman age.

In the mind of a Jew of Roman times, the personages of ancient Jewish history and legend, however far back in the past, were still as vividly alive as any of his own day, and continued many hundreds of years after their deaths to play a part in successive events: which, indeed, are incomprehensible unless the ever-continued prominence of these antique models in Jewish thought is constantly borne in mind. Least of all peoples in the whole world did the Jews heed the words of the Book of Isaiah:

> Cease to dwell on days gone by
> and to brood over past history.[4]

First of all, there had been Adam and his sons, of whom Seth, more prominent in Jewish tradition than the Old Testament suggests, was the centre of many legends; he was known as the first of the 'Patriarchs', the scriptural heroes before Moses. Often revered, too, in later times was Enoch, the son of Adam's eldest son Cain or a descendant of Seth – who 'walked with God . . . because God had taken him away',[5] a precedent for the ascensions ascribed to others, including Jesus, in later times. His great-grandson was believed to have been Noah, whose rescue from the waters of the Flood was a perpetual symbol of Deliverance by God's will. Noah's three sons were Shem, Ham and Japheth. From the eldest of them, Shem, sprang the peoples speaking Semitic tongues. They were descended through Abraham,

6

who was said to have migrated from Ur in Chaldaea,[6] the ancient land of the Sumerians near the Persian Gulf, to Haran in the north of Mesopotamia, and back to the south again to 'Canaan', the later Israel; and then to the more fertile land of Egypt, before he turned northwards to Israel once more, and died at Hebron. His name and saga stands for authentic migrations that took place, over a considerable period, in the troubled centuries of the early second millennium BC; and they bring him and his people symbolically in touch with both the Mesopotamian and Egyptian centres of this near-eastern world.

In Jewish tradition, God gave Abraham a preliminary assurance of the Covenant which was destined to single out the Jews from other nations. 'This is how you shall keep my Covenant between myself and you and your descendants after you: circumcise yourselves, every male among you. You shall circumcise the flesh of your foreskin, and it shall be the sign of covenant between us.'[7] Where circumcision originated is a matter of dispute, but the Greeks and Romans believed that the Jews, like the Phoenicians who dwelt along the coast to their north, had learnt it from Egypt. The initial purpose of the institution, too, is obscure; but perhaps it was a sacrifice to the god of fertility, an initiation-rite which symbolized the individual's incorporation into the life of the group. At all events, circumcision came to be a national mark of consecration, the sign of a man who belonged to the service of God. Moreover, as the centuries passed, it gained rather than lost in significance, continuing even in Roman times to play a large part in successive events and crises. For, as in Israel today, it was still widely thought to constitute the most essential sign of Jewishness.

In about the sixteenth century BC the legendary Isaac, son of Abraham, reputedly had two sons, whose strife impinged upon all later times: Esau who was also called Edom and was regarded as the forefather of the Edomites and Idumaeans, and Jacob who was named Israel, the 'man who prevails with God', 'because you strove with God and with men, and prevailed'.[8] The story of Jacob's favourite son Joseph, the traveller to Egypt who became the vizier of one of its pharaohs and was invited by him to bring his father Jacob and his brothers to Egypt, is a genuine reflection of Jewish emigrations. And so Egypt, once again, cast its shadow on Palestinian history from the south, just as Mesopotamia cast its shadow from the north and east. The pharaoh who made Joseph his vizier may well have been the sun-worshipper Akhnaton, who, if so, could have set his stamp on subsequent

7

Jewish monotheism; and his successor who invited Joseph's family to the country was perhaps Tutankhamen.

Then, some time between 1450 and 1200 BC, many of the descendants of these Jewish settlers in Egypt returned to Canaan or Israel, to rejoin their compatriots there. This Exodus remained the most famous event in Jewish history, and in later centuries served countless Jews settled in foreign lands as a perpetual symbol of reunion with the home country. 'In every generation,' declared a rabbinical leader of Roman times, 'it behoves a man to see himself as if he personally had come out of Egypt.'[9] The Exodus was the decisive divine act of deliverance by which the nation was constituted, prefiguring the Salvation to come. Its leader, who was said to be the grandson of Jacob and son of Levi, possessed the Egyptian name of Moses, but was considered ever afterwards as the greatest of all Jewish heroes. The departure of the Jews was made possible, according to the tradition, by God's engulfment and annihilation of the pursuing Egyptian army in the 'Red Sea', and the Jews' rejoicings because of this event, repeated annually at the Festival of the Passover (Pesah), contributed largely to their unpopularity in Egypt in Roman times.

> The Lord ... opened the way in the sea
> And a path through mighty waters,
> And drew on chariot and horse to their destruction,
> A whole army, men of valour;
> There they lay, never to rise again;
> They were crushed, snuffed out like a wick.

Later, after the Jews reached the Sinai desert on the other side, Moses was given miraculous food, manna, from heaven. Moreover, when he smote the rock, fresh water gushed out; and this further illustration of God-sent deliverance can still be seen over and over again today depicted on the wall-paintings of the Christian catacombs of Rome, where these miracles were taken over from the Jews as prefigurations of Jesus' Last Supper and baptism. And then, as they moved forward to the part of Transjordan opposite Jericho, the soothsayer Balaam was said to have uttered to the king of Moab a Messianic prophecy which was never forgotten, 'that a star shall come forth out of Jacob, and a sceptre shall rise out of Israel'.[10]

But above all it was believed that God entrusted to Moses, upon Mount Sinai, the Covenant, of which advance notice, according to the

tradition, had already been granted to Abraham; and Moses trans-
mitted knowledge of it to the whole people. This Covenant, which no
Jews of later times have ever forgotten, and which later profoundly
affected their relations with the Romans as with every other great
state, was, in its origins, a spiritual echo of the type of relation which
these west Semitic tribes saw existing between themselves and the major
powers which exercised suzerainty over them. It was not a commercial
bargain or legal contract, but the Israelites' unconditional, eternal
pledge of loyalty to the God who had chosen them for deliverance. God
makes exclusive demands on man's will, and although the Covenant is
unilateral, laying no obligation upon the divine power in return, the
revelation supposedly conveyed to Moses explicitly added that their
fulfilment of their own duties of obedience (represented by the Ten
Commandments) would single them out as recipients of God's special
protection and guidance. 'If only,' God was understood to declare, 'you
will now listen to me and keep my Covenant, then out of all peoples
you shall become my special possession; for the whole earth is mine.
You shall be my kingdom of priests, my holy nation.'[11] Those words
were written centuries after the legendary time of Moses: but they
present a doctrine that had been present very early in Jewish religion.
This was the doctrine that the Jews were the Chosen People – the
belief which has dominated all their subsequent history, inspiring and
encouraging them to perpetual pride and endurance, and profoundly
affecting the story that is to be told in the present book. 'Chosen',
however, is a less accurate rendering than 'holy' – that is to say invested
with a special vocation, the nation through which the inscrutable way
and will of God were destined to take effect.

The result was unmistakably, and deliberately, the creation of a
barrier, a separateness. In the words ascribed to Balaam,

> I see a people that dwells alone,
> That has not made itself one with the nations.[12]

'Their Laws', a Persian minister later told his monarch, 'are different
from those of every nation; they do not keep your majesty's laws.'[13]
These 'Laws' of the Jews were handed to Moses on Mount Sinai by
God, who, as the supreme event and cornerstone of the Jewish conception of world history, 'gave him the two tablets of the Tokens, tablets
of stone written with the finger of God'. According to this vivid myth
the tablets were held to contain the first five books of the Jewish (and

subsequently Christian) faith, the Pentateuch: the books of Genesis, Exodus, Leviticus, Numbers and Deuteronomy. Reputed to have been composed before the creation of the world,[14] they relate the primitive history of man; the stories of Abraham and the other earlier Hebrew heroes; the Exodus and return as far as the border of the Promised Land; and God's transmission of the Pentateuch, the Torah, to Moses.

This Torah is the foundation of the Jewish religion, and everything else in all other scriptual books was held to be revealed or implied in its contents. The word is often translated as 'Law', and so it will be here, but its meaning is much wider – since religion and law were inseparable. In origin, 'Torah' probably meant 'instruction', by means of the divine revelation, and then it came to be understood in terms of the legislation which gradually grew around this nucleus – the vast interlocking system of observances upon which the continuity of Judaism throughout the millennia has depended. This design for an entire way of life, divine in origin and human in discipline, has irradiated every field of Jewish life, thought, feeling and action:

'See, I set before you this day a blessing and a curse' . . . . To know the Law and keep it in its entirety was the assured way of perfect blessedness. To infringe the least of its precepts was to bring down the vengeance of a justly incensed God, 'an eye for an eye, and a tooth for a tooth.' Such was the eternal justice, which God must vindicate, because he was God.[15]

When the Jews first formed such convictions, we cannot tell; the story of Moses dramatizes and conceals a prolonged period of growth and development. But, once formed, these beliefs were never abandoned. As Jewish writers of Roman times were still asserting – though their assertions contributed to the hostility which their people inspired in others – this Torah seemed to them immeasurably superior to anything the Greeks or Romans ever produced.

Its original custodian, when the Ark (coffer) to contain it had been constructed on Mount Sinai, was later believed to be the first high priest, Moses' own brother Aaron. His prominence, perhaps, was only magnified to that degree some eight or nine hundred years after these alleged events. But in Greek and Roman times much insistence was placed upon the Aaronic, high-priestly descent, and this caused embarrassment to successive regimes which could not lay a genealogical claim to its inheritance.

Jewish tradition (though not the Bible itself) tells how Moses, when he died, was taken up to the sky in a cloud,[16] thus joining the revered figures of the past who had likewise ascended to heaven. He had lived, it was believed, long enough to conduct the Israelites back as far as Transjordan, but not west of the river to the Promised Land itself. After his death this duty fell to Joshua – 'God is salvation', the same name as Jesus. The sagas attributed to his legendary personality stand for the militant thread in Jewish tradition: and his entry into the Holy Land, though presented as a 'single act under God's guidance', depicts a historical process in which successive groups of Jewish migrants from Egypt filtered into the country and took, one by one, the more vulnerable cities – as other peoples, notably the non-Semitic Philistines who gave Palestine its name, were doing at this same troubled time.

The next great figure, surely authentic, is Saul, who in the second half of the eleventh century BC established himself as ruler over a substantial nucleus of territory in Israel. He assumed the title of king, a status which, almost apologetically, was admitted to be a borrowing from other nations.[17] But perhaps the most influential of all the traditions associated with Saul was the story that one of the prophets of the time, Samuel, had anointed him:[18] for the Hebrew word for the anointed one was 'Messiah', a term which echoed through all subsequent Jewish history, most of all during the period that will be considered in this book.

Saul was succeeded by David, under whom the Jewish nation reached the peak of its political and military vigour, expanding into an empire which has remained in the minds of its militants ever since. David also founded the fortunes of the royal house of Judah (the southernmost of the twelve Israelite tribes, giving its name to the Roman Judaea). This family was revered as the keystone of Israel's ideal continuity,[19] and it was believed that the Messiah of the future would come from it: it was the house to which Christians claimed that Jesus belonged. Our accounts of the reign of David are relatively full, and represent the initiation, and at the same time the climax, of Hebrew historiography, of which one of the two main streams may date back almost to his own time. The principal historical events ascribed to David's rule were the absorption of part of the coastal strip and the capture of Jerusalem from the warrior tribe of Jebusites who had been its previous occupants. Jerusalem was not a new city; an idealized figure, Melchizedek, who was priest and king and was later seen as a forerunner of

Jesus, had ruled 'Salem' some eight centuries earlier. But henceforward, as David decided by a far-reaching and fateful act of statesmanship, this place was to be his capital – chosen because, situated on the border between the tribes of Judah and Benjamin (the names of two of Jacob's sons), it had no close, partisan, association with these or any others of the twelve Israelite tribes. And there in Jerusalem, henceforward, dwelt not only the king but the hereditary high priests. In David's time, it was said, there were two, descended from different branches of the family of Aaron; one of them, Zadok,[20] still had his followers a millennium later.

David's son Solomon converted his father's expanded Israel into a large and civilized and sophisticated state such as it has never been again until modern times. But the Jewish tradition, being kept alive by orthodox religious devotees, did not approve of his receptive cosmopolitanism, and out of all his many activities singled out only one for high praise: the construction of the First Temple at Jerusalem, which housed the Ark of the Law and became the revered centre of the Jewish religion.

After Solomon, the kingdom split into two. The ten northernmost Israelite tribes established a new dynasty, the house of Ephraim, to form the kingdom of Israel, which before long established its capital at Samaria, a new royal city in the middle of the land of that name. On the other hand the two southern tribes of Judah and Benjamin remained under the house of David as the kingdom of Judah, with its capital at Jerusalem. Though both these little states were harassed by successive great powers, Israel survived for over two hundred years and Judah for well over three hundred. Yet their only feature which imposed itself permanently upon subsequent tradition was the rise of the prophets. These were outspoken religious and social reformers who, for all their devotion to the Torah, separated themselves from the ritual functions of the priests and turned to wider aspects of the national life. By a phenomenon characteristic of Jewish history at many periods, these men of religion were by no means afraid to criticize their contemporary monarch, whoever he might be, judging his conduct according to the single yardstick of what they believed to be God's will. As the prophets saw it, there was a tripartite agreement between God, his people and the ruler – who might well forfeit the throne if he breached his part of the contract. So the prophets possessed the power to topple dynasties. Nathan had spoken out against David, and Elijah attacked

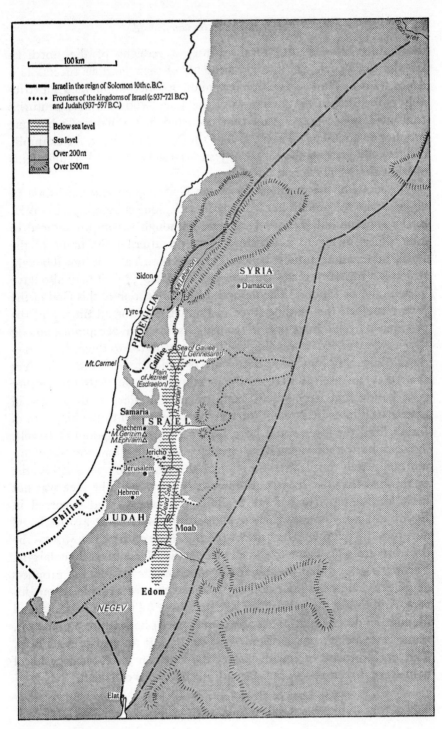

100 km

━━ Israel in the reign of Solomon 10th c. B.C.
•••• Frontiers of the kingdoms of Israel (c.937–721 B.C.) and Judah (937–597 B.C.)

Below sea level
Sea level
Over 200m
Over 1500m

SYRIA

• Damascus

Sidon •

PHOENICIA

Tyre •

Mt. Lebanon

Galilee

Sea of Galilee (L. Gennesaret)

Mt. Carmel

Plain of Jezreel (Esdraelon)

R. Jordan

Samaria

ISRAEL

Shechem •
M. Gerizim △
M. Ephraim △

Jericho •

Jerusalem •

Dead Sea

Hebron •

JUDAH

Moab

Philistia

Edom

NEGEV

Elat •

Euphrates

Biblical Israel and Judah

the immoralities of the ninth-century sovereigns of the northern kingdom of Israel. The pronouncements of their glorious successors – Amos, Hosea, the two Isaiahs, Jeremiah, Ezekiel – remained inextricably embedded in the memories of the Jews, who for many centuries continued to see every event that occurred in the light of what one prophet or another had said: so that the New Testament, for example, deliberately presents the career of Jesus as a mass of detailed fulfilments of what the prophets had forecast.

The name of the prophets' God, the God of Jews and Christians in all centuries to come, is known only from its four consonants, YHWH, in the consonantal Hebrew language. Although left unpronounced in later times, owing to a scriptural veto on uttering the name of the Lord,[21] the name is usually believed to have been Yahweh (not Jehovah, which is a mistaken reconstruction by Christians); but it may also have been Yahu, or Jahoh.[22] The monotheistic conception of this God of the Jews remained the guiding force in their history for all time, and the prophets played a huge part in securing its universal acceptance among the people. Indeed, in reading the books attributed to them, it is sometimes difficult to remember that matters had ever been otherwise. Yet even they themselves were ready to admit that, in their time, other gods beside him were still worshipped in Palestine, as they were in Greece and later in Rome. 'For you,' says Jeremiah to the kingdom of Judah (and the same could have been said to the kingdom of Israel), 'have as many gods as you have towns.'[23] Gradually, however – perhaps not completely until after the end of the prophetic age – it became established that the Jews could have only one God. The idea was not new, for attempts to enforce a similar conception had occurred in Egypt and Babylonia as early as the second millennium BC. In Israel and Judah – to some extent under the influence of those countries – the doctrine probably came to the fore in the eighth century. By enlarging Yahweh's rule so that it extended over the entire people, the prophets emphasized that the poor and oppressed were not excluded from his care. And unlike the gods of Greece and Rome (of which the traditional foundation date was at about this same epoch) he was not a detached, immovable being, not a distant first cause, but an ever-present help. The world-process of Jewish history did not run in classical cycles of vain eternal recurrence, but instead, in the words of Isaiah,

> The Lord of Hosts has prepared his plan:
> Who shall frustrate it?

14

His is the hand stretched out, and who shall
turn it back?[24]

It was a decisive moment, though we cannot pinpoint it in time, when certain Jews began to believe that Yahweh was the God not only of their own people – a familiar enough notion – but of all other peoples as well. And this was a somewhat surprising conception in states as politically insignificant as those of Palestine. In great countries like Egypt and Mesopotamia, it had been easy to regard the gods of less powerful peoples as inferior imitations, and then to ignore them altogether. But when people in diminutive Israel and Judah chose to take the same view, this indicated a remarkable amount of faith and assurance. After that, it was only a further step to the conclusion that there could be no real Golden Age, no final establishment of God's will, until all men had been converted to a belief in this one, universal God. And that was how people interpreted, as time went on, his declaration to Abraham that 'all the families on earth will pray to be blessed as you are blessed'.

Yet this conception implied, indeed indicated, that pending such a fulfilment all other peoples were misguided and benighted. This sentiment contributed greatly to the hostility encountered by the ancient Jews, particularly in the classical times which are the subject of this book; and in return Rufus Learsi, for example, still views the Greek and Roman religions in as sinister a light as any modern aberration. 'The basic historical fact,' he declares, 'is still the struggle in the human heart and in human society between the holy and righteous God of Abraham, Moses and Isaiah, and the idols of paganism. And they are essentially the same, those idol broods, whether they disport themselves elegantly on Mount Olympus or practise their savage lusts in the forests of Germany.' However this may be, Learsi's subsequent conclusion is indubitably correct: 'It was those spiritual possessions which, in the words of the well-known benediction, have "kept us alive, and preserved us, and enabled us to reach this season".'[25]

Above all, it was the great achievement of the prophets to endow this monotheism with an ethical, moral quality. There is One God: he is good: because of his Covenant he requires his worshippers to be good also. The rudiments of this idea had appeared in earlier forms of the Jewish faith: the prophets brought out its implications, and made them explicit.

And so their names reverberated down the centuries, and were never

15

out of the minds of later Jews in all the crises of the Greco-Roman age, whenever they felt themselves confronted with tyrannical or blasphemous demands. The earliest prophets seemed to have been something more than human. After Elijah had died, he 'was carried up in the whirlwind to heaven',[26] heralding (like Enoch and Moses) the miraculous deaths attributed to later holy men and Messiahs, and encouraging the belief that he himself would later descend upon the earth once again.[27] His disciple from the Sea of Galilee, Elisha, by instructing Naaman, the commander of the Syrian army, to bathe in Jordan to cure his leprosy, was setting a precedent for John the Baptist.

But the sagas about Elisha display a savage intolerance which the eighth-century sheep farmer and prophet Amos, who came to Israel from Tekoa in Judah, discarded and superseded. His were the first prophetic pronouncements to be recorded in writing – within a generation or two after his own lifetime – and they already show awareness that Yahweh is interested in Philistines and other foreigners.[28] Hosea, likewise active in the north, strikes a keynote of the Jewish faith by condemning the worship of images,[29] an attitude which later remained incomprehensible to numerous Greeks and Romans, who could not understand this imageless faith. But Hosea went further than Amos in stressing God's love and mercy, a doctrine subsequently enlarged upon by Jesus. Isaiah, who played a prominent part in eighth-century Judah, gave advice in the face of a growing Assyrian danger, but above all envisaged a future ideal ruler who would inaugurate a regime of justice and gentleness for Jews and Gentiles alike.[30] Though he did not call him the Messiah, certain of his words suggesting such a conception[31] were later interpreted by Christians as a prediction of Jesus.

In Isaiah's lifetime, Israel was annexed by Sargon II of Assyria (722–721 BC). He also removed 27,290 of its more prosperous inhabitants, thus launching the Jews upon their historic Dispersion (Diaspora) to other countries. These 'Ten Lost Tribes' were swallowed up in the Assyrian empire and disappeared without a trace, though legends of their survival, and hopes of their eventual miraculous restoration, have always persisted. The Jews who remained in Israel also fell into oblivion, and were merged with new immigrants, so that in later centuries the racial and religious status of the Samaritans remained a subject of embittered dispute.

Meanwhile Judah precariously held on. Its king Hezekiah escaped the Assyrian Sennacherib (701) by the payment of tribute and by a reputed miracle.[32] As the Assyrians were replaced as dominant power by Babylon (in what is now central Iraq), the anxious monarchs of Judah turned to the prophet Jeremiah for advice. He lived to witness their downfall, for in 597–586 BC Jerusalem succumbed to the Babylonian king Nebuchadrezzar (Nebuchadnezzar) II. Traditionally known as the prophet of disaster, Jeremiah, throughout his career, had to face the dilemma which has so often confronted theologians, and the Jews most of all:

> Why do the wicked prosper,
>   And traitors live at ease?
> Thou hast planted them, and their roots strike deep,
>   They grow up and bear fruit.[33]

But he drew what consolation he could from the assurance of a future New Covenant which God, through the Jews, would ultimately establish, after all peoples had been converted to his worship.

Meanwhile Judah had come to the end of its existence as a nation. Its capital and Temple were destroyed, and many thousands of its inhabitants were taken off to Babylonia. These were events which never disappeared from the national consciousness, and returned sharply to its surface when later conquerors, such as the Romans, revived their memory. To Jeremiah, once again, are ascribed the sombre *Lamentations* which, in characteristic prophetic fashion, blame the catastrophe not on the enemy but on the manifold failures of her people to honour God's Covenant: 'Jerusalem had sinned greatly, and so she was treated like a filthy rag ... Uncleanness clung to her skirts.'[34] And so for Palestinian Jewry the Dispersion, which from now onwards was such a leading feature of the nation's history, always remained the *galut*, exile, captivity: a curse, inflicted by God on a sinful people; just as the Fire of London was ascribed to gluttony, and the Messina earthquake to immorality.

Yet meanwhile Judaism lived on in its places of exile; and there were others besides Assyria and Babylonia. For in addition to the deportations to those countries, the stormy period preceding the ultimate destruction of Judah witnessed migrations to Egypt, where a Temple at Elephantine (Yeb), a fortress garrisoned by Jews, accommodated Yahweh as well as four other deities. There are also possible traces of fifth-century settlement in Asia Minor, notably at Sardis (Sart) in

Lydia;[35] and certainly before long this region, too, became a centre of the Dispersion.

The Jewish settlers in these countries did not assimilate very extensively with the native populations, which therefore regarded them as separate, a conclusion that they themselves were happy to accept: and so anti-Semitism soon began to rear its head, and the Jewish problem had begun. Nevertheless, their continued existence in surroundings divorced from any Hebrew political entity or cult centre brought about permanent changes in their own ways of thinking and their institutions. Since the Temple was far away and no more, the Jews in Babylonia established new meeting places, the forerunners of the synagogues. Yet it was towards Jerusalem and its vanished Temple that their eyes were turned. 'By the rivers of Babylon,' cried the Psalmist, 'we sat down and wept when we remembered Zion . . . If I forget you, O Jerusalem, let my right hand wither away.'[36] And when Israel was reasserting its national life in 1948, the same words were to be seen chalked up on the sides of lorries. This preservation by the exiled Jews of their national and religious habits, amended by geographical circumstances but still intact, is one of the strangest phenomena in history. For although they came to grasp the full significance of the words of their prophets, that even a Temple was not indispensable, they never lost their roots in their own distant land.

The first priest–prophet of the new order was Ezekiel, who had been one of the earliest group of deportees to Babylonia in 598–597. If the Book of Ezekiel goes back to his day, as is not improbable, he took the lead in pointing out, with specific reference to the recent disaster, that worldly power is less important than spiritual. And the same book strikes a significant note for the future by rejecting the concept of collective guilt and retribution: each individual, the writer asserts, is responsible for his own actions.[37] But the reason why the Book of Ezekiel was pored over more than any other work in later Greek and Roman times was because it prophesied a future end of the world in which, after dire destruction, a prince of the house of David would humble the Gentiles and bring salvation to Israel.[38]

Then, in the middle of the sixth century BC, there appeared one of the greatest of all Jewish prophets and writers, the man who wrote chapters 40–55 of the *Book of Isaiah*: since we do not know his name, he can only be called the Second Isaiah (Deutero-Isaiah). Writing, perhaps, in Babylonia, he profoundly and stirringly proclaimed the imminent return of the exiles to a restored Jerusalem, under the guidance of Yahweh, the one and only God. The missionary ideal is strongly proclaimed, even from Captivity, and many modern dreams of universal peace go back to this prophet of comfort and hope. The inspiring splendours of his message inured the Jews to the idea that the whole nation must endure untold hardships for its beliefs. Moreover, the same prophet, with even greater effects on future Jewish thoughts and actions – most of all in Greek and Roman times – envisages a Suffering Servant, who is chosen by God to preside over the universal salvation, and who, despite the mystery in which his figure is shrouded, seems to stand both for the personified community and for an individual who will bring its mission to fulfilment. And this may also be the period of the finalization of the *Second Book of Samuel* (the kingmaker of Israel five centuries earlier), in which God prophesies to David that he will establish the throne of a future monarch of his house for ever, 'and your kingdom shall stand for all time in my sight'.[39] This was the seedbed for future hopes of a Messiah destined to arise from the family of David.

Soon afterwards, the Persians (Achaemenids) violently displaced the Babylonians as the imperial power controlling the middle east, and their monarch Cyrus I the Great repatriated fifty thousand Jews, of the families that had been exiled from Judah, to Jerusalem and the surrounding area. Many more were left behind in Babylonia, but it was always a Jewish doctrine that the community could be narrowed down to a part, which would suffice to continue the nation's inheritance. This was a moment of triumph, for, in the words of David Ben Gurion (1957), 'the ingathering of the exiles is the beginning of the realization of the Messianic vision'. But the immediate practical and spiritual result of the return from exile was the reconstruction of the Temple, initiated by Zerubbabel of David's royal house and completed in 515 BC. The Second Temple had a life of 585 years (in the course of which there was a further rebuilding by Herod the Great) before its obliteration by the Romans. Despite the poverty of its construction and its architectural inferiority to its Solomonian model, it was an achievement of which the Jews never ceased to be proud.

But its building was accompanied by an intentionally divisive measure. This was a period of new national consciousness, when the term 'Jew' first came into use, meaning a descendant of Judah and his tribe. It was at this juncture, when the new Temple was being planned, that the Samaritans asked to join in the enterprise. Zerubbabel and his colleagues, however, seeing Jewry as a matter of racial as well as religious unity (a matter of permanent controversy thereafter), were so insistent upon ethnic purity and the prohibition of intermarriage that they felt unable to comply. In consequence, the Samaritans' offer of help was rejected. 'The House', the Jewish leaders declared, 'which we are building for our God is no concern of yours.'[40] Thus the tiny country of Israel was split irrevocably and permanently into two hostile halves. The Samaritans, for their part, retreated into their own interpretation of the Jewish faith, in which the only books they accepted as inspired were the Pentateuch and the *Book of Joshua*, relying with literal, puritanical Fundamentalism upon their own distinctive idea of eventual salvation, which had no use for a Messiah of the House of David. Excluded from Jerusalem, they built their own shrine (now or somewhat later) on Mount Gerizim, where about one hundred and fifty of their survivors, living on the western fringes of the town of Nablus (Neapolis, the ancient Shechem), still follow the same doctrines today.[41] But in ancient times the Samaritans were abundant, and the division, whether theologically inevitable or not, was destined to weaken the resistance of Israel to successive external enemies.

Nevertheless, the new Jerusalem community was a notable experiment. It was based on the idea of the People of God ruling themselves without an earthly monarch; the term 'theocracy' was later coined to describe the conception.[42] For the high priest, advised by a Council of Elders (the forerunner of the later Sanhedrin), was God's viceregent upon earth – a formula looked back upon longingly by Jewish leaders in subsequent Roman times. Zechariah, a prophet who did much to forward the reconstruction of the Temple, saw *both* a Davidic prince *and* a high priest of Aaron's stock as future anointed ones (Messiahs) – a doctrine of which a good deal more would be heard later on. But meanwhile another prophet, Malachi, in the middle of the fifth century BC, had to battle against discouragements that threatened to overcome the infant community. While castigating the shortcomings of his fellow Jews, Malachi struck a memorable universal note: 'Have we not all one father? Did not one God create us?'[43] For this was a time of rapidly developing attitudes. The revival of Jerusalem seemed conclusive proof of the prophetic view that history was working out the purpose of God; and so the written biblical versions of history, which were greatly advanced at this epoch, decisively reflect the same view – and it continued to prevail throughout the periods that will be discussed in this book. The Jews always continued to explain the present according to a carefully interpreted past: time was seen to move in a straight line, with ups and downs but with a clearly perceptible direction, leading to God's ultimate deliverance of Israel and, through Israel, of the world.

The new Temple was the focus for the whole movement, and it was now that every male Jew from the age of twenty, wherever he might be, began to be expected to make an annual contribution to its upkeep.[44] In the fifth century BC the community of Jerusalem was greatly strengthened by new and important arrivals from Babylonia, led by Nehemiah and Ezra; and in later times these halcyon days of the Persian monarchs, who sponsored this revival, were looked back upon as a golden age – especially at times when a Persian empire had arisen once again.

Ezra and his colleagues consolidated the religious and legal code of the small community, setting monotheism on a firmer basis than ever before, laying the foundations for the later development of Judaism as a creed and way of life, and giving the Jews the courage to fight the apparently hopeless battles of the future. 'Greater is Torah,' it was still declared in Roman times, 'than the priesthood, and than the king-dom',[45] and the reason why this doctrine prevailed was largely because Ezra had so emphatically proclaimed it to be the law. Interpretation and instruction were no longer monopolized by priests. And these tasks were now urgently necessary: for whereas almost all of the Old Testa-ment had been written in Hebrew, the common spoken tongue was now another Semitic language, Aramaic, related to both Hebrew and Phoenician, and less closely to Arabic (it is still spoken in the mountains of Lebanon and Anti-Lebanon today). Hebrew never died, and was to revive, but its employment had now become limited, for the most part, to literary, legal and liturgical purposes. Yet the men who hence-forward acted as the expounders of its holy books were the forerunners of the rabbis with whom the future of Judaism lay.

2

Liberation from the Greeks: the Maccabees

Our literary knowledge of Israel from 400 BC until the time when the Romans first began to impinge upon its history is sparse, and archaeology does not give much help either. Only isolated pieces of information emerge. For example, we learn that the Dispersion was swelled in the middle of the fourth century BC when a Persian monarch, Artaxerxes III (358–338), settled Jews in Hyrcania beside the Caspian – the origin of the name of later Jewish kings called Hyrcanus. This may also be the epoch of the *Book of Jonah* (perhaps identifiable with a prophet of some four centuries earlier), whose swallowing up by a monstrous fish, and emergence after three days and three nights, became a favourite symbol of deliverance and of Jesus' resurrection. The writer of *Jonah*, an unknown Jew in Assyria, is unique in the Old Testament for the completeness of his freedom from particularist bias. God shows mercy even to Assyrian Nineveh, when it repents, for he is the God of all nations. And so the book became a missionary appeal encouraging Jews to spread their religion throughout the pagan world.

When Alexander the Great of Macedonia overwhelmed the Persian (Achaemenid) empire (332), Israel lost one overlord and gained another, and the words of *Genesis* seemed fulfilled: 'May God extend the bounds of Japheth [Noah's son who was the legendary founder of the northern peoples]: let him dwell in the tents of Shem [the ancestor of the Semites].'[1] For the first time the Jews had felt the impact of the

European continent which was to dominate world history for more than two millennia. As Alexander passed through Palestine on his way to annex Egypt, there were stories of his kind treatment of the Jews, some of whom were allowed to settle on Egyptian territory; and there were also gratifying tales of his hostility towards the Samaritans.

When he died (323), the gigantic empire which he had established from the Adriatic to the Indus split up into the kingdoms of three principal dynasties of Macedonian (that is to say partly Greek) race, and wholly Greek culture: the Antigonids in Macedonia, the Seleucids based on Syria and Mesopotamia, and the Ptolemies in Egypt. Each of these kingdoms extended its tentacles as far afield as it could, the Antigonids into Greece, the Seleucids into parts of Asia Minor and Persia and the Ptolemies into other Asiatic territories. Among these Ptolemaic territories was not only Phoenicia (the modern Lebanon) but Israel; and it remained under Ptolemaic rule for more than a century.

The capital of the Ptolemies was at Alexander's new foundation, Alexandria, and this rapidly became one of the most important centres of Jewish settlement in the world. Ptolemy I introduced many Jews and Samaritans to the city, where they occupied a quarter of their own behind the palace (not a ghetto, but the result of voluntary settlement); and they inhabited other parts of the city as well. The place made a strong appeal to Jewish immigrants, partly because of Egypt's association with the origins of their faith, but especially in view of the favourable conditions offered them by the Ptolemies. These privileges included a largely autonomous Jewish civic organization – not possessing Alexandrian citizenship, but existing alongside the Greek citizen-community of the city, and above the native Egyptian community. Jews were ruled by their own Council of Elders, headed (from an unknown date during the period) by a community president or ethnarch. The earliest synagogue for which we have evidence (anywhere in the world) was at Schedia, fourteen miles from Alexandria (c. 225 BC).[2] The services in this and other synagogues were often conducted in Greek, which soon superseded Aramaic as the ordinary language of the local Jewish community.

In Jerusalem the Council of Elders that had existed since the time of Nehemiah and Ezra was maintained by the Ptolemies' governors, perhaps under the presidency of the high priest. The Council was granted the power to enforce the Torah and keep foreign cults out of the country, and even to a limited extent to conduct external relations.

Under this loose Ptolemaic suzerainty the country enjoyed an economic efflorescence (concealed by Jewish sources). After the middle of the third century BC, the most notable figures in this revival were the Tobiads – the family of Tobias, a Transjordanian chieftain's descendant who advised the high priest and rose to a high position in the Ptolemaic hierarchy in Israel (*c.* 230).

The Tobiads displayed leanings towards the Greek way of life: and indeed this was now available to many Jews. For example, the Ptolemies commenced the foundation of a ring of non-Jewish, Greco-Macedonian cities round the fringe of the Jewish homeland itself, particularly on the Mediterranean coast and in Transjordan, and this policy of urbanization brought the influences of Greek culture to bear upon the nucleus of Israel itself.[3] Hellenism and Judaism had begun their prolonged confrontation, which forms part of the millennial tension between the Greek and Syrian cultures, and is one of the principal themes of this book. Moreover, if the Jews were becoming familiar with Greek ideas, a few Greeks were also by now becoming at least dimly acquainted with Jewish institutions. The historian Hecataeus of Abdera in Thrace (*c.* 300 BC) (or someone else using his name) wrote about the Jews, either as a separate work or as part of a history of Egypt. He indicated that their way of living, which had been initiated (despite subsequent modifications) by Moses, was devoted to seclusion from human kind and hatred of non-Jews.[4] He also compared the training of their young men to the discipline of Sparta. A certain tendency was also arising to see the Jews as philosophers, or to study them from a philosophical viewpoint. Thus Clearchus of Soli in Cyprus (d. *c.* 250 BC) reported a belief on the part of his master Aristotle that the ancestors of the Jewish race had been Indian philosophers, though he suggested an alternative descent from Persian holy men (magi).[5]

But this was also the period of the first known anti-Jewish literature, with its vast and fatefully influential future history. Manetho, the Egyptian high priest at Heliopolis (On), dedicated to King Ptolemy II Philadelphus (d. 246 BC) a history of Egypt wherein he reacted strongly against the Jewish account of the Exodus, which caused such offence to Egyptian pride. Far from leaving Egypt triumphantly under God's guidance, as the Jews themselves asserted, Manetho declared that, after ruling the country brutally for thirteen years, tradition declared that they had been expelled from it, owing to their infection with leprosy and other illnesses.

Not long afterwards, the Alexandrian Jews (probably not Palestinians, as was alleged) were producing the Greek translation of the Old Testament known (because of its legendary seventy-two verbally inspired translators) as the Septuagint.[6] In addition to translations from the Hebrew scriptures (which had now practically assumed their present form) or from Aramaic versions, the Septuagint included the books later described by Protestants as the Apocrypha, comprising certain writings composed in Greek and others translated from lost Semitic originals. Composed at various times from the third century BC onwards (not all at once under Ptolemy II, as the legend suggested), the Septuagint laid down the language, concepts and general background which made it possible to create a Jewish literature in Greek, thus making Judaism much more accessible to the philosophical and mystical beliefs of the pagans. For the first time in history the Bible had moved beyond the closed circle of the people of Israel.

The Jewish philosopher Philo asserted that the Septuagint was intended to convince the Greeks. But it exercised little missionary effect on them, and they would have found it hard and puzzling to read. The almost complete absence of references to the work in Greek and Latin writings[7] is a striking illustration of the gulf that was fixed between pagans and Jews – even in Alexandria, where so many of them lived together. For the Alexandrian Jews themselves, on the other hand, the Septuagint became their Bible; and it remained the greatest monument of Greek Judaism until, centuries later, this form of the Jewish faith failed to maintain itself as a rival to the Palestinian and Babylonian rabbis.

From about 275 BC the favourable situation of Ptolemaic Palestine came to an end, and for the next century it became a tramping ground disputed between the Ptolemies and their Seleucid neighbours and enemies in Syria. In these struggles, the Ptolemies relied on the warlike Idumaeans as mercenary troops. However, after various changes of fortune, the Seleucid monarch Antiochus III the Great decisively defeated the Ptolemaic army at Panion (Banyas) on Israel's northern border, and the country passed into Seleucid hands (200 BC).

When this occurred, the Council of Elders was permitted to keep its position, and at first a broad degree of self-determination was maintained. But taxation soon became heavier, the land-tax amounting to as much as one third of the crop. Moreover, in the days of Seleucus IV

(187–175 BC), the Temple treasury at Jerusalem was plundered, or nearly plundered,[8] by a Seleucid representative. This is the point at which, indirectly, we first encounter Rome. For the reason why Seleucus IV was obliged to have recourse to these severe measures was in order to raise the heavy tribute imposed by the Romans upon his father Antiochus III, defeated heavily by them in a series of battles (191–190) which deprived the Seleucids of their position as a Mediterranean power.

It had taken the Romans a long time to reach the position in which they could dictate to one of the great kingdoms of the east, thus casting their shadow as far as Israel. Three hundred years earlier, their territories around Rome had been no larger than Israel itself. But before the end of the fourth century BC they had become the dominant power throughout the greater part of Italy, and before 200, by their conquest of Carthage (north African offshoot of Israel's Phoenician neighbour Tyre), they had gained control of the entire western Mediterranean area. During this Second Punic War against Carthage they became increasingly concerned with the affairs of the eastern Mediterranean also. The Antigonids were the first to suffer defeat at their hands; and it was almost immediately afterwards that the Seleucid Antiochus III, after crossing over aggressively into Europe, paid the penalty at the hands of the Romans.

His defeat was one of a number of factors which swelled the Jewish Dispersion. This further expansion of the Jews had already gained increasing momentum under the Seleucids. It was probably at about this time that their great foundation Antioch in Syria (now Antakya, in south-eastern Turkey) began to become a leading and favoured Jewish centre,[9] and Antiochus III appears to have settled two thousand Jewish families in the western regions of central Asia Minor (Lydia, Phrygia). Now, after his defeat, it is possible, though not certain, that Jewish prisoners of war were brought to Rome, to become the founding fathers of its large Jewish community. And it was because of the same defeat and the indemnities which it incurred that the Jewish homeland itself encountered severe financial pressure from his son Seleucus IV.

Inside Israel, the clash between Judaism and Hellenism had continued to develop. There was, by now, a keen difference of opinion between the Jews who believed in the complete rejection of Greek influence and those who felt that some infusion of it was essential if Jewry was not to fall behind the modern world. In the former category was Joshua ben Sira (Jesus the son of Sirach), the conservative author of the *Wisdom of Jesus*, or *Ecclesiasticus*, a moving meditation upon the eternity of the Torah. On the other side were those who declared: 'Let us enter upon a covenant with the Gentiles round about, because disaster after disaster has overtaken us since we segregated ourselves from them.'[10] This latter trend became particularly prominent after the accession of Antiochus IV Epiphanes (175–163), from whom the Hellenizers in Jerusalem obtained permission to build a gymnasium in the Greek fashion. This was a crucial issue, because orthodox Jews disliked nakedness, and Greeks found circumcision distasteful: so that young Jews eager to participate in athletic contests were sometimes prepared to have themselves operated upon to abolish this mark of their national identity, a proceeding which deeply offended Jewish religious opinion.

In an attempt to seize Egypt, Antiochus IV was rudely rebuffed by the Romans. He then turned his attention towards the Parthians, the Iranian power which during the previous century had established itself in Mesopotamia and Persia. If he was to proceed in that direction, however, a well disciplined Palestine in his rear was indispensable. This was a theme which will be constantly encountered in centuries to come: one of the vital aspects of Israel's role was its strategic importance in wars between the powers occupying Syria and Mesopotamia. Antiochus IV decided, therefore, that he must control Palestine closely. His way of doing so was to support the Hellenizers, because he believed in Hellenism as a universal instrument of rule and civilization. As for the Jews, he saw no reason why they should wish, or be allowed, to escape from the beneficent sway of these Hellenizing influences.

Meanwhile the Jews, as so often during their history in these Greco-Roman times, were so disunited among themselves that the path of intervention from outside was all too easy. At this particular juncture, moderate and extreme Hellenists were at odds with one another, and there was a background of economic discontent. These divisions gave Antiochus IV a classic opportunity, and he sent one of his generals to Jerusalem. The walls were razed, the treasury seized and a fortified citadel was built to house a permanent garrison. Moreover, the observance of the Sabbath and the rite of circumcision were banned, and a statue of Olympian Zeus was set up in the Holy of Holies of the Temple (168). Antiochus IV may have been misled, by his experience of the Dispersion's less exacting forms of Judaism, to accept assurances from rich Hellenizing leaders at Jerusalem – and of anti-Jewish Greek cities round about – that his 'reforms' could be enforced. But, if so, the advice he received was wrong, and his imprudent desecration echoed down the centuries. The *Book of Daniel* described it as the 'Abomination of Desolation', or abomination which appals; and many a dirge bewailed the horror.[11] Antiochus IV issued edicts of the same repressive character in every town throughout Palestine; and it was not even a consolation that the Samaritans too were compelled to dedicate their shrine on Mount Gerizim to Olympian Zeus.[12] The savage persecutions by which, according to Jewish tradition, all these decrees were enforced created a great exaltation of religious martyrdom, as a vicarious suffering for Israel. This concept was to dominate Jewish (and then Christian) minds for many generations, and most notably in Roman times when it often rose to the state of a mass psychosis. 'I, like my brothers,' one of the martyrs was alleged to have cried to Antiochus IV, 'surrender my body and my life for the laws of our fathers. I appeal to God to shew mercy speedily to his people, and by whips and scourges to bring you to admit that he alone is God!'[13]

Under the impact of this passion for martyrdom, there now broke out the Maccabaean revolt, a rebellion which, although it struck too secular a note to find much place in rabbinical writings, exercised an undying effect upon the national consciousness of the Jews. For it was hailed not only as the movement which saved their monotheism from imminent destruction, but as the first occasion on which a people had risen up in arms to defend its religious freedom and conscience – and a classic example of a patriotic struggle which succeeded against all the apparent odds. Moreover, the rising was a popular movement, with class over-tones based on the support of the lower urban population. The name of the Maccabee house, which took the lead, may mean 'hammerers'; and they were also called Hasmonaeans, perhaps after an ancestor Hasmon: or the word may mean 'princes'. Their family was not of the leading nobility, but belonged to a priestly clan named Joarib, though not to the house of Aaron which would have enabled them to claim the Davidic high priesthood.

The outbreak began partly as a civil war between Jews when the aged Hasmonaean priest Mattathias, at his birthplace Modein (El-Medieh), not only refused to take the first pagan sacrifice but slew an apostate Jew who was willing to step into the breach. Having thus raised the standard of revolt, Mattathias took to the mountains with his five sons, and many rallied to their side. Mattathias enjoyed a very special position in the hearts of contemporary and later Jews because he seemed the arch-hero of resistance movements, the prototype of ruthless zeal, like the legendary high priest Phineas of Moses' time who, in defence of monotheism, had seized his spear, attacked an Israelite cohabiting with a foreign woman and pinned them together in death.[14]

When Mattathias died (166), he was succeeded by his son Judas (Yehudah) Maccabaeus, one of the great military heroes on whom subsequent Jewish nationalists looked back with admiration. Judas retook and reconsecrated the Temple (165–164), an occasion commemorated ever since by the Festival of the Dedication (Hanukkah). Seleucid persecution was brought to an end, but not yet Seleucid rule, and not the hostility of the Greek cities of the Levant. As a counterweight, therefore, Judas Maccabaeus made a treaty with the Romans (*c.* 161 BC), whom he knew to be ever anxious to weaken Seleucid power. This significant act, which seemed prudent but was perhaps, like all appeals to the Romans, short-sighted, may provide one of the reasons why Judas Maccabaeus, for all his heroic triumphs, is never mentioned in the Hebrew Mishnah. The Roman version of the treaty, which should not be dismissed as wholly fictitious but was a declaration of friendship rather than a formal alliance, is recorded by the unknown author of the *First Book of the Maccabees* (surviving in a Greek translation) as follows:

Success to the Romans and the Jewish nation by sea and land for ever! May sword and foe be far from them! But if war breaks out first against Rome or any of her allies throughout her dominion, then the Jewish nation shall support them wholeheartedly as occasion may require. To the enemies of Rome or of her allies the Jews shall neither give nor supply provisions, arms, moneys, or ships; so Rome has decided; and they shall observe their commitments, without compensation.

Similarly, if war breaks out first against the Jewish nation, then the Romans shall give them hearty support as occasion may require. To their enemies there shall be given neither provisions, arms, money nor ships; so Rome has decided. These commitments shall be kept without breach of faith . . .[15]

The writer of this book *I Maccabees*, who recounts events up to 135 BC with a strongly pro-Jewish bias, may in retrospect have endowed the treaty with a colouring which is exaggeratedly complimentary to Jewish nationalist sentiment. But the agreement was confirmed by Judas' successors, and remained the canonical document of those Jews, influential but disliked by their compatriots, who favoured collaboration with the Romans. There were also treaties with the nominally 'free' Greek city of Sparta,[16] with which the alleged similarities of educational discipline provided sentimental ties.

The exciting events of these years exercised their effects on the Jewish Dispersion; for example the persecutions of Antiochus IV accelerated the flow of emigrants from Israel. But the Jews of the Dispersion did not at first take part in the Maccabaean revolt because, not being persecuted themselves in the various territories where they had settled, they failed to see its significance as a national revival. This only became clear to them after the desecration of the Temple, which stimulated greater enthusiasm for the cause. It expressed itself, as it had ever since the rebuilding of the Temple by Zerubbabel, in the dispatch of great sums of money for its upkeep every year, in the form of the half-shekel tax, sent or brought by large convoys of pilgrims;[17] and now the contributions were no doubt increased, and the campaign for them intensified. Modern Israel, as Nahum Goldmann commented recently, is economically dependent on world Jewry. So was the Israel of Hellenistic and Roman times.

Judas Maccabaeus, owing to his lack of the appropriate birth qualification, had never ventured to become high-priest; and now a quarrel concerning that office, which had become vacant, produced a major effect on the Dispersion. It was apparently in 162–160 that a certain Onias IV, an unsuccessful contender for the high priesthood, fled to Egypt and was allowed by the Ptolemies to build a smaller duplicate of the Jerusalem Temple at Leontopolis on the eastern edge of the Nile delta, twenty-two miles from Memphis. This was a unique event, since no Jewish colony elsewhere had ever possessed such a Temple, and the Torah ordained that there should be a single sanctuary only. The foundation of Leontopolis indicated that the Jewish settlements in Lower Egypt were by no means restricted to Alexandria, but must also have included sizeable settlements on the eastern marshes. In spite of the existence of this new Temple, however, the Egyptian Jews, like all other communities of the Dispersion, continued to pay their annual tax to the Temple at Jerusalem.

In Israel Judas Maccabaeus fell in battle, and was succeeded by his brother Jonathan, who secured access to the sea by the conquest of Joppa (Jaffa) and showed diplomatic talent in securing practical, though still not theoretical, independence from the Seleucids. One of them, Alexander Balas, 150–145 BC, made him high priest,[18] an appointment which the Jews themselves had not been ready to confer on him, and which was therefore destined to cause trouble in times to come.

After Jonathan, like Judas, had been killed in battle, their last surviving brother Simon secured full independence from the Seleucids (142), and the Hasmonaean princes henceforward assumed the hereditary titles of 'High Priest and Leader [ethnarch, national ruler] of the Jews'. In this development the Seleucid monarch Demetrius II (145–139 and 129–125) concurred; and indeed Simon had succeeded in expelling his garrison, so that Hellenism was reduced to a merely cultural and no longer a political force. A new national state had come into existence – though it still did not include Samaria, Galilee or Idumaea. The Romans now renewed their agreement with the Jews on more definite terms (139), writing to all neighbouring monarchs that 'if any traitors have escaped from their country to you, they should hand them over to Simon the High Priest to be punished by him according to the Law of the Jews'.[19]

This was also, perhaps, the time when these agreements between Rome and Israel began to include a clause guaranteeing freedom of worship for the Jews throughout the Roman empire and the lands of its allies. Such measures may have been inherited from the Ptolemaic and Seleucid regimes, but they constituted a remarkable concession all the same, considering that the Jewish cult was so wholly different and distinct from the worships prescribed by the various pagan cities in all these territories. Moreover, this tolerance is all the more noteworthy in view of the restrictive action that was taken against the Jews of Rome itself. For in 139 BC they were said to have been expelled from Rome and Italy 'for attempting to corrupt Roman customs'.[20] The report has been doubted, but it is likely enough that an attempt was made to stop Jewish proselytism. That is to say, while policy throughout the empire was to be tolerant, it was also felt that the national way of life, in its capital at least, must not be encroached on by these alien institutions, which had not received the official sanction of the Roman State and might, therefore, become the cause of political or social irregularities. When the Jews were expelled from Rome, it was stated that the soothsaying magicians called Chaldaeans (originating in southern Mesopotamia) were turned out as well. The classification of the Jews with practitioners of magic is not altogether surprising, since Judaism in these epochs was greatly affected by demonology, resulting from the belief – increased, not diminished, by monotheism – that there must be numerous spirits or angels, good and evil alike, acting as intermediaries between so lofty a divinity and mankind. There was also, among the Jews, an enormously extensive magical literature, noted with scorn and denounced as superstitious by many of their pagan enemies.

Simon's elimination of the Seleucids was still not quite the end of their interference, for after Simon had been murdered by his own son-in-law the Seleucid monarch Antiochus VII Sidetes, anxious to consolidate the Levant before attacking Parthia, succeeded in reconquering the Jewish state for himself (135–134). Owing to Roman intervention, however, he imposed mild terms, and after his death (129) Simon's son John (Jehohanan) Hyrcanus I, though Antiochus VII obliged him to join an expedition against the Parthians, reasserted the national independence. He did so by appealing to Rome, probably not once only but twice; and the Romans were still eager to undermine the Seleucids in any way they could. On the first occasion they duly warned the Seleucids, and the Egyptians as well, against encroaching on John Hyrcanus' territories and coasts. At the same time, in a decree of its own, the city of Pergamum (Bergama) in the Roman province of Asia (western Asia Minor) dutifully echoes and endorses this pronouncement, referring to a legendary friendship between the Greeks and Jews supposedly going back to the time of Abraham. The Pergamum decree also alludes to commercial privileges conferred upon John Hyrcanus by the Romans.[21] Then, in its second intervention, Rome squashed a Seleucid plan to reannex Israel.

Having thus secured his position with Roman help, John Hyrcanus I proceeded to extend his rule into Samaria, Idumaea and Galilee, by aggressions which contained profound significance for the future. The Samaritans, remembering past enmities, had been openly hostile to the Hasmonaean revolt, and John Hyrcanus I now destroyed their capital Samaria, as well as the national shrine on Mount Gerizim. Invading Idumaea, he forcibly converted its people to Judaism and ordered them to be circumcised, thus admitting them officially to the faith, though Jewish public opinion never fully ratified their enrolment. And it was once again John Hyrcanus I, apparently, who undertook the full absorption of Galilee, at the other extremity of the country. Although there may have been partial Judaization at an earlier period, this was the epoch at which full conquest and conversion of the Galileans took place, so that it was into Jewry, a century later, that Jesus the Galilean was born.

These annexations increased the state to dimensions which justified its self-description as a new Israel. True, the mass-conversions also introduced many tough elements, which were later destined to show resistance to successive governmental authorities. But for the present the numerous additional soldiers thus provided for John Hyrcanus I's army made Israel the most important military power between Roman Asia and Egypt.

There the Ptolemies, though still rich, had become increasingly dependent on Rome, and the country was suffering from internecine strife within the royal house. In the course of these struggles, the large Jewish community at Alexandria became involved. Ptolemy VI, who had sanctioned the foundation of the temple at Leontopolis, employed Jews not only as soldiers but as generals, and used them against his brother Ptolemy VIII (164–116 BC) who thus entertained a bitter grudge against the Jewish population. Indeed, he would have trampled down a large number of its members with his elephants if his mistress had not intervened to save them.

The concern of the Maccabee state for the Dispersion, which had already become a feature of its policy under Simon, is now reflected in documents relating to Greek cities of Asia. Laodicea ad Lycum, for example – near the modern Denizli – is obliged to accept a Roman request, apparently prompted by John Hyrcanus I, 'that it shall be lawful for the Jews to observe their Sabbaths and perform their other rites in accordance with their native laws, and that no one shall give orders to them, because they are our friends and allies, and that none shall do them an injury in our province' (Asia).[22] But the Laodicean declaration is particularly significant for the future because it specifically indicates that another city of the province, Tralles (Aydin), had previously objected to allowing its Jewish community these privileges, and that Rome had been obliged to overrule its objection.

Moreover, this anti-Jewish tendency, as on earlier occasions, was finding expression in literature. It was perhaps in *c.* 120 BC that Apollonius Molon, a rhetorician from Alabanda (Araphisar, in south-western Asia Minor), wrote an influential *Diatribe against the Jews*, whom he described as a cowardly and insolent lot without ability, the only 'barbarian' race which had never achieved a useful invention or produced any great artists or sages. Furthermore, when the Jews attacked the Seleucids for profaning the Holy of Holies, their enemies retaliated (since they found its imageless emptiness inexplicable) by saying it was a place of human sacrifice, where the victims were foreigners whom, every seven years, the Jews kidnapped, killed and cut into small pieces.[23] There were also reports that a donkey was worshipped in the shrine.[24]

But the real reason why these ignorant rumours arose was because the Jews kept so much to themselves, as many an ancient writer stressed. It was an irritant that they refused to eat with Gentiles. Economic considerations were not yet a major factor, since they had not yet acquired their reputation as traders and moneylenders, but their specific institutions were severely criticized. The Sabbath, for example, was said to be an excuse for idleness which had originated in a disease contracted in the wilderness, and meant that a day could now be spent sleeping with foreign women (though there was also the contradictory complaint that the Jews were too arrogant to sleep with foreigners, or marry them!). They kept up these customs of their own, people protested, with ostentatious display. But the real cause of this hostility towards them was because, allegedly, they hated all other peoples but themselves.[25] Such are the penalties of those who seek, corporatively, to maintain their own ways in alien communities. It is true that racial and cultural mixtures and antagonisms were nothing strange or new in this Hellenistic world. But A. N. Sherwin-White is right to conclude that 'it was only between Greeks and Jews that racial prejudice manifested itself at full strength'.

When the Greeks or Romans delivered abusive attacks on foreign peoples, as they frequently did, their targets were usually nations which had little or no literature of their own to express their own points of view and beliefs. But the situation was emphatically different with regard to the Jews, who during the last two centuries BC produced an enormous literature, not only in Aramaic and Hebrew, but in Greek: in the wake of the Septuagint came a host of other writings. Their authors were commonly inclined to claim that Judaism, not Hellenism, was the fountainhead of all human knowledge[26] – or, more tactfully, that the best Gentiles had always held the Jewish people in esteem – and

34

that the Jews accepted and admired (though with the addition of monotheism) all that was most valuable in Gentile thought.

Since the Jewish apologists adopted this approach, it seems evident that they expected their works to be read not only by their Hellenized co-religionists but by pagan Greeks. The same hopes, apparently, had been entertained for the Septuagint; but they had not been fulfilled then, and they were not very thoroughly fulfilled now. True, to judge by the large numbers of pagans who, as time went on, came at least as far as the fringes of Judaism, the propaganda must have had at least some effect. But what attracted people was the institutional way of life of the Jews, and there is very little evidence that their literary justifications often reached Gentile writers or their publics. Despite converts and semi-converts, the gulf between the two sorts of civilization remained great. Although the more scrupulous Jewish writers refrained from direct polemics against pagan religion, pagans could not be expected to feel much sympathy when they read, in the *Letter of Aristeas*, that 'the lawgiver fenced us about with impregnable palisades and walls of iron, so that we should in no way have dealings with other nations'.[27] And when these apologists dogmatically affirmed, as they were obliged to affirm, that the Law had been given to Moses by God himself, the Greeks and Romans found the effort of belief altogether too great.

Nevertheless, a number of Greek-speaking Jews continued to make the attempt, though the results of their efforts are now lost. Already while the Septuagint was still taking shape, at the end of the third century BC, a Jew named Demetrius inaugurated the composition of Jewish history in Greek, without attempting to Hellenize the great figures of Jewish history. Then his co-religionist Aristobulus (who was acquainted with the philosophy of Aristotle) may – if the tradition is correct – have written an *Explanation of the Mosaic Law* promoting the idea, later adapted by Christian Fathers, that Pythagoras and Socrates had been students of Moses. Eupolemus, an envoy of Judas Maccabaeus, tried his hand at a historical approach, treating the biblical tradition more freely, though his command of literary Greek apparently left much to be desired. Philo the elder was a Jewish epic poet. Artapanus invited trouble by claiming that Moses was the creator of the entire Egyptian civilization; but the *Wisdom of Solomon* more tactfully assured the Alexandrians that the Exodus, so far from being a humiliation for the Egyptians, had been sped on its way with their favour.[28] There were also numerous Jewish writings masquerading, as was the contemporary custom,[29] under false names, among which even those of Aeschylus and Sophocles are found. Moreover, a whole series of anonymous Jewish pronouncements and prophecies, once again in the Greek language, got incorporated in the collections of so-called Sibylline Oracles. Among these short poems of many epochs, one notable early example proclaims the widespread extent of the Dispersion – and its unpopularity as well: 'every sea and every land is full of you, and every one hates you, because of your ways . . . every man shall hold your ordinances in hatred'.[30]

The technique of the Sibylline oracles is to demonstrate their reliability by safely predicting *past* events, and then to foretell, happily, the future downfall of the great kings and empires. This is an apocalyptic theme, offering revelations relating to the end of the world and the disasters and marvels that will be its accompaniments: and in the Hebrew literature of the time, too, the apocalyptic writings are the most significant feature of the age. The orthodox view, repeated in *I Maccabees*, announced that the time for such prophecies and prophets had now passed. But the apocalyptists, their imagination sharpened by sufferings under Antiochus Epiphanes, believed that they stood, once again, right in the centre of the antique prophetic tradition. Their predictions provided spiritual consolation and psychological escape, in times of poverty and disturbance. And their hopeful visions of the world's end were sometimes interpreted, by their readers and by governmental and religious authorities, as politically subversive.

3

The Divisions within Judaism in Maccabaean Times

The principal surviving apocalyptic work of the time (*c.* 160 BC) is the *Book of Daniel*, in which an unknown author, writing in Aramaic and Hebrew, presents a collection of legendary popular stories about a Jew named Daniel, attached to the Babylonian court at a date five hundred years previously, who was supposedly vouchsafed miraculous deliverances and visions. Although the stories are attributed discreetly to this remote epoch, Daniel's salvation from the den of lions, and the rescue of his three companions Shadrach, Meshach and Abednego from the fiery furnace, are intended to refer to the oppressions of Antiochus Epiphanes. Throughout centuries to come, these tales, and Daniel's visions, stirred the emotions of oppressed Jews and then Christians: and so did the declaration that followed, proclaiming a future end of Israel's tribulation and the inauguration of God's kingdom. 'In *Daniel*,' declared Nicolas Berdyaev, 'we are made to feel dramatically that mankind is engaged in a process that tends towards a definite goal.' But, although *Daniel* encouraged the enthusiasm for martyrdom, the goal it had in mind was not the specific rebellion of the Maccabees – since they are not perfect, but need to be 'tested, refined and made shining white'.[1] For in the view of this writer, God will intervene at the right time without the need of any human assistance.

The outcome of his intervention – and this is far the most influential passage in *Daniel* – will be the survival of the individual dead. This was to be not just a question of ascensions to Heaven, like those of Enoch, Moses and Elijah, but of actual bodily resurrection, by no means limited to a few venerated figures. Of this idea, with its immense repercussions upon subsequent religious thought, *Daniel* gives us the only clear and undisputed reference in the entire Old Testament:

> Many of those who sleep in the dust of the
> earth will wake,
> Some to everlasting life
> And some to the reproach of eternal abhorrence.[2]

Unlike the immortality of the soul, which was a Greek doctrine, this resurrection of the body seems to have been an idea of the Jews, who thought in terms of the survival not merely of the spirit but of entire psychosomatic unities.

This insistence on survival came from a familiar problem: why do the unrighteous flourish? Since the Jews were certain there is a God who cares, they concluded that there must, in the future, be another life, in which a Last Judgment will redress the balance. Individual salvation was a common enough view among Gentiles: but the Jews attributed it to God's concern for his People. In epochs to come, this conviction was to encourage defiance of their worldly overlords. And the same implication could be read into *Daniel*'s belief in the eventual coming of a Liberator or Liberators. The end of the world would be heralded by 'the appearance of one anointed [Messiah], a prince'.[3] He, however, shall 'be removed with none to take his part': so the ultimate saviour will be another. For a vision also revealed to Daniel that One Like a Man, or a Son of Man, would come with the clouds of heaven to be presented to the Ancient of years: and 'sovereignty and glory and kingly power were given to him'.[4] This difficult conception, perhaps deriving ultimately from non-Jewish Canaanite beliefs of the enthrone-ment of one god (Baal) by another (El), seems to be intended by *Daniel* not so much to indicate an individual saviour, but rather to symbolize the Elect Community as a whole. However, it was soon interpreted as foretelling the visitation of a personal Redeemer: though he could not, according to the thought of the Jews, be divine, since divinity was reserved for the one God.

These themes return in the *First Book of Enoch*. In this work of the second and first centuries BC, written originally in Hebrew or Aramaic and now preserved in an Ethiopian version based on a Greek translation, one of the various names under which a series of prophecies is collected is that of Enoch, who was Adam's grandson, or seventh in descent from him (Chapter 1, n. 5). Once again the future empire of the Almighty is described, and once again there is reference to the Son of Man, who is now clearly envisaged as an individual saviour: the Son of Man in the Gospels is the direct heir to this conception.

While these books were being written, Judaism was going through a period of intense differences of opinion, principally caused by the pull of Hellenistic, Greek ways, and the counter-pull exerted by strict interpretations of the Torah. Every element, it is true, in the kaleidoscope of national life protested utter devotion to the Torah. Yet during the three hundred years that now lay ahead, overt divisions within Jewry were more numerous than in any previous epoch, or in any subsequent epoch either, at least until the nineteenth century. New texts of the period are frequently coming to light, and many of them suggest that still further additions will have to be made to our list of deviant or dissident sects and groups. This tolerance of the 'both-this-and-that' approach, in contrast to the Greek 'either-or', made for marked religious liveliness and important theological achievement, and prepared the way for Christianity. On the other hand it also meant that the Jews, thus split, were peculiarly ill-equipped to resist the great encroaching power of the Romans.

When, therefore, the Jewish historian Josephus, contemptuous of the far-out groups, chooses to classify the religious thinking of the age according to a merely three-fold, or at most four-fold, division, he is gravely misleading, since the variety was really much greater – though it was subsequently lost sight of when Jewish orthodoxy eliminated non-normative sources in the late first century AD. Yet Josephus' three or four major groups were certainly pre-eminent, and the destiny of the Jews in the Greco-Roman world depended upon the political implications of their divergent beliefs.

First of all, there were the Sadducees. Their name may, though this is not quite certain, come from Zadok, the high priest of David. They were a relatively small and select group of influential and wealthy men, mostly landed magnates, and they also included the hereditary priests in control of the Temple. The Temple's ceremonies seemed to them more important than hair-splittings about the Torah, which they accepted in its written form just as it was, without glosses. Morality did not interest them a great deal, and speculations about the end of world and resurrection not at all – these they dismissed as late and unauthoritative, and a likely source of subversive thinking. The Sadducees were attached to the Hasmonaean house and (in spite of the mob-support which it had at first engaged) formed the core of its party, tolerating the surface Hellenism which, for all its nationalist origins, the regime increasingly manifested. It is hard to look at the Sadducees from the inside, because only hostile versions of what they stood for have survived – notably the version put out by the Christians. For Sadducee ways did not eventually prevail. If they had, the result would have been a lack of spiritual development. Yet the catastrophic future wars against the Romans would also have been avoided.

By the time of John Hyrcanus I, and probably already to some extent under his uncle Jonathan, the Sadducees were ceasing to have the field to themselves. Indeed, since the very beginning of the Hasmonaean dynasty, a group of 'Pious men' (Hasidim, Assidaeans), while on the whole supporting the new regime, had frowned on its increasing tolerance of cultural Hellenism. And now, owing something to these 'Pious', the Pharisees too were taking shape.[5] Their name is likely to come from a word meaning 'separated', that is to say detached from what is sinful or unclean. They themselves preferred to be called Haberim, signifying equals or associates or fellow-members. Representing, initially at least, not so much a separate sect from the Sadducees as a different attitude within a common legal and religious framework, they arose as a party opposed to the Hasmonaean dynasty's combination of the kingship with the high priesthood, to which, according to the scriptures, it was not entitled (Ch. 2, n. 18). Moreover, while stressing their passionate love of the Law, the Pharisees insisted that its written canon had to be augmented by oral interpretations; indeed they believed that God had imparted to Moses an oral Torah as well as a written one.[6]

But where political considerations, affecting the order of society, could arise was in their agreement with the *Book of Daniel*'s belief in an ultimate resurrection of the body. Since, however, they were eager to achieve the kingdom of God in this world, they did not, for a long while, go all the way with the writer of *Daniel* and other apocalyptics in prophesying an ultimate holocaust. That is one of the reasons why they were later described, for instance in the Gospels, as hypocritical: like the Hasmonaeans – criticized by *Daniel* for this reason – they fought only for civil and religious liberties, and not for the ultimate, apocalyptic kingdom.[7] Nevertheless, the Pharisees' belief in resurrection, since it appealed to those who were oppressed in their present lives, was one of the reasons why the Sadducees accused them of playing up to the lower classes. And whereas the Sadducees' strength resided in the Temple, the Pharisees, essentially a lay and middle-class movement, provided the synagogues with their largely hereditary presbyters (the name later adopted by the Calvinists for their own elders). In the synagogues, the Law was interpreted and studied; and, sometimes, too, various material amenities were offered, such as guest accommodation.

The Pharisees attached great importance to morals and education – on which the Jews concentrated more intensively than the Greeks or Romans. And they were also eager to make religion a source of joy and satisfaction: their dismissal as dry formalists came from later developments, exaggerated by their enemies.[8] The Pharisees' agents and assistants, and indeed many Pharisees themselves, were lay scribes (Sopherim) or professional lawyers. It was they who decided what was required, in all details of conduct, in order to give practical effect to the Law – as interpreted by themselves.[9] This was a particularly necessary task, since biblical Hebrew was no longer widely understood. The scribes were not men of wealth or property; yet this was a responsibility which gave them, and their Pharisee associates, powerful influence not only in the Council of Elders which advised the monarchs,[10] but over public opinion as well.

The Pharisees were eager to adapt their faith to modern needs, and the result was that the synagogues became the media through which Judaism was adapted to the changing world. Yet they remained, on the whole, opposed to Hellenizing relaxations, since they were the party most anxious to preserve the distinctively religious and theocratic character of Jewish life in defiance of Greek and Roman ways. In spite, therefore, of their scathing references to the rabble or scum who failed to understand the Law, they were popular. This was not so much because of their precepts but because, in their own way, they acted as a focus for natural hopes and aspirations. They were the principal spiritual leaders, and their urge to keep up with the times gave them particular authority, as Stewart Perowne noted, in 'that undefined realm between religion and politics which is always the danger zone in any country'.

Although not necessarily in complete harmony with the policies of the secular power, they tended to avoid active opposition towards its

regime, instead advocating 'inner emigration' and submissive acceptance of the divine will – even if this meant endurance of worldly
oppression. That is to say, provided a government did not interfere
with their own beliefs, they were prepared to put up with it – whether
it was national or foreign. This was one of the reasons why they became
a remarkable expansive force in the Jewish Dispersion. As the anti-
Jewish *Gospel according to St Matthew* makes Jesus declare, 'You travel
over sea and land to win one convert; and when you have won him you
make him twice as fit for hell as you are yourselves.'[11]

The third of the principal groups indicated by Josephus comprised
the Essenes, who may have developed from a pacific, quietist branch
of the 'Pious' of earlier times.[12] The Essenes, who were said to number
four thousand, possessed a political importance of their own, but only
for the negative reason that they were unlikely to give the authorities
any trouble. Withdrawn, at least in part, into semi-monastic communities,[13] they made it their practice to refrain from disobedience to the
political power of the day, actually going so far as to maintain that no
ruler holds his office except by the will of God;[14] and Philo (the
younger), in the first century AD, said they had never clashed with any
ruler of Palestine, however tyrannical he might be.[15] This passivity,
however, did not necessarily imply agreement with the regimes they
so conspicuously failed to oppose. For one thing, they were at the
opposite pole from the collaborating Hellenizers. Secondly, sharing
the Pharisees' belief in bodily resurrection, they cloaked the doctrine
in potentially more disturbing terms by claiming to be prophets[16]
and laying emphatic stress upon the coming end of the world. And
above all they rejected the Hasmonaeans' assumption of the high-
priestly office, for they claimed that the *true* high priesthood, which
went back to David's nominee Zadok but had been in abeyance since
the time of Antiochus IV Epiphanes,[17] was represented only by themselves. The Temple cult, therefore, as now celebrated, meant nothing
to the Essenes. Their dedication to the exact ritual fulfilment of the
Torah, on the other hand, went to such extreme lengths that on the
Sabbath they were even forbidden to excrete.

Among the discoveries of recent years which have done most to
destroy Josephus' neat tripartite or quadripartite pattern* and to
provide a glimpse of the great variety which subsequently disappeared,
are the Hebrew scrolls of the Qumran sect. These scrolls, written in

* For his 'Fourth Philosophy', not relevant to this period, see p. 90.

ink on the hairy side of pieces of leather sown together with flaxen threads, were found in eleven caves in the vicinity of what was once the community of Khirbet Qumran, not far from the northern end of the Dead Sea.[18] New scrolls from this frightening wasteland, one of the deepest lying places upon earth yet a frequent setting for Jewish religious experience, have continued to come to light. Unfortunately, however, their employment for purposes of historical reconstruction must still be extremely limited, since even their approximate dates remain the subject of profound dispute. 'New material,' observed Victor Tcherikover, 'may furnish us with fresh data and at last produce the necessary certainty; but as long as this certainty is remote, we shall do well to be content with the dictum *ignoramus*.'[19] All that can be said is that many or most of the scrolls seem to belong to the later second or first centuries B C, that is to say to middle or late Hasmonaean times: a conclusion that does not disagree with the archaeologists' view that the settlement came into existence in *c.* 140–130 B C.

Whether there were other settlements belonging to the same movement, or to kindred movements, we are not yet in a position to say. The geographical position of Qumran has suggested to many that its members were Essenes, since an Essene community, perhaps the principal Essene community, is known to have existed nearby. And in many ways the attitudes of the two groups were not dissimilar. For example, the Qumran community, like the Essenes, broke away from central Judaism because they believed that the religious leaders of the day had failed and become corrupt. They also believed that the public worship at Jerusalem was conducted according to an erroneous calendar and by unworthy priests. Moreover, in the spirit of the earlier 'Pious', they were determined to resist the tides of invading Hellenism: 'the unfaithful wife is the Jewish people, and her lovers are the Gentiles who have led the nation astray'.[20] But the writings of the Qumran sect also show that they were a good deal more militant against the ruling power, whether Hasmonaean or (later) Roman, than the Essenes had normally been. It was evidently an indispensable part of their faith, and of their revelation concerning a future liberating end of the world, to resist the powers that be, here and now.

Once again, then, at Qumran, there reappears the 'Son of Man' of *Daniel* and *Enoch*, but now with sharper contours. To bring his empire into being, hatred must be fostered against the nation's enemies (who are ambiguously named), and at the appointed time, when an apocalyptic war shall be waged against the whole lot of them, God will make his terrible visitation,[21] and the bodies of the dead will be resurrected.[22] There are also references to a mysterious Teacher of Righteousness, a priest and recipient of divine revelation. He may, originally, have been the founder of Qumran, or at least one of its honoured leaders; but thereafter, perhaps, his name was perpetuated by his successors. Subsequently, however, the Teacher may have become associated in the minds of the sectaries with One who will return at the end of time. For a Redeemer is going to be born.[23] However, it is also declared, echoing *Zechariah*,[24] that there will not be one Messiah but two – preceded by a prophet: 'then shall come a prophet and the Messiahs of Aaron and Israel'.[25] The prophet may be the Teacher of Righteousness come again, or he may not. As for the Messiah of Aaron, he – unlike the Hasmonaeans – will be a high priest of the high-priestly stock of Aaron and Zadok. The Messiah of Israel, on the other hand, will be a layman, the traditional king of the house of David. Moreover, the Priestly Messiah, symbol of the devoted priests who are called to protect the legitimacy of the chief religious office, is placed above the Royal Messiah, who will obey him:[26] a significant and potentially subversive claim for the superiority of the religious over the worldly arm. The doctrine of a personal Messiah has now assumed an increasingly explicit form, and one which could not be welcome to the secular authorities.

Here, then, is an isolated glimpse of one of the numerous Jewish groups which subsequently disappeared from view. The Qumran community were convinced that they were the true heirs of the Covenant, and the faithful Remnant for whose benefit the Covenant was renewed, the 'sanctuary for Israel and the Holy of Holies for Aaron'. Although not strictly monastic – for the skeletons of women and a child of the second century B C have been found – they were some of the most exclusive sectarians the world has ever seen. Their Community Rule sets the severest standards of personal austerity and purity, unrelentingly subjecting human nature to the Law (in contrast to the Pharisees who tried to adapt the Law to human needs), and laying powerful stress on communal ownership and labour. Like other Jews, the Qumran community never allowed the scriptures to be out of their minds; and some of their practices partially foreshadow later Christian developments. When they took their common meal after a council meeting, they thought of the Messianic banquet foretold in a late passage of *Isaiah*. And when, to symbolize their entry into the Covenant, they underwent the ablutions of purificatory baptism, they remembered how Elisha, too, had ordered cleansing by these same waters.[27]

According to the so-called *Zadokite Fragment* or *Damascus Document* (or *Rule*), a work of completely uncertain date of which pieces from a number of copies have been found at Qumran in addition to a much larger section which turned up at Cairo, a group of exiles from Jerusalem were led by the Teacher of Righteousness to the 'land of Damascus'. It has often been assumed, therefore, that the document refers to another of these quasi-monastic groups which made its home at Damascus (in the same way as we hear of a settlement of refugees in 88 BC at Chalcis beneath Lebanon). This is possible, but the reference to the land of Damascus may also be metaphorical, in fulfilment of Amos' declaration that God would drive those in his disfavour 'into exile beyond Damascus'.[28] In that case, the real reference may be to some quite different place – and perhaps to Qumran, where so many fragments of this *Document* have been found:[29] indeed, whether the group which produced it was part of the Qumran sect or not, the work is strikingly similar in many respects to that community's Rule. The Jewish official caste is once more attacked[30] – as it was to be attacked in the Gospels – and there are various Messianic calculations.

Whether the emigration to Damascus really took place or not, Israel was not the only country where such quasi-monastic settlements existed. In Greek lands this tradition of seclusion went back, traditionally, as far as the sixth-century sage Pythagoras, and in the second century pagan recluses were appearing in Ptolemaic Egypt. There were also, near Alexandria and in numerous parts of Egypt ascetics of both sexes known as Therapeutae (Worshippers). Said to be of Jewish stock,[31] these devotees seem reminiscent of the Essenes and particularly of Qumran – though the Therapeutae were more philosophical in their general approach. They met only on the Sabbath, and for nocturnal festivals, at which they performed musical liturgies. A subtle allegory into which they converted the Jews' Crossing of the Red Sea may, by ironing out provocative features, have commended them to the Egyptians.

Whatever the exact relations of the Therapeutae with Judaism, they were only an outlying, secluded element among the vast number of Jews in Egypt. These had already been drawn into politics, and in 102 BC they played a vital part when the Ptolemaic queen Cleopatra III was deterred from a plan to reannex Israel by receiving a warning that this would be unacceptable to the Egyptian Jews.[32]

John Hyrcanus I was now dead, and so was his son Aristobulus I (104–103), a lover of Greek culture. His brother and successor Alexander I Jannaeus (Jehonathan or Jonathan, 103–76) was an exceedingly tough and ferocious character who, with the help of numerous mercenaries from southern Asia Minor, expanded Hasmonaean Israel to its largest extent.[33] These aggressions infuriated the Gentiles, but he rebutted their anger by claiming that he was only reviving the inheritance of his forefathers. To his high-priestly office he added the title of king, if his predecessor had not done so already, and he was the first of his royal line to issue coins.[34] These employ an archaic Hebrew script, to stress his nationalistic piety, and on other issues he tactfully couples his name with that of his Council of Elders.[35] These pieces, however, display Greek as well as Jewish inscriptions, and depict the un-Jewish maritime design of an anchor. This coin-type, imitated from Seleucid issues, stresses the achievement of Alexander Jannaeus in having established control of the entire coastline from Mount Carmel to the borders of Egypt, with the single exception of the city of Ascalon (Ashkelon), which remained free.

Alexander Jannaeus also introduced a new theme, which would henceforward be recurrent in his country's history, by coming into violent contact with its eastern and southern neighbour, the Nabataeans. This highly gifted people, whose territory included not only north western Arabia but the Negev and the greater part of Sinai, were Arab in race and speech, though their inscriptions show that they used a dialect of Aramaic, akin to the Aramaic of Israel, as their official and literary language. At first they were nomadic, but then as their customs became more settled they established their capital at Petra (*c.* 312 BC) on Mount Edom, now in Jordan, half-way between the Red Sea and the Gulf of Elat or Akaba. At Petra and elsewhere they developed not only great agricultural skill but a fascinating Greco-oriental architecture and art. Evading absorption by the Ptolemies and Seleucids, they controlled the spice and perfume caravan route from southern Arabia to the Mediterranean port of Gaza, and continued, during the last two centuries BC, to amass great wealth. But these successes, and their firm adherence to paganism, brought them into sharp conflict with the expansionist ambitions of Alexander Jannaeus.

The subsequent battles had various results, but in the end the Nabataeans were forced to cede him not only twelve cities across the Jordan but the terminal of Gaza itself.

These confrontations between Israel and the Nabataean Arabs also

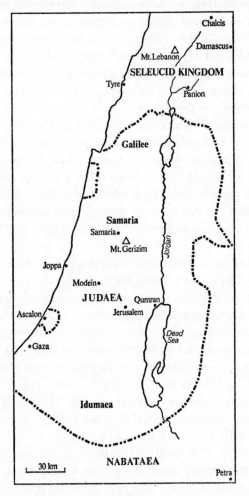

Judaea under the Hasmonaeans

(second and early first centuries B C)

possessed a further significance, because they could not fail to bring Jannaeus into closer contact with the greater Parthian power beyond. The control by the Parthians of the central route from India to the Mediterranean had played a great part in making Nabataean Petra one of the principal markets in Asia; and it was therefore a matter of concern to them when the Jews clashed with the Nabataeans and

47

seized from them maritime and other territory which encroached upon Parthian trade.

In consequence, the Parthians now proceeded to send a deputation to Alexander Jannaeus.[36] This was a particularly important event, seeing that they themselves, in Mesopotamia, harboured such large Jewish colonies that they could almost be regarded as a sort of 'reserve' Israel – like west European Jewry in the fifth and sixth centuries, when Byzantine and Babylonian Jewry were suffering, and American Jewry in the twentieth century, when European Jewry was decimated. These densely populated Mesopotamian colonies, extending over hundreds of miles, consisted mainly of the descendants of the Jews deported there by Babylonian monarchs in the sixth century BC. The Parthians, although adherents of a different sort of religion, the sun-cult of Zoroaster, regarded these settlers with tolerance, even if the loose-knit character of the realm meant that they could not always afford them sufficient protection against the Babylonians, who hated the Jews for their separateness. But the existence of these Jewish communities profoundly affected the relations of Parthia with other powers. Of this the Jews themselves were well aware, for they generally refused to commit themselves fully either to the Parthians or their more western suzerains, and this helped them to survive under both.

The communities in Parthia also possessed great economic significance for Israel, since they contributed on a massive scale to the Temple tax. The safe transmission of these funds to Jerusalem presented no mean problem. The custom arose, at an uncertain date, of employing two Babylonian cities, Nehardea on the Euphrates and Nisibis on a neighbouring island, as centres in which this tribute, once it had been collected, was kept safe under an elaborate guard. Then, finally, when everything was ready, great convoys of armed pilgrims carried the money every year to Jerusalem, a two-week journey by way of Sura, Palmyra and Damascus. The leading Jewish personages of Babylonia vied with one another for the honour of undertaking these missions, which often filled Jerusalem with more pilgrims than inhabitants.[37]

When the Parthian delegates visited Alexander Jannaeus, they did not omit to call on the religious leaders also. But they must have found them disaffected since this was the reign when disapproval of the secularization of the high priesthood, due to its amalgamation with the kingship, spread from the more rigorous groups to other elements in the population, including the Pharisees. One of them, Judah ben

Gedidiah, explicitly bade a monarch, probably Alexander Jannaeus, to be content with his royal crown, and to leave the priestly crown to the sons of Aaron.[38] Moreover, it was an additional source of dissatisfaction that he relied so exclusively upon the Sadducees for his support. Finally, eight hundred Pharisees broke into active disloyalty against him – and, after a savage civil war (94–89 B c), paid for this betrayal by crucifixion.

It is possible that this crisis produced the *Similitudes* (or *Parables*) *of Enoch* (*I Enoch*, Chs. 37–71). The writer seems to despair of earthly help, for he sees the awaited Messiah, the Son of Man, not as a saviour in this world but as a heavenly, transcendental figure. However, this refuge in apocalyptic escapism proved unnecessary, since Alexander Jannaeus' widow and successor Salome Alexandra (Shelomziyyon) (76–67), reputedly in accordance with her husband's deathbed advice,[39] reversed his hostility towards the Pharisees and treated them with favour. During her reign they and their friends the scribes dominated her Council of Elders and inflicted retaliatory persecutions upon the Sadducees, so that later Pharisaic writers looked back upon the queen's reign as a golden age.

However, it was most unusual, indeed exceptional, for the Jews to be ruled by a woman,[40] and this of course meant the temporary divorcement of the monarchy and the high priesthood. The latter office consequently had to go to her elder son John (Jehohanan) Hyrcanus II, a weak character guided by a brilliant Idumaean hereditary chieftain, Antipater. When the queen fell ill and then died, John Hyrcanus II, under pressure from Antipater, came to blows with his brother Aristobulus II, whereupon Antipater invited the Nabataean Arabs to march on Jerusalem. Their success was already assured when news came that revolutionized the situation. The Romans had arrived in Syria.

Part II

Herod and his Successors

4

The Jews under Pompey, Caesar and the Parthians[1]

During the latter part of the second century BC, the Roman republic had virtually completed its assertion of control over the entire Mediterranean region, east and west alike: a feat which no other power had ever achieved before or would ever achieve again. Yet, although great states succumbed to them, the Ptolemies and Seleucids were still allowed to pursue an attenuated existence. When Pompey the Great, the outstanding Roman military leader of the day, arrived in the east in order to suppress Rome's recalcitrant enemy Mithridates VI of Pontus (66–63 BC), the Ptolemies still had over thirty years of troubled existence ahead of them. But the Seleucids, deeply rent by dynastic quarrels and almost destroyed by a transient great power under Tigranes I of Armenia, had come to the end of the road. For Pompey, fresh from suppressing both Mithridates and Tigranes, now proceeded to move into Syria and annex it as a Roman province, abolishing the Seleucid monarchy altogether (63 BC): this new Roman dominion was to serve as a bastion against the only major power that Rome had to contend with anywhere in the world, the kingdom of Parthia.

Israel would clearly be the next region to come under some sort of Roman control, since it, too, was needed to safeguard the eastern frontier against the Parthians. At this stage, therefore, John Hyrcanus II and his brother Aristobulus II both thought it best to settle their struggle with one another by appealing to Pompey – an action which was obviously risky, though perhaps by now they could see no alternative. However, a third Jewish delegation, significantly enough, requested Pompey to place neither of the contenders on the throne, but to set up a priestly regime,[2] reminiscent of the ancient days of Ezra. Before reaching a decision upon this subject, Pompey wanted first to suppress and annex Nabataean Arabia, thus securing the frontier still further, but was obliged to postpone this action (indeed, it took another 169 years to achieve it) owing to the hostile behaviour of Aristobulus II in Jerusalem. Before long Pompey was besieging Aristobulus in the Temple itself, and soon it fell to him by storm. A general massacre followed. The priests were struck down in the middle of their holy office, and Pompey, though he preserved the Temple treasure, did not hesitate to set foot in the Holy of Holies itself. Probably he just wanted to see for himself what secrets this mysterious, imageless place contained. But his visit was an intolerable affront to the Jews – even worse than the profanation by the troops of Antiochus Epiphanes – since no one but the high priest was permitted to enter the place. Pompey was execrated for ever afterwards; and Roman suzerainty had started badly.

After occupying Jerusalem, he reinstated John Hyrcanus II. But Hyrcanus' principality was drastically shorn: he was deprived of numerous possessions including not only the plain of Jezreel (Esdraelon) and Samaria (or at least the parts round its Hellenized capital of the same name), but also Transjordan (where a league of ten Greek cities, the Decapolis, was established), and, on the other side, the entire Mediterranean coastal strip. These territories were placed under the local control of Greek city authorities, under the ultimate supervision of the new Roman governorship of Syria. Israel was thus reduced to its diminutive Jewish core, with Jezreel and Samaria as a Roman corridor between its principal remaining component parts, Judaea and Galilee. The country was also compelled to pay an annual tax to Rome.[3]

Moreover John Hyrcanus II, while retaining the high priesthood, became, officially, a dependant or vassal ('client') of Rome – and at the same time he was demoted from king to prince (ethnarch). In compensation, however, this title of ethnarch, ruler of the nation, was interpreted as confirming his inherited rights of intervention in matters affecting the Jews of the Dispersion, where he 'shall be the protector of those Jews who are unjustly treated'.[4] Perhaps unwittingly, Pompey had helped to lay the basis for the Jewish patriarchate of Judaea, to which the Romans, in the distant future, were to allow similar powers.

He had also swelled the Dispersion, for during the upheavals of this time many Jews emigrated from Israel. They included peasants who fled from the territories he transferred to Gentile control; and there was an influx of Jewish prisoners of war into Rome. For the most part, however, they did not remain prisoners for long, because it was a religious duty of local Jews, and especially synagogues, to ransom them and set them free,[5] whereupon they continued to reside in Rome as free citizens. The orator Cicero, in his speech *In Defence of Flaccus* (59 BC), complains, perhaps with exaggeration, of the large size of the Jewish community, and the influence it had acquired in the city.[6] Cicero's speech also reveals one of the ways in which the Jews of the Dispersion were subjected to harassment. His client on this occasion, Lucius Valerius Flaccus, had taken steps, while governor of Asia, to prevent the large Jewish communities there from sending their annual tax contribution to the Jerusalem Temple, and Jewish funds had been seized at a number of the Greek cities of the province. While such action by governors was normally frowned upon by the central Roman authorities, it was popular with the Greek and Hellenized inhabitants and leaders of the local cities, who continually resented this diversion of funds for purposes that lay right outside their own territories and were devoted, moreover, to a religion which seemed deliberately to set itself apart. Cicero defends Flaccus on the economic grounds that the transfer of money from one country to another for commercial purposes was forbidden, and that it was a good thing for such exportations of funds to be prevented.

Moreover, he remarks elsewhere, voicing a widespread view at the time, that Judaism had shown the emptiness of its claim to enjoy divine privilege when it suffered such a total defeat at the hands of the Romans under Pompey:

Each state has its own religious scruples, we have ours. Even while Jerusalem was standing and the Jews were at peace with us, the practice of their sacred rites was at variance with the glory of our empire, the dignity of our name, the customs of our ancestors. But now it is even more so, when that nation by its armed resistance has shown what it thinks of our rule; how dear it was to the immortal gods is shown by the fact that it has been conquered, let out for taxes, made a slave.[7]

One of Cicero's teachers, the philosopher Posidonius, who was a keen supporter of Pompey, infused his Greek *Histories* with even more strongly anti-Jewish views, claiming that Antiochus IV Epiphanes had found, in the Holy of Holies, a statue of a bearded man holding a book and riding on a donkey:[8] and that this was Moses, who gave the Jews their laws of hatred towards the whole of mankind.

Meanwhile Jewish literature had its own contributions to make to the traumatic capture of Jerusalem. One of the *Psalms of Solomon*, a collection of eighteen poems extant in Greek and Syrian versions, refers to the event, and to the developments that preceded it.[9] Pompey, like earlier enemies, is the providential Scourge of God come to punish the unworthy Jews. But, although strong partisanship is lacking – the authors seem to be Pharisees of the more pacific variety – the main burden of disapproval seems to fall upon the Hasmonaeans. There is a clear affirmation of the weak, illegitimate priestly foundations of the Hasmonaean dynasty, and a detailed description of the very different king, of David's house, who is to come when the greatness, goodness and justice of God will make Israel the ruler of the world – presumably by overthrowing the Romans. The expected leader is described as the Messiah, and this, as far as our knowledge goes, is the first occasion on which such a description is applied to the Davidic leader who is going to bring about the new order. In these works he is envisaged as a human figure who will actually rule in Jerusalem. 'And who can stand up against him? He is mighty in his works and strong in the fear of God, tending the flock of the Lord with faith and righteousness; and he shall suffer none among them to faint in their pasture.'[10]

The dates of the scrolls belonging to the community of Qumran, as we have seen, are still impossible to establish. But some of them may well belong to the grim time after Pompey's capture of Jerusalem. One such document (a religious calendar) specifically refers, among earlier historical personages, to Scaurus, the general whom Pompey left behind in Judaea.[11] Many of the Qumran hymns, which tell of hope in spite of disaster, and of future victory, can also be referred to this period, though not with any certainty. Of the same date, too, could be Qumran's *War of the Sons of Light and the Sons of Darkness*, otherwise known as the *War Scroll* or *War Rule*. In this curious work, the powers of good and evil are pitted against each other in a fierce struggle of vengeance, with ultimate judgment upon the stubborn-hearted to be exercised by the weak-kneed and oppressed, the 'poor' or 'downcast in spirit'[12] – a phrase which was to become so familiar in Christian theology. Relevance to Pompey's invasion has also been seen, quite plausibly, in a

Qumran *Commentary* (or *Exegesis*) *on the Book of Habakkuk*, a prophet of Judah of the late seventh century B C. This commentary, while once again indicating an external enemy, turns inwards as well, and insists on careful discernment between true and false aspirants to benefits under the Covenant. It also denounces with particular outspokenness the fiscal oppression and exploitation of the poor that was a continuing feature of life in Israel.

However the Idumaean Antipater, who retained his position as John Hyrcanus II's counsellor and guide, took the view that the country's recent severe treatment at the hands of the Romans made it necessary not by any means to attempt sedition against them, but to collaborate with them all the more closely. He therefore helped Scaurus in an attack on the Nabataean Arabs which, although not entirely successful, did at least result in the Nabataeans becoming 'clients' of Rome, even if somewhat independent ones (62). Five years later, after rebellions by the Hasmonaean faction which Pompey had rejected, another of his supporters, Gabinius, became governor of Syria and introduced far-reaching constitutional changes into the diminished Israeli state. John Hyrcanus II was deprived of his ethnarchy, retaining only the high priesthood, and his truncated country was divided into five small units, each under a council of local Jewish notables.

This unusual arrangement (which Rome had applied on an earlier occasion to Macedonia) was popular among the Sadducee aristocracy, who found themselves in a position of power. Moreover, they were allowed, outside Jerusalem at least, the lucrative task of collecting Rome's taxes in place of Pompey's Roman tax-collectors. But they must have been less pleased when Gabinius embarked on an expensive restoration of the largely paganized city of Samaria, as well as a number of other cities. Antipater, who seems to have been granted Idumaea as a personal fief, continued to collaborate with the Romans. First, he helped Gabinius to undertake an expedition against Egypt – persuading a Jewish section of the Egyptian army at the frontier town of Pelusium not to oppose the Roman force. Then, after a further Hasmonaean revolt, Antipater was entrusted by the Romans with some kind of official supervision of Jerusalem, including the responsibility for the collection of its taxes.

The years that followed were very uncomfortable for Israel. In Rome, the First Triumvirate of Pompey, Caesar and Crassus had virtually superseded the traditional republican institutions and was ruling the empire in autocratic fashion. Crassus was given the task of invading Parthia, and on his way he plundered the Treasury of the Jerusalem Temple, which even Pompey had respected. Then, while Crassus was thus engaged, yet another local rebellion had to be crushed by Roman intervention, this time, significantly, in Galilee, which in future years was to witness many such revolts; its purpose, this time, was to espouse the cause of Hyrcanus' dispossessed brother. Next came the sensational news that Crassus had been defeated and killed by the Parthians at Carrhae (Haran) in northern Mesopotamia. Syria and Israel now seemed wide open to their attack, and there were, as always, Jews who were willing to welcome them. But Crassus' lieutenant Cassius, who had put down the Galilean revolt, showed such severity that no internal disloyalty was able to show its head, and owing to the Parthians' weak internal organization their attack never materialized.

Soon after Crassus' death the two surviving triumvirs, Pompey and Caesar, drifted into empire-wide Civil War (49). In spite of Pompey's never-to-be forgotten offence against Judaism in Jerusalem, John Hyrcanus II and Antipater were obliged to take his side.[13] In return, the Pompeian consul Lentulus Crus exempted such Jews of Asia as were Roman citizens from military service; we hear of those of Ephesus (Selçuk),[14] but no doubt the same concession was granted at other Greek cities also. Although Jews had served in the armies of the Ptolemies and other powers, Lentulus Crus was no doubt influenced by the unsuitability for the profession of war, since the Law, in addition to its dietetic requirements, forbade them to carry arms or march on the Sabbath. But these Pompeian privileges to the Jews did them little good, since in the following year Pompey's total defeat at Pharsalus in Thessaly placed Hyrcanus and Antipater, like his other supporters, in a highly dangerous situation.

However, they soon found a chance to redeem themselves. For after Pompey had fled to Egypt and was murdered by the representatives of young Ptolemy XIII upon its shore, Caesar, who had pursued him there, found his new-formed alliance and amorous friendship with Ptolemy's half-sister Cleopatra VII interrupted by fierce armed opposition in Alexandria. He sent to Asia Minor for help, but the relief column was held up on Israel's southern border. At this point, however, Antipater, accompanied by the high priest Hyrcanus himself, arrived in timely fashion at Ascalon with at least fifteen hundred Jewish soldiers, to clear the way ahead. And during the five to eight days' desert journey onwards into Egypt, it was Antipater, once again, who kept the relief army supplied with food and drink. Furthermore, the presence of this Jewish force, escorting the high priest in person, stimulated the numerous Egyptian Jews around the temple city of Leontopolis to rally to Caesar: Jewish units in the Egyptian army at Heliopolis and Memphis did the same.

When, therefore, Caesar had overcome his enemies and restored Cleopatra to the Egyptian throne as a Roman ally, he showed marked gratitude towards the Jews. First, he caused Cleopatra to confer some improvement of status (its exact nature is unidentifiable) upon the Jewish community of Alexandria, a measure which was no doubt unpopular with the Greek and Egyptian populations but could be enforced by the garrison Caesar left behind him in the city. The powerful Jewish minorities elsewhere in Egypt, and in the Cyrenaican cities of Cyrene and Berenice (Benghazi), no doubt benefited as well. Then, at Rome, he arranged for the senate to exempt synagogues from a general ban on associations. Moreover, he promulgated a series of measures confirming the freedom of worship and privileged autonomous status of Jewish communities in Phoenicia and Asia Minor. Such decrees were not new, but the extent and detailed character of the edicts attributed to Caesar seem to justify their description as 'a veritable Magna Carta' guaranteeing the privileges of the Jewish Dispersion.

Caesar's measures were followed, over the next eighty years, by a series of similar decrees issued by other Roman leaders, beginning with an announcement of 44–43 B C issued to all the Roman officials in Asia. These documents, taken as a whole, enjoin the Greek cities to guarantee their Jews exemption from military service, protection of Sabbath observance (when Jews were not expected to attend the law-courts), freedom to hold religious meetings, freedom to send their money contributions to the Jerusalem Temple without molestation, the right to settle their internal legal controversies by their own jurisdiction, and instructions that their funds and sacred books should not be stolen from their synagogues.

This tolerance to the Jews of the Dispersion – men who were, on the whole, unwilling to participate in civic and imperial institutions – is a significant feature of the Roman empire. Admittedly, it was due partly to administrative conservatism: the Romans tolerated the Jews because they found them tolerated already. It owed something, also, to the desire for a quiet life, since this very certainly would not be attainable if ever the Jews felt aggrieved. But it was also an emphatic principle of Roman rule that every community should, as far as possible, be allowed to maintain its national customs, including the worship of its own gods in its own way. Pagan cults, after all, tolerated one another; religious exclusiveness was regarded as weird. And so, paradoxically, the Roman authorities issued tolerant dispensations in favour of the intolerant Jewish God.

As the constant need to repeat the decrees suggests, this policy of tolerance ran into a good deal of opposition from the Greeks who ruled and dwelt in the cities where such Jewish communities existed. For, as A.N.Sherwin-White observes:

these privileges represented a considerable diminution of the ordinary powers of the local government over resident foreigners, and were resented. So the Greek city officials had long been trying to suppress all these activities. At Miletus and Parium (in western Asia Minor) a specific decree had been passed by the city assemblies to this end. At Sardis the importation of Jewish foodstuffs had been prohibited. At Ephesus Jews had been fined for celebrating the Sabbath ... At Halicarnassus and Ephesus Roman pressure secured the sanction of a fine against any magistrate who prevented the Jewish faithful from keeping the Sabbath ... No fewer than eight cities came under Roman pressure for their anti-Semitic activities, some of them more than once.[15]

The documents to which he refers, collected by Josephus, all happen to relate to the province of Asia,[16] but no doubt similar dossiers once existed for the other eastern provinces too, and perhaps for some western regions as well. And so the Dispersion survived, and modestly flourished. The number of Jews in the world in Julius Caesar's time is impossible to determine: perhaps there were about eight million, as against fourteen million today. Out of these, it may be estimated that a million lived outside the Roman empire – mainly in the Parthian kingdom, and most of all in Babylonia. Out of the remaining (conjectural) seven million living within the Roman empire, and representing between six and nine per cent of its inhabitants, there may have been two and a half million in Israel itself. Of the rest, perhaps there were a million in Egypt, one and a half million in Syria and Asia Minor combined and 100,000 each in Italy and Cyrenaica. It is likely that in the eastern provinces as a whole the Jews comprised nearly twenty per cent of the total population; and there were many Samaritans as well.

This number was attained by the winning of proselytes, an activity to which as has been seen, the Pharisees devoted themselves with particular enthusiasm.[17] 'God sent Israel into Exile among the nations,' observed a rabbi, 'only for the purpose of acquiring converts.'[18] This was an age in which men, and especially women, had a fierce longing for supernatural inspiration and help. Judaism gave them what they needed. And it possessed many other attractions too – simple moral rules, an impressive Holy Book, a strictly regulated way of life (including a weekly day of rest) and a tightly knit community. In the Dispersion, life was not made too difficult for a convert, because there were a number of Hellenic relaxations: at Miletus for example, despite orthodox Jewish prohibitions of the drama, good seats in the front row of the theatre were reserved for the Jews. Nevertheless, the proselyte was expected gradually to become a thoroughgoing Jew – it was declared that he must truly abandon kin and country.[19] Whether he was also expected to undergo circumcision was disputable, and disputed.[20] Circumcision presented little difficulty to certain eastern peoples, notably the Phoenicians, many of whom had long since followed the practice. But elsewhere it was a step which many pagans, otherwise favourably inclined to Judaism, were not prepared to take, while some were nervous that such a very thoroughgoing conversion would draw censure from their Greek neighbours. In such conditions, the idea that circumcision could be dispensed with gained ground in the Dispersion.

There was also a further category of *sebomenoi*, 'god-fearers' who sympathized with Judaism and enjoyed a recognized status upon its fringes. And it was largely through these half-way groups that the Jews of the Dispersion, as Salo Baron observed, 'more than any other population group, seem to have served as the yeast in this fermenting world'.[21] Nevertheless, in spite of every variation of local circumstances, the Jewish communities of the Dispersion persistently retained those autonomous institutions – independent of the host city – which Caesar and others were at such remarkable pains to protect, while at the same time maintaining a strong but ill-defined allegiance to Jerusalem, half-religious and half-political in character.

In general, these communities were run by well-born families whose hereditary boards of administrative and judicial functionaries showed little sympathy for democratic ideas.[22] This was the case, for example, in Ptolemaic Egypt. In that country, the Jews were almost everywhere.[23]

In Alexandria, they probably comprised one third of the city's population; their government, quite distinct from the Greek municipal organization,[24] was unitary, with its own Jewish council, under a president (ethnarch), who 'ruled the people, judged its cases and supervised the implementation of contracts and orders like the ruler of an independent state'.[25] The many Alexandrian synagogues, including the magnificent principal building,[26] came under this central control.[27] At Rome, on the other hand, the synagogues, of which thirteen of various epochs are known, seem to have operated separately as independent units. The absence of a unified Jewish organization in Rome may have been due to the comparatively small size of the community, which, in spite of Cicero's assertions of its power, was far smaller than Alexandria's; perhaps there were between twenty and forty thousand Jews in Rome at the beginning of our era.[28] But there may also have been a Roman feeling that, in the capital, any too compact or too tightly knit central organization of an alien race and religion were impermissible.

Nevertheless, the Roman synagogues, each under its own council chaired by a president (*archisynagogus*),[29] were granted autonomous administration of their communal property, with a right to levy their own obligatory contributions and to inflict fines for offences such as burial-violation. When there were Roman distributions of grain and oil, the Jews were given a double portion on Friday so that they need not attend on the Sabbath; and, since some Jewish authorities prohibited the dietary use of heathen oil, they were authorized (at least by Augustus' time) to demand money instead. It was not a very wealthy community. The inscriptions, dating from the imperial epoch, of the Jewish underground burial-places (catacombs), which existed at Rome as elsewhere,[30] show weavers, tent-makers, dyers, butchers, painters, jewellers and doctors – not yet the moneylenders and financiers who were characteristic of later communities. In other words, Jews followed most of the usual professions (outside the cities, they engaged extensively in agriculture). At Rome as elsewhere, they paid great attention to education; though little Hebrew was evidently spoken, since most of the inscriptions are in Greek. Jewish slaves were rare, partly because their communities were so quick to ransom prisoners and partly because their religious institutions were hard for slavemasters to cope with. The community was spread fairly widely in the city, mostly on its fringes, but there was a considerable concentration in what is now Trastevere, on the right bank of the Tiber. Young Romans, the poet Ovid tells us, hung around synagogues in the hope of romantic adventures.[31] Elsewhere in Italy, there is fairly certain evidence for *kosher* food at Pompeii,[32] and at the great neighbouring port of Puteoli (Pozzuoli) there was already in Caesar's time a well-to-do Jewish colony.

Caesar's measures in favour of the Jewish communities of the Dispersion were evidently prompted by his friendship for the Jewish leaders in Israel itself, Antipater and the high priest John Hyrcanus II. And meanwhile in Israel itself he took decisive steps to revive, under their leadership, the little state that had been split by Gabinius into five parts. This division was abolished, and the borders of the re-amalgamated state were enlarged by the return of Joppa and the Jezreel (Esdraelon) plain to Jewish rule, though a Roman enclave in Samaria still separated the country's two main component parts, Judaea and Galilee. John Hyrcanus II was given back the title of prince (ethnarch) of which Pompey had deprived him, together with other privileges specified in surviving decrees of Caesar. Moreover, his coinage now describes him as President of his Council of Elders.[33] Antipater, too, obtained a more explicitly recognized role as chief minister, with the duty of collecting the Roman land-tax throughout the whole country. At the same time this was diminished from one third of the sown corn, the figure under the Seleucids, to one quarter.[34]

Antipater was also authorized to entrust key posts to his two extremely able eldest sons, the first, Phasael, being made governor of Jerusalem, and the second, the twenty-five-year-old Herod (later the Great), obtaining the governorship of the detached province of Galilee. Among the volatile population of this recently converted region, Herod had to deal with a serious rising, led by a certain Hezekiah (Ezekias). Such risings, except in periods of unusual calm, were often more or less continuous, and nowhere more than in Galilee. However, there is a wide difference of opinion about their character. Should they be regarded as a series of independent outbursts of mere banditry and brigandage, such as was readily facilitated by Galilee's proximity to Mount Lebanon? This, as Josephus shows us, is how the disturbances tended to be regarded by the political power. Or should they, on the other hand, be thought of as the continuing and more or less coherent manifestations of patriotic, nationalistic, freedom-fighting, in the tradition of the hero Judas Maccabaeus? That, in general, is how modern Israeli historians treat these outbreaks. The two interpretations, however, do not exclude one another, and most of the risings perhaps shared elements of both attitudes, complicated by the extreme regionalism of the entire area, which meant that a Galilean, for example, was more likely to be fighting for Galilee than for anything or anywhere else.

At all events, Herod defeated and captured Hezekiah, and put him and many of his followers to death. This taking of the law into his own hands got him into grave trouble with the Jewish Council in Jerusalem. Although John Hyrcanus II, its president, was prince and high priest, and Herod's own father Antipater was the most powerful man in the country, the Council, seventy-one members strong, was the only body entitled to administer the Law throughout the territory of Israel. After the death of Salome Alexandra, the Sadducees had reasserted their dominance over its deliberations, though there was still a strong minority of Pharisees. One of these, the conservative Shammai,[35] now proceeded to launch an attack on Herod's conduct; and the Council, not sorry to have an opportunity to weaken the Idumaean house of Antipater, adopted such a threatening attitude towards the young prince that, after a brief and perilous visit to Jerusalem, he fled to the free city of Damascus. Once outside Israel, however, he easily gained the support of the Roman governor of Syria, Sextus Julius Caesar. A relative of Gaius Julius Caesar himself, Sextus appreciated his distinguished kinsman's attachment to the Idumaean house, and now proceeded to give Herod a significant command, comprising not only the Golan heights but the Roman territory of Samaria between Jerusalem and Galilee.

The subsequent murder of the dictator Caesar was, understandably, lamented by the Jews.[36] It also necessitated a painful readjustment by Antipater and his sons, since almost immediately afterwards Caesar's assassins Brutus and Cassius arrived in the east, and asserted control over the whole area. A reckoning was bound to come with the late dictator's supporters, Antony and Octavian (the future Augustus), and Cassius required the Jews to contribute large sums for the coming campaign. Herod keenly collected money for him in Galilee, whereupon Cassius confirmed his command in south Syria and Samaria and gave him a post in Judaea as well. But anti-Idumaean feelings in the country were still strong, and after a series of internal crises Antipater was murdered. However, Herod, presumably with the connivance of Cassius, murdered his father's murderer, and then had to meet a dangerous in-

vasion of Judaea by a rival. This was Antigonus, son of that brother of
Hyrcanus whom Pompey had driven out, and a standard-bearer of
traditional Hasmonaean nationalism. Herod repelled Antigonus, and
was rewarded by Hyrcanus with a Hasmonaean fiancée, Mariamme
(Miriam).

However, Cassius and Brutus succumbed to Antony and Octavian
at Philippi in Macedonia (42); and, with Antony now entrusted by his
colleagues in the Second Triumvirate (Octavian and Lepidus) with the
eastern regions of the empire, Hyrcanus and his Idumaean advisers had
to adjust their loyalties once again. They were duly permitted to do so,
and Phasael and Herod were confirmed in their appointments in
Jerusalem and Galilee respectively, with the status of tetrarch – a
princely title next in importance to Hyrcanus' own ethnarchy. Huge
Jewish delegations urging Antony to withdraw these favours towards
the Idumaeans were rebuffed and dispersed by him with numerous
casualties.

But shortly afterwards the entire situation was changed when the
Parthians, who had so shatteringly defeated Crassus thirteen years
earlier, burst through the Roman defences into Asia Minor and Syria
(40). Then they pressed onwards into Israel as well, where they set
Antigonus on the throne.

This sudden, violent re-entry of the eastern power into Palestinian
history was an event which the Romans never forgot, for it opened up
the horrifying possibility, indeed probability, that when the Parthians
intervened in this way they would always find dissident populations in
the Levant, and particularly in Israel, to support them. That is what
happened now. There was no lack of Jews to applaud Antigonus' policy
of anti-Roman, Hasmonaean, nationalism. Once he was installed, he or
the Parthians inflicted a bizarre retribution upon John Hyrcanus II,
cutting off or mutilating his ears. This meant that he could no longer
be high priest, since according to the Torah such a physical defect was a
disqualification for that office.[37] He was deported by the Parthians to
Babylonia, and Antigonus became high priest as well as king: his coins
call him by the royal title in Greek, and 'Mattathias the high priest' in
Hebrew.[38] The Idumaean brothers were also swept from the scene.
Phasael was killed, and Herod fled to Idumaea, and then to Cleopatra –
who offered him a job, which he refused. Then Herod moved onwards,
to Rome.

5

The Kingship of Herod the Great

When Herod came to Rome, he came primarily to see Antony, who was in charge of the east. Antony now persuaded his fellow-triumvirs and the senate to make Herod not only a 'friend and ally of the Roman people', but king as well – the first king of Israel, or Judaea, recognized by the Romans since the suspension of the kingship by Pompey. Herod was given the appointment in order that he should win his country back from Antigonus and the Parthians, and make it a Roman client state once again. This conferment of the royal title upon him was a fateful decision, since it meant the termination of the national Hasmonaean dynasty in favour of an Idumaean house of recent conversion and Arab race. It also meant that the kingship and high priesthood must become definitively separated, since Herod lacked even a shred of family quali-fication for the priestly office.

And so he returned to the near east with an army of non-Jewish mer-cenaries. The long haul to recover all the territories seized by Parthia had now begun.[1] It was greatly assisted because Antony, who did not take the field himself, had a general of genius in Ventidius: two decisive engagements (39, 38) drove the Parthians out of Syria. Antigonus still held out – issuing coins which uniquely display the seven-branched candlestick (Menorah),[2] and denouncing Herod as a commoner and a mere 'half-Jew':[3] this is a term which Jews say cannot exist, but Anti-gonus meant that he was a foreigner whom it was unlawful for Israel to have as its ruler. Nevertheless, after a series of difficult campaigns, in which the Roman assistance to Herod at times seemed half-hearted and corrupt, Antigonus finally succumbed in 37 to Antony's general Sosius, who sent him to his master for execution and installed Herod as Rome's client king in Jerusalem.

Antony trusted him to provide the bastion, and the rear communications, which his forthcoming expeditions against Parthia were going to need. He was also allowed to reannex Samaria, and for a short time a coastal strip. But Herod was no more successful than John Hyrcanus ii in asserting his claim to most of the Gentile and semi-Gentile territories bordering on Judaea, whether on the coast or in the interior, since Antony gave them to his mistress Cleopatra. At the same time she pleaded with Antony to give her the whole of Israel – so that she could revive the territories of her Ptolemaic ancestors. Cleopatra was risking the displeasure of the Alexandrian Jews when she made this appeal; but she never had to test their reaction, since Antony persistently rejected or evaded her pleas. For his middle eastern and Parthian policy seemed to him to require a dependent monarch in Jerusalem as well as in Alexandria.

Having established himself on the throne, Herod did not forget that the Jewish Council of Elders had threatened his life ten years earlier, after his operations in Galilee, and had subsequently supported his enemy Antigonus. So forty-five of its seventy-one members were executed, and the Council itself was deprived of all its political power and superseded by a private council of Herod's friends (supplemented, when propaganda required it, by mass rallies). The casualties were mainly Sadducees, and the old type of pro-Hasmonaean Sadducee was virtually exterminated. It might have been thought that the Council's Pharisaic members would also suffer, seeing that one of their leading members, Shammai, had led the movement against Herod in 47. But he and the second great Pharisee, the more cheerful, practical and progressive Hillel (of Babylonian origin),[4] were spared because during the last days of the war with Antigonus they had urged their fellow-Jews to submit to Herod.

Hillel and Shammai, two of the outstanding and most revered Jewish leaders of all time, were the directors, and perhaps something like founders, of two academies for the exposition of the Torah. Such studies flourished during the years to come, under the Tannaim (Teachers), as they had never flourished before; and this was partly owing to the good understanding that these Pharisees achieved with Herod.[5] True, they declared that he was an infliction from heaven, God's scourge and an instrument of judgement. But Herod did not mind that; the sentiment was not a new one, and it was more important when they went on to say that the scourge just had to be endured. In other words, they confirmed a tradition among the Pharisees, or at least among an important section of them, that the rulers of the day should not be opposed: the tradition of Hillel's teacher Shemaiah, who advised the Jews to 'love work and shun authority and have nothing to do with the ruling power'.[6] Having nothing to do with it meant doing nothing to oppose it; and so they constituted a kind of passive pro-Herodian party. A more radical group of Pharisees might fulminate against the secular power, in this respect (though not in others) resembling the withdrawn Qumran community, but for the moment not very much was heard of this actively hostile element. As for that other semi-monastic group, the Essenes, they too were sufficiently quietist to present no difficulty, and Herod is on record as admiring them and respecting their prophetic gifts. Indeed, at a later stage of his reign (*c.* 17 BC) he actually exempted Essenes and Pharisees alike from taking a general oath of allegiance to himself, the former because they objected to oaths on principle and the latter because they disliked using the name of God in an oath. This deliberate mark of tolerance ensured that for a long time neither group would move into open opposition.

With this measure of backing behind him, Herod was able to turn to the problem of the high priesthood. The problem was a considerable one, because the Hasmonaean incumbent, King Antigonus, had been executed, and the Sadducees, who had always been the main props of the high-priestly office, had suffered terrible casualties. Nor did rumours spread by Herod's own friends that his family had been priestly after all cut any ice, or persuade him to take the fatal step of becoming high priest himself. John Hyrcanus II, at this stage, was invited back from Parthia by Herod, and came. The mutilation of his ears still disqualified him from resuming the office on his own account, however, so it had to go to someone else. But this must be someone loyal and obedient – and suggestions that Herod should restore the secular powers of the post seemed to him wholly unacceptable. On the contrary, he even proposed to retain under his own control the sacred vestments, which were said to be copied from those with which God himself had invested Aaron,[7] and were ascribed magical powers. So the high-priestly vestments, with all their powers of arousing popular emotion, were only to be handed over to the high priests for the services on the three major holidays and the Day of Atonement – a complicated arrangement, because a seven-day period of purification was required before each feast.

With these precautions arranged, Herod proceeded to bestow the high priesthood upon an obscure Jew from Babylonia named Hananel. This was an ingenious decision, since he was able to point out that the claim of Hananel, who was reputed to be a descendant of Aaron himself through David's high priest Zadok, was actually better than the title of the Hasmonaeans. Furthermore, there was precedent for giving Mesopotamian Jews high religious office in Israel[8] and it was tactful to the Pharisees to do so since their leader Hillel was also of Babylonian origin.

But like many of Herod's ideas, it was too clever by half. In particular it greatly infuriated his Hasmonaean mother-in-law Alexandra, mother of Mariamme. Indeed, after Alexandra had appealed to Cleopatra, he was forced to revoke the appointment in favour of his mother-in-law's seventeen-year-old son Aristobulus. However, when Antony was safely out of the way in the wilds of Armenia and Media, Herod arranged a bathing party at Jericho at which Aristobulus was drowned (36). When the inevitable outcry arose, Antony summoned him to offer some sort of an explanation. Yet Herod was retained in his confidence and in power – though by now he was humiliatingly paying rent to Cleopatra for his own valuable Jericho plantations, which he had been compelled to transfer to her possession. However, he had also been given a good opportunity to interfere in the affairs of the Nabataean Arabs. For they, likewise, had been forced to cede important properties to her, namely their Dead Sea bitumen deposits, and now Herod himself offered to collect the rent on Cleopatra's behalf. The high priesthood was restored to Hananel; and when he abdicated or died his successors were derived, for the greater part of the next century, from the members of two Sadducee families, with a few members from a third.[9] Some of their co-religionists bemoaned the arrogance and violence of these high-priestly dynasties,[10] but they suited Herod very well. Tenures were kept short, and former high priests retained the same privileged status as the actual incumbents. In this way there was built up, in due course, quite a nucleus of 'new', subservient Sadducees, replacing those whose Hasmonaean sympathies had cost them their lives.

Cleopatra's constant pressure on Antony to destroy Herod never succeeded, though at times it may have been close to bringing him down – especially when she fomented rebellion in Idumaea, while continuing at the same time to encourage the king's Hasmonaean relatives-in-law to sedition. But in the end he survived, and Cleopatra did not. It had been clear for some time that Antony and Cleopatra were destined to clash with Octavian, who now held sole control of the western Roman empire. When the final breach came, and all the eastern client kings flocked to join Antony's army and navy guarding western Greece from the expected Italian invasion, Cleopatra prevented Herod from coming too. Instead, she induced Antony to send him against the Nabataean Arabs who had failed to pay her bitumen rent – and at the same time she sent a general of her own to make sure Herod would not defeat them too completely.

But meanwhile Antony and Cleopatra were worsted by Octavian's admiral Marcus Agrippa in the preliminaries to the naval battle of Actium (31). When the battle took place, they tried to break out, but only a relatively small proportion of their fleet, and none of their army, was able to escape with them back to Egypt; when Octavian arrived there in pursuit in the following year they both committed suicide. By this time, the eastern client monarchs had already hastened to change sides – mostly with success, since Octavian's opinion of them (other than Cleopatra) was, on the whole, as high as Antony's. Among those who succeeded in joining the victorious cause was Herod: after taking the precaution of executing Hyrcanus in case of a Hasmonaean revolt, he sailed to Rhodes to meet the conqueror and have his kingship confirmed. At the same time, he received back by far the greater part of the lands of which Israel had been shorn thirty-two years earlier by Pompey, including the entire coastal strip and two of the Greek Ten Cities (Decapolis) across Jordan, namely Hippos (Susita) and Gadara. His triumph was only damped by grave family troubles, resulting in the execution of his Hasmonaean wife Mariamme and her mother Alexandra. Moreover, the governor of Idumaea, Costobarus, earlier tampered with by Cleopatra, once again came under suspicion for alleged pro-Hasmonaean sympathies, and was likewise put to death.

Herod's path was indeed a difficult one. He had to show himself a good enough Jew to retain sympathy at home. At the same time, he had to be a good enough pro-Roman to retain the favour of Octavian who now, as universal autocrat, assumed the grandiose name of

Augustus (27 BC). In pursuit of this loyal, modern, pro-Augustan policy, Herod instituted commemorative Actian Games. These were on the Greek model, and constituted, as it were, an attempt to drag his country into the current world of the Hellenistic first century BC. But the gymnastics and wrestling which such functions included had already become a principal target of anti-Hellenizing opinion at the time of the nationalist Maccabaean revolt. Moreover, these Games and similar ceremonies required the construction of a theatre and amphitheatre at Jerusalem, and Herod had every intention that his buildings should compete in architectural and sculptural grandeur with the finest products of the Greco-Roman world. But orthodox Jews feared that this would mean adorning these edifices with images of men and beasts, which was forbidden according to the strictest interpretation of the Commandment banning graven images.[11] When a scare about this arose, Herod was able to show the theologians, whose sight was perhaps faulty, that all he had, in fact, put up was an imageless trophy of arms. But trophies displayed representations of weapons, and these too could be interpreted as impious objects of pagan worship. For such reasons, an attempt was made to assassinate Herod, right inside his new theatre. But it failed, and the religious opposition went underground for more than twenty years.

Eager not to rely too extensively on his touchy capital of Jerusalem, Herod turned to Samaria, and converted its capital of the same name into the fine new city of Sebaste, named after the 'Sebastos', the Greek equivalent of 'Augustus'. The population of Sebaste was at least half Samaritan, but the buildings, including a stadium, were Greek, and so was the ruling class. In consequence Herod, less tactful to Jewish opinion in this predominantly non-Jewish milieu, saw no objection to erecting a temple in honour of Rome and Augustus, such as were to be found in other parts of the Roman world. He also married a Samaritan woman, Malthace (whose sons ultimately became his successors), and the settlers he planted in the district provided him with an important military force.

Sebaste was powerfully walled, and other formidable fortresses and splendid palaces sprang up at a number of strategic points in Herod's dominions, including Masada, Herodium and Jericho. Not long afterwards (22 BC), Herod began work on a second great city, Caesarea Maritima (Sdot Yam), which rapidly became a splendid port utterly dwarfing the feeble roadsteads of the past. Here too, ruling over a partly Jewish population, the dominant class was Greek, and here too, in addition to the customary Greek theatre and amphitheatre, was a Temple of Rome and Augustus: so the country had two Holy Cities of the emperor, as well as the City of God at Jerusalem. Moreover, like Sebaste, Caesarea Maritima supplied a unit for Herod's army. Like the armies of the Hasmonaeans, this, apart from a stiffening of his own Idumaean compatriots, was largely made up of foreigners. His government, too, was organized on non-Jewish models, in accordance with the systems bequeathed by the Ptolemies and Seleucids.

Such aspects of his rule, however, were unlikely to ingratiate him with the Jews, and this he determined to achieve by a scheme of breathtaking vastness – the total and magnificent reconstruction of the Jerusalem Temple. The project was announced in *c.* 22 BC, and the building of the Sanctuary was completed in 18; the immense surrounding courtyards, now the platform of the Haram-al-Sharif, were completed ten years later. The whole sacred complex, of which visitors to somewhat similar precincts at Palmyra (Tadmor) and Gerasa (Jerash) can get an idea today, was an imposing fusion of Jewish and Greek architectural styles, the very symbol of his efforts to link east and west. Together with his other achievements in the same field, the Temple entitles Herod to be described as one of the great builders of antiquity. Yet later Jewish writers, detesting him as a Roman collaborator, tended to express admiration of the Temple while neither indicating its association with Herod nor allowing it the designation of the Third Temple; or it was suggested that such reconstruction as he undertook was not his own idea.[12] Yet there grew up a proverb 'He who has not seen the Temple of Herod has never seen anything beautiful'; and Herod himself was not slow to point out that the Hasmonaeans, during their regime of a hundred and twenty-five years, had never even attempted anything of the kind.

In 23, Augustus presented him with a north-eastern extension of territory, covering a large area of southern Syria (east of the Golan Heights) which was important for the Babylonian pilgrim traffic to the Temple.[13] Then, in the winter of 22–21 BC, Herod proceeded to the island of Lesbos (Mytilene) to confer with Augustus' viceroy Marcus Agrippa, who was temporarily residing in the east; subsequently, in 20, he went to Antioch to see Augustus himself. At this moment Augustus, like so many other Roman leaders of all periods when they visited the near east, was primarily concerned with relations with

Parthia. Roman dignity required that the death of Crassus thirty-three years earlier should be avenged, but Augustus had the novel and sensible idea that the principal bone of contention, Armenia, should be disposed of by diplomatic rather than military means. At the same time Herod's Israel, still an important element in the frontier system, was granted yet another territorial extension on its northern border.[14] He also obtained Augustus' agreement to the installation of his brother Pheroras as a dependent prince (tetrarch) in the Transjordanian territory of Peraea: though Pheroras preferred to remain in Jerusalem, closer to the ever-thickening domestic intrigues of the court.

While Augustus was in Antioch, the Greek city of Gadara complained to him about the way it had been treated by Herod. This was an exceptional event, since the king's Greek subjects were on the whole content enough with the favourable economic conditions they enjoyed under his rule. But it is possible that his governors exercised a somewhat stricter supervision of their affairs than they were accustomed to.

Whether Herod's *Jewish* subjects were contented is a question which has been very variously answered. Certainly, orthodox Jews regarded his dealings with Romans and Greeks as suspect; and the ordinary populace, of all races, was intimidated by secret policemen and financial officials. Moreover, taxation was by no means light. All ancient taxation was non-progressive and therefore inequitable, and Judaea had to provide both for the Romans and for Herod's own costly projects, as well as paying the Temple tax and other contributions normally made to Jewish causes, such as tithes for the poor. On the other hand, Herod was capable of showing spectacular generosity, for example in times of famine; and the existence of his self-governing regime did at least mean that the tax-collectors were not men appointed by Rome. But, above all, what he conferred upon his country was the astonishing, unprecedented phenomenon of peace for thirty years. And with peace went prosperity on a scale which would have been regarded as inconceivable ever before.

For example, without straining his efficient economy, Herod was able to offer substantial loans, from which even the Nabataean Arabs, who bore him no love, were glad to benefit. Nor did all his expenditure strain the economy, as his vast bequests amply demonstrated. Like his father, Antipater, who had taught him the advantages of this policy,

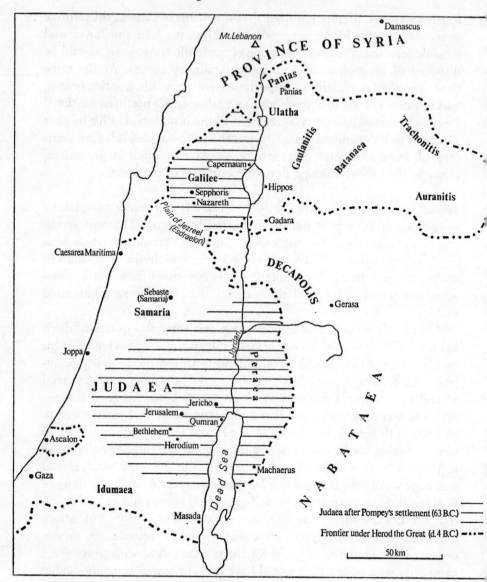

Judaea under Pompey and Herod

Herod was a financier and speculator on a monumental scale; and in addition to the Temple at Jerusalem, which served as a national bank for the government and its officials, he founded royal banks at administrative centres in many parts of the country. He also possessed business contacts throughout the Greek east, upon whose cities he showered lavish buildings, thus earning useful gratitude. In 12 BC he arranged a highly lucrative deal with Augustus himself, according to which he paid the emperor a lump sum, and in return received half the revenue of the copper mines of Cyprus – mines which were so extensive and productive that they even supplied the Indian market.

Meanwhile, however, Augustus' chief lieutenant Marcus Agrippa had undertaken a second tour of duty in the east; and in the course of this visit he came to Herod's kingdom (15 BC). After touring the principal royal foundations and fortresses, the imperial viceroy went on to Jerusalem, where his suite in Herod's magnificent new palace was named after him; and so was one of the gates of the new Temple itself. Marcus Agrippa visited the Temple, and although entry to the Sanctuary was of course out of the question he was able to enter the outer Court of the Gentiles, which was still under construction. There, in accordance with a tradition accepting and regulating sacrifices by non-Jews, he offered up a hundred oxen as victims. It is conceivable that Augustus, while generally approving this complimentary treatment of a loyal client king, nevertheless felt that Marcus Agrippa was on this occasion going just a little far, for some years later the emperor himself publicly complimented one of his grandsons (Gaius Caesar) for *not* stopping to see the Temple when he passed through the country.

Nevertheless, Marcus Agrippa's visit represented the climax of Herod's pro-Roman policy, and indeed the climactic moment, for all time, of Jewish collaboration with Rome. Herod also used the occasion to increase in spectacular fashion the influence which, as monarch of Israel, he had inherited over the Jews of the Dispersion. The opportunity came when Marcus Agrippa left his kingdom and moved northwards to conduct naval operations in the Black Sea. The target of the campaign was a usurper who had seized power in the Cimmerian Bosphorus (Crimea), a client kingdom of great importance to Rome owing to the enormous production of grain in its hinterland. Herod followed after Marcus Agrippa to the north coast of Asia Minor, and took with him the fleet – proudly commemorated on his coinage – which his new port of Caesarea Maritima had enabled him to construct; the principal Greek cities on the way were loaded with his gifts. The naval move against the Crimeans proved unnecessary, since they disposed of their usurper themselves. But when Marcus Agrippa returned through Asia

Minor by land he took Herod with him as his honoured companion and friend.

As they came towards the province of Asia in the west, it became clear that the Jewish communities in its cities were labouring under vigorous grievances; and letters to similar effect were received from the communities of Cyrenaica,[15] in spite of their remarkably close relation with pagans.[16] Although a spate of Roman decrees had insisted, for many years past, that Jewish autonomy and privileges should be maintained, Greek city governments were still resenting this special treatment and encroaching upon the status of the Jews.[17] At the time of the visit of Marcus Agrippa and Herod, for example, the Asian city-governments were said to be forcing them to appear in court on the Sabbath, interfering with their dispatch of the Temple tax to Jerusalem, and 'compelling them to participate in military service and civic duties and to spend their sacred funds for these things'.[18]

Herod persuaded Marcus Agrippa to hear the case of these Asian Jews – even though it might seem that the king was trespassing on the preserves of the governor of Asia – and instructed his own chief minister, Nicolaus of Damascus, to defend their cause at the hearing. Nicolaus was not a Jew himself; he had formerly been the tutor of Cleopatra's children, and had passed into the service of Herod. One of the most talented Greek writers of the age, he was the author of a Universal History, the most important work of such a kind for over three centuries. He was also the chief source employed by Josephus for many of the events of Herod's reign, so that when Josephus offers us a detailed account of the speech Nicolaus now delivered before Marcus Agrippa it is likely to be authentic – or at least an authentic rendering of the literary version into which it was subsequently cast. Nicolaus elaborates all the main arguments in favour of treating the Jews well. He points out to Marcus Agrippa not only the excellence of the Hebrew Law but its antiquity. He leaves him in no doubt concerning the policy of his master Herod, as pro-Roman as his father Antipater. But at the same time he emphasizes that the Pax Romana owes its glory to Rome's custom of 'allowing every country to live and prosper while respecting its own traditions'.[19]

The representatives of the Greek cities, perhaps somewhat daunted by Herod's power and Nicolaus' rhetoric, did not attempt to deny the anti-Jewish measures they had taken. However, they did venture to reply that the Jewish communities in their midst were doing them a great deal of harm, and although Josephus dismisses their case in one sentence,[20] in contrast to the many thousands of words in which he reproduces the speech of Nicolaus, it is to be presumed that they went into full detail. Nevertheless, Marcus Agrippa decided in favour of the Jews. In one of his two accounts Josephus, relying on Nicolaus, attributes this decision to the influence of Herod. In the other he quotes Marcus Agrippa as stating that his verdict was based on the precedents which authorized the Jews to observe their own customs without ill-treatment.

No doubt Agrippa would have come to the same, characteristically Roman, decision even if Herod and Nicolaus had not intervened at all. But no doubt also their intervention caused Rome to implement the policy of tolerance with particular vigour. The decrees which Marcus Agrippa now sent to Ephesus and Cyrene have survived; they follow the familiar lines.[21] However, like earlier edicts, they still do not seem to have been entirely effective, since a series of further similar decrees by Augustus and his Asian governors in subsequent decades[22] shows that the sources of irritation still remained. These documents are quoted by Josephus with the over-hopeful comment that, 'if I frequently mention such decrees, it is to reconcile the other nations to us and to remove the causes of hatred which have taken root in thoughtless persons among us as well as among them'.[23] Augustus also turned his attention to the Jewish community of Alexandria, perhaps restive since Rome's annexation of Egypt had subjected them, but not the Greeks of the place, to poll-tax: he now reformed their constitution, and apparently increased the powers of their elders.[24] Herod's role as protector of the Dispersion had been strikingly affirmed. Moreover his intervention in Asia, though directed against the Greeks, did not diminish his general popularity in Greek cities, to which he continued to show great generosity; in 12 BC he consented to be President of the Olympic Games.

But the brilliant successes of Herod's reign were gradually blighted, especially in the eyes of his Roman patron Augustus, by the appalling quarrels and disturbances which took place within his own family. This was nothing new, since his Hasmonaean wife Mariamme and mother-in-law had long ago succumbed, and others as well. But now Mariamme's half-Hasmonaean sons likewise came under suspicion; and the last

77

years of the reign witnessed their violent deaths, and the death of Herod's eldest son by another wife,[25] and the downfall of other close relatives as well. These troubles confronted Augustus with a problem. He was prepared to allow his client kings a very free hand in dealing with their domestic upheavals. But where questions relating to the succession to their kingly thrones became involved, he could not remain unconcerned, for this was a nomination which the emperor normally reserved for himself. He may not have been unaffected by reports, however unwarranted, that both Herod and his brother Pheroras were in secret touch with Parthia. In Herod's heyday, Augustus had granted him the unique privilege of being allowed to make his own choice from among his numerous sons and thus to nominate his own successor. But this privilege at some stage was revoked,[26] and meanwhile his prestige at Rome suffered greatly when Roman governors of Syria, and even Augustus himself, found themselves drawn with increasing frequency into these desperately unsavoury disputes.

But Herod's worst moment with the emperor came in 9 BC; it was caused by the king's clash with the Nabataean Arabs, owing to the non-payment of one of their debts to him. Believing he had the authority of the governor of Syria behind him, Herod attacked the Nabataeans and inflicted some casualties, subsequently settling three thousand Idumaeans and five hundred Babylonian Jewish horse-archers in his north-eastern territories, to keep the border area (and its pilgrim traffic) under control.[27] But the powerful Nabataean prime minister Syllaeus had long borne a bitter grudge against Herod, who had prevented him from marrying his sister, and Syllaeus now went to Rome and protested to Augustus about the invasion. Herod's Roman backing for the operation turned out to have been illusory, and the emperor was very gravely displeased. That a client king, whose foreign policy was supposed to be conducted not by himself but by Rome, should actually make war upon another monarch in the same category was the very height of impropriety.[28] So Augustus now wrote to Herod in the harshest terms, indicating that, whereas up to now he had treated him as a friend, he would henceforward treat him as a subject.

Very fortunately for Herod, however, the Nabataeans now proceeded to commit an offence which put them even more in the wrong than he had put himself. For when the old Nabataean king Obodas III died, a usurper Aretas IV seized the throne without awaiting the decision of Rome (9 BC). Now Aretas was very hostile to Syllaeus; this proved a bond which brought the usurper and Herod together, and they happily collaborated in the task of destroying Syllaeus' reputation in the eyes of Augustus. Their chosen instrument was Herod's chief minister Nicolaus of Damascus, and when he delivered his formidable indictment of Syllaeus he succeeded in convincing the emperor that the Nabataean had grossly exaggerated Herod's incursion into his country. So Syllaeus was ruined, and Herod came back, or at least part of the way back, into imperial favour.[29]

As the disarray in Herod's family became worse and worse, religious opposition to his rule in Jewish circles, a problem which had been in abeyance for twenty years, became active once again. The first crisis occurred in 7 or 6 BC, when the king ordered his people to swear a joint oath of loyalty to Augustus and himself. This was an attempt to complete the restoration of his prestige with the emperor and to demonstrate afresh the solid pro-Roman position on which his whole policy was based. Such demonstrations of loyalty, in other forms, were nothing new. Already at an earlier date Herod had revived the Persian and Seleucid practice of twice-daily Temple sacrifices of a bull and two lambs in honour of the suzerain emperor, who had consented to meet the costs of the victims himself. The oath that was now required had likewise been a Seleucid custom. It also seems to have been regular practice in the other client kingdoms of Rome. Yet in those kingdoms, as in the Roman provinces, worship of the emperor's statue was required,[30] and this prospect was a nightmare to the Jews, because it was the complete negation of their monotheism and all it stood for. The issue was an old and traditional one, because in *Daniel* it was the refusal of his three companions to worship Nebuchadnezzar's golden image that had condemned them to the fiery furnace.[31] However, the Jews of Augustus' time had not had to worry about this particular problem, since he – to the indignation of Greek loyalists – had exempted them from any such obligations.[32] Instead, in their synagogues, they addressed prayers to God for the safety of the emperor.[33] And now they were required to swear an oath to him, coupling his name with that of their own ruler Herod.

Ten years earlier, when an oath to Herod alone (not the emperor) had been administered throughout the country, the king had excused the Essenes and Pharisees. Now however, when the emperor's name had to be included, further exemption was out of the question. How the Essenes reactee we do not know, but six thousand Pharisees again refused to swear. Strangely enough Herod, who was not famous for his leniency, punished them with nothing worse than a fine. It was promptly paid off by the wife of his own brother Pheroras, the titular prince of Peraea – which indicated that religious opposition was now added to the other causes of dissension within Herod's own family.

Herod did not at first take direct action against his sister-in-law, apart from telling Pheroras to send her away, which he refused to do. Yet it soon proved possible for the king to unearth an alleged conspiracy among the Pharisees, which he proceeded to suppress with considerable loss of life.

Considering that these events occurred at a date within a few years, or even a few months, of the birth of Jesus Christ, there is a curious interest in the fact that these plotters, if plotters they were, endowed their enterprise with a Messianic character. For the Pharisees convinced Bagoas, an important official of the royal household, that although he was a eunuch he was destined to become the father and guide of the coming Messianic king, in accordance with the admonition of the Second Isaiah, 'the eunuch must not say, "I am nothing but a barren tree"'.[34]

Messianism, and the accompanying belief in an end of the world and a last judgment, had not figured in the central trends of Pharisaic opinion during Herod's time, since the leading Pharisee Hillel, averse to raising potentially subversive hopes, had implicitly rejected such views by his assertion: 'He who has acquired for himself words of the Torah has acquired life in the coming world.'[35] But now this last period of Herod's reign, when his power had become weakened, was witnessing the emergence of a new and much more radical wing of the Pharisees, politically closer to the militancy of the Qumran community than to the pacific wisdom of Hillel and Shammai. Such men regarded Herod as no better than oppressive Hasmonaeans such as Alexander Jannaeus. And in any case, Herod for his part regarded Messianism of this type as deeply unsatisfactory. For his own view was that if anyone should be declared the Messiah it must be himself, as *de facto* heir to the house of David; and, indeed, flatterers could be found that he actually belonged to David's family by birth. So a star which appears on his coinage[36] may well be the star which, according to Balaam's prophecy in *Numbers*, shall come out of Jacob, to foreshadow the Messianic coming.[37]

The conspirators, including Bagoas, were captured and executed. Pheroras retired to Peraea and died (5 BC); and after inquiries in his household had allegedly implicated his wife in a plot to assassinate

Herod, she too was killed. Her fate at Herod's hands no doubt alienated still further the radical section of the Pharisees who were her friends. At all events, in the following year the Jewish resistance to Herod broke out into open violence. This took the form of serious student demonstrations, instigated by senior Pharisee professors. The pretext for the upheaval was a large gilt-bronze representation of an eagle which Herod had erected over the great gate of the Temple,[38] perhaps at the time of its initial construction (he had also placed a representation of an eagle on his coinage).[39] In spite of reverent allusions to eagles in the Torah[40] and other Jewish writings, Herod's action in erecting this piece of sculpture could be regarded, according to the strict interpretation, as an infringement of the commandment forbidding graven images – and the strongly Roman associations of eagles added fuel to the flames. When, two decades earlier, there had been signs of similar agitation, Herod had been able to put a stop to them. Now, however, he was sixty-eight, and losing his grip. His health was failing, and the radical Pharisees were irremediably disaffected. Rioters pulled the eagle down, and Herod, ill though he was, travelled to Jericho, where the atmosphere was less tense, to condemn them to execution. Soon afterwards he ordered the death of his own eldest son, whom he had earlier imprisoned for high treason; and then he himself died.

The internal and domestic upheavals of Herod's last years had got completely out of hand, assuming terrifying proportions. But they should not, and did not, efface the effects of thirty years of a flourishing peace such as was totally unfamiliar to Israel. Herod is often condemned as a collaborator with Rome, a quisling who preferred subservience to heroic rebellion. Collaborator with Rome he was, but to call him a quisling ignores a fundamental difference between the conditions of Herod's lifetime and the great wars of our own. Vidkun Quisling, during a war that might be lost or won, sided with the foreign power that would enslave his nation against those who would liberate it. Herod had no such choice. There was no great war in which he could select the side he preferred. After the brief flash-in-the-pan of his enemy Antigonus who chose Parthia and was defeated, there was one power and one power only, Rome, in charge of Israel's destiny, and the chances of escaping from its domination were so small as to be nonexistent. The only alternative was a rebellion which, as was shown seventy and again a hundred and thirty-five years later, could only end in defeat, immeasurable hardship and obliteration. Herod saw this clearly, and in order to save his people from the catastrophe he settled for the best terms he could get. In spite of all the seedy compromises this policy involved, it seemed to him better than the miserable deaths of countless Jewish men, women and children, in a cause that could not be won.

6

Principalities and Province

In view of all the horrors that had taken place within Herod's family, it was hardly to be expected that his own arrangements for his succession would be accepted by Augustus without very careful consideration and, probably, modification. Moreover, as each fresh household disturbance occurred, the king wrote a new will, distributing the inheritance in some different way among the sons of his ten wives; and the will he finally left behind him was his fourth. It sought to provide, subject to the emperor's agreement, that the eighteen-year-old Archelaus, one of his sons by the Samaritan Malthace, should become king in his place, but that within his kingdom there were to be two autonomous principalities (tetrarchies). One of these, comprising the two separate territories of Galilee and Peraea (Transjordan), was to go to Archelaus' younger brother Antipas, and the other, consisting of the recently acquired north-eastern territories, was to be ruled by their half-brother Philip, son of a Jewish woman named Cleopatra.

It must be supposed that these final arrangements of Herod, at least in their general lines, had received the advance approval of Augustus, and on the king's death he duly sanctioned them – with the single vital exception that the young Archelaus was not allowed any control over his brother and half-brother. For the three principalities were to be distinct and separate. Nor was Archelaus, though ruler of the central region of Judaea itself, permitted the title of king enjoyed by his father.

Instead, he had to rest content with a princely title (ethnarch), one grade above the tetrarchic title of his two fellow-princes. It was suggested that he might earn promotion when he had proved himself. But Augustus was evidently convinced, at least at this stage, that none of Herod's sons was capable of taking on his mantle.

Conscious of his need to live up to this responsibility, Archelaus at once proceeded to assume the name of Herod, and Antipas later did the same. Evidently they, at least, did not feel that their father's reign had been an unpopular disaster. With one another, however, they entirely failed to cooperate. Both Archelaus and Antipas hastened to Rome, where Antipas, who in one of Herod's earlier wills had for a brief period been accorded the top place, did everything to undermine Archelaus' position with Augustus – until a Jewish delegation requested the abolition of the Herodian dynasty in favour of a resumption of priestly rule, whereupon the two princes abandoned their quarrel.

But the emperor's decision did not come immediately, and while it was awaited serious bloodshed broke out in various parts of Israel. In Jerusalem a very grave situation developed almost at once:

The feast of unleavened bread, which the Jews call Passover, came round; it is an occasion for the contribution of a multitude of sacrifices, and a vast crowd streamed in from the country for the ceremony. The promoters of the mourning for the executed Pharisees stood in a body in the temple, procuring recruits for their faction. This alarmed Archelaus, who, wishing to prevent the contagion from spreading to the whole crowd, sent in a tribune in command of a cohort, with orders to restrain by force the ringleaders of the sedition. Indignant at the appearance of the troops, the whole crowd pelted them with stones; most of the cohort were killed, while their commander was wounded and escaped with difficulty. Then, as if nothing serious had happened, the rioters returned to their sacrifices. Archelaus, however, now felt it would be impossible to restrain the mob without bloodshed, and let loose upon them his entire army, the infantry advancing in close order through the city, the cavalry by way of the plain. The soldiers falling unexpectedly upon the various parties busy with their sacrifices slew about three thousand of them and dispersed the remainder among the neighbouring hills.[1]

Outside Jerusalem, the situation was no better. The authorities in Antipas' territories had to deal with revolts in Galilee and Peraea, the former led by Judas, the learned son of the Hezekiah whom Julius

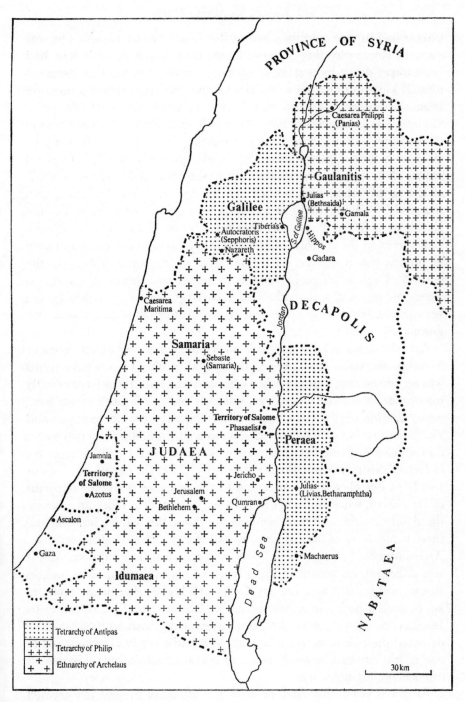

PROVINCE OF SYRIA

Caesarea Philippi
(Panias)

+Gaulanitis

Julias
(Bethsaida)
•Gamala

Galilee

Tibérias•
Autocratoris
(Sepphoris)
•Nazareth
Hippos
•Gadara

S. of Galilee

DECAPOLIS

Jordan

•Caesarea
Maritima

+Samaria+

Sebaste
(Samaria)

Territory of Salome
•Phasaelis

Peraea

JUDAEA

Jamnia•
Jericho•

Territory
of Salome
•Azotus
Jerusalem•
Bethlehem•
Qumran•

Julias
(Livias, Betharamphtha)

•Ascalon

Dead Sea

•Gaza

•Machaerus

NABATAEA

Idumaea

Tetrarchy of Antipas
Tetrarchy of Philip
Ethnarchy of Archelaus

30 km

Judea under Herod's sons

Caesar had suppressed fifty years earlier.[2] And Archelaus, while he was away in Rome pleading his case, learnt that his palace at Jericho had been burnt down by a slave of his father called Simon, who declared himself king and created a sufficient impression to warrant a mention from the historian Tacitus well over a century later.[3] At this point Sabinus, the principal finance officer of Roman Syria, descended upon the country, with the intention of combating these movements that proclaimed 'national independence';[4] he also proposed to seize the royal estates of Archelaus, presumably for the emperor. Sabinus took control of the royal palace and robbed the Temple treasury, but then, surrounded by Jewish troops and crowds, was compelled to appeal to the governor of Syria, Publius Quinctilius Varus. Varus, a man already well versed in the troubles of Herod's family, had to intervene not only in Judaea but in Galilee, where he burnt the capital Sepphoris to the ground. The campaign he fought, in which two thousand insurgents were crucified and many others sold as slaves, was later ranked by the Jews as comparable with the outrages of Antiochus IV Epiphanes and Pompey.[5]

Archelaus, when he returned from Rome, was never able to recover from his bad start. He had everything against him. One of his parents was an Idumaean, and the other a Samaritan: both races were equally unpopular in Judaea. Moreover, not only had his father's realm been vastly diminished by the carving out of principalities for Antipas and Philip, but its Greek fringes had gone as well. In addition to two towns on the coast and one in the interior which became the private property of Herod's sister Salome, the other Greek cities of the peripheral regions had been detached and reallocated to the province of Syria.[6] Nicolaus of Damascus, who continued to help Archelaus for a short time before thankfully retiring, advised him not to oppose this. Since, however, all these truncations of his principality had sharply decreased his revenue, Archelaus could not pay his soldiers, and soon lost their support. And it was difficult for a youth who had received his education, as he had, in Rome, and wanted to carry out his father's Hellenizing programme, to adopt such a policy in a state which had been virtually reduced to its Jewish core. Furthermore, Archelaus alienated Jewish opinion when he divorced his wife to marry a woman who had already been married to one of his late half-brothers and had borne him children; this was an offence against the Torah.

After ten years of Archelaus' rule, the affairs of the country seemed to be going so badly that Augustus launched a general investigation. This was extended to the affairs of Antipas and Philip, who were summoned to Rome with him; but they cleared themselves, and returned to rule over their states once again. Archelaus, however, was less successful. The protests against his regime which Augustus received actually included a joint complaint by Judaeans and Samaritans.[7] This unprecedented unity, in which the people of his mother's country joined, shows that he must indeed have been a failure. At any rate that is what the emperor decided. Archelaus was banished to Vienna (Vienne) in Gaul, and Rome annexed his principality.

At long last, sixty-nine years after Pompey had entered Jerusalem, Israel had ceased to exist as a self-governing client state, and the Roman province of Judaea was now in existence. The new province possessed a certain connexion with the governors of Syria, to the extent that, in special emergencies, the emperor would instruct them to intervene in Judaean affairs. But otherwise Judaea was independent of Syria, and its governors, who bore the title of prefect, were directly responsible to the emperor. They were not, however, great men like the governors of Syria, whose past careers had always included a consulship. Indeed, the prefect of Judaea was not even a member of the senate, as the great majority of provincial governors were, but belonged to the next social order, that of the knights. The governors of Egypt, exceptionally, were also knights, because the imperial government did not care to entrust so rich a province to a senator. But the knights who governed Egypt were important and exceptional. Such other provinces as had knightly governors were unimportant third-class affairs, and that is how the Romans regarded their new province of Judaea. The prefects, therefore, though well enough qualified to run Herod's bureaucratic machine, were not for the most part men of outstanding ability or experience: which was unfortunate, since Jewish affairs possessed so complex a character and erupted so easily into trouble and violence.

Besides, leading Jews were affronted because of the low rank of these Roman governors who had been forced on them. Disappointed because the fall of the dynasty had not led to priestly rule, some of them took a second and more favourable look at the vanished monarchy, and formed a nostalgic party aiming at the restoration of Herod's house: a new political party of Herodians came into existence.[8] More Hellenizing in character than the Sadducees, but in spite of their monarchic yearnings equally collaborative with Rome, the Herodians probably originated in the principality of Antipas, whose adoption of the name of Herod, already mentioned, probably occurred after the deposition of Archelaus. But before long the monarchic movement spread into the Judaean province. No doubt it received encouragement from the promotion of a grandson of Herod and stepson of Antipas named Tigranes v, whom Augustus had recently made king of Armenia (*c.* AD 6–12).[9]

Another shade of opinion is represented by the *Assumption of Moses*, preserved in Latin but originally written in Hebrew or Aramaic. The writer of this work spreads his criticisms widely, disliking Herod, and the later Hasmonaeans, and the Romans, as well as the Sadducees and their priestly caste. Horrible details are given of the martyrdoms of early Maccabaean times. Yet the *Assumption* concludes that, although martyrdoms are sweet, militancy is not, and counsels that it is best to refrain from causing disturbances.[10] The author was a pious Pharisee, possibly of Greek background (from Antioch?), representing the traditional quietist, pacifist wing of the party, not the new radical wing which was going to continue to cause so much trouble.

The only people, on the other hand, who were actually pleased by the eclipse of Jewish autonomy were the Samaritans. Encouraged by Augustus' reception of their protest against Archelaus, they showed their elation by scattering bones in the precinct of the Temple, and substituting two rats for its sacrificial pigeons (AD 7 or 8).[11]

Provincial status involved not only the oath of loyalty to the emperor, which Herod had experienced such difficulty in enforcing, but permanent Roman military occupation, taxation by Roman officials, and Roman supervision of public order. The prefects, of whom the first was a certain Coponius, resided normally at Caesarea Maritima but employed Jerusalem as the mint for the bronze coinage they issued for the province. When they themselves came to the city for the great festivals, they were accustomed to reside in Herod's palace at the western end of the city, just inside what is now the Jaffa Gate. During the ceremonies, troops were posted in full battle-kit around the porticos of the Temple, thus presenting a distasteful and sacrilegious spectacle to the Jews. The prefects were the commanders-in-chief of the provincial troops, which consisted of the corps raised by Herod at Caesarea and Sebaste (Samaria), amounting to five cohorts of five hundred infantry and a cavalry wing of five hundred. One of the cohorts and a cavalry contingent were normally stationed at Jerusalem, mainly in the Antonia fortress overlooking the Temple and Lower City.[12]

To enable the new administration to get under way, it was arranged that the governor of Syria – not the new prefect – should organize the confiscation of Archelaus' property, including the valuable date and balsam groves of Jericho. At the same time he was to conduct a census of the province.[13] This was not an altogether new experience for the Jews, since Herod the Great, too, must have held censuses, just as they had been a regular administrative feature of the Hellenistic kingdoms. But in the atmosphere of tension accompanying the Roman annexation, feeling ran high against the census. For one thing, it reminded everyone that they would now be paying their taxes to the Romans, which seemed a stinging brand of servitude. Moreover, it was strongly suspected that taxation would now increase – and the suspicion may have been justified.[14] At all events, with Herod's prosperity fading, taxes seemed heavy indeed, amounting perhaps to as much as forty per cent of production. Furthermore, it was possible, as so often, to point to unhappy scriptural precedents, which helped further to blacken the census. For example, it had been laid down in the Torah that the earth belonged to God,[15] and surely the census operations must infringe on this. Moreover, it was recalled that a census conducted a thousand years previously by David had caused the Lord to bring pestilence upon the land.[16]

At this juncture, therefore, a guerrilla war broke out. Its leader was a certain Judas or Judah who came from Gamala in Gaulanitis (Golan), east of the Sea of Galilee. But he was known as 'the Galilean', which sounded roughly equivalent to 'anarchist'. Whether he was the same Judas, the son of Hezekiah, who had stirred up trouble in Galilee after the death of Herod ten years earlier is unclear. If he was, then we should be justified in envisaging a single, more or less continuous and homogeneous movement of resistance, perhaps under one single family. But this cannot be demonstrated with any certainty, and it seems that the Judas of AD 6 was operating not in Galilee – which was unaffected by the census since it formed part of the principality of Antipas – but, as one might expect, in the new province of Judaea.[17]

There were bandits and robbers and murderers on all sides, reduced to destitution or violence by the deteriorating economic conditions of the country. There were also resistance groups, freedom fighters and fervent nationalists, some with worldly and some with Messianic aspirations.[18] However, as on earlier occasions, too exact an attribution of this or that guerrilla movement to this or that category should not be attempted, since often a single individual simultaneously displayed the characteristics of more than one of these groups, and there were complex shifts of underground alliances from year to year. From the ancient writers two names of these movements have survived: Zealots and *sicarii*. 'Zealot', the Aramaic *gan'an* or Hebrew *ganna* (sometimes Hellenized as *Kananaios*) is a Greek word meaning zealous admirer or emulator (with overtones of jealousy, enmity, opposition, rebellion). The term was deliberately reminiscent of Phineas, whose punishment of a backsliding Jew had inspired Mattathias the Hasmonaean to have recourse to a similar violent action, thus triggering off the Maccabaean revolt.[19] *Sicarius* is a Latin description of a dagger-man or professional assassin.[20] But unfortunately it is hard to say which of the groups we hear about at one period or another can rightly be described by either term, because our ancient authority, Josephus, felt such aversion to all these violent and excited men, such anxiety to dissociate himself from them all, and such eagerness to show that the Jews in the first years of the province had behaved reasonably, that his information is inadequate and misleading.

In consequence, there is disagreement among modern scholars about the dates when the two sets of dissidents came into existence, and who they were. Indeed it is possible that 'Zealot' and *sicarius* are both vague designations denoting extremists in general, undefined terms. As for the followers of Judas the Galilean in AD 6, Josephus mysteriously indicates that they represented an unspecified 'Fourth Philosophy' (the other three comprising Sadducees, Pharisees and Essenes) from which every evil stemmed.[21] It is possible enough that Judas' supporters were loosely described, or described themselves, as Zealots or *sicarii* or both, but it has recently been suggested that they may more formally have labelled their movement as plain 'Israel'. Josephus' evidently reluctant elevation of their ideology to a philosophical status may be meant to point out that Judas was the first, in the new province, to declare resistance against the alien ruler to be a religious duty. Judas presumably stressed that the oath to the emperor was incompatible with the absolute sovereignty of God laid down by the Covenant. True, resistance to alien regimes had often been preached before, but the recent Roman annexation of Judaea enormously sharpened the message, and Judas the Galilean was able to propose an axiomatic non-acceptance of Roman rule.

He was joined by a Pharisee named Zadok, evidently of that radical branch of Pharisaism which had emerged in the last days of Herod. The revolt seemed likely to attain considerable proportions. But it was put down, largely because the high priest Joazar influenced the people against it. The high-priestly houses, which had collaborated with Herod, were now proposing to collaborate with the Romans. It seems a little harsh perhaps that Joazar, after this action as mediator and peacemaker, was almost immediately dismissed (as he had been after a previous brief tenure, ten years earlier). From now onwards, in general, appointments to this office, and dismissals from it, were in the hands of the Roman prefects of Judaea. But in this case the dismissal was carried out by the governor of Syria, Quirinius, before he departed for Syria and left the new prefect Coponius to carry on.

Perhaps Joazar had made himself *too* pro-Roman to be acceptable – or possibly he was too closely associated with the dynasty of Herod. In any case, it was now decided to get away from the pro-Herodian family of Boethus, to which he and a whole series of his predecessors had belonged, and the member of another house of collaborating Sadducees was appointed instead. This influential personage, Ananus, and his relatives almost monopolized the office for the next thirty-five years. The Jewish tradition preserves a hostile feeling towards both families alike: 'Woe is me because of the house of Boethus! Woe is me because of their slaves! Woe is me because of the house of Ananus! Woe is me because of their whisperings!'[22] And there followed critical comments upon the ways in which the high-priestly clans use not only their pens but their fists.

The high priests, drawn from this narrow Sadducee circle, were regarded by the Roman governors as their chief intermediaries in dealing with the Jewish inhabitants of Judaea. Of necessity, they were more or less pro-Roman. Nevertheless, in view of the traditional nature of their office, many Jews now looked to them for leadership, as they had looked to them long ago in Seleucid times. Indeed, each successive holder of the office, together with the former high priests who were their principal advisers, enjoyed a quasi-regal status as the chief representatives of the nation. They were astute enough experts in the shadowy spheres of politico-religious diplomacy in which they operated. Their role was a difficult and delicate one; and survival, for themselves as well as their people, was their principal aim. To achieve both parts of this aim at the same time, they had to back the Romans – but not too much.

Nor did the Romans ever trust a high priest very fully; or at least they did not trust the aspirations which he might, consciously or unconsciously, arouse. They showed this openly when they decided to follow Herod's policy of retaining custody of the high-priestly vestments, except for major religious festivals. It was bad enough when Herod had kept the vestments under his control, but for the Romans to do so was much worse. For one thing, they were kept in the Antonia castle, which was actually a Roman fortress – and besides, though adjoining the Temple, it was not part of the Temple area, whereas it was forbidden to take the robes outside the Temple.[23] In such circumstances, it could never be certain that non-Jews might not handle the robes – which would constitute a grave pollution.[24] This whole business seemed a deliberate offence, a continual provocation, and remained a source of profound disquiet and discontent.

There was also another limitation upon the power of the high priests. For, in spite of their prestige, they were not the sole repositories of Jewish national opinion. They had to reckon also with a revival of the Council of Elders, meeting in the Temple as successor to the Councils of ancient times and forerunner of the Sanhedrin. Herod the Great had relegated the Council to obscurity or non-existence, but now, in AD 6, it was resuscitated as an advisory body to assist the prefect and the high priest. Moreover, although advisory, it was permitted legislative and executive authority – much more than was usual in non-autonomous communities of the Roman empire. The Council possessed its own treasury. It also regained some of its former powers as a law court, for the maintenance of Jewish law. It did not, however, apparently possess powers of capital jurisdiction, except in the altogether specialized case of action by judicial process, or perhaps by authorized lynching, against pagans who trespassed into the inner courts of the Temple, beyond the permitted Court of the Gentiles.[25] This absence of capital jurisdiction, scarcely mitigated by a probable right to try capital cases and pass them on to the prefect for implementation, served to underline the transfer of real sovereignty elsewhere. In spite of the Council's powers, they were obviously limited by the presence of a Roman governor in the land. So the revival of its other activities did not prevent Jews from feeling discontented with this tantalizing but somewhat empty show.

It is uncertain whether the Council's chairman was normally the high priest or a lawyer-teacher. At all events, although its members included the Sadducee aristocracy, it also contained a substantial representation of the more moderate sort of Pharisees and their associates the scribes. Moreover, these two closely allied groups exerted a more profound and fundamental influence on public opinion than the Sadducees were now able to achieve, so that their influence in the Council continually increased. Yet their power, just like the power of the Sadducee high priests, was not as vigorously exerted as it might have been, and for the same reason: it was exerted too passively. On the one hand they were not militantly anti-Roman, but on the other they failed to demonstrate to the people the advantages of collaboration with the Romans; this meant that they abandoned the political arena to the militants. And the Romans, for their part, lacked effective contact with the Pharisees, and failed to recognize that, if the numerous dissident movements were ever to be suppressed, these were the people on whom they could best rely to help them in this task.

In AD 14 Augustus died, after forty-five years of supremacy. His stepson Tiberius, who had been virtual co-regent during the previous decade, became his successor. The peoples of Syria and Judaea begged the new emperor to lessen their tribute (AD 17),[26] but when Tiberius' nephew Germanicus visited the east two years later, with extended powers, there is no evidence that he took any remedial action. Nor, on a visit to Alexandria, did Germanicus do anything to help the Jewish community there. He made a distribution of grain, but in this the Jews, not being citizens, had no share. 'In the chorus of praise,' as J.P.V.D. Balsdon remarks, 'which was raised from all quarters of the Empire in his honour, the voice of the Jews alone is absent.'[27] Before long, however, Germanicus died at Antioch, in mysterious circumstances that were thought to implicate the governor of Syria.

By this time there could be seen signs of changes at Rome which were to exercise a considerable effect upon policy towards the Jews. These changes were due to the rise to power of the emperor's adviser Sejanus. Not long after Tiberius' accession, he had become joint, and then sole, commander of the imperial bodyguard (the praetorian cohorts); and thereafter his influence continually increased. There is good reason to regard him as ill-disposed to the Jews,[28] whose failure to conform to the loyal customs of other peoples seemed to him inconvenient and undesirable. His responsibility, therefore, can be detected in a senatorial decree of AD 19 deporting four thousand adult Jewish and Egyptian freedmen to Sardinia, where they could be put to good use in extirpating banditry. 'If the unhealthy climate killed them,' comments Tacitus, 'the loss would be small. The rest, unless they repudiated their unholy practices by a given date, must leave Italy.'[29]

Josephus, who refers only to Jews and not Egyptians, speaks of banishment not from Italy but from Rome. But he mentions that a good many refused to go to Sardinia – for fear of breaking the Jewish law during their military activities – and were consequently penalized. He adds the further information that this disciplinary measure was due to the behaviour of a Jewish crook who, together with three confederates, had embezzled purple and gold handed over by a Roman noble lady, a convert to Judaism, for the Jerusalem Temple.[30] Evidently the Roman action, like a similar decree in 139 BC, was prompted by a desire that Jewish proselytism should not spread, and above all that it should not spread among the upper class, which had become so unfortunately involved in this incident. But the repressive measures were only temporary, perhaps because the emperor's sister-in-law Antonia had friends in the family of Herod.[31]

Rome was watching the Jews with especial care, because in the neighbouring empire of Parthia the affairs of their co-religionists had taken a strange turn. Upon the banks of the Babylonian Euphrates, west of Ctesiphon, at the point where the royal canal joined the river, lay the town of Nehardea (Nearda), which possessed a large Jewish community. Two members of this community, the brothers Hasinai (Asinaeus) and Hanilai (Anilaeus), now seized control of the town. Moreover, this pair actually set up a sort of free state of their own, which was conceded autonomy by the Parthian monarch Artabanus III and lasted for fifteen years.[32] These surprising events were bound to have their reactions upon the Jews on the Roman side of the frontier, so that the affairs of Judaea needed to be conducted with especial vigilance – as Sejanus in any case intended.

The first three prefects of Judaea had only stayed in office for about three years each. But then came one of Sejanus' nominees, Valerius Gratus, who remained for eleven. This was characteristic of the provincial arrangements of Tiberius, who liked his governors to retain their posts for a long time – comparing them to flies that suck their fill at a wound and stay there, keeping other flies away.[33] We know virtually nothing of Gratus' administration. He names Tiberius and his mother Livia on his coinage,[34] but its designs do not conflict with Jewish susceptibilities. However, the fact that three high priests whom he appointed[35] had extremely short tenures indicates that things were not going altogether smoothly.

Part III

*Threats from Romans, Greeks
and Christians*

Part II

[title illegible]

7

The Problems of Pontius Pilate

About the troubles that beset Gratus' successor, Pontius Pilatus, we know a great deal more – though, tantalizingly, nothing like enough. Pilate, member of a family from central Italy (Samnium), was another nominee of Sejanus, and he too enjoyed a long tenure, staying in Judaea for more than ten years (*c*. 25–36). This suggests that the highly damaging view of him taken by the Jewish writer Philo,[1] and the impression of feebleness given by New Testament authors, was not shared by the emperor Tiberius, who, for all his tastes for long governorships, was both exacting and efficient, and would not have kept him there if he had failed to give satisfaction. Nor can Pilate's relations with the Jewish authorities have been conspicuously bad, since he retained a single high priest, Ananus' son-in-law Joseph Caiaphas – whom he had found in office on his arrival – throughout the entire decade of his rule. Josephus does not share Philo's attitude, commenting on Pilate in terms varying from slightly critical to neutral.[2] Nevertheless, the course of events, in so far as we are able to reconstruct it, does give some reason to suppose that Pilate was influenced by Sejanus' lack of sympathy for Jewish separatist manifestations. Moreover, such a tendency is displayed by the prefect's coinage, which, breaking with more tactful precedents that had avoided un-Jewish designs, displays the augur's staff and sacrificial ladle of specifically Roman ritual.[3]

Not altogether surprisingly, then, his tenure was punctuated by a series of unpleasant incidents. One of them, probably the first (*c.* AD 26), is described by Josephus as follows:

When Pilate brought his army from Caesarea Maritima and removed it to winter quarters in Jerusalem, he took a bold step in subversion of the Jewish practices by introducing into the city the busts [medallions] of the emperor that were attached to the military standards, for our law forbids the making of images. It was for this reason that the previous prefects, when they entered the city, had ordered their troops to carry standards that displayed no such ornaments. Pilate was the first to bring the images into Jerusalem and set them up, doing it without the knowledge of the people, for he entered by night.[4]

Pilate, in Roman fashion, regarded the standards as the essential emblems of loyalty to Rome and its emperor. Either he or Sejanus, or perhaps Tiberius himself, felt that the imperial dignity had been slighted by the care taken in Jerusalem by his predecessors only to employ the aniconic type of standard which did not incorporate medallions showing the ruler's features. The Jews, on the other hand, objected very strongly to Pilate's new course of action, not only because the importation of these medallions seemed an infringement of the commandment relating to images, but because these standards were 'the particular gods of the legions'.[5] Furthermore, they were set up in the Antonia fortress, the place that housed the high-priestly garments, which would consequently have their sanctity gravely compromised.

Results followed thick and fast. First, there were excited demonstrations at Jerusalem, joined by numerous people who flocked in from the country. Then hordes of people followed Pilate back to Caesarea Maritima, where they staged the first recorded example of civil disobedience by lying on the ground all round his residence and refusing for five days and nights to get up. Then Pilate managed to draw them to the stadium, where they expected him to deliver them an address; but instead he surrounded them with troops. Once again, they all fell prostrate. But now Pilate had had enough, and ordered the standards to be removed from Jerusalem and sent back to Caesarea. If his original action had been prompted by Rome, it had presumably been accompanied by the indication, explicit or tacit, that the matter was not to be pressed, at least at present, if this meant that the situation was going to get out of hand – as had now happened.

'On a later occasion,' says Josephus, Pilate 'provoked a fresh uproar by expending upon the construction of an aqueduct the sacred treasure known as *Corbonas*.'[6] Pilate presumably thought he was not infringing upon Jewish custom, since water-channels were among the objects specifically mentioned in the instructions (of later date, but presumably already existing in these times) which prescribed how the Temple treasure might be expended.[7] Moreover, the channels specified in these rules were those running through the Temple court, and it was into the Temple cisterns that Pilate's aqueduct was going to deliver its water. It is therefore to be supposed that his proposal had been supported by the priestly authorities. However, Korban is the Hebrew word for sacrifices, and militant Jews were therefore able to assert that he was drawing the funds from a section of the treasury which should not have been employed for this purpose, but ought to have been reserved for the purchase of sacrificial animals.

Once again, therefore, his action proved inflammatory. Pilate was visiting Jerusalem at the time, and found his tribunal surrounded by an angry mob. This time, however, he had improved upon his previous method of using uniformed troops to keep order, and instead his soldiers infiltrated among the demonstrators disguised in Jewish civilian clothes beneath which clubs were hidden. When Pilate signalled to them to act, they laid into the Jews with such violence that a good many casualties resulted. The rest of the crowd melted away.

Before very long, a third unpleasant incident followed. It is not mentioned by Josephus, but his fellow Jew, Philo, provides a description. According to him, Pilate 'set up gilded shields in Herod's palace in the Holy City. They bore no figure and nothing else that was forbidden, but only the briefest possible inscription, which stated two things – the name of the dedicator and that of the person in whose honour the dedication was made.'[8] Philo's additional comment that Pilate was acting 'with the intention of annoying the Jews rather than of honouring Tiberius' need not, perhaps, be taken too seriously. Nevertheless, the Jews *were* very annoyed indeed. Alleging a grave violation of their national customs, they sent Pilate a powerful deputation including four sons of Herod the Great – two of whom were presumably the ruling princes Antipas and Philip.

But why were the Jews so agitated? There was no question of setting up the shields in the Temple, and they did not offend orthodox opinion by displaying images (not that Antipas could very easily have objected to this, since he had paintings of animals in his own palace). It can only be supposed that the 'brief inscription' on the shields either referred to the divinity of the emperor, or more probably cited his official nomenclature – which pronounced him, not indeed a divinity, but, since the divine Augustus had adopted him, the son of one (*divi Augusti filius*). Hyper-orthodox opinion might detect in this an affront to Jewish monotheism, though Josephus' omission of the incident suggests that he himself found the complaint unreasonable. Whether the shields were Pilate's idea (as Philo suggests) or Rome's, we cannot say. But at all events when the Jewish leaders appealed to Tiberius he gave way and ordered the shields to be moved back to his provincial capital Caesarea Maritima, where the Greek municipal administration would in no way find them distressing.

Infinitely more important, in its eventual repercussions, than these various incidents was a further problem which arose not in Pilate's province of Judaea but in one of the adjoining principalities. After escaping involvement in Archelaus' downfall, the two rulers of these little states, Philip and Antipas, had managed to carry on with some success. Philip ruled his north-eastern lands, including difficult mountain territories, quietly and conscientiously, and does not seem to have travelled outside them at all frequently. He had brought the Babylonian Jewish settlers imported by his father Herod under discreet control. He had also converted the little town of Bethsaida (slightly north of the Sea of Galilee, possibly but not certainly the Bethsaida of the Gospels) into a city named Julias, after Tiberius' mother Livia who was now called Julia Augusta. Philip had also 'refounded' his capital Panias under the name of Caesarea Philippi, depicting on his coinage the temple of Augustus which he erected there.[9] This exceedingly un-Jewish coin-type was possible because the mixture of races inhabiting his principality included very few Jews. For the same reason he was able to place Roman imperial portraits on his coins, the first ever to appear on the coinage of a Jewish prince. Augustus, Tiberius and Livia are all represented.

Antipas, who had been given Galilee and Peraea in 4 BC, seems to have been the ablest of all Herod's sons. Jesus Christ was said to have described him as a fox[10] – not as a compliment, though Jewish tradition regarded the fox as the cleverest of the beasts.[11] After the revolts immediately following his father's death had been put down, he dealt effectively with the arduous task of controlling two unconnected territories, one of which, moreover, was inhabited by the unruly Galileans. Since his subjects were mainly Jews, the designs on his coinage were selected so as to avoid offending Jewish susceptibilities. Nevertheless, when Antipas rebuilt his father's Peraean residence, Betharamphtha, which had been burnt down in the troubles of 4 BC, he called it Livias – later changed to Julias, when Livia changed her name. He also renamed his first capital, Sepphoris, in Galilee, calling it Autocratoris ('Of the Emperor');[12] and when he built himself a new capital (AD 19–20) on the west bank of the Sea of Galilee (on a site upon which orthodox Jews were at first reluctant to settle, because it included an ancient burial ground) he called it Tiberias, and placed the name on his coins.[13] It was a fitting enough name, since it reminded his subjects and others that he enjoyed the confidence of Tiberius, to whom he supplied intelligence reports supplementing or correcting those of the prefects of Judaea. His was probably the decisive intervention that caused Tiberius to reverse Pilate's action over the gilded shields, and as a result the relations between Pilate and Antipas now became strained.

Already before those developments occurred, Antipas had experienced a major security problem owing to the activities of John, son of Zechariah, nicknamed 'the Baptist', whose mission perhaps began in AD 27–9. The Gospels are likely to underestimate John's significance, owing to their anxiety to subordinate him to the figure of Jesus. Even the places where he preached and baptized remain unidentifiable. But he was active beyond the Jordan and perhaps in many parts of the Jordan valley: partly, that is to say, in the territories of the Greek Ten Cities (Decapolis), and partly in the principality of Antipas.

It is possible that John was at one time a member of the Essene or Qumran communities, though if so he did not withdraw from the masses, as they did, but addressed himself to all Israel. If we can believe the New Testament, he disclaimed Messianic ambitions, though one of the Gospels seems to concede the existence of a group which believed him to be the Messiah.[14] More probably, he saw himself as the direct descendant of the prophets, and a living witness that the long suspension of prophetic activity[15] had ended.

In particular, however, John was felt to be in the succession to Elijah and Elisha, and one reason why he chose the Jordan area as his special sphere, and baptized with the river's waters, was because this was where Elijah had ascended to heaven, and this was the stream in which Elisha had ordered the leper Naaman to be washed. Ritual ablutions were well known, and John may have encountered them at Qumran, but his own baptism was not administered to himself but to others, and was not a repeated act but a single and unique one, a drastic innovation. For it was the symbol, for those who underwent the experience, of repentance and atonement, such as the prophets had so often demanded: it signified a drastic entry into a world of renewed ideas and purposes, like the Crossing of the Red Sea in ancient times. Every Jewish reformer was obliged to cite scriptural support, and John apparently saw himself as the Second Isaiah's 'voice crying in the wilderness, "Prepare a way for the Lord, clear a straight path for him"'.[16] And his baptism – 'in token of repentance for the forgiveness of sins' – dramatized the willingness of the penitent to subject himself to the coming divine judgment.

This baptism was an emergency measure – an apocalyptic sign of immediately impending crisis. Whether or not John the Baptist saw himself as a political revolutionary we cannot say; *Matthew* seems to suggest as much, but Josephus is anxious to deny it.[17] But at any rate to Antipas, and secular rulers in general, the other-worldly, catastrophic political implications of John's message inevitably seemed to represent a tendency, indeed an invitation, towards disorder and sedition. Indeed, the various disturbances with which Pilate had to contend may not be altogether unconnected with the excitement caused by John's preaching and baptism, for at one point he seems to have moved out of Antipas' dominions into Samaria, which was part of the Roman province. It was probably not without encouragement from Antipas himself that John had left his principality, but later on he returned to it once again and involved himself in a controversy about the prince's matrimonial affairs. Antipas had divorced his Nabataean Arab wife (who fled back to Arabia), marrying the widow of one of his own brothers instead. This, if she had borne his brother children (as she had), was forbidden by the Torah;[18] and John, like the prophets of old addressing the kings of Israel and Judah, now proceeded to denounce him for the impiety. Antipas may already have been suspicious of John for his activities near the Nabataean border, which the collapse of his Nabataean marriage had made a very sensitive area, and he was also greatly disturbed by the effect of John's sermons, which raised such violent emotions in their audiences that a revolt seemed an immediate possibility.[19] When therefore his second wife's daughter, Salome, asked for John's head as the reward for her dancing at a party, he agreed. And so John met his death at Herod's border fortress of Machaerus, close to the desert place where Moses had died, and not far from the traditional site of Elijah's ascension. It was believed that he, too, rose from the dead.[20]

While John still remained at large, he was said to have baptized Jesus. In itself, this is probable – just because it does not 'fit in'. It does not fit in because Jesus himself, subsequently, was not known to have practised baptism, and indeed was stated to have refrained from it.[21] When, therefore, we are told that he himself underwent a rite that was admittedly uncharacteristic of his programme, this deserves attention. But as soon as we pass to John's alleged recognition of Jesus as his superior, the two Gospels which refer to the point give entirely different accounts.[22] One of these seems to imply, somewhat vaguely, that they eventually became disunited – perhaps because of their different views about baptism. It is also suggested that the Baptist's asceticism did not conform with Jesus' practice.[23] But Antipas, at any rate – whose steward was married to one of Jesus' early converts[24] – was advised of reports that Jesus was being spoken of as John (or Elijah) risen from the dead. And it was at this point, according to one tradition, that Jesus 'withdrew privately by boat to a lonely place':[25] that is to say, he crossed the Sea of Galilee to a point outside Antipas' dominions, in the principality of Philip.

But these are all conjectural assertions, because the New Testament, like earlier Jewish literature, was not written to tell secular history. Its purpose, instead, was to bear witness to superhuman, miraculous events, which defy historical analysis and require faith: namely, the deeds by which Jesus manifested himself as the Son of God. The existence of Jesus can be called as likely a historical fact as most others.[26] True, the argument that our picture of him is too vivid to be attributable to mere myth is inconclusive. Yet not only the authors of the Gospels, but pagan writers, too, knew of his career. However, the testimonies of pagans and Christians alike date from many years, indeed decades, after his death. Tacitus was writing his *Annals*, and Pliny the younger his letters, after the beginning of the second century AD (the alleged references to Jesus by Josephus are forged).[27] The earliest of the Gospels, too, was written more than thirty years after Jesus' death.

A further problem is the sharp disagreement between one Gospel and another, even on the most fundamental points. Some common ground, of course, there is; and it raises the question of the sources of the Gospels. Did the authors of the Gospels depend on a lengthy oral tradition, or were there written sources, now lost? Now an oral tradition, if it is concerned with material relating to religious and miraculous beliefs, stands no chance of surviving unchanged for more than thirty years. As to written sources, it seems only too likely that those who listened to Jesus had no idea of writing down his words or actions at the time, for transmission to posterity; and if there is a written background behind the Gospels, we cannot identify it. The earliest *Epistles of Paul*, it is true, may have been written less than two decades after Jesus' death. But they present a disconcertingly different picture, almost wholly divorced from the alleged events of his lifetime, and quite useless, in consequence, for any reconstruction of the sources of the Gospels.

Whether Christianity becomes any the less acceptable if the Gospels are shown to be unrelated to historical facts is a much debated question; not every theologian agrees that it suffers at all. But in any case we are obliged to conclude, with Hans Conzelmann, that 'it is no longer possible to establish the sequence of events in the life of Jesus, to write a biography of Jesus, and to provide a picture of the figure of Jesus'.[28] The evidence is too little and too late. All that we have is the picture of a picture, or rather of several substantially discordant pictures. And all the learned study that can ever be applied to the subject only bridges, to some extent, the gap between the reader and the Gospels, and never between the Gospels and the events they are purporting to describe.

Since blood-purity was regarded as a vital mark of distinction, *Matthew* and *Luke* stress that through Joseph, the husband of his mother Mary, Jesus belonged to the house of David, which according to tradition would provide the earthly Messiah.[29] However, the genealogies these works provide are completely at variance over long stretches: even the father of Joseph is differently named.[30] Attempts were made, later on, to reconcile the two versions, but they could not prevent hostile pagans from continuing to dwell on their divergences.[31] There is a similar discrepancy about Jesus' birthplace. Whereas *Matthew* and *Luke* name it as Bethlehem,[32] *John* takes a different view. The Messiah, this Gospel concedes, was *expected* to come from Bethlehem, because that place, according to *I Samuel*, had been the home of David's father Jesse, and the *Book of the Prophet Micah* had declared that it would produce a 'governor for Israel'. Nevertheless, *John* continues, Jesus was not born there at all, but came from Galilee.[33] Elsewhere, the same Gospel indicates that his Galilean place of origin was Nazareth. *Mark* seems to imply agreement,[34] and according to *Luke*, Nazareth had been Joseph's home before he and Mary came to Bethlehem.[35] *Matthew*, it is true, seems quite unaware that this was so; but otherwise the unanimity regarding Nazareth is considerable, and it was as Nazarenes that many Jews described the early followers of Jesus.

It is remarkable, therefore, that Nazareth, a little place which lay in a hollow on the Galilean hills above the Plain of Jezreel, is mentioned neither in the Old Testament, nor by Josephus, nor by the Talmud. Because of this, it has been suggested that Jesus' real connexion was not with Nazareth but with the Nazirites. These 'separated' or 'dedicated' ones are referred to in *Numbers* and elsewhere as men and women who have made a special vow to dedicate themselves to God;[36] they may, in some degree, have constituted a special sect, possibly Messianic in nature. Alternatively, Nazareth may be a synonym for all Galilee, since Jesus was later described as the Galilean.[37] Modern conjectures have suggested that the place with which he had the closest connexions seems to have been Capernaum on the north shore of the Sea, just inside the principality of Antipas.

The belief that Jesus was born in AD I only originated in the sixth century AD, when a monk from south Russia living in Italy, Dionysius Exiguus, made a miscalculation when he was trying to reconcile differing accounts. *Luke* causes a notorious confusion by linking Jesus' birth with a census undertaken by Sulpicius Quirinius, who had not become governor of Syria until Rome's annexation of Judaea in AD 6 (and did not conduct any census there at an earlier date). The choice of so late a year for the birth of Jesus creates chronological impossibilities at subsequent stages; and although Herod's Massacre of the Innocents[38] cannot be regarded as historically plausible, Jesus is likely to have been born before Herod's death in 4 BC. Arguments have been variously put forward in favour of the years 11 or 7, or (more plausibly) 6, 5 or 4.

The date of his death is attributed to AD 28, or 29, or 30 or 33. His mission is variously estimated by the Gospels as lasting approximately three years or one. It took place, for the most part, in Galilee, though this phase underwent a temporary break after John the Baptist had been executed, and perhaps another interruption after the spreading of the report that he had miraculously fed five thousand people: this caused great excitement, whereupon Jesus 'withdrew again to the hills by himself'.[39] While preaching in Galilee, he did not enter the larger Hellenized capital towns such as Autocratoris (Sepphoris) or Tiberias, but directed his message mainly to the highlands, with their purely Jewish population. Among a people as volatile as the Galileans, preachers readily stirred up high religious and patriotic emotions, and the reason why he withdrew from their midst on the second occasion was specifically because the local people 'meant to come and seize him to proclaim him king'. Whether he himself, in any sense, claimed to be the Messiah (Christos) cannot, of course, be determined from our late and strongly coloured sources. But it seems likely enough that some of his followers in Galilee already believed him to be a Messiah, and that they chose to interpret his sayings as indicating that he believed the same. But what sort of a Messiah they saw in him we cannot tell, and indeed the substance and nature of the sayings he uttered remains obscure. As Rudolf Bultmann concludes, 'definite proof of authenticity can never be provided for a single individual saying of Jesus'.[40]

Whether Jesus' ministry alternated between Galilee and Jerusalem (as *John* indicates) or more simply moved once and for all from the one to the other (in accordance with the other Gospels), his entry into Jerusalem – the only large city in which he is recorded as preaching – was manifestly the climax and crux of his career. Whether, previously, he had been greeted as the Messiah or not, it was almost inevitable that a politico-religious leader with the reputation that he had now acquired would be greeted in this way, and it is difficult to believe that he did not realize this. The timing of his entry just before Passover ensured that he would be seen by the greatest possible number of Jews. Moreover, there is evidence that this was a time of serious political trouble. We cannot, it is true, synchronize Jesus' entry with any of the specific Jewish disturbances which confronted Pilate, though their coincidence in date is far from improbable. But *Mark* tells us it was at a time when the prison contained 'rebels who had committed murder in the rising' (including a certain Barabbas whose true story, in spite of varied speculations, is irrecoverable from the Gospel legends). And *Luke* records that people were speaking of 'the Galileans whose blood Pilate had mixed with their sacrifices'.[41]

It was evidently believed by the Jewish and Roman authorities that Jesus, after his entrance into Jerusalem, posed some threat to the Temple, and made some reference to its impermanence and ultimate destruction.[42] But most remarkable of all is the testimony of the Gospels that this supposedly pacific man – who had, however, reportedly declared that he came not to bring peace to the earth, but a sword[43] – drove out the money-changers and traders who thronged the precincts of the Temple, employing force to do so, and indeed making use, according to *John*, of a whip of cords.[44] Though their details vary, the Gospels are unanimous that this incident took place, and the surprising character of their reports suggests that they reflected an authentic tradition. If that is so, Jesus was committing a breach of the Roman provincial administration's public order. Moreover, at the same time he was attacking the Jewish priestly aristocracy, which controlled the affairs of the Temple and, incidentally, derived profits from the money-changers' tables he was overturning. It has been argued that he was directly associated with one of the politico-religious resistance movements, especially since one of his followers was said to be Simon 'the Zealot'.[45] There is no proof of any such affiliation, but that may well be the direction in which his sympathies lay. Certainly the Gospels, which so lavishly indicate his alleged attacks on various branches of the Jewish establishment, never record any criticism of the Zealots or *sicarii*, or of other subversive groups such as the Qumran sect.

At all events, Jesus' relations with the Roman and Jewish authorities were now at breaking point. *Luke* twice admits, in passages so alien to the general 'image' that they once again probably represent a reliable record, that at least some of his disciples were armed,[46] and his popular following at Jerusalem was apparently considerable.[47] When, therefore, steps were now taken to arrest him, this was done secretly. Temple police were employed for the purpose, and, according to *John*, Roman soldiers as well.[48]

Then Jesus was condemned to death. The relative parts played in his condemnation by the Romans and Jews already constituted a major emotional issue at the period when the Gospels were written (Chapter 13). They were written during or after the First Revolt (AD 66–70), at a time when Roman feelings against the Jews were very strong, and when, in consequence, the Gospel writers were eager to incriminate the Jews rather than Pilate – who even, according to the tradition of various churches, died (like his wife) a Christian! And the problem has been passionately discussed ever since, prompting many Jewish persecutions at Christian hands. The Jews themselves, according to their earlier traditions, were only too glad to take the responsibility upon themselves, readily asserting that the trial was an exclusively

Jewish matter, and adding that its outcome was amply justified.[49] In fact, however, the responsibility must have been divided between themselves and the Roman provincial government. In an occupied country, the ruling power and the collaborationist authorities act hand in hand, since it is in both their interests to do so;[50] on this occasion they must have been completely agreed on the treatment that should be accorded to popular preachers and reformist movements. As the high priest Joseph Caiaphas is very plausibly said to have observed to his Council, 'it is more to your interest that one man should die for the people, than that the whole nation should be destroyed'.[51] In other words, unless he and his colleagues cooperated with the Romans in suppressing Jesus, relations with the occupying power would be imperilled.

The exact procedure that was followed is obscure. Students of the Roman and particularly the Jewish legal systems have found it possible to pick very numerous holes in the legal procedures of the alleged trial, or two trials, described in the Gospels. But in all probability Jesus underwent no trial at all, in any formal or technical sense of the term. He is likely to have been subjected to informal examinations, first by the Jewish leaders, the high priest Caiaphas and his father-in-law the ex-high-priest Ananus (Annas in the Gospels), and then by Pilate.[52] One of the most convincing touches in the story is that Pilate did not take a part in the action until he had vainly endeavoured to shelve the problem on to Antipas, who was in Jerusalem for the Passover. For Jesus 'belonged to Antipas' jurisdiction',[53] and Pilate hoped in this way to restore his damaged relations with the prince.

There has also been an enormous amount of debate about the charge on which Jesus was tried. Was it blasphemy, on the grounds that he had made sinister remarks about the Temple and had set himself up as a Messianic impostor, under the name of the Son of God, or even of God himself, or a god?[54] If so, this was a matter on which the Jewish Council could or should give a ruling. Or was Jesus accused of treason against the Roman regime, in that he had committed and encouraged public disorder and claimed a kingship which constituted sedition? But the problem is not really a meaningful one, since in Judaea any challenge to the Jewish religious authority inevitably seemed to imply political opposition to the Romans – and the reverse was true as well.

The Council, as we have seen, was probably not entitled to carry out capital punishments (except for the execution, perhaps, by authorized lynchings, of Gentiles who had entered the inner courts of the Temple). But its judicial powers are likely to have included the right to *try* capital cases and to present those whom it condemned to the prefect for pronouncement of sentence and execution (though a Jewish source records the withdrawal of such a power at just about this time).[55] But that does not seem quite what happened now. More probably there were hurried and informal hearings, overshadowed by a threat to public order; and in the course of them, or after them, an administrative decision was taken to execute Jesus.

In the old days, when the Council had been entitled to inflict capital punishment for blasphemy, it had employed the traditional method of stoning. However, that was not how Jesus died.[56] His form of execution, on the contrary, was the agonizing penalty of crucifixion,[57] and on this occasion it was agreed by all to have been a Roman penalty imposed by the Romans and carried out by Roman soldiers.[58] This crucifixion of Jesus is unlikely to be an invention, since the criminal and degrading nature of such a death utterly alienated, for a time, almost all those who had believed in him – not least because it was widely held that a Messiah could only prove himself by success. Even centuries later, Christian artists were still avoiding the shocking theme. The damaging admission that Jesus had been crucified would never have been made if it was not true.

Pilate had restored his relations with Antipas, not so much perhaps by offering to transfer the case of Jesus to the latter's jurisdiction – which was embarrassing – as by having this troublesome Galilean executed. Shortly afterwards, Antipas received a great compliment from his Roman patron Tiberius: he was selected to act as mediator between the new governor of Syria, Lucius Vitellius, and the king of Parthia, Artabanus III (*c.* AD 12–38), who had recently, it would appear, suppressed the Jewish secessionist state at Nehardea. Antipas, whose knowledge of Aramaic and influence with the Babylonian Jews made him useful, gave a great banquet for the governor and the king upon a bridge over the Euphrates – and then got his dispatch on the subject to Rome in advance of the report of Vitellius, who was in consequence gravely annoyed. While Antipas was away, however, Aretas IV, the king of Nabataean Arabia, still harbouring a grudge owing to Antipas' repudiation of his royal Nabataean wife, invaded Peraea and heavily defeated that prince's generals – a defeat attributed by those who had admired John the Baptist to Antipas' responsibility for his death.[59] Tiberius was greatly angered by this behaviour, which was so improper for a client king, and instructed Vitellius to go to war with Aretas and execute or arrest him.

Meanwhile, Pilate's troubles, too, were not at an end, for yet another disturbance now occurred in his province, this time in Samaria. 'For a man there who made light of mendacity,' according to Josephus, 'and in all his designs catered to the mob, rallied them, bidding them go in a body with him to Mount Gerizim, which in their belief is the most sacred of mountains. He assured them that on their arrival he would show them the sacred vessels which were buried there, where Moses had deposited them.' This was in accordance with the Samaritans' particular interpretation of a passage of *Deuteronomy*,[60] which was regarded by them as a Commandment and indicated that a prophet would come out of Moses' tribe of Levi and would discover the hidden vessels of the Temple. But when a huge crowd began climbing the mountain, Pilate blocked their way with a detachment of cavalry and heavy infantry, and the subsequent clash resulted in fatal casualties, arrests and executions.

Shortly afterwards, Pilate terminated his governorship and returned to Rome (AD 36). According to Josephus, he was recalled because of a complaint by the Samaritans to Lucius Vitellius. It is probable enough that they complained, but not certain that their complaint caused his recall, since even under Tiberius, who preferred not to change his governors often, Pilate's ten- or eleven-year term of office meant he was due for a change. By the time he arrived in Rome, however, the emperor was dead, and Pilate passed from history into legend. Vitellius temporarily replaced him by an acting governor of Judaea, named Marcellus.

During the first years after Jesus' death, the group of Jews who had been his followers, greatly diminished in numbers by the catastrophe of his downfall and punishment, disappeared from view for a time. It was later said, perhaps correctly, that their surviving leaders were temporarily arrested, but released owing to the intervention of the greatest Pharisee of the day, Gamaliel I, who was the grandson of Hillel and president of the academy which he had founded or developed.[61] The reported version of Gamaliel's speech displays a characteristic Pharisaic ambiguity about Messiahs. 'Keep clear of these men, I tell you! Leave them alone. For if this idea of theirs, or its execution, is of human origin, it will collapse. But if it is from God, you will never be able to put them down, and you risk finding yourself at war with God.'[62] This advice corresponds with the known Pharisaic doctrine that the supreme power of God leaves some room for freewill among men. Moreover, its relatively sympathetic attitude towards Christian opinions, conflicting with the frequent emphasis, elsewhere in the New Testament, upon the unfriendly wrongheadedness of the Pharisees, gives the words an authentic ring.

Meanwhile those few Jews who remained faithful to Jesus' memory began to buoy themselves up with the belief that, in spite of his catastrophic downfall, he had subsequently risen from the dead, and had made a number of reappearances upon the earth.[63] Perhaps in the most primitive tradition of all he had appeared in a vision or visions. But then there grew up the belief in his bodily resurrection or resuscitation (the women among Jesus' followers, who 'found the tomb empty', played an active part in the transmission of this belief). It was, of course, by no means a new idea in Jewish thought – and only very recently Antipas had heard a report that John the Baptist had risen from the dead.[64] But to find a Messiah who had suffered earthly defeat and execution was something new. Reference was made to the Second Isaiah's Suffering Servant to explain this, and the doctrine of Jesus' resurrection on the Third Day owed a great deal to the prophet Hosea: 'after two days he will revive us, on the third day he will restore us, that in his presence we may live'.[65]

Doubters, symbolized by the figure of Thomas, could not believe that such a resurrection had taken place.[66] But those who did not doubt marked the first step in the eventual detachment of Christianity from Judaism and its establishment as a separate religion. For whereas Jesus' teaching, whatever its precise content, cannot have aimed at anything more than an enlargement of Jewish doctrine, the idea of a Christ who had already Risen, which Judaism, still awaiting its Messiah, could not accept, made an ultimate breach inevitable. Furthermore, there was a very early belief that it was from Jesus' resurrection, and not from his origins, that his position as the Messiah had its beginning. Although a Messiah was judged by results – which, in Jesus' case, had been catastrophic – that was now remedied, and he became the Messiah 'by a mighty act in that he rose from the dead'. It was from this belief, and its subsequent elaborations, that the whole tradition about Jesus arose – growing up backwards from his resurrection to his crucifixion and then to his life.

Moreover, since he had risen from the dead and reappeared upon earth, it was easy to go further and to declare that, like Enoch, Moses, Elijah and John the Baptist, he had also subsequently ascended to heaven.[67] And it was claimed, probably in the early days after his crucifixion, that this ascension or translation of Jesus had been witnessed – either on the very same day as his bodily resurrection (Easter) or, according to the canonical account, on the fortieth day thereafter.[68] Such were the seeds of the future religion, which would, among many other results, alter the whole place of Judaism in the future history of the world.

The birth of the church was later symbolized by the miracle of the Feast of Pentecost (Shabuoth),[69] when a divine power was believed to have descended collectively upon those assembled, conferring the Gift of Tongues. Yet this, with its strong universalist implications, was an attempt to reverse historical fact, since the earliest church of these years was wholly Jewish. This was the time of the first development of the Judaeo-Christians, the believers in Jesus who possessed and maintained their roots in the Jewish milieu in which he himself had been born. Their leading members derived their title of apostle from a Jewish office, the *shaliach*, and their number twelve was related to the twelve tribes and to the twelve patriarchs of early Hebrew history and legend.

The earliest leader of this deviant Jewish group seems to have been Jesus' former associate Peter, at least for some seven or ten years. In all the lists of the apostles, and all the numerous miracles attributed to this time, Peter comes first.[70] It is he whom visitors (notably Paul, of whom more shortly) came to see at Antioch. To Peter was ascribed the credit for the first missionary journeys, down the coast from Antioch to Gaza.[71] In the course of these journeys, as later tradition insisted, he baptized certain of the Gentiles who predominated in this area; though this may merely represent an attempt to palliate and contradict Peter's later opposition to Gentile proselytism. Peter apparently had his own personal following over a wide area, presumably among Jews; even at Corinth in Greece there were those who specifically described themselves as his supporters.[72]

Yet in these years of shock, shortly after the crucifixion, there was great disarray upon the fringes of the little group or groups who believed in Jesus. In particular, there arose a whole host of new Messianic claimants. One of them was a Samaritan named Dositheus, about whom the New Testament says nothing. He still revered the memory of John the Baptist, in whose name a separate sect may have been constituted. And there was Dositheus' compatriot Simon Magus, a 'sorcerer' regarded by his devotees as a god, whom later church historians denounced as the fountainhead of all heresy.[73] However, a Christian tradition also claimed that Simon Magus was converted by Philip the Evangelist. Philip (not the Apostle of that name) was one of the Seven, a group separate from the Twelve – and perhaps not appointed by them, as was later officially claimed. The Seven were concerned specifically with Gentile converts – those who spoke Greek and not the Aramaic 'language of the Jews'[74] – after a disagreement between the two groups had already arisen. Here are early indications of a deliberate extension of the cult of Jesus to Gentiles, in spite of all the objections this aroused among many Jews.

Another of the Seven was Stephen, and with him the break became manifest. The speech he is reported to have made when hauled before the Jewish Council contains material of great importance to the future of Christianity and Judaism. In view of the essentially non-historical purpose of the *Acts of the Apostles*, and the unlikelihood that an accurate record was kept, the oration cannot be regarded as wholly authentic. Yet its substance may faithfully represent new beliefs that were arising at this early stage in the life of the Jewish groups that revered the memory of Jesus. Stephen is made to declare that he saw Jesus standing at God's right hand, and he refers to his impending return to the earth. It was in the tradition of certain Jewish schools of thought, notably the Qumran sect, to associate the end of the world with the coming of a Messiah (in this case a Second Coming, since Jesus had appeared once upon the earth already). When that time arrived, he would participate in the Last Judgment. The time would arrive very soon, as many would fervently hope and agree, in the midst of their profound discontent with Roman rule and economic hardship: Stephen and other early Christians believed that the hoped-for Judgment would follow at any moment.

But Stephen was said to have expressed these sentiments in a shocking way. For he apparently asserted that, since the Temple, being manmade, was not essential, Jesus, when he came again, would destroy it. Or so at least his enemies said: and even a friendly tradition attributed to him the statement that 'the Most High does not live in houses made by men'. [75]

This could be, and was, cloaked in the respectable form of an interpretation of biblical passages. [76] But it remained, in effect, a direct attack on the authorities of the Temple, and an assertion that converted Gentiles, who could not use the Temple, had as much right to be called true believers as the Jews themselves. Significantly enough, those who were quoted as having prompted the proceedings against Stephen were Jews of the Dispersion, who stood the greatest risk of being swamped if Gentile converts were given excessive encouragement. For the leaders of the protest were the members of the Synagogue of Freedmen, including men from Cyrene, Alexandria and Asia Minor – Jews who may, or may not, have fully accepted Jesus as Messiah, but who at any rate regarded Stephen's attitude as too revolutionary a shift in favour of non-Jewish converts.

Stephen accordingly died at the hands of his fellow Jews. His death resulted in a fateful takeover, by his admirers, of the fervent Jewish ideal of martyrdom. What legal preliminaries, if any, preceded his killing, cannot now be determined. He was evidently stoned to death – and that was the Council's traditional punishment for blasphemy. However, it was not a punishment which the Council was any longer entitled to inflict. Either, then, the matter was presented as (and perhaps was) an unauthorized lynching, or the Council acted with deliberate illegality. In the latter case, it may well have been taking advantage of the virtual interregnum in the Roman governorship of Judaea due to the departure of Pilate (end of 36 or early 37 AD). If so, the high priest may not have troubled to consult Pilate's successor Marcellus, who was only holding office in an acting capacity.

Besides, there was a feeling of freedom in the air. For Lucius Vitellius, who visited Jerusalem at this time, had gained Tiberius' permission to accede to a Jewish request that the vestments of the high priesthood should be returned to the custody of the high priest himself, a major triumph for the Jewish authorities.

Moreover, Vitellius had also shown delicate feeling towards the Jews in another way. Ordered by Tiberius to come to Antipas' help against the Nabataeans, he did not bring his army with him to Jerusalem – which he visited for a second time at Passover, 37 – but sent it by a detour through the coastal plain. Although there is no evidence that the Jews had extended their objection to Roman military standards beyond Jerusalem itself, this looked like a tactful desire to avoid any repetition of the disturbances which had occurred when Pilate imported them into Jerusalem – a wise precaution for a commander about to plunge into the Nabataean desert. But Vitellius' gesture may well also have been prompted by a personal reluctance to rush to the help of Antipas, who had angered him by reporting so rapidly to the emperor about the Parthian conference. And now Vitellius was given the opportunity to avoid assisting Antipas at all. For while paying his second visit to Jerusalem he learnt of Tiberius' death, and gave up the expedition altogether.

Vitellius also made changes in the high priesthood. Perhaps the high priest largely responsible for the death of Stephen was still Caiaphas, who had played a leading part in Jesus' execution as well. But that is uncertain, since early in 37 Caiaphas was replaced – on the order of Vitellius, since the acting prefect Marcellus lacked the necessary authority. It is possible that the unauthorized killing of Stephen (if it had already occurred) was partly responsible for this change, but such a conclusion is not necessary since Caiaphas' tenure had already been abnormally long. His successor Jonathan however (his brother-in-law, and Ananus' son) was only high priest for a few months or weeks before Vitellius deposed him during his second visit.[77] Why this second change was made so quickly we cannot tell; perhaps Jonathan (whether responsible for Stephen's execution or not) had shown himself too independent and nationalistic. He was succeeded by his brother Theophilus.

As these high priests soon found, their difficulties with the groups of Jews who revered Jesus and shared the feelings of Stephen were only beginning. Before very long, perhaps because of the persecution of Stephen in Jerusalem, there was a group of these sectarians at Antioch. The Jews, in this stronghold of the Dispersion, had already been the object of a missionary visit from Peter, and Antioch may also have been the first place where Gentiles were approached by Jesus' followers on a substantial scale. The same wave of emigration of Hellenizing Christians from Jerusalem also led to the establishment of a colony at Damascus, and this attracted such unfavourable attention from the Jewish Council that they sent an envoy to bring it to order. This was Paul, a Jew from Tarsus in Cilicia (south eastern Asia Minor), who claimed descent from the tribe of Benjamin.[78] He came of a strict Pharisaic family, and had been a student of the principal Pharisee of the day,

Gamaliel I. His home town Tarsus, however, was a cultured Greek city, so that while Aramaic was the principal language of his speech and thoughts, Paul was also familiar enough with the Greek tongue: the style in which he wrote his Greek suggests that he learnt it in a Jewish environment less Hellenized, for example, than that of Alexandria.

Paul was not one of the small body of Jews who became, in their individual capacity, citizens of Greek cities, though he may have been the potential beneficiary of an arrangement (going back to Seleucid times) by which he could become a citizen on demand, if he worshipped the city's gods: a right which he did not choose to exercise.[79] On the other hand he belonged to one of the families, found in small numbers at many such places, which possessed Roman citizenship; it had been acquired by his father, either as a reward for services rendered to the Romans or because he was a freed slave.[80] Paul therefore belonged to three different worlds, and united them in his own person, as could not have been possible before the extension of the *Pax Romana*. His original Jewish name was Saul, and he probably chose Paul as its Roman equivalent because it was the Latin name which most closely resembled Saul.

The stoning of Stephen had taken place during the virtual interregnum in Judaea after the departure of Pilate, and the Council's further initiative in sending Paul to Damascus – which lay outside Judaea altogether, under the loose control of the governor of Syria – is probably another manifestation of Jewish freedom at the same epoch. Paul was later said, perhaps for the sake of dramatic effect, to have been the young man at whose feet the men who stoned Stephen laid their coats.[81] At all events, he himself declared that he had persecuted the Christians[82] – either at Jerusalem or his native Tarsus. The reason why he felt called upon to do so is clear. In the first place, Stephen's blasphemies about the Temple were deeply offensive to all firm believers in the Torah. Secondly, the threat from the Gentiles, which Stephen encouraged, seemed greatest in countries full of Greek cities like Paul's homeland Cilicia, which, as we have seen, contributed its quota of members to the synagogue that took the lead in the denunciations of Stephen. But there was also a more fundamental aspect of Paul's reasoning – a process to which his Greek background gave a sharper edge. The Jews, many of them, awaited a Messiah, as they do today. Either Jesus was the Messiah, or he was not. Since, in Paul's view, it was impossible for a condemned and executed criminal to be anything of the kind, he had been an impostor. And if he was an impostor, his followers must be extirpated, for otherwise they would be grievous stumbling-blocks to Israel, and would hamper its salvation.

But on the road to Damascus, Paul claimed that he saw a blinding light which felled him to the ground, and miraculously converted him to Christianity. Paul does not claim that he had known Jesus personally.[83] The light came to him out of his own psychological wrestlings. As it turned out, his conversion was the death-knell of Judaism's hopes to supersede paganism as the religion of the near-eastern and western worlds. But that only became apparent at a later stage. For the time being Paul retired to Damascus, which at this juncture (AD 37) was ceded or leased by the Romans to King Aretas IV of Nabataean Arabia. Paul also travelled round other parts of Arabia, presumably describing the conversion he had experienced, and in that distant area he remained for three years.[84]

8

The Peril from Caligula and the Greeks

The year AD 37, in which Tiberius died and Caligula came to the imperial throne, made a forty-seven-year-old Herodian prince Agrippa I the most important man in the Jewish world. A grandson of Herod the Great and Mariamme, and a nephew of the ruling princes Antipas and Philip, Agrippa I had been named after the great Roman Marcus Agrippa, Herod's friend, who had died about two years before he was born.

Sent to Rome at the age of about five, Agrippa I was brought up there with Tiberius' son Drusus the younger. Very popular in Roman society, this witty, charming, versatile Jewish youth ran into heavy debt, partly because of his extensive bribery of the imperial household; after Drusus' death in AD 23 he found it necessary to leave Rome in a hurry. He retired to a remote place in Idumaea, but was rescued by his uncle Antipas who gave him an appointment as notary at Tiberias. However, Agrippa quarrelled with Antipas, whose job he found boring, and placed himself under the protection of the governor of Syria, Lucius Pomponius Flaccus (AD 32–5). But then he quarrelled with Flaccus, too, and moved southwards again to Ptolemais Ace, with the intention of returning to Italy – if only he could collect the necessary funds. In this latter task he was successful, for he managed to raise a loan locally from a freedman of the emperor's sister-in-law Antonia, who had been friendly with his mother. Then he made his way to a family property at Anthedon (near Gaza), so as to leave unobtrusively from its small port. But there the procurator in charge of the neighbouring imperial estate of Jamnia (Yavne), Herennius Capito, placed him under detention, claiming that he owed a large sum to the Roman treasury. However, Agrippa I slipped away to Alexandria, where with some difficulty he extracted a further large loan from a very rich Jewish commercial and customs official named Alexander, brother of the philosopher Philo.[1]

Agrippa now sailed back to Italy, arriving in spring 36 at the island of Capreae (Capri) where the aged emperor Tiberius was residing. Tiberius received him kindly, but on the very next day there arrived a letter from Herennius Capito giving news of the circumstances of his debt and flight. Dismissed from court until he could raise the money, Agrippa borrowed it from Antonia. Then the emperor, drawing a veil over this unfortunate affair, entrusted him with the care of his own grandson Tiberius Gemellus – son of the Drusus who had been Agrippa's friend. Gemellus was spoken of as a possible heir to the throne, but a stronger candidate was Tiberius' grand-nephew Gaius (Caligula); and so Agrippa I took pains to strike up a friendship with this peculiar young man, to whom he presented part of the funds he had received from Antonia. But some careless words of flattery Agrippa uttered to Caligula, expressing hopes of his early accession, were overheard, and he was arrested. Six months later, however, Tiberius died, and Caligula not only released him but gave him the principality of Philip, vacant since his recent death. Moreover, Caligula not only enlarged this Transjordanian territory by adding a strip of southern Syria (Abilene in Anti-Lebanon), but made Agrippa I a king – not merely a prince (tetrarch) as Philip had been. He was also given the honorary rank of praetor, which was second only in the Roman hierarchy to the consulship.

Agrippa was at first in no hurry to leave the luxuries of Rome and of imperial favour for his native land, of which he had unpleasant, though comparatively brief, recollections. By the end of the year, however, he had changed his mind, since Caligula was showing such marked eccentricities that Agrippa considered it a good investment to put some distance between them. And so he sailed off to the near east.

On the way, he called in at Alexandria. In recent years relations between the Greeks and Jews in that city had gravely deteriorated.

The Greeks nursed many long-standing grudges against the huge local Jewish community – religious, racial, economic and social alike. But what they objected to most of all was that the Jews collaborated so willingly with the Roman authorities. For the Greeks, disillusioned after half a century of Roman rule, had now produced a party of extreme anti-Roman nationalists. Being anti-Roman, they were strongly anti-Jewish as well – influenced still further in this direction by the native Egyptians, who were known to exceed all other peoples in the hatred they felt for the Jews.[2] Nor, probably, did the Alexandrian Jews themselves altogether lack responsibility for this sharp worsening of relations with the Greeks. For, although their propagandist Philo does not tell us so, it seems that a modernist party among them, not content with its community's existing privileges, was also demanding – and perhaps partially usurping – the Alexandrian citizenship which, except as far as a few individuals were concerned, had always been reserved for the Greeks. The Jews wanted to have an equal share in this communal citizenship, not only for reasons of prestige but because this would exempt them from the hated provincial poll-tax, which the Greeks were not required to pay.

Such were the mutual, deeply burning resentments which engaged the attention of Aulus Avillius Flaccus when he became prefect of Egypt in AD 32–3. Until Caligula's accession four years later, all went relatively well. But then Flaccus, who had been a friend of Tiberius and had played a part in the banishment of Caligula's mother Agrippina I,[3] felt obliged to take special steps to flatter the new emperor. The victims of these steps proved to be the Jewish community of Alexandria. Like similar communities elsewhere, it did not participate in the worship of the emperor; now, in consequence, it incurred new and severe sanctions from Flaccus. The extremist Greek leader in Alexandria, Isidorus, was a man of whom Flaccus stood in considerable fear. For Isidorus not only commanded gangs of local hooligans, but may even have been powerful enough to play a part in the downfall of Macro, the praetorian prefect (commander of the imperial guard) at Rome, whom Caligula had inherited from Tiberius but had subsequently dropped and driven to suicide. And now at this time, in the gymnasium of Alexandria – centre and symbol of the city's Hellenism – Isidorus' gangsters were reciting scurrilous poems against Flaccus; and this and other more menacing activities on their part frightened him into toeing the line and pursuing an increasingly anti-Jewish policy. Before long, he was refusing access to Jewish petitioners, and displaying obvious bias against them in lawsuits. When they gave him a letter of congratulation to forward to the new emperor, he failed to send it on.

It was at this juncture that Agrippa I arrived in Alexandria (August, 38). His status was very different from that of his last visit, when he had been a defaulting debtor, and his Jewish supporters in the city, led by his former benefactor Alexander, were jubilant. Agrippa himself, on his arrival, was anxious to avoid publicity, but he gave in to the pressure of the Jews and agreed to a military parade, hoping no doubt that this would impress Flaccus and the Greeks with Jewish pomp and might. But the Greeks chanted mocking, obscene verses and arranged an insulting counter-procession in which the local idiot, Carabas (Cabbage), masqueraded as king. With the connivance, it was said, of Avillius Flaccus, violence and casualties followed. At this stage Agrippa decided he had better leave Egypt straightaway, and so he continued upon his journey to his new kingdom – but not before he had sent a letter to Caligula complaining about Flaccus' retention of the Jews' congratulatory letter, and about his other hostile behaviour.

Then rioting of a more serious kind broke out: and so began the first serious pogrom of Roman times. In those quarters of Alexandria in which the Jews formed a minority, their synagogues were profaned and destroyed, and the Jewish inhabitants themselves were compelled to emigrate to the exclusively Jewish quarter in the Delta area, incurring heavy losses of life and property as they did so. This district, by now desperately overcrowded, overflowing into refuse heaps and cemeteries, assailed by famine and disease, became the first compulsory ghetto of the Mediterranean world: and the Jewish community in Alexandria, which had been by far the richest in the empire, was stricken by a dire poverty from which it never fully recovered.[4]

Next the Greeks invaded the Jewish quarter itself and, forcing their way into its synagogues, erected a statue of Caligula in every one of them. This was an act of profanation, but one which the emperor's uncertain temperament made it difficult for the Jews to protest against. Indeed, Flaccus himself may have sanctioned the desecrations, and the looting of Jewish shops and homes which accompanied them. At all events, he deliberately added fuel to the flames by proclaiming that the Jews were 'aliens and foreigners' at Alexandria. By this he meant that, so far from encouraging them to seek the citizenship reserved for the

Greeks, he considered them as demoted from their special autonomous privileges to the status of unprivileged native Egyptians. Next, after conducting a house-to-house search for arms, he arrested thirty-eight members of the Jewish Council, and on 31 August, AD 38 marched them to the theatre, where, as a choice item in a programme of music and dancing, they were publicly flogged, while their women folk were forced to eat pork in front of a vast crowd.

Meanwhile, however, Caligula had received Agrippa's letter written after his disastrous visit to Alexandria. As a result of it, Flaccus was recalled to Rome and placed on trial. Perhaps the charge was maladministration, although his earlier position among the enemies of the emperor's mother is also likely to have played a part. It is surprising to find Isidorus and his principal colleague Lampon among his accusers, for it would have seemed that Flaccus had been playing their game. No doubt, however, they wanted to be on the winning side. And Flaccus was duly convicted. His art collection was confiscated, and he himself was banished to the Greek island of Andros, and executed in the following year.

Such a reversal of fortune seemed to the Jews reminiscent of their Old Testament deliverances, of which the most famous of all had related to this same Egyptian land. The role of Agrippa I in these events had been triumphant. Although he was not king of Judaea itself, but only of a border country away to its north, his letter to Caligula shows him overtly acting as the politico-religious leader of world Jewry – and achieving spectacular results. After his arrival in his new kingdom, he issued a remarkable coin, probably at his capital Caesarea Philippi (AD 38–9), displaying his own name and portrait.[5] He was the first member of the Herodian house, indeed the first Jewish ruler of all time, to place his own head on his coins. Furthermore, on the reverse of the same issues, appears an equestrian figure labelled with the name of his ten-year-old son Agrippa, who later became Agrippa II; while on another piece the boy's childish portrait is depicted.[6] Caligula's head also appears on his coinage (though not apparently until AD 41),[7] and so confident was Agrippa of his goodwill that he ventures to place on his coinage this open declaration that his successor to the kingship – whom it was for the emperor to appoint – must in his view be his own son.

However, there was one quarter in which Agrippa I's title was causing intense jealousy, and that was at the court of Antipas at Tiberias. When

Agrippa was destitute and on the run, Antipas had given him modest but useful help, only to meet with quarrelsome ingratitude. Moreover, Antipas' wife Herodias was Agrippa's sister. Herodias, as her destruction of John the Baptist had shown, was a woman who favoured decisive action. And as Stewart Perowne rightly suggests, she could not bear to think that her scapegrace brother should now be ruling as a king, a bare thirty miles away, up in Caesarea Philippi, while her husband, after forty-three years of service to Rome and to his people, was still only a mere prince. Antipas himself, now in his sixties, was content with his lot – but Herodias was fatally determined that he should improve it. So in 39 the two of them set off for Rome, in the most magnificent style,[8] and Antipas requested Caligula to grant him the same kingly rank as Agrippa I.

Whether, at the same time, he was rash enough to offer abuse against Agrippa we do not know. But Agrippa was taking no risks, and one day after the arrival of the couple at the fashionable Campanian watering-place of Baiae, where Caligula was holding his court, a freedman of Agrippa arrived as well, with a message from his master. This accused Antipas, among other things, of having plotted against the life of Tiberius – in the company of Sejanus, who had been executed for this offence in AD 31. Secondly, the letter declared that Antipas was engaged, at this very moment, in concocting a treasonable conspiracy with King Artabanus III of Parthia. Accusations that Jewish leaders were conspiring with the Parthians often won a ready hearing from the suspicious Roman authorities. Moreover, it was a fact that Antipas had acted as mediator between Lucius Vitellius, governor of Syria, and Artabanus; and probably Vitellius, who had resented Antipas' behaviour on that occasion, was glad enough to confirm the report of his disloyalty. So Antipas was banished to Lugdunum Convenarum (S. Bertrand de Comminges) in Gaul – just as his brother Archelaus had long ago been banished to another town in the same country thirty-three years earlier. The service he had given for so long, to the satisfaction of three emperors, went for nothing. His wife Herodias was told she need not go with him, but she did. Antipas' principality of Galilee and Peraea was added to the dominions of Agrippa, which were thus nearly doubled in size and more than doubled in importance.

Meanwhile, at Alexandria, the synagogues remained closed, and Greeks and Jews alike showed desperate eagerness to send deputations to Rome so that Caligula could hear their cases. There was some delay before this was possible, probably because the new prefect of Egypt, Vitrasius Pollio, wanted to examine the quarrel before letting them leave for the capital. Finally, however, late in 39, both embassies sailed away. The Greek delegation, which included Isidorus and Lampon, was led by an erudite and industrious literary figure, a historian from upper Egypt named Apion. Currently head of the academy at Alexandria, Apion was well known at Rome, where his ostentatiousness had caused Tiberius to describe him as the tambourine or cymbals of the world. Primarily an Egyptian historian, he also wrote extensively about the Jews, though it is uncertain whether this was in his history of Egypt or in a separate work. But he expressed himself with exceptional hostility towards them, repeating and embroidering upon every form of attack that had ever been attempted. Even a half century later, his vituperations were still so well known that Josephus thought it necessary to refute them in great detail.

The leader of the Jewish delegation to Caligula was Philo, brother of the Alexander who had helped Agrippa I when he was in trouble. Philo was a very talented Jew with Greek training, whose numerous literary works clothed Judaism in Greek dress, emphasizing, with some exaggeration, that the Septuagint had been created in order to enlighten the Greek world. Although recognizing that his Jewish belief in the omnipotence of the one God conflicted with every school of Greek philosophy, he showed a strong desire somehow to harmonize the two points of view. This desire, stimulated by a strong taste for intellectual paradox, encouraged him to insist that, whereas the priority of the quasi-divine Moses was beyond question,[9] Pythagoras, Plato and Aristotle had all copied and echoed his pronouncements. And these same Greek philosophers, he added, had also displayed similarities to their forebears the Jewish Prophets – thus demonstrating that their doctrines, like those of the prophets, were of divine origin. One curious way in which he effected this Greco-Jewish amalgamation was by turning the Torah into allegories, after the fashion of Greek philosophers such as the Stoics. Thus circumcision represented the cutting off of passions and ungodly opinions, and the drowning of the Egyptians in the Red Sea during the Exodus was a mere symbol of the destruction of the true Israel's lower impulses.[10]

Philo's methods made him a remarkable protagonist of the Jews of the Dispersion, and on the Day of Deliverance, he assured them, salvation would be theirs as much as Israel's.[11] Whatever country they inhabited, he declared, *that* was their real fatherland – Jerusalem was very far from forgotten, yet the Dispersion was no longer its subordinate.[12] Moreover, Philo spoke with exceptional warmth about the welcome that must be given to proselytes. For although wavering, at times, between the doctrine of the Chosen Race and preference for insisting upon the universality of God,[13] he was convinced that Judaism is not a racial concept: any man is capable of 'seeing God'. Messianism did not fail to touch him, but not very forcibly: he sees the awaited Messiah as prophet-priest and saintly pacific leader, but by no means as a conquering hero.

Philo was not so much a philosopher as a religious preacher, a spiritual director. His abundant writings flow smoothly and mellifluously, but the smoothness conceals lengthy preliminary processes of discussion and disputation. For he lived at a time when the Jews, almost uniquely among the subjects of Rome, had produced and were still producing an extensive literature of their own, at which we can only guess from what he wrote. Seeking to resolve their problems in a spirit of large-minded kindness and serene belief, and firmly setting Jewish revelation beside Greek reason as the composite basis for a system of human thought, he emerges as the greatest exponent of that Hellenized Judaism which subsequently vanished from among the Jews almost without a trace, superseded by the rabbinical tradition. Although a number of Philo's themes can, with some difficulty, be detected in the Talmud and other Jewish works, he was in general anathema to Jewish theologians, who never mentioned him or his Greco-Jewish associates – though pagan philosophers of the later empire found him useful, and he was eagerly studied by the Christian fathers.

Such was the man who now found himself leader of an exceedingly delicate mission to the emperor Caligula. Already advanced in years at this time, he was a political conservative, who chooses as his objection to pagan polytheism its 'transference from earth to heaven mob-rule, that worst of evil forms of government'.[14] He represented the wealthier section of the Jews in Alexandria, that portion of the community which wanted good relations with the Romans – and even reconciliation with the Greeks, if it could possibly be achieved. And by a fortunate chance we have Philo's own record, not only of Avillius Flaccus' Egyptian governorship, but of the vicissitudes of his deputation to Rome.[15] Less fortunately, these works, for all their masses of valuable detail, are in the first instance not so much histories as explanations of how God's will is vindicated, and how he defends his Chosen People: the pro-secutors of the pious are punished, and first Avillius Flaccus falls and then Caligula himself.

While Philo and his colleagues and enemies were all on their way to Rome, the Jewish cause was gravely affected by deplorable events in Judaea. Caligula, on his accession, had replaced the acting prefect Marcellus by a substantive successor, Marullus.[16] But the crisis that now arose was so grave that it had to be handled, not by the local man, but by the very much more senior governor of Syria, who from 39 was Publius Petronius, a relative of his predecessor Lucius Vitellius.

The trouble began at Jamnia (Yavneh) on the coast. There the Greeks, though probably not a numerical majority, were the dominant element in the administration of the town. In the early days of 40, these Greeks, who hated the large local community of Jews, listened favour-ably to suggestions from the imperial agent Herennius Capito, the man who had made difficulties for Agrippa I in years gone by. Capito proposed, or agreed with the proposal, that they should erect an altar in honour of the godhead of the emperor, to commemorate his recently announced (though fictitious) victories in Germany. Caligula was insistent on the worship of himself as a universal imperial divinity, regarding ruler-cult as a suitable bond of unification for the numerous peoples of the empire. But for the monotheistic Jews, of course, such worship was out of the question, as the Greeks of Jamnia very well knew. Nevertheless, they erected the altar, building it solidly of brick. The Jews might perhaps have treated this structure as a phenomenon relating only to the Greeks, in which case it could have been ignored. Instead, however, they forcibly dismantled it.

Capito reported to Caligula what they had done, and the emperor consulted two advisers of near eastern origins, his chamberlain Helicon, who was probably an Alexandrian Greek, and Apelles, an actor from Ascalon. Philo described Helicon as a scorpion, and it was clear that neither he nor Apelles seemed likely to favour the Jewish case. After listening to their advice, Caligula decided upon a radical measure which would deal once and for all with this sort of problem, not only in Jamnia but everywhere else in Judaea as well. For he intended to make not only the synagogues, but the Temple at Jerusalem itself, into shrines of the imperial cult. The days of King Antiochus IV Epiphanes had come once again, and for much the same reason: because ruler worship was to be regarded as the common denominator of loyalty to the imperial state and its monarch. And so orders were given to Petronius to commission the construction of a colossal gilt statue of Caligula, in the guise of Zeus (Jupiter), and to place it in the Jerusalem Temple.

While these ominous decisions were being reached, the Jewish and Greek deputations from Alexandria had been making their way to Italy, where they disembarked, after an uncomfortable winter voyage, early in 40. There they found that nothing could be done for the present because Caligula was spending the winter in Gaul, and had not yet come back. While awaiting his return both parties set about bribing his chief counsellors. The Greeks enjoyed the greater success, especially with Helicon. But the Jews still intended to stake their claims high, for they apparently proposed to request not only the restoration of their violated rights in Alexandria, but also admission (for the first time) to the citizenship of the city. When Caligula got back he gave the Jewish deputation (and presumably the Greeks also) a short preliminary hearing at about the end of May. Then he left to spend the summer in Campania, and probably both deputations went with him. It was there, at Puteoli (Pozzuoli), that the Jews learnt of the intolerable decision to make the Temple a centre of imperial cult.

In due course Caligula returned to Rome, and after he had celebrated an Ovation for his alleged German victories (31 August) he received both sets of envoys in his gardens on the Esquiline Hill, where he was busy inspecting building operations. According to Philo, the story of the Greek desecration of the Alexandrian synagogues did not come up, but Caligula raised the question of their participation in emperor worship. The Jews carefully explained that whereas they could not sacrifice *to* him they were accustomed, very gladly, to make offerings *for* him. But Caligula replied: 'What is the good of that? You have not sacrificed *to* me.' Then he suddenly interrupted his renewed study of the building by asking why Jews refused to eat pork. Soon afterwards, the meeting ended on an indeterminate but by no means encouraging note, with Caligula pointedly inquiring about the legal basis of the Jews' organization in Alexandria, and finally observing that failure to recognize his divinity showed them not so much to be criminals as lunatics.[17]

Meanwhile Petronius, in Syria, had bowed to the imperial command

and ordered the construction, at Sidon, of a statue of Caligula-Zeus for the Jerusalem Temple. He hinted, however, that the sculptor and workmen need not exert themselves to finish the image too quickly, since he was painfully aware of the disturbances its erection would raise. When the imperial decision became known, Petronius had summoned the Jewish leaders to Antioch to inform them of it; their reaction left him in no doubt concerning the inevitable outcome. Indeed, this was also no secret to the emperor himself. However, he did not change his mind, but instead instructed Petronius to take with him two of the four legions of the Syrian garrison, with auxiliary troops to match, when he moved southwards to install the statue.

Petronius had some heart-searchings before removing these legions from Syria, since he was afraid that this might encourage the Parthians to invade Syria – though fortunately for him a series of rapid changes in the Parthian kingship (after the death of Artabanus III in AD 38) prevented this, and indeed such a state of anarchy prevailed that for seven years the city of Seleucia on the Tigris was virtually independent.[18] But Petronius was particularly afraid that if the Jews in Judaea revolted they would receive assistance from the Jewish communities in Babylonia.[19] These had received a serious setback when their little state at Nehardea, which had survived in a state of virtual independence for fifteen years, had been crushed and its leader Anilaeus killed (*c.* 35–6). But the upheavals accompanying this development had produced a flood of refugees and emigrants, and Petronius must obviously have been afraid that they would flock into Judaea.

The Judaean Jews themselves were prepared to stop at nothing in order to reverse Caligula's decision. They had already proclaimed an agricultural strike, and when Petronius brought his legions southwards as far as Ptolemais Ace he was confronted by a deputation from the province, probably led by the high priest Theophilus himself. Hordes of demonstrators also arrived, and threatened mass-martyrdom.[20] Petronius was no doubt keeping Caligula informed of developments as tactfully as possible, but he felt it inadvisable to allow the Jews to send another deputation to the emperor, since this might only infuriate him. In due course he continued his journey and came to Tiberias, where a further series of large-scale demonstrations awaited him. Agrippa I was not available to support these appeals, since he had left for Italy once again, in order to expedite matters relating to his recent annexation of Antipas' principality. However, the mass-protests were duly backed by Agrippa's brother and regent Aristobulus, who begged Petronius to avoid installing the statue at all costs. And Petronius now concluded that it was the lesser of two evils – though still a very perilous course – to write to the emperor and urge him to countermand his order, so as to avoid general war.

Josephus, in describing these events, stresses the dignified protests of the legitimate Jewish authorities, and says nothing of any threats of violence from political extremists. But this is only because he is so eager to show the patient forbearance of the Jews in the face of the tyranny of Caligula, whose memory, Roman emperor though he had been, it was perfectly safe and acceptable to execrate. The historian Tacitus confirms that an open rising was, in fact, imminent;[21] and, as even Josephus does at one point admit, Petronius felt obliged to warn Caligula that such a rebellion might break out at any moment. The main preoccupation of his dispatches to his imperial master at this time, however, was a desire to explain that the delay in setting up the statue was due not to his own negligence but to the slowness of those engaged in its construction; though at the same time he did venture to suggest that it would be best to avoid any action which might risk sabotage to the grain and fruit harvest. This was a useful argument, since the emperor himself was planning an early visit to the near east,[22] and any shortage of supplies or famine in the area would cause him personal inconvenience.

However, Caligula sent Petronius a letter pointing out that by the time it reached him the harvest would already be in, and once again he ordered that the statue should be erected and dedicated forthwith. Meanwhile, Agrippa I had arrived in Italy (September, 40), where he learnt with horror what Caligula had written to Petronius. The news caused him to suffer a nervous breakdown, or perhaps a stroke, but as soon as he had somewhat recovered from the shock he thought it right, as the leading Jew (although not officially concerned with the affairs of Judaea), to address the emperor a long, careful memorandum explaining why the erection of the statue was inadvisable.[23] Caligula was to some extent impressed by his arguments, and wrote to Petronius cancelling his order. But he added that the Jews in other parts of Judaea outside Jerusalem, must not, as those of Jamnia had endeavoured to do, raise obstacles to the celebration of the imperial cult by Gentiles in their areas.

That probably was the end of the story. But the Jewish writers were unwilling to give Caligula the credit of reversing a policy that had proved mistaken; they chose instead to invent vivid touches of melodrama that would provide a more suitable climax. Thus, according to Philo, Caligula despotically changed his mind once again and arranged to have a vast statue of himself, in the guise of Zeus, made in Italy, so that when he left for the east it could be set up in the Temple after all. Josephus adds that the emperor, infuriated by Petronius' reluctance to obey, wrote ordering him to commit suicide; but that the ship carrying this message only arrived after the news that Caligula had been assassinated, so that Petronius' life was saved. These, probably, are fairy tales.[24] But it is true enough that the death of Caligula, on 24 January 41, saved a very great deal of disturbance and loss of life. For if he had not died when he did, the date of the First Jewish Revolt would have been advanced by twenty-five years.

Upon Jewish (and later Christian) thought this crisis exercised a traumatic and lasting effect. The day on which the news of Caligula's murder became known was kept by the Jews as a day of rejoicing.[25] Moreover, his threats had given the whole idea of martyrdom, inherited from Maccabaean times, a fresh boost, because the counter-threats of martyrdom by the Jews at Ptolemais and Tiberias seemed, by God's mercy, to have brought about the deliverance of their suffering people. However, these events also possessed a sinister political significance. Although the part played in the crisis by nationalistic extremists remains so obscure, the menace of Caligula had greatly strengthened their hand, for it had demonstrated the essential logicality of their case: Roman rule, intolerable in theory, could at any moment become intolerable in practice as well – and must therefore be resisted at all times.

9

The Kingship of Agrippa I and After

In Rome, after the murder of Caligula, there was a period of crisis before his uncle Claudius secured recognition as his successor. Agrippa I was still in the city at this time, and in the hasty and vital negotiation between the senate, the praetorian guard and Claudius himself, he discreetly performed an indispensable role as intermediary.[1] Claudius, a pedantic figure of ridiculous physical appearance, had never before, during his fifty-one years, been taken seriously in court or senatorial circles. But Agrippa I had the foresight to recognize that he had latent gifts. And no doubt Agrippa also reasoned that timely assistance to the successful candidate for the throne would stand himself, and his fellow Jews, in good stead.

Shortly after his accession, Claudius interviewed the delegations of Greeks and Jews who had come to Rome in order to see Caligula. The Greeks, no longer benefiting from the anti-Jewish feelings of the late emperor, were now in deep disgrace owing to their violent conduct in Alexandria. In the proceedings before Claudius, it was therefore most unwise of Isidorus and Lampon to take the thoroughly aggressive line recorded in the *Acts of the Pagan Martyrs*, which seems to have drawn upon more or less accurate summaries. It indicates that Isidorus spoke in the most unrestrained fashion when he was given a hearing, describing Agrippa I as just a twopenny-halfpenny Jew and even declaring that the emperor himself was a half-Jewish, cast-off bastard.[2] His main argument, however, was that the Jews of Alexandria were trouble-makers on a world-wide scale, and should undoubtedly be classified with tribute-paying Egyptians rather than with the Greeks who were the only citizens of the place. In view of his other remarks, it is hardly surprising that these arguments proved unsuccessful, and that Isidorus and Lampon, transformed from accusers into defendants, found themselves convicted and executed for bringing a fraudulent accusation (*calumnia*) – a fate which earned them, in Greek circles, a reputation as martyred heroes. At this point, too, Claudius issued a provisional edict in which he criticized the policy of his predecessor and confirmed the privileges of the Jews in Alexandria.

Meanwhile, however, there had already been fresh trouble in that city, where the Jews, without waiting for this confirmation from Claudius, had wanted to get their own back on their Greek enemies immediately. So after collecting together an armoury of weapons and calling in gangs of their co-religionists from other parts of Egypt and from Syria[3] – a particularly alarming step in the eyes of the Roman authorities – they proceeded to launch a savage attack upon the Greek majority in the city. Somehow or other the fighting was suppressed, and then each side sent further sets of envoys to Rome. The Greek delegates were eleven or twelve in number, but the Jews actually sent two separate deputations: one may have represented the conservatives, the other the more radical schools of Jewish thought; or the division may have been between those Jews who (on an individual basis) possessed the Alexandrian citizenship, and those who did not, or between natives and immigrants respectively. Ostensibly each of the delegations wanted to congratulate Claudius on his accession. But the Greeks, on this occasion, also had a special further demand to make, for they requested the establishment of a municipal senate – a body which, if it had ever existed, was already in abeyance since long before Roman rule began. As for the Jews, they once again demanded, as a communal right, the Alexandrian citizenship which had never been theirs.

Claudius' reply, preserved in an unscrupulously doctored version by Josephus and in its authentic form by a papyrus, is a significant record of a sorely tried emperor's attempt to be fair. The Greek demand for a senate is diplomatically shelved; that is to say, it is referred to a special commission. The Jews, for their part, learnt that their existing rights were reaffirmed, but that their request for Alexandrian citizenship was explicitly turned down:

As for the question which party was responsible for the riots and feud (or rather, if the truth must be told, the war) with the Jews, although in confrontation with their opponents your ambassadors, and particularly Dionysius son of Theon, contended with great zeal, nevertheless I was unwilling to make a strict inquiry, though guarding within me a store of immutable indignation against whichever party renews the conflict; and I tell you once and for all that unless you put a stop to this ruinous and obstinate enmity against each other, I shall be driven to show what a benevolent prince can be when turned to righteous indignation.

Wherefore once again I conjure you that on the one hand the Alexandrians show themselves forbearing and kindly towards the Jews who for many years have dwelt in the same city, and dishonour none of the rites observed by them in the worship of their god, but allow them to observe their customs as in the time of the deified Augustus, which customs I also, after hearing both sides, have sanctioned; and on the other hand I explicitly order the Jews not to agitate for more privileges than they formerly possessed, and not in future to send out a separate embassy as if they lived in a separate city, a thing unprecedented, and not to force their way into the gymnasiarchies or the games given by the cosmetes, while enjoying their own privileges and sharing a great abundance of advantages in a city not their own, and not to bring in or admit Jews who sail in from Syria or Egypt, a proceeding which will compel me to conceive serious suspicions; otherwise I will by all means take vengeance on them as fomenters of what is a general plague infecting the whole world.

If, desisting from these courses, you consent to live with mutual forbearance and kindliness, I on my side will exercise a solicitude of very long standing for the city, as one which is bound to us by traditional friendship. I bear witness to my friend Balbillus of the solicitude which he has always shown for you in my presence and of the extreme zeal with which he has now advocated your cause, and likewise to my friend Tiberius Claudius Archibius. Farewell.[4]

Thus Claudius lays down the principle, perhaps never so explicitly stated before, that the Jews must repay toleration with toleration. And his edict was followed up by another addressed to Jewish communities throughout the entire Roman empire, in which he requests that they should not 'behave with contempt towards the gods of other peoples', but assures them of his sympathy all the same.[5] This was sufficient to please Philo, who winds up his *Embassy to Gaius* (*Caligula*) with a 'palinode'[6] induced by the great change for the better that these words of Claudius had announced; and Josephus, too, hails his attitude as pro-

Jewish. But what the new emperor is really trying to do, as most Roman emperors except Caligula tried to do, is to strike a fair balance.

In Palestine itself, on the other hand, Claudius acted in a markedly, indeed sensationally, pro-Jewish fashion – in order to do favour to Agrippa I. He was deeply grateful to Agrippa for his invaluable help in securing his succession to the imperial throne, and it is also likely that Agrippa had helped Claudius to draft his edicts about Jewish affairs.[7] In consequence, his kingdom was now enlarged by no less a gift than the whole province of Judaea itself. The provincial status of the country was abolished and the prefect removed, and the entire territory passed into the hands of Agrippa I, now elevated to consular rank. Agrippa's dominions, governed once again from Jerusalem, were practically the same as those of Herod the Great, and indeed, towards the north, were even more extensive. Furthermore Agrippa's brother, likewise called Herod, was declared king in his turn, and was presented with the land of Chalcis (Anjar) in Lebanon, at the foot of Mount Hermon. He was granted the rank of praetor, and given his brother Agrippa's daughter Berenice as his wife. Meanwhile, however, in order to distinguish himself from the new monarch and other kings of lesser rank, Agrippa adopted the ancient and imposing, though lately much devalued, title of Great King.[8]

Back in Jerusalem in October 41, Agrippa proceeded with considerable skill. In order to overcome Hellenic hostility incurred through his support of the Alexandrian Jews against the Greeks, he made magnificent gifts to Greek cities such as Berytus (Beirut).[9] At the same time, he went to great pains to demonstrate his loyalty to Rome and its emperor. The pattern was set by his mint of Caesarea Maritima, where the coinage (mainly employed for external trade) bore the heads both of Claudius and of Agrippa himself, the latter being inscribed Philocaesar, Lover of the Emperor.[10] Even more explicit is another coin of the same mint which shows a figure of Agrippa, sacrificing at an altar, and two clasped hands inscribed 'The Friendship of King Agrippa with the Senate and Roman People', referring to a treaty with Rome that he had recently solemnized in the Forum.[11]

At Caesarea Maritima, where Jews were not the dominant element, Agrippa felt fairly free to adopt Greco-Roman habits. For example he ignored the commandments by setting up statues of his three daughters (Drusilla, Mariamme (III) and Berenice) in the palace. Yet when Greeks set up an image of the emperor at a synagogue of Phoenician Dora, he was quick to protest to the governor of Syria;[12] and at Jerusalem above all, learning from the mistakes of his predecessors, he behaved with great care. Thus his coins of Jerusalem, intended for circulation inside Judaea, impeccably substituted a royal canopy for a royal head, and omitted the title 'Lover of the Emperor'.[13] For in his capital Agrippa I observed Jewish law very strictly,[14] and the Pharisees and scribes, whose view is echoed in the Talmud, regarded his reign as a return to the Golden Age of Queen Salome Alexandra (76–67 BC), who had done so much to support their cause.

Agrippa I had a remarkable way with him. When, for example, a Jewish lawyer named Simon demanded his exclusion from the Temple 'as a foreigner', Agrippa charmed even this hyper-orthodox personage into behaving more amiably. Simon's point, indeed, was a narrow and unreasonable one, since although Agrippa, being a Herodian, was of Idumaean origin, an Idumaean whose family had been converted as far back as his could not sensibly be regarded as anything but out-and-out Jewish. Moreover, Agrippa's gift for theatricality enabled him to turn even his Idumaean origin to good account. At the Feast of Tabernacles in AD 41, while he was reading out a passage in *Deuteronomy*, 'you shall appoint over you a man of your own race; you must not appoint a foreigner, one who is not of your own race',[15] Agrippa, according to the Mishnah, burst into tears, whereupon the congregation cried out, 'Be comforted, Agrippa! You are our brother!'[16]

This restoration of the monarchy, after thirty-five years of Roman rule, was profoundly reassuring and exciting to most Jews. The only quarter in which some readjustment was necessary was the Sadducee high priesthood, which had stood for Jewish national aspirations under the Roman provincial regime; now, although Agrippa lacked the birth qualifications to become high priest himself, it had inevitably to take second place to him. The current holder of the office, Theophilus, like four out of the six high priests just before him, had belonged to the powerful family of Ananus. But Agrippa now replaced him by Simon Cantheras, a member of the second great high-priestly dynasty, the house of Boethus on which the king's grandfather Herod the Great had so largely relied. But for some reason the appointment was not a success, and Agrippa reverted to the family of Ananus. First he tried to reappoint Theophilus' brother and immediate predecessor, Jonathan. But Jonathan declined on the grounds that 'a man of greater piety was needed'[17] – which was probably his way of saying that if the high priest was now to be reduced to a second-rate figure no longer permitted to play the leading political part, then he was not interested.[18] But a third brother, Matthias, proved more complaisant, and was appointed instead of him.[19]

In order to ingratiate himself with this Sadducee aristocracy, Agrippa I turned against a small group of dissident Jews, the 'Nazarenes' who believed in the Messiahship of Jesus. Some six years earlier, these had suffered a reverse when Stephen was done to death, but soon afterwards they had scored a remarkable success by the conversion of their former violent enemy Paul. Since then Paul, after spending three mysterious years among the Arabians, had made his way to Antioch, which had become one of the principal centres of congregation for the holders of these opinions. He was joined there for a year by his future collaborator Barnabas, a former Levite, and they preached to Gentiles as well as to Jews. It was at this period, according to the *Acts of the Apostles*, that the group at Antioch were first described as Christianoi.[20] It is a curious term, composed of the Greek 'Christos' and the Grecized Latin termination -*anus*, like the name of the royalist party of the *Herodiani*; for the Christians too were regarded as a Jewish party or faction by the pagans of Antioch, and it is to them that the term is owed. It only appears twice more in the New Testament, and on both occasions it is derisive, conveying semi-political or conspiratorial overtones.[21] Christians themselves do not appear to have used the word until the second century A D.

These Antiochene 'Christians' were beyond the reach of King Agrippa I. But those who held similar views at Jerusalem were within his sphere of control, and incurred his disapproval. First of all, at a time when the Passover was being celebrated, he arrested and executed James the son of Zebedee, who was one of the 'apostles' who had been the personal associates of Jesus. The fact that James was beheaded indicates condemnation for a political offence,[22] so that it must be assumed that he held Messianic views which were interpreted as a potential disturbance of public order. Since this act of repression met with the approval of the Jewish authorities,[23] Agrippa I next felt himself encouraged to place the leader of the entire group, Peter, under arrest – though perhaps not until the pilgrims attending the Passover had left the city, so as to avoid demonstrations.

Peter was soon released, in circumstances concealed by miraculous legends. Then, according to the *Acts of the Apostles*, after telling his friends to report for duty to Jesus' own brother James the Just, he 'went off elsewhere'.[24] That is to say – although the statement seems embarrassed and consequently cryptic – Peter appears at this stage to have handed over the headship of the community to the brother oj Jesus. James the Just, who possessed a reputation as a strict ascetic, had not been mentioned as one of Jesus' associates, but he was said to be a firm believer in his brother's imminent return, and this family relationship, a factor on which Jews were accustomed to place strong emphasis, made him a natural claimant to the leadership.[25] And so James became, in succession to Peter, the director of that specifically Jewish branch of Christianity, the Judaeo-Christians of the circumcision, who were later eclipsed by the wider movement of uncircumcised Christians inspired largely by Paul.

Agrippa's repressive action against the followers of Jesus was one of the many measures that reassured the Jewish establishment about his soundness. However, the recently appointed governor of Syria, Gaius Vibius Marsus (42–5), felt much less confident about this. To him, Agrippa I seemed altogether too active. The first suspicions arose, as far as we know, when the king began constructing a new wall in order to enclose and fortify the New City of Jerusalem, at the point (north of Herod's ramparts) where the potential defences of the city were weakest.[26] Understandably, the governor of Syria felt inclined to ask: against whom were these fortifications designed? Agrippa I might have answered that they were intended against invasion from Parthia – where there had been recent massacres of Jews at Seleucia on the Tigris – but in that case one would have expected him to consult Rome's Syrian governor, who was entrusted with the general control of frontier defence. But probably Agrippa was mainly concerned to initiate a grandiose project which would enhance his prestige, as well as providing employment to a large number of Jews. Vibius Marsus, however, reported the project to Claudius.

And he reported to him another of Agrippa's initiatives as well. For in AD 44 the king decided to hold a conference of client kings, to which he invited his brother Herod of Chalcis and five other monarchs and princes of Syria and eastern Asia Minor. The meeting was to be held at Tiberias, where Agrippa, in days gone by, had worked as a humble official employed by his uncle Antipas. Apart from the simple satisfaction of displaying to the Tiberians how his fortunes had changed, it is not very easy to see what Agrippa's motive for holding the conference can have been. Perhaps, like the building of the wall, it was largely a matter of ostentation – and Agrippa was a restless, dynamic type, always eager to be doing something. It is also possible that, without the slightest treasonable intentions against Rome, he had seen advantage in forming closer relations with his fellow client princes – in the hope that they would develop a vested interest in the survival of the Jewish state.

At all events, Vibius Marsus, though he too had been invited to the conference, did not view it with favour. It was a principle of Roman policy that the whole position of client monarchs should be based on bilateral treaties of friendship with Rome, and that their foreign relations should be exclusively in Rome's hands; that was why Augustus had been so angry with Agrippa I's grandfather Herod the Great when he ventured to wage war as a private enterprise. Marsus was also nervous, as governors of Syria always were, that the client kings might be discussing schemes that could involve treasonable connexions with Parthia. As a result, therefore, of all these considerations, he 'took it for granted that a close friendly relationship among so many heads of state was prejudicial to Roman interests'.[27] On the other hand, he did not like to break up the conference openly. So instead he sent friends to approach the invited rulers privately, and request them to return to their homes.

Agrippa I, however, had no intention of allowing this rebuff to damp his policy of friendship with Claudius. The emperor's generals had just won important military successes in Britain, annexing the entire southern part of the country; Agrippa I now proceeded to Caesarea Maritima to launch magnificent celebrations of the victory.[28] The festivities at Caesarea were the counterpart of a Triumph that was being celebrated by Claudius in Rome. They were also, in one particular respect, a triumph for Agrippa I. For some time his relations with certain of the Greek cities of Phoenicia had been strained. To Berytus, it is true, he had shown munificence, but Tyre and Sidon had been hostile to him ever since, in the days of Tiberius, he had sided against Tyre (a notoriously anti-Jewish city) in a border dispute it was waging against Damascus.[29] These cities, with their extensive hinterlands, were under the general supervision of the governor of Syria. Nevertheless, in his annoyance with Vibius Marsus, Agrippa had recently placed an embargo on the food exports the Tyrians and Sidonians were accustomed to receive from his kingdom. What Marsus said or thought, we do not know. But so great was the dependence of Tyre and Sidon on their supplies from Agrippa's territories that they had now sent deputations to Caesarea to sue for peace.

But his success was short-lived, for on the second day of the Victory Games, while he was presiding over the proceedings in a robe made wholly of silver, he suddenly fell ill and died. Why and how he died, at this comparatively early age of fifty-four, it is impossible to say. The indication in the *Acts of the Apostles*, that he was struck down by an angel of the Lord and eaten up with worms,[30] is manifestly due to the action he had taken against the Christians. Certainly the Jews did not share such hostile sentiments towards him. Unlike his grandfather Herod the Great, he had succeeded remarkably well in retaining their affections. It is true that Herod had reigned for over thirty years, and Agrippa I for only three; and what might have happened later we cannot tell. Nevertheless, it seems likely that Agrippa's more tactful version of the Herodian state-formula was the best arrangement the Jews had ever had, or were ever likely to have again. When, therefore, they lamented his death, they had good reason to do so.

Where things might have gone wrong, however, and indeed were already beginning to go wrong, was in his relations with the Greeks. In this respect he did not achieve such good results as Herod. His generosity to individual cities was more than counterbalanced by the quarrel with Tyre and Sidon, and at Alexandria his attitude had been entirely pro-Jewish and anti-Greek – not surprisingly, since the Greeks had insulted him. His coins at Caesarea Maritima might assume an unabashedly pagan tone, designed to commend itself to its Greek inhabitants, yet once he was dead the Caesarean Greeks jubilantly rioted, removing the statues of his daughters from his palace and setting them up in brothels, where they were subjected to indecent affronts. And at Herod's other pagan foundation Samaria (Sebaste) the Greeks, including the Sebastean soldiery, likewise rejoiced at the news that Agrippa was dead.

The Roman authorities, when they heard the same news, may have found it difficult to decide if they were pleased or sorry. On the one hand Agrippa had enjoyed Claudius' confidence, had given him invaluable personal assistance at his accession, had proclaimed impeccably pro-

Roman sentiments, and had shown a remarkable talent for managing his notoriously recalcitrant Jewish subjects; on the other, not only had he inspired the Greeks with a great deal less affectionate feelings, but he had twice aroused the suspicions of the Roman governor of Syria. Moreover, he had gained the reputation of not being altogether efficient. In particular, he was too extravagant to be regarded as a reliable financial administrator.[31] Herod the Great had been a very good one, and Agrippa I's substantial revenue, larger than his grandfather's, was the result of that excellence. For example, Herod's various agricultural and industrial enterprises were now paying nicely, and Agrippa was even able to mitigate the taxes which the former Roman provincial administration had levied. But his expenditure was more lavish than Herod's and had begun to cause the imperial government a good deal of concern.

On his very first coinages under Caligula, Agrippa I had announced that he intended his son Agrippa II to become his eventual successor. But his sudden and early death created a problem, for Agrippa II was scarcely seventeen, and the Romans remembered that when Herod the Great had been succeeded by a son of similar age the results had been disastrous. In spite of this precedent Claudius, it was said, wanted Agrippa II to take over his father's throne, but his chief freedmen and friends dissuaded him on the grounds that the burden was excessive for such a young man.[32] They recommended, therefore, that Judaea should revert to Roman provincial rule; and their motives may not have been wholly disinterested, since the governorships of such provinces were a valuable source of patronage. At all events, Claudius accepted this proposal, and direct rule was reintroduced.

With hindsight, it seems that this was the decision which finally made a violent clash between the Romans inevitable – if indeed it had not already become inevitable when Agrippa I died. The revived province covered the entire area of his kingdom, so that the new Roman Judaea was much larger than the Roman Judaea of AD 6–41. And the knightly governors who were sent bore the title, no longer of prefect, but of procurator, as was normal for governors of provinces of the third class. Here a second chance was missed; for the experiences of the earlier province had shown that only a governor of higher rank and wider experience could hope to deal with the special problems presented by the Jews. Claudius also made another bad and fateful decision. He had intended to replace the provincial garrison, consisting of local pagans from Caesarea and Sebaste, by other, less inflammatory units But he was overborne. His touch in Judaea was less sure than it had been in Alexandria.

As was entirely predictable – to those who remembered what had happened when the province had originally been inaugurated in AD 6 – the first procurator, Cuspius Fadus, encountered insurrections, religious or political or both, on many sides. The Greeks and Jews in Peraea came to blows, and Fadus executed the Jewish ringleader, who had the Phoenician name of Hannibal. A ferocious individual named Tholomaeus terrorized Idumaea and carried out raids into Nabataean Arabia. Moreover, a self-styled prophet, Theudas, collected a huge crowd at the River Jordan, which he proposed to divide so that they could cross dry-shod, as their ancestors had crossed the Red Sea in the time of Moses. These migrants were carrying their possessions with them, so that it seemed as if they proposed to settle down somewhere and establish a semi-independent community.[33] It might have been wiser for Fadus to wait, so that the miracle of the river-crossing could be seen to have failed. But instead he sent his cavalry against the multitude, and many people were killed and arrested. Theudas was treated as a political offender, and beheaded.

Cuspius Fadus also involved himself in serious trouble concerning the high priests' vestments. Even before the earlier province ceased to exist, Lucius Vitellius had handed these robes back to the Jews. Now, however, their retention by the Jews was considered dangerous, and Fadus requested them back again – presumably on the instructions of the emperor. Since, however, this decision was certain to cause trouble, the new governor of Syria, an eminent jurist named Gaius Cassius Longinus, decided to inquire more fully into the matter, and came to Jerusalem with a considerable military force (AD 45). As a result of his consultations it was agreed that a Jewish deputation should go to Rome and place the issue before Claudius. Agrippa II, not having been allowed his father's kingdom, was in Rome, and his pleas and those of his family proved decisive; the emperor concluded that the envoys' request was reasonable, and the vestments remained in Jewish hands.

They were entrusted to the care of the young Agrippa II's uncle, King Herod of Chalcis. When Judaea reverted to the Romans, he had retained his Lebanese kingdom, and coined with the title Philoclaudios, lover of Claudius. Herod also received another signal honour, which once again showed that he had become the leading Jew in the world.

This new honour related to the high priests at Jerusalem. Herod's brother Agrippa I had been made responsible for appointing and dismissing them. But now he was dead, and Claudius wisely decided not to revive the unpalatable earlier procedure according to which these appointments had been in the hands of the Roman provincial governors. So he resolved instead to place this responsibility in the hands of Herod, who, although king of Chalcis and not Judaea, was invested with the 'guardianship' of the Temple and its treasury, which carried with it the power of appointing high priests. During the next three years he made two changes in the office.[34]

Meanwhile, however, there had been a change in the governorship (AD 46). The new procurator was Tiberius Julius Alexander. This man, a scholar or patron of letters,[35] owed the job to a former marriage connexion with Herod of Chalcis' wife Berenice.[36] Although born of an eminent Alexandrian Jewish family, of which his uncle Philo was the leading luminary, Alexander had abandoned Judaism and become a pagan. This might seem to have made him a strange choice for the Jerusalem appointment. However, although an apostate, he earned the approval of responsible Jews, and preserved peace, 'by refraining from interference with the customs of the country'.[37] He also rounded on two sons of Judas the Galilean, who had led a revolt in AD 6, and crucified them, presumably for leading yet another popular revolt.

But his major problem was a famine, which took place at some stage during the first two years of his tenure.[38] Relief came from a country belonging to Parthia, namely Adiabene or Assyria, the fertile modern province of Erbil lying between two rivers known as the Great and Little Zab. There, during the past few years, an event of great interest to the Jewish world had occurred. For the country's ruler, Izates, and his mother Helena (whose husband had been her own brother) become converted to Judaism, thus creating a second Jewish state on Parthian territory in succession to the Babylonian principality which, after an existence of fifteen years, had recently collapsed.

The conversion of this royal dynasty – in itself almost a whole tribe, since Izates had forty-eight children – must have caused Jewish nationalists and proselytizers in Judaea great satisfaction, especially as it seemed like a historic, God-given reversal of the ancient downfall of Israel at Assyria's hands. The leading Adiabenians, however, do not seem to have welcomed the conversion, and in this they were supported by the prince of the neighbouring Mesopotamian state Edessa (Urfa). In consequence, Izates' Jewish adviser, a merchant and missionary named Ananias, disagreed with the suggestion made by a Galilean, named Eleazar, that Izates should be circumcised. Ananias counselled the king to refrain from circumcision, at least at first, so as not to stir up popular feeling. Izates agreed, but later, after stabilizing his regime, he felt able to go on to this final stage, in the company of his brother and heir Monobazus.[39] It is a sign of the good relations at this time between the Parthians and their Jewish communities that the Parthian king apparently raised no objection to the conversion.

Izates tactfully sent brothers as hostages both to the Parthian king and to the emperor of Rome. But Jewish events of such a kind in Parthian territory were always watched with keen and suspicious attention by Roman governors of Syria and Judaea, who feared treasonable communications between the Jews of the two empires. On this occasion, however, Tiberius Alexander must have been grateful, since while Judaea was in the grip of the famine Helena made a pilgrimage to Jerusalem bringing grain from Alexandria and figs from Cyprus. The city became her family's favourite place of residence. But when, after a reign of twenty-four years, Izates died, his mother returned home to Adiabene. Soon afterwards she, too, died, and her remains were sent to Jerusalem, where they were laid in a burial place that can still be seen, the so-called 'Tombs of the Kings'. In 48, Tiberius Alexander was succeeded as procurator by Ventidius Cumanus, whose four-year tenure was destined to be a troubled one.[40] In the same year King Herod of Chalcis exercised once again his prerogative of appointing high priests. This time his choice fell on a certain Ananias, a rich and powerful personage of unknown family who was to retain the office for the uniquely long duration of eleven years. But very soon afterwards his appointer, Herod of Chalcis, died. Claudius now felt that the time had come for Agrippa II, who was about twenty years of age, to be brought onto the scene. So two years later he gave the young man the vacant kingdom of Chalcis, together with the same rank of praetor that his uncle had enjoyed. Moreover shortly afterwards, in 50, Agrippa II inherited his uncle's important rights to supervise the Temple and its treasury and to appoint the high priests, and owing to his possession of these powers he often came to Jerusalem. Fortified by the support of Claudius' new wife Agrippina the younger (49),[41] Agrippa II let himself be known by the Romanized name of Marcus Julius Agrippa.[42]

At Rome, at this time (though some would attribute the incident to an earlier stage in Claudius' reign), there seems to have been some trouble relating to the Jews, and apparently affecting the group which offered allegiance to Jesus Christ as well. The *Acts of the Apostles* report an edict by Claudius 'that all Jews should leave the city';[43] whereas Dio Cassius says that Claudius forbade the Jews to hold meetings.[44] The biographer Suetonius, writing three quarters of a century after the event, offers a different version again: 'since the Jews constantly made disturbances at the instigation of Chrestus, Claudius expelled them from Rome'.[45] This wording might seem to suggest that Suetonius believed 'Chrestus' to be still alive, and it is possible that he is not referring to Jesus Christ at all, but to a Jewish agitator of Claudian date. But it seems more likely that he is referring to Jesus (unaware, perhaps, that he was dead), and to the Christians – 'Chrestus' being a mispronunciation that was still current in the third century AD[46] – and that it is they whom he believes to have been expelled from the city.

In view of these discordant and ambiguous accounts, it is hard to say what really happened. Were the Jews expelled (as they had been temporarily expelled under Tiberius), or was it only their Christian faction that was ejected (perhaps at the request of the Jews), or did Jews and Christians alike have to leave, and if so why? It is impossible to say. Perhaps Jewish proselytizing activities had antagonized the Romans, as had happened on previous occasions. Or perhaps there had been trouble between those Jews who rejected Christianity and those who accepted it – if there were enough of the latter at Rome at this time to create such an issue, as we cannot determine. But one may perhaps tentatively assume that these events, whatever their precise character, were concerned in some way with vitally important developments affecting the Jews and Christians which were now taking place in Judaea and the eastern provinces, and will be described in the next chapter.

I0

Paul's Bid to Change the Jews

Paul's conversion to belief in Jesus as the Messiah had occurred in AD 36–7. But within the following decade, as some of the earliest passages of the New Testament show, the youthful Jewish movement which accepted his Messiahship had already become dramatically split, between those who wished to keep it within the Judaism of Judaea, and those who sought to extend it to the great outer world of Gentile Greeks.[1]

James the Just and Peter were the leaders of the former school of thought; James was probably by now the more important of the two, though later tradition retained Peter in the primacy, and he may still have directed the missionary movement to the Jews.[2] The leader of the mission to the Gentiles was Paul. For although Paul was a Pharisee by birth and upbringing, and proud of it,[3] and although he agreed strongly that his mission was *first* for the Jews, his background of Hellenistic Judaism pulled the other way and left him subject to profound psychological tensions. At first he had been convinced that the Gentile mission, as exemplified by Stephen, was utterly wrong. But his conversion reversed this belief, and from now on he believed that the church of Christ should not be Jewish, but universal, and that its followers ought not to be limited to the circumcised, but must include the uncircumcised as well.[4]

After his conversion and subsequent retirement to Arabia, Paul spent ten years as an independent missionary in Syria and his native land of Cilicia.[5] During this time his conviction evidently deepened, and it was perhaps now, at Antioch, which he always regarded as his base of operations, that he and others of like mind first formulated the idea of *seeking out* Gentile converts. 'For God,' said Paul, 'whose action made Peter an apostle to the Jews, also made me an apostle to the Gentiles.' The conflict between the two groups was, and is, undeniable; and it took on additional sharpness because of the worsening relations between Jews and Gentiles after the return of Judaea to provincial status (44). In *c.* 47 Paul and Barnabas, who for the most part shared his views,[6] were commissioned to proselytize pagans in Syria, Cyprus and Asia Minor; this was Paul's First Journey. But those who commissioned them were surely not James and Peter, and soon afterwards came the major confrontation between the two factions. It is recorded, historically or symbolically, by the description of a conference or council at Jerusalem (*c.* 49).[7] The *Acts of the Apostles*, still looking back at a legendary time when primitive Christians were of one heart and soul,[8] minimized the rift, but Paul in his *Letter to the Galatians* makes no attempt to conceal its seriousness. The result seems to have been a compromise, between James and Peter on the one hand (James is mentioned first) and Paul and Barnabas on the other:[9] Jewish converts to Christianity remained bound by the full provisions of the Torah, but pagan converts were exempted from circumcision. Soon afterwards, Paul returned to his principal headquarters at Antioch. But then Peter, too, came to Antioch, and Paul declared: 'I opposed him to his face because he was clearly in the wrong.'[10] James had persuaded Peter not to take meals with Gentiles, and even Paul's associate Barnabas succumbed to similar pressure; but Paul remained adamant against segregation of this type.

Perhaps Paul was disappointed by the Antioch compromise. But at least the other faction, the Judaeo-Christians, had not repudiated his work; and now he resumed it, with the utmost energy and defiance. 'Do you suppose God is the God of the Jews alone? Is he not the God of the Gentiles also? Certainly, of Gentiles also, if it be true that God is one . . .[11] Because they [the Jews] offended, salvation has come to the Gentiles, to stir Israel to emulation.'[12]

Meanwhile, for reasons unrelated to these small Christian groups, the procurator of Judaea, Ventidius Cumanus, was encountering

serious difficulties. First, at the Passover of AD 48 or 49, one of the soldiers guarding the Temple, a non-Jew from the corps raised at Caesarea
or Samaria (Sebaste), 'raising his robe, stooped in an indecent attitude,
so as to turn his backside to the Jews, and made a noise in keeping with
this posture'.[13] Rioting followed, the governor called in reinforcements, and as the huge crowds turned to flee from the Temple precinct,
thousands of people were trampled to death. Then, in 51 or 52, on the
road to Beth-Horon, brigands attacked one of the emperor's slaves and
seized his baggage, whereupon Cumanus made numerous arrests in
the region. In the course of this operation a soldier, finding in one
village a copy of the sacred Law, tore the book to pieces and flung
it into the fire. At that, the Jews were roused 'as though it were their
whole country which had been consumed in the flames'. They flocked
in thousands to Caesarea Maritima, and the governor ordered the
execution of the offender.

Next, a Galilean pilgrim was murdered by the Samaritans as he was
on his way to Jerusalem, and some said that more than one were
killed. The angry Jews, engaging as their commander a certain
Eleazar ben Dinai – who had been terrorizing the country for nearly
twenty years[14] and was described in the Mishnah as the Son of a
Murderer – poured northwards out of the capital bent on vengeance.
Cumanus sent Sebastian cavalry to kill or arrest these Jewish
marchers, and fighting between Jews and Samaritans now broke out in
many areas. The leading Samaritans hastened to Tyre to appeal to
the governor of Syria, who was now Gaius Ummidius Quadratus. A
deputation of Jews also appeared, led by the ex-high priest Jonathan,
and put the blame on Cumanus.

Quadratus, however, entered the province of Judaea, and crucified
Cumanus' Jewish prisoners. Next, moving to Lydda, he ordered that
eighteen further Jews should be beheaded. Perhaps he also wanted to
discipline the Samaritans, but since he could not do so without blaming
Cumanus he now referred the whole matter to Rome and the emperor.
Samaritans and Jews alike, the latter including their high priest
Ananias as well as Jonathan, were among those dispatched to the
capital to state their cases. Quadratus also ordered Cumanus and a
Roman officer called Celer, whose alleged offence is not specified, to
proceed to Rome and give an account of themselves to their imperial
master. Some of Claudius' freedmen were sympathetic to the Samaritans. But the emperor himself, influenced by the young Agrippa II of

Chalcis who enjoyed the patronage of the empress Agrippina, decided in favour of the Jews.[15] He ordered three Samaritan leaders to be executed, banished Cumanus, and sent Celer back in chains to Jerusalem, where the Jews – in punishment of his offence, whatever it may have been – were allowed to drag him round the city and cut off his head. It is also possible that in 52–3 Claudius heard an Alexandrian dispute, involving some complaint against Agrippa II, and, if so, it seems that he settled in favour of the Jews.[16]

Meanwhile Paul, after his dispute with the Judaeo-Christians, was away on his Second Journey. This great tour, with a third to follow, covered huge areas of the near east and the Balkans – a spectacular, often painfully laborious series of travels made possible, first, by the *Pax Romana*,[17] and, secondly, by the Jewish communities in the numerous cities of the Dispersion – communities round which Paul's Gentile converts could gather.

The first journey is approximately dated by Paul's encounter at Corinth with Gallio, a man with an oratorical reputation who was brother of the philosopher Seneca and held the governorship of Achaia (Greece) in *c.* AD 52.[18] The meeting, as plausibly described in the *Acts of the Apostles*, illuminates the attitude of Roman officials. The Corinthian Jews were outraged by Paul's insistence that Jesus was the Messiah. When Gallio was proconsul of Achaia, the Jews set upon Paul in a body and brought him into court. 'This man,' they said, 'is inducing people to worship God in ways that are against the Law.' Paul was just about to speak when Gallio said to them, 'If it had been a question of crime or grave misdemeanour, I should, of course, have given you Jews a patient hearing, but if it is some bickering about words and names and your Jewish Law, you may see to it yourselves; I have no mind to be a judge of these matters.' And he had them ejected from the court. Then there was a general attack on Sosthenes, who held office in the synagogue, and he was given a beating in full view of the bench. 'But all this left Gallio quite unconcerned.'[19] For it seemed to him an internal quarrel, within the Jewish community. On the whole the pagan communities in the various cities were less hostile to the missionaries than the Jews were – or paid them less attention. The conspicuous exception was Ephesus, where riots were instigated, for obvious reasons, by a silver-smith whose manufacture of silver shrines for the city's famous cult of Artemis provided a great deal of local employment.[20]

It was in these years of the fifties AD that Paul spread the Christian

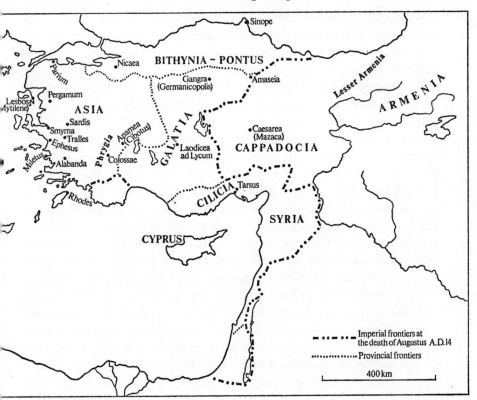

Asia Minor at the death of Augustus (AD. 14)

variant of Judaism throughout vast areas of the Greek world, a task to
which his peculiar Greco-Jewish genius was singularly well adapted.
The immediate results were not always conspicuous, but the seeds were
sown in readiness for a subsequent time when Judaism, weakened by
rebellion against Rome, would be too weak to compete against the new
movement. Meanwhile, Paul and his collaborators were making their
interpretation of its main lines abundantly clear: it must be a movement in which uncircumcised Gentiles were permitted to play the same
part as circumcised Jews. Whether the *Epistle to the Ephesians* was written
by Paul himself we cannot say, but his is the conclusion it firmly states:
'Gentiles and Jews, he [Christ Jesus] had made the two one, and in his
own body of flesh and blood has broken down the enmity which stood
like a dividing wall between them.'[21] The enmity had not, in fact, been
broken down. In the end, it was to result in the triumph of the pro-

Gentile element in the church over the Judaeo-Christian faction, for Christianity has never influenced the Semitic world deeply or widely, and Paul pointed the way to a decisive shift of the balance. But the shift still lay in the future. Jerusalem still remained the mother church, and, although Paul formally recognized that this was so, he devoted all his powers of argument to the assertion of his view against Jerusalem's.

How massive these powers were is to be seen in the first surviving records of Christianity, his Epistles (letters to the Christian communities of various cities in Asia Minor and Europe), which date from the very years of his travels. Whereas it is impossible to identify, with certainty, any passages in the New Testament dating back to an earlier period – to the first fifteen or twenty years, that is to say, after Jesus' crucifixion – the Epistles bring Christianity into the realms of history and literature. It is true that their dating is notoriously difficult, all the more so because they contain later, interpolated passages. Yet a good deal of this material is truly attributable to Paul, and belongs to the epoch of his Second and Third Journeys. In particular, the *First Epistle to the Thessalonians* (the Christian community of Thessalonica in Macedonia, the modern Salonica) seems to have been written from Corinth in *c.* 50–1, and may be the earliest of all extant Christian documents. Some place *Galatians* even earlier, but more probably it belongs to *c.* 55–7. The same dating is probable for *I Corinthians* and parts of *Romans*, a composition which contains various strata but amounts, in sum total, to the most complete statement of Paul's teaching that we possess.[22]

To those who have even the vaguest familiarity with the alleged facts of Jesus' career as they were described, at a considerably later date, by the Gospels, the presentation of him in the Epistles is highly disconcerting. For Paul says nothing about his life on earth at all, and appears to have no knowledge whatever of any of its happenings before the Last Supper. The only events concerning Jesus of which he speaks are his crucifixion and subsequent resurrection.[23] Indeed, at first, in *I Thessalonians*, except for a brief passage that is probably a later interpolation,[24] there is nothing even to show that Paul knew about the crucifixion. The Lord Jesus, the Messiah, is seen as a divine being, the Son of God. The names of God and Jesus even govern a singular verb,[25] though to the Jews Paul seemed to be implying that Jesus, as Son of God was a second God – a doctrine which denied the unity of God and the monotheism of their faith. And then the *Epistle to the*

Philippians, a composite work of which part may have been written by Paul, envisages Jesus as a pre-existent celestial being.[26]

In that work, as in others from *c.* 55 onwards, there is immense stress upon the crucifixion, and constant emphasis on its salvation-bringing humiliation. 'Jews call for miracles, Greeks look for wisdom; but we proclaim Christ – yes, Christ nailed to the cross; and though this is a stumbling-block to Jews and Greeks alike, he is the power of God and the wisdom of God.' The methods by which Paul arrived at this paradox are suggested by A. D. Nock.

He was a natural extremist, and he took an extreme view of the claim that the Anointed One of God was to be found in the person of a criminal handed over by the religious authorities of the nation to the Romans to die what could be regarded as an accursed death...[27] Paul could not treat this movement with polite indifference or contempt as something ephemeral that would run its course. Further, analogies suggest that his conversion was not the sudden thing which it seemed to him: the movement had probably fascinated him at the same time that it excited his deepest animosity, and it must have been the question, if the unvoiced question, of his life for some time. 'Why dost thou kick against the pricks?'[28] is the truth of psychology, if not of history. On the face of it, Christianity was not only wrong but enig-matic . . . it was illogical, incomprehensible; and that Stephen should die for it, as readily as Pharisees had died rather than fail to protest against Herod's defiance of the Law, was the height of illogicality. Paul's conversion meant for him the recognition that the condemned criminal was in fact the Anointed One of God, living now in the glory of the Spirit world.[29]

'Christos', the anointed, is used almost as a personal name – so firmly established already is the idea of Jesus' Messiahship. Yet this is a super-natural, esoteric Messiah, wholly unattached to any of the facts and events later attributed by the Gospels to Jesus' earthly career. At one point, Paul even ceases to attribute Jesus' death to any agents so worldly as the Roman or Jewish authorities (though he blames the latter fiercely enough elsewhere). Instead, he ascribes the respon-sibility for the crucifixion to 'the powers that rule the world',[30] by which he means the demonic powers or *daimones* – elemental spirits, discarnate intelligences, which stand, like the angels, as indispensable intermediaries between God and human beings. Here we are very remote from the biographical approach of the Gospels. For from contemporary Jewish and other sects – called Gnostic, from *gnosis*, knowledge, because of their conviction that they had received private revelations – Paul had absorbed a deep sense of the dualist struggle between the powers of light and darkness.

The Cross itself played a major part in these mystic and magical ways of thought, appearing countless times on Jewish and Christian artefacts as a charm, a protection against the evil eye and a symbol of power. As the last letter of the Hebrew alphabet, it was the cruciform *Tau* which in *Ezekiel* was marked on the foreheads of those to be spared;[31] and as the coins of Herod the Great confirm,[32] a sign in the form of the Greek letter Chi (X) figured on the crowns of kings and priests.

In keeping with the Jews' constant interpretation of everything that happened, past, present and future, in the light of the Bible, Paul wove a huge number of Old Testament prophecies into the Christian fabric: the Epistles, like the Gospels, display stereoscopic depth of meaning which requires, at every point, interpretation in terms not only of its own story but of the whole legendary and historical tradition of the Jewish nation.[33] It was in the light of this Biblical background that Paul pondered on the crucifixion. It was a stumbling-block to the Jews partly because there was no room for a failed Messiah, but partly also because, in the words of *Deuteronomy*, 'a hanged [and so also a crucified] man is offensive [or accursed] in the sight of God'.[34] But the conversion of Paul, whose mind was ever given to the sharpest paradox, provided him with an answer. It has often been suggested that he found his answer in the annually Dying and Saving Gods of pagan Mystery Cults – Osiris, Attis and Adonis – or in Greek heroes carried up to heaven because of their virtues; and indeed it would have been strange if the widespread contemporary susceptibility to ideas of this kind had altogether failed to influence a brain as receptive as his. But in the mystery religions death was a temporary defeat, not a triumph as Paul declared it to be; where he found his real solution was in the scriptures of the Jews. Most of all, the Suffering Servant of the Second Isaiah provided him with his model. The story of the crucifixion also owes something to a passage in *Zechariah*, where it was written: 'they shall look on me, on him whom they have pierced'.[35] And a part was played, too, by the reverence accorded to those who had died a martyr's death for the sake of their beliefs.

The stories about Jesus' tomb, found later in all four Gospels, were apparently quite unknown to Paul. Yet he whole-heartedly adopted the belief that his Saviour had not only died but had risen bodily from the dead. This belief is already incorporated in *I Thessalonians* and *I Corinthians*, where the Passover is identified with what will soon be called Easter,[36] and Paul testified that he himself, despite his record as a persecutor, had finally been accorded the sight of the risen Lord.[37] He recognizes this resurrection as an utterly radical assault on the categories of our usual perception. Nevertheless he insists that this was precisely the way in which God bore witness to his Son:[38] without belief in the resurrection of Jesus, he asserts, it is no use believing in anything else at all.

Paul also worked out, with forcible unremitting repetition, the difficult concept that the death of Jesus, followed by his resurrection, possessed a redemptive value for all mankind – or in the first instance 'for those who died as Christians: whom God will bring to life with Jesus'.[39] (After the resurrection, Jesus had ascended to heaven, like Enoch and the others, but Paul points out to the Corinthians the wrongness of deducing that he had *avoided* death by so doing: since that would mean that the doctrine of redemption lost its point.)[40] The redemption would come to pass at the Last Judgment, at the end of the world, when 'we shall be changed in a flash, in the twinkling of an eye, at the last trumpet-call'. Writing at a time of famines, earthquakes and disturbances, Paul believed at first (though later he modified this view)[41] that the end of the world was likely to come at any moment in the immediate future. All sufferings would then cease – except for those who are destined to receive savage vengeance.[42]

Meanwhile, declared Paul, we can have communion with our Saviour through the institutions of the Eucharist (Last Supper) and Baptism. In his emphasis on these links between the Christian and his faith (known subsequently as sacraments) is mirrored the mysticism that emerges so strongly in Paul, and though it is a mysticism which shared features with contemporary pagan cults, its roots are Jewish:

In a Jewish home, especially on a social occasion, special thanksgivings were attached to the bread broken by the host at the beginning of the meal, and the 'Cup of Blessing' drunk at its close. This is the beginning of Christian Eucharistic worship. The very name *eucharist* (*berakah*), 'thanksgiving' (customary from the end of the first century), and the opening of the central prayer in many liturgies with 'We thank Thee, God' ... indicate the ultimate derivation of the ceremony from a Jewish benediction of shared food: so does the Pauline phrase 'the cup of blessing',[43] where the word for blessing, *eulogia,* is that which appears on a Jewish cup.[44]

The second of these rituals, later known as sacraments, was baptism, received by Jesus from John the Baptist who had used the rite as a symbol of 'repentance', that is to say of a completely changed attitude. And now, in the baptism applied to all Christians, Paul imagined that the individual actually died with the Lord and rose with him and in him. He envisaged Moses' Exodus as a prefiguration of baptism and the Eucharist alike: 'our ancestors all received baptism into the fellowship of Moses in cloud and sea. They all ate the same supernatural food [manna], and all drank the same supernatural drink; I mean, they all drank from the supernatural rock . . . – and that rock was Christ.'[45]

This Christ who would redeem us was, in Jewish fashion, interpreted according to the Scriptures, since the Second Isaiah's Suffering Servant had 'borne the sin of many and interceded for their transgressions',[46] and 'the new path of life' upon which Jesus set the feet of mankind was the same as the New Covenant which the Lord had told Jeremiah he would establish for Israel and Judah.[47] 'The sacrifice is offered: Christ himself! . . . You were bought at a price!'[48] Paul knew that there were those who would find the idea impossible: but he attempted to show them how wrong they were to doubt it.[49]

Having once accepted its truth, the believer is bound by the sternest moral obligation. 'Christ suffered on your behalf, and thereby left you an example: it is for you to follow in his steps.'[50] This logical conclusion was fundamental in Paul's thought since, like the Qumran sect though with an added intensity that was all his own, he possessed a profound consciousness of sin. He believed that all men have been sinful since Adam's Fall, and, by appealing to various Old Testament texts, concluded that the crucifixion of Jesus made possible the forgiveness of men's sins: vast structures of varying doctrine have been built on the few short paragraphs of *Romans* that develop this argument.[51] For all Paul's Pharisaic background, it was an argument singularly unacceptable to the Jews, because belief in the expiatory death of Jesus clashed with the great prophetic doctrine according to which God vouchsafed the penitent sinner his free forgiveness – a doctrine which, according to Jewish thought, was the only real remedy of sin.

But Paul, for his part, retaliated fiercely against this and other attacks launched against him by Jewish theologians. The question of the validity of the Law and the prophets was a problem that clearly caused him, as a Jew and a Pharisee, profound anxiety and contradictory emotions.

At one point, in order to show that ritual is no use without goodness, he declares that circumcision is only of value if you keep the Law – which implies that the Law is the essential basis of conduct.[52] But other emphatic passages tell an entirely different story, and culminate in a violent contrast in which the rift between Judaism and its aberrant Christian members yawns wide open: 'by becoming for our sake an accursed thing, Christ brought us freedom from the curse of the Law'.[53]

In more sober terms, observance of the Law is described, at the very most, as a discipline for something higher.[54] That something higher is faith – belief in Jesus. There was nothing new or un-Jewish about faith: it had been a cardinal Jewish requirement ever since Abraham had first been described as its outstanding exponent.[55] But the faith that was now demanded was in something new. 'For our argument is that a man is justified by faith *quite apart from success in keeping the Law.*[56] Does this mean that we are using faith to undermine Law? By no means: we are placing Law itself on a firmer footing.' In the words of *Galatians*, hailed by Christians (including Martin Luther) as the Magna Carta of Christian liberty and its defence against Jewish legalism, 'we ourselves are Jews by birth, not Gentiles and sinners. But we know that no man is ever justified by doing what the Law demands, but only through faith in Christ Jesus . . . If righteousness comes by law, then Christ died for nothing.'[57]

The proper basis for membership of 'Israel', announced Paul, had never been observance of the Law, or for that matter descent from the patriarchs, but faith. And in a passage of *I Thessalonians*, ominously significant for the future, he attacked the whole Jewish nation, his own people, for having been the slayers of Jesus. He sympathizes with the Thessalonians because they have received similar treatment. 'You have been treated by your countrymen as they are treated by the Jews, who killed the Lord Jesus and the prophet [or 'their own prophets'] and drove us out: the Jews who are heedless of God's will and enemies of their fellow-men, hindering us from speaking to the Gentiles to lead them to salvation.'[58] The guilt of the Jews was later strongly confirmed by the Gospels, and in due course the Good Friday and Easter services took on a tone of strong hostility to all Jews. It was only in 1959 that their description as 'perfidious' was omitted from a defamatory Good Friday intercession. In 1963, during the Second Vatican Council, Pope John XXIII published a penitential prayer withdrawing the curse pronounced upon the whole Jewish nation for ever; and yet even then the Syriac Patriarch of Antioch could still cry out to the Council: 'the creed of the Church is that responsibility . . . lies with the Jewish people until the world ends!'

When Paul preached his startling doctrines, the Jews in many centres were utterly scandalized, and, even apart from his personal attacks on their views, it is easy to see why. He accepted a Messiah whom they rejected. He interpreted his Messiahship in a way that flouted both their concept of monotheism and their central doctrine of repentance – and he accused them of murdering him. Furthermore, the Jews always distrusted policies of too easy conversion, and although the Pharisees, from whom Paul came, were notable for their proselytism, his vast, deliberate campaign of Gentile conversions seemed to them to violate the doctrine of the Chosen People, the elect. Paul's relations with the Jews to whom he had belonged, and to whom he and every other Christian would still claim to belong for years ahead, had become disastrous.

His attitude to the Romans was far more favourable. True, to say that we must 'follow in Jesus' footsteps' might sound to some an invitation to martyrdom, and the Romans knew only too well that such invitations meant political subversion. Yet this was by no means Paul's intention, since he never saw Jesus as a Messiah who would restore its earthly kingdom to Israel. Although fully prepared to suffer flogging and imprisonment for Jesus' sake, he explicitly, and at length, counsels obedience to the political authorities, who seem to him to owe their powers to the act of God.[59] This is an echo of the attitude of the moderate Pharisees to Herod the Great; in the same spirit, Paul's stress on other-worldly salvation sometimes suggests that he deliberately inoculated his contemporaries against Messianic propaganda in favour of revolution in this world. Slavery, too, is not condemned by Paul – if the *Epistle to Philemon* is his. Like pagan contemporaries such as Seneca, the writer hopes for a human relationship between master and slave, but the whole approach is far from revolutionary.

While Paul was still away on his second journey, and his third lay in the early future, there were important changes in Judaea. To fill the vacancy in the governorship left by Cumanus' disgrace, Claudius appointed Antonius Felix (*c.* 52). His profoundly troubled eight-year tenure of office was destined to lead to a point of no return. At first sight, the appointment looked like a downgrading of the post, since Felix was not a knight but only a freedman. But, in fact, the opposite conclusion should be drawn, since Felix was the brother of Claudius' freedman Pallas, who was one of the two or three most important men in the entire Roman world, and the ally of the empress Agrippina. Furthermore, since the first wife of Felix, Drusilla I, was the grand-daughter of Mark Antony, Felix was a relative by marriage of the emperor himself, whose mother Antonia was Antony's daughter.[60] So on his coins issued in Jerusalem Felix tactfully (though with some risk to Jewish sentiment) copies a design of two shields and two spears which Claudius' coins had depicted in honour of his father, Antonia's husband Drusus the elder.[61] And the coinage of Felix looks ahead as well. Faced, like all Romans, with the delicate task of deciding which of the two possible heirs to the throne to commemorate, the emperor's own son Britannicus (by a former marriage), or Nero the son of Claudius' present wife Agrippina (likewise by a former marriage), Felix dis-creetly names both. It was fortunate for him that he did not omit to name Nero, since it was Nero, shortly afterwards, who succeeded to the throne (54), whereupon Felix gave Sepphoris, now the Roman capital of Galilee, the name of Neronias.[62] Felix also shows his attachment to Agrippina by naming her emphatically on a series of coins.[63]

Felix possessed exceptionally important Jewish connexions as well. He enjoyed the friendship of the powerful ex-high priest Jonathan, who had supposedly helped him to secure the post; and his second wife, Drusilla (II), was the sister of Agrippa II. That king, in the very next year (53), was moved by Claudius from his kingdom of Chalcis to a larger state comprising not only parts of Anti-Lebanon, and a fertile strip north-west of Damascus, but the extensive northern area of Trans-jordan which his great uncle Philip had ruled under Augustus and Tiberius; it was at the chief city of this region, Caesarea Philippi, that he now proceeded to establish his capital. In addition to the sister who was married to Felix, Agrippa II had another sister, Berenice. Her brother's relationship with her was so close that the association was widely regarded as incestuous.[64] However that may be, she played a very important part in Agrippa's regime, and her name even precedes his in some inscriptions, since one of her three marriages, to his late uncle Herod of Chalcis, meant that she had achieved royal rank before he did.

Felix took vigorous measures against the murderous brigand Eleazar,

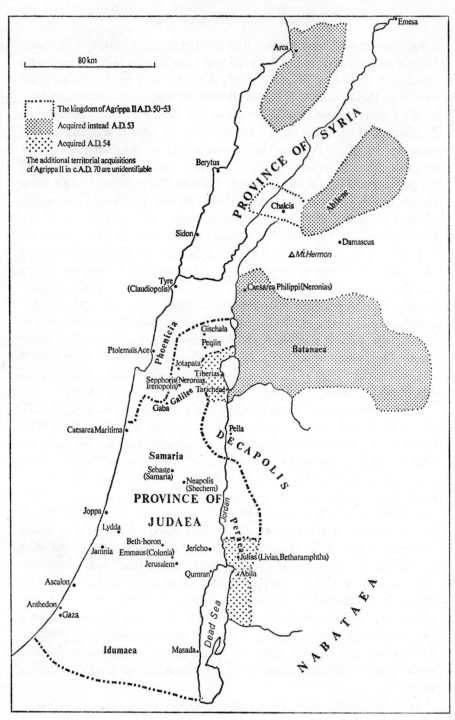

The Kingdom of Agrippa II (AD. 50–c. 93/4)

capturing him and many of his associates and sending them to Rome for trial, while a large number of others were crucified in Judaea. But he also had to face a very unpleasant new development, the rise of a terrorist urban guerrilla group in the capital. It was these men, according to Josephus, who were specifically known as *sicarii* (assassins), though the term had already been used loosely for other types of political extremity. The speciality of the new movement, according to the same historian, was to:

commit murders in broad daylight in the heart of the city. The festivals were their special seasons, when they would mingle with the crowd, carrying short curved daggers [*sicae*] concealed under their clothing, with which they stabbed their enemies. Then, when they fell, the murderers joined in the cries of indignation, and through this plausible behaviour were never discovered. The first to be assassinated by them was Jonathan the ex-high priest. After his death, there were numerous daily murders. The panic created was more alarming than the calamity itself – everyone, as on the battlefield, hourly expecting death.[65]

Josephus in one of his major works, though not the other, asserts that Jonathan's murder was arranged by his own protégé Felix, who resented his patronizing interference.[66] But the insinuation is implausible, since it was in the interests of Felix to maintain public order, to which the assassination of an eminent former high priest was scarcely likely to contribute.

The next problem of Felix was a host of 'deceivers and impostors, who, fostering revolutionary changes under the pretence of divine inspiration, persuaded the multitude to act like madmen, and led them out into the desert under the belief that God would there give them tokens of deliverance'.[67] These were neither the first nor the last of such prophets in the wilderness, men posing as miracle-workers and Messiahs. But Felix treated their activities as a serious subversive threat, and sent a force of cavalry and infantry to suppress them and their followers. Yet even this was nothing like the end of his difficulties, for there now appeared on the scene a very troublesome Egyptian Jew, whose name is not known. Winning a great reputation as a prophet, he collected round himself a horde of followers – variously estimated as four thousand and thirty thousand – and led them from the desert to the Mount of Olives. There he was reported to be planning a military attack on Jerusalem so as to set himself up as the ruler of an independent

Judaea. According to other reports, he proposed to knock the city walls down by a miracle, thus enabling his followers to take possession.[68] Troops sent against him by Felix killed four hundred of his men and captured two hundred others, but the Egyptian himself managed to escape and disappear. The belief persisted that he would come back, and anarchy continued to spread throughout the province. The large estates, in particular, suffered from a campaign of systematic plundering.

Felix also had to deal with serious problems relating to the Christian movement. These were concerned, chiefly, with Paul. Paul's journeys through the near east had come to an end. It is difficult to estimate the measure of their immediate success. Hints in the *Acts* suggest that it was not so great as the rest of that work asserts: there was a good deal of opposition and, at sophisticated Athens for example, contemptuous rejection. The time when Paul's cause would prevail had not arrived yet. But meanwhile he had become quite well known. When his Third Journey was completed, he revisited Jerusalem (*c.* 58). On the way, he had passed through the cities of Tyre, now called Claudiopolis after the late emperor, and Ptolemais Ace, which Claudius had made into a Roman 'colony', settling there a substantial number of ex-soldier settlers. Paul's visits to these essentially pagan cities were a final demonstration that his mission was largely directed to the Gentiles.

As a reminder, however, of the material profits Jews might derive from his attention to the Dispersion, he took with him to Jerusalem, for the benefit of the Judaeo-Christians there, the sums of money which he had received in the course of his journeys. When he arrived, James the Just, leader of the Jerusalem church, suggested that in order to allay suspicions of his unorthodoxy, Paul should pay the expenses of a ritual purification which four Judaeo-Christians wished to undertake, and that he should also share their fast himself. This was agreed, but on the last day of the fast Paul was recognized by four Jews from Asia who strongly disagreed with his pro-Gentile policy and were no doubt well informed about his attempts to forward it in their own country. They seized hold of him, and charged him with speaking against the Jewish people, the Law and the Temple. They also added the allegation that he had introduced into the Temple a Gentile – a certain Trophimus of Ephesus – thus causing it to suffer defilement.[69] The importation of a non-Jew even so far as the inner courts surrounding the Temple had always been regarded as a particularly grave offence, so grave indeed that the Romans had always allowed the Jews, who otherwise lacked capital jurisdiction, to put offenders to death.

An enormous, excitable crowd soon gathered, and dragged Paul out of the Temple. There he would undoubtedly have been lynched if the Roman garrison commander, Claudius Lysias, had not rescued him. Lysias was apparently under the impression that Paul might be the Egyptian Jew who had escaped from a Roman military operation a short time previously. In any case, he planned to have his detainee flogged, a normal preliminary to a judicial examination. But Paul claimed the immunity which was his entitlement as a Roman citizen. Thereupon, according to a plausible enough account in the *Acts of the Apostles*, Lysias arranged for the Jewish Council to see him, in order to obtain from them a clearer definition of the case against him: the case, that is to say, in the religious field, which came within their competence – as sedition did not. Whether, at the meeting, the *Acts* were truthful in reporting that the high priest Ananias ordered Paul to be struck, and that he retorted 'God will strike you, you whitewashed wall!' must be regarded as less certain.[70] But the further assertion that Paul claimed to be a believer in resurrection like any other Pharisee, and that this gained him a measure of support from the Pharisees on the Council, and corresponding disapproval from the Sadducee members, is likely enough. On the charge of bringing a Gentile into the Temple nothing further is said at this stage.

As vigorous argument raged, the Council, or the crowds surrounding its chamber, broke into uproar. Lysias, fearing that Paul would be torn in pieces, once again had him rescued, and he was escorted to the Roman barracks. However, information reached the commander on the next day that more than forty Jews had come to the high priest and his advisers, and had sworn an oath that they would not taste food and drink until they had assassinated Paul. Lysias, well aware that he must not take risks with a Roman citizen, was disturbed by this news, and decided to send Paul down to the provincial capital Caesarea Maritima. He provided him, for the journey, with an escort of four hundred infantry and seventy cavalry: this was the third time within twenty-four hours that he had used Roman troops to save his life.

On arrival at Caesarea, Paul was taken into custody by the governor Felix. Felix also read Lysias' letter indicating that the Jews wanted to prefer a charge against him. Undeterred by the possible technical difficulty that Paul came from another province (and indeed from a 'free' city), the governor consented to conduct the investigation, and requested the attendance of the high priest Ananias. When Ananias arrived from Jerusalem, he did not present the Jewish case in person, but arranged that an orator named Tertullus should act as spokesman. Knowing that Roman governors were unwilling to convict on Jewish religious offences, Tertullus instead developed the argument that Paul, by stirring up disturbances and profaning the Temple, was guilty not only of an offence of this religious category but also of the *Roman* offence of causing a riot, that is to say of treasonable, subversive activity.

After a preliminary hearing Felix decided that he must have not only the personal evidence of Lysias but the advice of his own wife Drusilla (II), who was Jewish; since although the charge was political, the evidence was theological, and therefore difficult for a Roman official, even one so well informed as Felix, to understand. Lysias, presumably, arrived and testified, and then Felix and Drusilla heard Paul together. But Felix found the encounter too much for him. 'When the discourse turned to questions of morals, self-control, and the coming judgment, Felix became alarmed and exclaimed, "That will do for the present; when I find it convenient I will send for you again."'

The fact was that he felt highly unwilling to pronounce on this matter. He was sure to be recalled to Rome before long, and the loss of influence at court by his brother Pallas and his patron Agrippina (culminating in the latter's violent death at the hand of her son Nero in 59) had weakened his position. At this juncture, then, any verdict on Paul seemed likely to cause trouble – his condemnation because of possible Christian turbulence, and his acquittal because the Jewish authorities might then write to Rome bringing charges against Felix himself for maladministration. So he decided, as was his entitlement, to defer his verdict altogether. Paul was left 'on a charge', so that the Jews could not say he had been let off, and he seems to have remained in prison at Caesarea Maritima for two years.[71] It may possibly have been here (rather than during earlier prison sentences, or at Rome later on) that he composed some of the Epistles attributed to his captivity (if, indeed, they are really his work): *Philippians, Colossians, Ephesians* and *Philemon.*

While he was still under guard at Caesarea, the city erupted into serious disturbances, apparently for reasons unconnected with his presence. For at this juncture the large Jewish population, still deeply resenting its exclusion from the citizenship of the place, proceeded to come to blows with the Greeks. As Josephus explained it, 'the older members of the Jewish community were incapable of restraining their turbulent partisans'.[72] The Jews had the advantage in wealth and physical force, but the Greeks enjoyed the support of the pagan garrison, and Felix himself intervened on their side. However, the quarrel still dragged on, and in the end Felix arranged for the leaders of both factions to be sent to Nero to advance their claims – no doubt hoping that the case of the Jews would not prevail, since they were certain to criticize him severely.[73]

At this juncture King Agrippa II exercised his prerogative of appointing high priests, putting an end to the record tenure of Ananias (or accepting his resignation), and appointing Ishmael ben Phiabi (*c.* 59–61) in his stead. Ishmael was a member not of the houses of Boethus or Ananus, which had generally shared the high priesthood during the past eighty years, but of a third family, which appears to have included two holders of the office in earlier generations.[74] The Jewish tradition seems divided on his merits. In one passage, he is spoken of as the last representative of 'the splendour of the priesthood';[75] and he is also described as the disciple of Phineas, who had struck down the unfaithful Jew and provided a model for the Maccabees. But it is also said, almost in the same breath, 'Woe is me because of the house of Ishmael the son of Phiabi; woe is me because of their fists! For they (and other high priests have been mentioned too) are high priests, and their sons are Temple treasurers, and their sons-in-law are trustees, and their servants beat the people with staves.'

The two conflicting versions reflect accurately a deep split, highly ominous for the future, which had now appeared within the ranks of the Jewish priesthood itself. Josephus explains:

For now there was kindled mutual enmity and class warfare between the high priests, on the one hand, and the priests and the leaders of the populace of Jerusalem on the other. Each of the factions formed and collected for itself a band of the most reckless revolutionaries and acted as their leader. And when they clashed, they used abusive language and pelted each other with stones . . .

The cause of the conflict was the priests' entitlement to a percentage of the grain harvest, a contribution on which the humbler members of the priesthood largely depended for their sustenance.[76] The collection of these assets had been centralized by John Hyrcanus I, but now, as Josephus continues, 'such was the shamelessness and effrontery which possessed the high priests that they actually were so brazen as to send slaves to the threshing floors to receive the tithes that were due to the priests, with the result that the poorer priests starved to death'.[77] The incident significantly revealed that the economic disparity in the community as a whole was matched by an equally or even more serious cleavage within the ranks of the priests (as in France on the eve of the Revolution). In consequence, the priestly class could no longer be regarded as providing anything approaching a national front against Roman encroachment or oppression.

Soon afterwards Felix had to answer for himself at Rome. The *Acts of the Apostles* do not speak of him unfavourably. The historian Tacitus, on the other hand, though far from pro-Jewish, is savagely critical of his conduct;[78] but that may only be because Tacitus was a snob in the old Roman conservative tradition, and disapproved of freedmen holding important offices and enjoying influence in Roman circles. The influence of Felix, although damaged by the fall of Agrippina, was still considerable. The fact that his wife Drusilla (II) was a sister of Agrippa II played an important part (though Agrippa's even more influential sister Berenice did not like her). Moreover the brother of Felix, Pallas, although removed by now from the centre of political power, could still scarcely be ignored by Nero. So no unfortunate fate befell Felix; but he did not return to Judaea.

His successor as procurator was Porcius Festus (*c.* 60–2), a prudent politician capable of speedy and vigorous action. These qualities were immediately put to the test owing to an extension of the dagger-carrying, murderous, extremists, already so prominent in Jerusalem, to many parts of the countryside. Furthermore, there arose yet another Messianic figure, enticing the population into the wilderness. But Festus sent troops who eliminated this new Messiah and his followers.

At this period, all governors of Judaea, however influential at home, had to reckon more and more seriously with their northern neighbour, King Agrippa II. By the time of Claudius' death, his kingdom had extended from the southern Lebanon over large tracts of northern Transjordan; and in AD 56 Nero transferred to him, from the Roman province of Judaea, not only two towns further south in Transjordan (Peraea), namely Julias (Betharamphtha) and Abila (close beside it), but also two places in Galilee, namely Tiberias and Taricheae (Migdal), the centre of the lucrative salt-fish industry on the Sea of Galilee. These accessions of territory considerably augmented the proportion of Jews in Agrippa II's kingdom, and his influence over Jewish affairs became proportionately greater. His coins date a new era from this moment.

It now remained for Festus to deal with the problem of Paul, who was still in prison at Caesarea Maritima. During a visit to Jerusalem immediately after his arrival, the high priest Ishmael and his associates had pressed Festus to send Paul back to them for a Jewish trial of his alleged religious offences: according to Christian tradition, they planned to assassinate him on the way.[79] But Festus said that they themselves could come to Caesarea instead, and that he personally would hear the case, as affecting a secular issue of law and order. Paul, however, while glad to escape a Jewish trial, was not eager to be tried by Festus either. It was not that he objected to his jurisdiction, but if and when he exercised it he was certain to summon a committee (*consilium*) to advise him, and Paul did not fancy the prospect of finding leading figures of the Jerusalem establishment on this body. Instead, therefore, he appealed to the emperor. The term 'appeal' may seem confusing seeing that there was not yet any sentence to appeal against. But a Roman citizen was protected, probably by a Law of Augustus (the *Lex Julia de vi*), from arrest or trial or summary punishment by Roman officials outside Italy, and was therefore entitled to appeal to be protected from a provincial governor's disciplinary measures and capital jurisdiction. Consequently Festus, after consulting assessors, granted his request, declaring: 'You have appealed to Caesar: to Caesar you shall go.'[80]

A few days later, however, King Agrippa II happened to arrive at Caesarea to pay a courtesy visit to the new governor. His sister Berenice, who had not cared to visit the place while her sister Drusilla (II), the wife of Felix, was in residence, accompanied him. Like Felix before him, Festus decided that in a tricky case such as Paul's it would be as well to consult authoritative (and royal) Jewish opinion, and he also – in case of subsequent repercussions – wanted Agrippa to be fully briefed before Paul departed for Rome. So it was arranged that the king and Berenice should give a hearing to the prisoner. If we can believe the *Acts*, Paul emphasized his Jewish and Pharisaic background, explained that his subsequent conduct was the inevitable outcome of the heavenly vision that had been vouchsafed to him and then added: 'I assert nothing beyond what was foretold by the prophets and by Moses: that the Messiah must suffer, and that he, the first to rise from the dead, would announce the dawn to Israel and to the Gentiles.'[81]

The reactions of the Roman governor and the Jewish monarch, as reported by *Acts*, have an authentic ring. Festus, at sea with all this Jewish theology, called out: 'Paul, you are raving! Too much learning is driving you mad!' Paul, however, turned to Agrippa II and asked him if he believed in the prophets: whereupon Agrippa, finding this question somewhat impertinent, replied: 'You appear to be of the opinion that it would be quite easy to win me over and make a Christian of me.' But after the court had risen Agrippa expressed the view to Festus that Paul need not, after all, have gone to such lengths to avoid trial either by the Jewish priestly authorities, or by Festus himself, since 'the fellow could have been discharged, if he had not appealed to the emperor'.[82] Festus, however, aware of rumours that Paul might never reach Jerusalem alive, may well have been of the opinion that this was out of the question. But it would hardly be tactful to tell Agrippa that Ishmael, the high priest he had himself appointed, was suspected of planning Paul's assassination on the road.

And so Paul went to Italy instead. The journey, with all the hazards which reveal the perils of Mediterranean communications even under the Roman Peace, is one of the masterpieces of the *Acts*. When he finally arrived at Rome, we are told that he spent two years there at his own expense.[83] But there the *Acts* tantalizingly stop, without indicating how Paul's trial (if it eventually took place, as seems probable enough) came to a conclusion. Tradition maintains that he subsequently travelled to 'the furthest limb of the west', perhaps Spain,[84] but that he then returned to Rome, where he and Peter, who despite their disagreements was believed to have joined him in Italy, were subsequently martyred.[85] Although, by the second century AD, the tradition of these martyrdoms was unanimous, early historical evidence on the subject is lacking. Nor is it possible to justify, or contradict, the further conjecture that if Peter and Paul died violent deaths these may have been due to internecine rivalries among the Jews and Christians themselves, in which the Romans played little or no part.[86] At all events, the visit of Paul to Rome, and the story that Peter visited it as well, caused that city, in the end, to replace Jerusalem as the geographical focus of the whole life of the church.

Part IV

The Wars Against the Romans

I I

The Prelude to the First Revolt

This was a period in which King Agrippa II seemed on the crest of the wave. To show his loyalty to the emperor, he re-named his capital Caesarea Philippi as Neronias – and celebrated the occasion by starting a new royal era (AD 61).[1] Yet in Jerusalem, where he was entrusted with the supervision of Temple affairs, he now became involved in a highly embarrassing dispute. During his visits to the city for religious festivals it was his custom to reside in the old palace of the Hasmonaeans, which was separated from the Temple by the Tyropoeon valley. To this palace he now added a tower containing a dining-room from which he could directly overlook the Temple and all that happened there. The high priest Ishmael and his colleagues, however, strongly opposed this action, claiming (according to what law or tradition we do not know) that it was improper for these proceedings, and especially the sacrifices, to be spied upon – or perhaps they objected to the spying being directed from a secular building. So they proceeded to erect a high wall at the western end of the Temple enclosure, in order to block Agrippa's view. This annoyed him greatly, but it also annoyed Festus, because it obstructed the view not only of Agrippa but of the Roman soldiers whose task it was to supervise the Temple during festivals. Festus consequently ordered the Jews to pull the wall down, but they objected, and he then allowed them to send a deputation to Nero. It consisted of ten men, including Ishmael the high priest and Helcias the Temple treasurer. Their appeal was successful, and the emperor permitted the wall to remain standing.

Most of the delegates now returned in triumph to Judaea. But in order to mitigate the snub to Agrippa II, Nero ordered that Ishmael and Helcias should remain behind in his palace at Rome as hostages. This gave Agrippa the opportunity to depose Ishmael from the high priesthood. In his place he appointed a certain Joseph Cabi, the son of Simon.[2] Nothing is known of him but his name, but these changes and other recent events had left an impression of the disunity that prevailed among the Jews – a disquieting situation when the maximum unity was required to face Romans and Christians alike.

Unfortunately for the future of Judaea, Porcius Festus, who if not actively pro-Jewish was at least efficient, died in office in AD 62. It was learnt that another procurator, Lucceius Albinus, had been appointed and was on the way. Before he arrived, however, Agrippa II deposed Josephus Cabi, after an extremely short tenure, and replaced him by Ananus II, the son of Ananus I and a member of the house of that name which had held so many high priesthoods during the earlier days of the province. It is impossible to say why he made this further rapid change, but it may be conjectured, in view of Ananus' evident strength of character,[3] that during the interregnum between governors the Sadducee leadership prevailed on him to appoint a forceful high priest who could get something done before Albinus arrived. The opportunity for Sadducee action seemed particularly favourable because the leader of the Pharisee party in the Council, the very eminent Gamaliel I, grandson of Hillel himself, had recently died, so that the moderate Pharisaic element was momentarily too weak to exercise a check.

Ananus II duly took the vigorous action required; for what he did was to proceed against the Christians. Evidently he had decided that their development now constituted a major threat to the Jews. With hindsight, we might have thought that the real peril was constituted by the Hellenizing branch of the Christians, whose most vigorous exponent Paul, even if the immediate results of his journeys were limited, had sown the seed which would ultimately prevent Judaism from achieving its largest aspirations. But whether Ananus was aware of this or not, Paul had escaped the clutches of the Jews. So the high priest turned, not against Paul's successor as leader of the Gentile mission (who is unidentifiable), but against the head of the other, Judaeo-Christian, faction which was based on Jerusalem itself. This group was still led by James the Just, the brother of Jesus; it was he who became the target of Ananus' attack.

Ananus may well have been prompted in this move by the recent dispute between the high priesthood and the lower clergy, since the Christians, being poor themselves, would naturally have espoused the cause of the poor priests. But in any case a pretext for action was easy enough to find, seeing that the belief that Jesus had been the Messiah could be interpreted as blasphemous. So James the Just and certain of his followers were hauled before the Council, and stoned to death – the antique punishment for religious offences.[4] The fact that the *Acts of the Apostles* remains strangely silent about this martyrdom is a measure of the gulf that existed between the views of Paul, the hero of the *Acts*, and the Judaeo-Christian leader James. But later Christians blamed this deed for all the disasters which were shortly to befall the Jews.[5] Meanwhile, a funerary inscription was erected to James on the site of his violent death, and he was succeeded by his cousin, Simeon the son of Cleophas – so that the leadership remained in Jesus' family.[6] Although nothing is said about this in the New Testament, these anti-Pauline Judaeo-Christians were still the dominant group in Palestine, and indeed retained this position for more than seven decades to come;[7] they probably would have prevailed over the Gentile faction everywhere but for the violence in Judaea that lay ahead.

Ananus' execution of James the Just caused dismay among a certain Jewish element at Jerusalem. It is not stated that they felt sorry for James, but although Josephus' account is somewhat obscure it is evident that they clearly, and rightly, felt that it was illegal for the high priest to inflict such a death penalty on his own account.[8] The fact that this had occurred during an interregnum in the governorship – when there was no Roman governor present to confirm the high priest's action – did not alter the illegality: indeed it gave the unmistakable impression that Ananus was deliberately taking advantage of the interregnum. The execution also lent fuel to the opposition which the lower priests were increasingly displaying towards the high priesthood. These lower priests were no doubt prominent among the group of Jews, hostile to Ananus, who went to greet Albinus the new governor while he was still on his way to the province (summer 62), and assailed him with vigorous complaints.

Albinus was probably bringing inflammable news to Judaea; or at any rate it must have come at about this time. For the emperor Nero had now considered the dispute between the Greeks and Jews of Caesarea Maritima, and, counselled by his Greek secretary, Beryllus, had refused to accept the Jewish request for Caesarean citizenship.

Whether this decision reflected any personal unfriendliness of Nero to the Jews, we cannot say. Everything about Nero was later enveloped in fantastic legends, and none of them was more fantastic than the Jewish stories that he himself became a convert to Judaism – and that an eminent Jewish scholar, Rabbi Meir, was one of his descendants! A glance at the situation prevailing in Nero's court suggests a more balanced picture. On the one hand, it is true that his love of things Greek, which caused him to surround himself with Greeks, was not promising. Nor was the strongly anti-Jewish attitude of his educator and (until 62) chief minister Seneca. The smoking lamps on the Sabbath, and the wastefulness of this institution in losing one seventh of man's labour, caused Seneca great annoyance, and he complained that 'the customs of that most criminal nation have gained such strength that they have now been received in all lands: the conquered have given laws to the conquerors'.[9] And contemporaries of Seneca, including Nero's friend Petronius, join in the sneers at the Sabbath.[10] Another prominent figure was Tiberius Claudius Balbillus, a prefect of Egypt who had probably led the anti-Jewish delegation sent by the Alexandrians in the previous reign. Furthermore, a certain Chaeremon, whose *History of Egypt* was very hostile to the Jews, has been identified, probably rightly, with Nero's tutor of that name.[11]

On the other hand the empress Poppaea, whom Nero married in 62, is described by the Jewish historian Josephus as 'god-fearing'.[12] This term is evidently intended to mean that, although not a proselyte or a Judaizer, she was at least sympathetic to the Jewish cause. For she is also indicated as a contributor to the emperor's decision to leave the Temple wall intact, and as the sponsor of the young Josephus' success when, as we shall see later in this chapter, he went to Rome in 64 to plead a Jewish cause.[13] He had been introduced to her by a Jewish actor in Nero's service, Aliturus, who was evidently able to play some part in counteracting some of the anti-Jewish influences at court.

Nevertheless, the emperor decided against the Jews' demand that they should become citizens of Caesarea. One difficult Jewish city, Jerusalem, was quite enough; it was understandable that he should not want another, especially at the capital of the Roman province. Yet, as Josephus points out, this decision was one of the events that directly led to the increasingly grave troubles of the years ahead.[14] If, as seems likely, it became known at about the time of Albinus' arrival, the diffusion of the news did not make his task any easier. Nevertheless, on receiving the complaint by Ananus' Jewish enemies against his conduct during the interregnum, Albinus took a stand in their favour, at least to the extent of conveying to the high priest a severe reprimand. Meanwhile, the Jews had also complained to Agrippa II; he proceeded to depose Ananus – after he had held office for only three months.

The next high priest, Jesus son of Damnaeus, was overshadowed during his tenure (62–3) by one of his predecessors, Ananias (who had held office between 48 and 59). Ananias, a powerful and vigorous or indeed violent personage, was accused of reviving the practice, introduced by the last high priest but two (Ishmael), of stealing the tithes that ought to have gone to the lower priests; he employed hooligans, it was said, to seize these funds by force. However, Josephus, while attacking Ananias' conduct, is bound to admit that in spite of his browbeating of the junior priests, or perhaps because of it, there were certain circles in which he enjoyed considerable popularity.[15]

Ananias was also charged with bribing both the new high priest Jesus and Albinus himself. Whether the latter charge is true depends on our estimate of Albinus, which is hard to get right since Josephus assesses him differently in his two principal writings. In the earlier of these works, the *Jewish War*, he had not found a good word to say for the governor's character, whereas later on, in the *Jewish Antiquities*, he does at least credit him with an initial vigour in the suppression of guerrillas.[16] In this, however, Albinus was not completely successful, since they entered Jerusalem and captured the chief assistant to Eleazar, the captain of the Temple. Now Eleazar was Ananias' son, and the release of his assistant was obtained on Ananias' persuasion, at the cost of the release by the Romans of ten captured guerrillas. But this capitulation to violence encouraged the underground movement to kidnap further members of Ananias' staff, whom once again they refused to release until their own imprisoned fellow-guerrillas were set free.

The reputation of Agrippa II in Jerusalem, already damaged by the incident of the wall, was now deteriorating further, partly as a result of Jewish displeasure because of extensive gifts and subsidies he had presented to the Greek city of Berytus. Nor, evidently, was he satisfied by

the attitude of his recently appointed high priest, Jesus, for after scarcely
a year he replaced him by another man of the same name, the son of
Gamaliel (63–5). This second Jesus was said to have secured the post
by arranging that his fiancée Martha, daughter of Boethus, should
send the king a bribe.[17] At all events the change had a lamentable and
perhaps unprecedented result, for the deposed man took his removal
badly and the followers of the two Jesuses became involved in street
fighting. At the same time a third gang was mobilized by Saul and
Costobarus, two princes of the house of Agrippa II – they were presumably operating in the king's interests, though whether he supported
their activities we cannot say. Meanwhile Ananias seems to have used
his wealth to profit by these divisions and keep the ultimate power in
his own hands. It is also possible that he was playing a double game,
secretly sympathizing with subversive and potentially anti-Roman
elements and using his influence over Albinus to further their cause. But
this must remain a conjecture.

At this point Albinus learnt that a new governor was about to be
sent in his place. Evidently he avoided disgrace with Nero, since he was
soon appointed governor of Mauretania – having filled the emperor's
coffers as well as his own, so his enemies said. Albinus had also, before
leaving Judaea, taken steps to increase his popularity within the province itself, in order to prevent adverse reports from reaching Rome.
In particular, while executing internees whose guilty participation in
guerrilla warfare was unmistakable, he released many of the others.
His critics, however, alleged that he received fees from the released
men, and that 'the prison was cleared of inmates but the land became
infested with brigands'.[18]

Meanwhile Agrippa II persuaded the Council to grant a request by
the Temple choir (drawn from the Levites) that they should be allowed
to wear linen robes like the priests, and that part of the same tribe
'should be allowed to learn the hymns by heart'.[19] It is psychologically
significant, and significant of the low flash-point of those times, that
these seemingly esoteric concessions (the subject of much learned
ancient and modern disputation) caused Josephus, himself far from
parochial in many respects, to declare 'all this was contrary to the ancestral laws, and such transgression was bound to make us liable to
punishment!' Agrippa also lost favour with the Jews because of his bad
reception of their request that a large number of men in Jerusalem,
whom the completion of certain building operations relating to the

Temple had left without employment, should be set to work by him, for relief purposes, on the reconstruction of one of the outer porticos of the same building. The number of people involved was estimated as high as eighteen thousand – no doubt an exaggeration. Agrippa rejected the proposal as unnecessary and excessive, but was prepared to accept a further suggestion that they should repave the city's streets with white stone. Nevertheless, the controversy had caused unpleasantness, and he decided to replace the high priest yet again, appointing Matthias the son of Theophilus, of the house of Ananus.

Four years earlier, the high priest of the day had been prevented from taking disciplinary action against the Hellenizing Christian Paul because the Roman authorities had sent him to Rome, where he and Peter may, or may not, have lived on since that time among the Roman community of Christians. Now, in 64, this community incurred savage treatment from Nero. For Rome was partially wrecked by a terrible fire; and when the homeless refugees began to believe rumours (no doubt untruthful) that the emperor himself had deliberately started the conflagration owing to his passion to reconstruct the city, the government chose to blame the Christians as the incendiarists. Our account comes from the historian Tacitus, writing half a century later and relying on sources whose authenticity we cannot assess:

To suppress the sinister suspicions that the fire had been instigated, Nero fabricated scapegoats – and punished with every refinement the notoriously depraved Christians (as they were popularly called) ... Their originator, Christ, had been executed in Tiberius' reign by the governor of Judaea, Pontius Pilate. But in spite of this temporary setback the deadly superstition had broken out afresh, not only in Judaea (where the mischief had started) but even in Rome. All degraded and shameful practices collect and flourish in the capital.[20]

First, Nero had self-confessed Christians arrested. Then, upon their information, large numbers of others were condemned – not so much for incendiarism as for their anti-social tendencies. How many were executed we cannot tell; if we could, we should be better able to assess the numerical results which had been obtained by Paul's mission. But those who died suffered in horrible fashion. The historian records the view – seemingly attributed to popular opinion rather than to himself – that, although Nero behaved with excessive cruelty, 'their guilt as

Christians deserved ruthless punishment'. Suetonius, too, in referring to their repression by Nero, describes their beliefs as 'a new and mischievous superstition'.[21]

There is no independent evidence that the Christians started the fire. But Tacitus reports that, after it had broken out, efforts to extinguish it were met with mysterious obstruction. 'Attempts to fight the flames were prevented by menacing gangs. Torches, too, were openly thrown in, by men calling out that they were acting under orders.' The possibility cannot be altogether excluded that these gangs consisted, in whole or part, of Christians. Paul himself, whether or not he was still in Rome at this time, had voiced the belief that the end of the world might come at any moment, and although he may subsequently have modified this view it was still very widely held. There was also an intense conviction that the agent of this Day of Judgment was to be *fire*: the fire which would consume the wicked and the rich, and bring victory to all Christians. 'My dear friends, do not be bewildered by the fiery ordeal that is upon you . . . your joy will be triumphant.' Such metaphors of fire and flame persist.[22] It may well be that some of the Christians in Rome, seeing the conflagration already raging, felt it was their pious duty to make it rage more fiercely still.

Nevertheless, what precise offence the Roman authorities attributed to the Christians is not quite clear from Tacitus' account. His version seems to veer between the notion that they were convicted of arson and the view that they were attacked merely for being Christians. Tacitus' ambiguity may well have been deliberate, since this was a device in which he excelled. But his equivocal words also, in all likelihood, reflected a historical situation, since the same muddled attitude must have existed among the Roman populace at the time when the persecution took place. Indeed the Roman government too, in order to dispose of the slanders against Nero, probably tried to suggest that a confession of Christian belief amounted to the same thing as an admission of fire-raising. The Christians, in other words, were attacked for alleged arson, and not because they were Christians – not, that is to say, because they failed to perform the patriotic religious duties of paganism; for the Jews equally refrained from these duties, and they were not persecuted.

It is unlikely, therefore, that Nero passed any measure which outlawed Christianity as such. The question of their status presumably remained undefined. Yet their persecution is startling, because it was far worse than any treatment that the main body of Jews had ever received from the Romans. Even the destruction inflicted upon Jerusalem by Sosius in 37 BC had never equalled the cold-blooded brutality of this. Yet the Jewish community at Rome, and Jews elsewhere in the Dispersion, if they were long-sighted, had good reason to conclude that Nero's repression of the Christians was ominous for themselves. For when Tacitus observes – no doubt reflecting a view which had already prevailed in Nero's time – that the trouble with the Christians was that they hated the human race, he is only saying what pagans had continually said about the Jews. And if this belief was going to play a part in bringing trouble upon the Christians, the Jews might well be the next to suffer. Hating the human race was not, of course, a specific accusation in law, but in an inflamed situation it could very well lead to one. People who behaved with such suspicious strangeness and separateness might, at any time, find themselves accused of instigating civil strife (*majestas*) or stirring up public violence (*vis*). Meanwhile, however, the Jews were exempted. One of their synagogues, in the Subura quarter, must have been burnt down in the fire, and it hardly seemed plausible to suggest they had burnt it down themselves. Moreover, in the previous year, by careful diplomacy, Rome had terminated a long Parthian war, and the last thing it wanted to do was to stir up Parthia's large Jewish communities.

However, Jews taking a shorter view of what had happened – even if they shared to the full the pity which, according to Tacitus, this cruelty towards the Roman Christians aroused in the city populace – might not be altogether sorry about the fate which had suddenly descended upon them. It is not necessary to go so far as those who argue that the Jews of Rome actually instigated the persecution. Nevertheless, it was only two years since their own authorities at Jerusalem had done to death the leader of the Judaean Christians, James the Just. They considered him a blasphemer, and there is no reason to suppose that either they or their co-religionists at Rome regarded the Roman Christians in any other light.

One of the most significant aspects of these events lies in the evident ability of Nero's government, at this point of time, to assess the separate positions of the Christians and the Jews and discern that the two were no longer the same. And the distinction they drew did not operate to the Christians' advantage, since whereas the Jews were excusably following their ancestral national cult – with its recognized status in society – the Christians had of their own choice abandoned, or deviated from, this cult in favour of beliefs which, because novel, were likely to be revolutionary. The capacity of the Roman authorities, and so presumably of other elements in the population as well, to effect this differentiation heralded the eventual complete split between Judaism and Christianity. Indeed, the spectacular attention which Nero's action focused upon their divergence must have accelerated the split. The movement had already boasted its martyrs, and now it could point to more of them, in Rome itself. The Christians had inherited to the full the Jewish enthusiasm for martyrdom, so that Nero's oppression provided a great stimulus for their cause: 'martyrdom is the bait that wins men for our school . . . the blood of Christians is seed'.[23] By persecuting them, Nero had begun the process which would bring them, and not their Jewish teachers, to the eventual primacy of the Roman world.

With the arrival in Judaea of the new procurator Gessius Florus (64–66), Josephus' *Jewish Antiquities* comes to an end, whereas his *Jewish War* spreads itself in more elaborate detail than hitherto. Florus' position in history is a gloomy one, because it was during his governorship that the disaster which had for so long threatened Judaea finally materialized. According to Josephus, who gives him the worst possible character, Florus actually *wanted* a Jewish rebellion, and his brutalities and imprudences did a great deal to hasten it on. However, we must take these strictures with a special grain of salt since one reason why he hated Florus was surely because the governor was a Greek, and a despised Asian Greek at that, since he came from Clazomenae (Urla) on the west coast of Asia Minor.

If Florus was as violently anti-Jewish as Josephus says, it is a little difficult to understand why, as the historian also indicates, he owed his appointment to his wife's friendship with the empress Poppaea, who was not unsympathetic to the Jews. Josephus himself had occasion to appreciate this during the very year of Florus' appointment when, at the age of twenty-six, he went to Rome as a member of a Jewish deputation. Their task was to try to secure the release of some Jewish priests who had been dispatched there by Felix, and who in order to avoid eating meat (which might be left over from heathen sacrifices) had been subsisting miserably on nuts and figs.[24] At Puteoli (Pozzuoli) Josephus became a friend of Aliturus, the Jewish actor at the court of Nero and Poppaea. Aliturus introduced him to the empress, who arranged that his mission should be successful and sent him home laden with gifts: such were the means by which Roman personages won collaborators in the provinces. Josephus was an aristocratic Jew and a Pharisee, but he returned to Judaea fervently convinced that friendship with the Romans was the only possible policy.

He arrived to find that Florus had immediately become involved in serious difficulties. These had arisen in Caesarea Maritima, where Nero had ruled against the Jews' demand to share citizenship with the Greeks. Subsequently, the Greeks put up some shops blocking access to a synagogue, whereupon the builders had come under attack from gangs of Jewish youths. Florus accepted a bribe from the Jewish authorities, but took no action to help their cause and left Caesarea on a journey to Sebaste (Samaria). On the next day, a Sabbath, the Caesarean Jews assembled at the synagogue only to find that one of their Greek enemies had placed outside its doors an inverted chamber-pot, on which he was sacrificing birds: a reference to the widespread belief that the Jews whom Moses had led out of Egypt were lepers, since according to the Torah birds for lepers to eat had to be killed in an earthenware vessel.[25] Fighting broke out, and a Roman cavalry commander succeeded in removing the pot. But the Jews, afraid for their safety, moved out of Caesarea *en masse* into a Jewish suburb, carrying with them a copy of the Torah. From there they sent a deputation to Florus, 'delicately reminding him of the matter of the bribe'.[26] But Florus put them under arrest, on the grounds that they had committed an irregularity by removing the Torah from Caesarea; perhaps this action had not received the support of the Caesarean Jews as a whole.

Next Florus seized a large sum (more than twice the amount of the bribe) from the Temple treasury at Jerusalem. He did this, in all probability, because the Judaean payment of taxes, in a time of growing disorders and economic sufferings, was in arrears. When rioting followed, he brought up reinforcements to Jerusalem from Caesarea Maritima, consisting of a cohort (five hundred men) preceded by a cavalry vanguard. After an unsuccessful conference with the Jews in front of the palace, Roman troops conducted a house-to-house search of the Upper City. This resulted in bloodshed – and Florus committed the legal error of crucifying Jews who were Roman knights.

King Agrippa II was in Alexandria. He had gone there (with that alacrity which helped to keep Herodian princes on their thrones) in order to congratulate the ex-Jew Tiberius Julius Alexander, once procurator of Judaea, who had recently become prefect of Egypt. But

Agrippa's sister Berenice was in Jerusalem discharging a religious vow, and now, narrowly escaping the violent troops, she came barefoot to Florus' tribunal and urged him to call a halt to the repression. Meanwhile, however, Florus had sent for two more cohorts from Caesarea Maritima, and the high priest Matthias and his Council, after more or less successful efforts to calm the crowd, went to meet them, with a large company of priests and other Jews. This was intended, so it was said, as a conciliatory gesture, but the advancing troops, being anti-Jews of Caesarea and Sebaste, failed to return their salute, and scuffling broke out. A cavalry charge caused numerous casualties, but then the soldiers, greatly outnumbered, were forced to take refuge in their camp adjoining the palace. Florus now agreed with the high priest and Council that only one cohort should remain in Jerusalem – not the one which had recently ransacked the Upper City. Then he himself returned with the other cohorts to Caesarea.

The governor of Syria was now Gaius Cestius Gallus, who was not, unfortunately, as capable of dealing with a crisis as most of his predecessors in that important post. At this juncture Florus sent him a dispatch strongly critical of the Jews, and further reports presenting the other side of the case reached him from the Jewish Council and Berenice. Cestius Gallus decided to dispatch a senior officer to investigate the situation on the spot. This envoy, Neapolitanus, went first of all to meet Agrippa II, who was at Jamnia, on his way back to his kingdom from Alexandria. The high priest and members of the Council also made their way to Jamnia to see the king. Then they all moved up towards Jerusalem, where vast crowds met them outside the gates. Gessius Florus was not there, but Neapolitanus toured the city, urged the population to keep the peace, sacrificed in the section of the Temple permitted to Gentiles and returned to Syria. On his arrival there, although Josephus is careful to stress the pacific intentions of the Jewish leadership, Neapolitanus must have reported to Cestius Gallus that an open rising might not be very far off.

Now it was the turn of Agrippa II to try to deal with the emergency; according to Josephus he delivered a lengthy oration to the people of Jerusalem seeking to convince them of the uselessness of rebelling against the Romans. The words, and even the occasion, may be fictitious. But the substance of the alleged speech is of great interest, since it provides a detailed defence of the whole policy of collaboration for which Agrippa II so firmly stood – like his grandfather Herod the Great and other members of his family, and most other leading Jews, including Josephus himself. First, Agrippa pointed out, according to the historian, that complaints against individual Roman procurators were very far from justifying a revolt against Rome. Then he went on to explain that this enthusiasm for freedom was completely anachronistic:

Passing to your present passion for liberty, I say that it comes too late. The time is past when you ought to have striven never to lose it. For servitude is a painful experience, and a struggle to avoid it once for all is just; but the man who having once accepted the yoke then tries to cast it off is a contumacious slave, not a lover of liberty. There was, to be sure, a time when you should have strained every nerve to keep out the Romans; that was when Pompey invaded this country. But our forefathers and their kings, though in wealth and in vigour of body and soul far your superiors, yet failed to withstand a small fraction of the Roman army; and will you, to whom thraldom is hereditary, you who in resources fall so far short of those who first tendered their submission, will you, I say, defy the whole Roman empire? ... Myriads of other nations, swelling with greater pride in the assertion of their liberty, have yielded. And will you alone disdain to serve those to whom the universe is subject?

What are the troops, what is the armour, on which you rely? Where is your fleet to sweep the Roman seas? Where is your treasury to meet the cost of your campaigns? Do you really suppose that you are just going to war with Egyptians or Arabs? Will you shut your eyes to the might of the Roman empire and refuse to take the measure of your own weakness? Have not our forces been constantly defeated even by the neighbouring nations, while theirs have never met with a reverse throughout the whole known world?[27]

Nor was it any disgrace, Agrippa II is reported to have continued, to remain subordinate to the Roman empire, since all the greatest nations of the Mediterranean area, and even of central and northern Europe, have found it necessary to do the same. Then he turned to a point which must often have passed through the minds of the more optimistic Jewish nationalists, just as it constantly occurred to suspicious Roman governors of Syria and Judaea. This was the possibility of treasonable communications with the Parthians, and the hope the Jews might entertain of receiving assistance from that quarter – a matter of particular interest to Josephus, who may have written a separate work, now lost, about Parthian and Syrian history.

What allies do you then expect for this war? Will you recruit them from the uninhabited wilds? For in the habitable world all are Romans – unless, maybe, the hopes of some of you soar beyond the Euphrates and you count on obtaining aid from your kinsmen in Adiabene [Assyria]. But they will not, for any frivolous pretext, let themselves be embroiled in so serious a war, and, if they did contemplate such folly, the Parthian would not permit it; for he is careful to maintain the truce with the Romans, and would regard it as a violation of the treaty if any of his tributaries were to march against them.[28]

If you rebel, the speech supposedly continued, you will hazard not only yourselves but every Jewish community of the Dispersion, which stretches so widely over all the world. It will not have been they who made the fatal decision, yet they too will be among the sufferers: 'through the folly of a handful of men, every city will be drenched with Jewish blood'. Besides, Agrippa pointed out, think how utterly adverse such a step would be to your own interests. 'For all the reasonableness of the Romans now (except when there happens to be a bad procurator), once you have revolted against them you need not expect mercy. You are the people who have to show mercy to yourselves, and mercy to all those you hold dear. Even if you will not take pity on your children and your wives, by not deciding upon a catastrophic action under the guise of martyrdom, at least spare the Temple, preserve for yourselves your sanctuary and its holy places!' For it did not need hindsight to realize that rebellion would mean the total downfall of the religious centre of Jerusalem.

Although written by a Jewish historian and placed in the mouth of a Jewish king, the speech completely omits any expression of faith in Israel's role as God's chosen people. Instead, it is the Roman empire which is endowed with divine sanction. 'The only refuge left to you is divine assistance. But even this is ranged on the side of the Romans, for, without God's aid, so vast an empire could never have been built up.' This attitude has earned Agrippa ii's views, so sympathetically expressed by Josephus, a good deal of criticism and contempt. Stuart Perowne offers a more judicious estimate:

We have to admit we are disgusted by its argument. It is in reality no more than a glorification of slavery ... That is why the argument of Agrippa's speech, brilliantly as it is presented, is, on reflection, so repugnant to the modern reader. Yet, in Agrippa's defence, it must be asked: what else could he have advised? In a world where partnership, political equality, of any kind, was unknown, what were the alternatives?[29]

Modern Israeli historians, however, adopt a different attitude, and point out that the revolt which now followed was not by any means such a desperate prospect as all that. Citing their own three successes in modern times against their vastly more numerous Arab enemies, they argue that the Jews of AD 66 too might have prevailed, even against apparently desperate odds. But the parallel is a very inexact one. The Romans were firmly in control of the entire Mediterranean area, and would obviously continue to control it for an indefinite period to come; to succeed against them was beyond the bounds of possibility. The *Copper Scroll*, found at Qumran, purports to describe the treasures available to the Jews,[30] but it is a wildly imaginative picture, a product of optimistic fantasy.

In general terms, comparisons with the Maccabees' successful revolt against the Seleucids were misleading. At that time, guerrilla movements had enjoyed a better chance, since urbanization and road communications were undeveloped. Besides, the Seleucids were severely harassed by external powers – including the Romans, who were so much stronger than themselves. Moreover, the warning of Agrippa II that sufficient help would never be forthcoming from Parthia was basically correct, and never more correct than at this particular time. It is true that Parthia was Rome's only external enemy which possessed any real power, or could conceivably have provided assistance to the rebels; and that according to a widespread Jewish belief the ultimate collapse of the Roman empire would be heralded by a Parthian invasion, like the never-forgotten invasion of 40 BC. Yet, by the most unfortunate of all possible coincidences for the Jews, their revolt in AD 66 came at a time when Parthia, under King Vologases I, had just agreed upon a pact of friendship with Rome which would last for half a century! Indeed, in this very year of all years, Vologases' brother Tiridates, the king of Armenia, was actually in Rome as Nero's guest to solemnize the agreement. In the whole of Roman history it would have been impossible to find a year more unlikely than AD 66 to provide Parthian intervention in favour of a Jewish revolt against Rome. And meanwhile, the east was still unusually full of Roman troops – with no sign or possibility of a Parthian or Armenian enemy to distract their attention or provide a diversion.

It is true that Agrippa II was not quite accurate when he said that the Jews of Palestine would get no assistance whatever from within the borders of the Parthian empire. For, as it turned out, their co-religionists belonging to the royal house of Adiabene (Assyria) did provide what help they could in the persons of their present ruler Monobazus and his relatives. But although Monobazus managed to arrange for some supplies to be sent to the rebels, he was without any adequate backing from his own largely pagan subjects. In any case, his contribution was only a drop in the ocean. And as for Judaea's neighbours the Nabataean Arabs, they, like the Syrians, sent help *against* the Jews, who were the objects of their special hatred.[31]

Furthermore, it was out of the question for the Jews of Judaea to put up anything like an effective resistance to the united force of Rome unless they themselves, whose resources were infinitely smaller, could achieve unity in their own ranks. Instead, as the story of the next disastrous years will show, they were ludicrously, tragically disunited – more disunited than they had ever been before, or would ever be again.

In all these circumstances it is premature to dismiss Agrippa II, or for that matter Josephus, as a 'quisling' or 'collaborationist'. Certainly Agrippa II was not a particularly attractive figure; and Josephus' fascinating works, in many passages, show him up as self-congratulatory to the point of thoroughgoing mendacity. Nevertheless the fact remains that in the rebellion of AD 66 there was no possibility whatever of disrupting the long-lived, utterly solid Roman empire. No doubt many of those who rebelled fought with great bravery, and to that extent they were heroes. But one has to consider carefully before attributing true heroism to men whose actions, as Agrippa II pointed out, would imperil their co-religionists everywhere, would cause the deaths not only of themselves but of their wives and children, and would condemn their national and religious homeland to destruction.

Agrippa II and Josephus were not alone in realizing how matters stood. A strong quietist or pacifist group among the Pharisees appreciated the situation very clearly. One of them was the teacher and writer Hanina, 'lieutenant of high priests'. For it was he who uttered the plea, probably in this very year: 'Pray for the welfare of the government! For if it were not for the fear of it, men would swallow one another up alive!'[32]

12

The First Revolt

Moderation is always an unexciting policy, and Agrippa II's pleas to keep the peace ceased to engage attention when he went on to urge that, pending the arrival of a new procurator who would surely be better, Gessius Florus should not be resisted. Stones were thrown at Agrippa, and he retired to his kingdom.

Soon afterwards, the point of no return was reached. The decisive step was taken by Ananias' son Eleazar, the captain of the Temple and apparently a Sadducee. Eleazar was the man whose secretary had been kidnapped by extremists four years earlier. Now, however, he showed that he had gone over to their cause: he issued an announcement that henceforward no sacrifices would be accepted from any foreigner (August 66). This meant that the twice-daily sacrifices on behalf of Rome and the emperor would henceforward have to be abandoned, since it was the emperor who paid for them. In consequence, Eleazar's ruling was an act of rebellion.

The high priest Matthias and his supporters, after protesting in vain against this decision, withdrew from the Lower City and the Temple, where Eleazar, though overlooked by a small Roman garrison in the Antonia fortress, was now in control (see Plan of Jerusalem, on p. 198). Matthias, installing himself in the Upper City, sent a deputation to Gessius Florus; and three Herodian princes, Saul, Costobarus and Antipas, left to see Agrippa II. Since Florus did nothing, Agrippa, anxious to assert his authority over the Temple, felt he had to have recourse to forceful methods. So he now proceeded to dispatch two thousand cavalry to Jerusalem. Their instructions were to defend the high priest and his followers in the Upper City – and, as soon as they could, to expel Eleazar from the Lower City and the Temple. But before they could take any such action, Eleazar broke into the Upper City, forced out the newly arrived royal troops and burnt down the old Hasmonaean palace which was Agrippa's residence. The rebels also destroyed the record office,[1] thus deliberately demolishing the deeds of the mortgages which had caused many destitute Jews to rally to Eleazar in despair.

Many of the high priest's followers took refuge in the city's underground passages and sewers, while that dignitary himself, together with Agrippa's friends and soldiers, fled to the massive fortified palace which Herod the Great had erected beside the Jaffa gate; at this time it contained a modest garrison of the procurator's Roman troops, that is to say of men from Sebaste or Caesarea. However, before tackling this target, Eleazar dealt with a problem nearer at hand, and besieged that other Roman garrison which was in occupation of the Antonia castle overlooking the Temple. The castle was a great rectangular structure, with a frontage three hundred and seventy-five feet long; at each of its four corners a tower rose precipitously to the sky. Nevertheless, after a resistance of only two days the stronghold fell, and its defenders were massacred. Then Eleazar turned his attention to Herod's palace, and subjected it to a series of savage assaults.

But at this stage his successes were interrupted by the appearance of a rival. This was a certain Menahem, who had just won great prestige by a surprise attack on the fortress of Masada. Situated on a precipitous hill-top in the bleak Dead Sea desert, this formidable fortress had been surrounded by Herod the Great with a twenty-foot-high wall punctuated by thirty-eight towers. Yet Menahem contrived, by some trick or other, to seize it, slaughtering the Roman garrison and installing his own men. Large quantities of arms fell into his hands; and he subsequently occupied the monastic centre of Qumran as well, or enrolled its inmates. Now he appeared in Jerusalem. Menahem came of a line of resistance fighters, since he was a son of that Judas the Galilean who had led a rising sixty years earlier when the province was first instituted. He entered Jerusalem 'like a veritable king',[2] that is to say with pretensions to be either the Messiah himself or at least a forerunner, reminiscent of

Elijah. The time was ripe for such a claim, because there was a widely believed oracle indicating that a man from Judaea was going to become ruler of the world; the prophecy played a large part in triggering off the Jews' rebellion.[3]

So here was a man whose recent success, combined with his family background, could have made him an effective national leader – in so far as such a figure could be contemplated. Moreover, on his arrival in Jerusalem Menahem scored an early victory by accepting the surrender of Agrippa's Jewish troops in Herod's palace. They were allowed to march out and return to their king. The Roman units in the palace declined to surrender, but retreated into the building's three great towers. Then Menahem succeeded in laying hands on Ananias and his brother, and had them murdered. Even if the ex-high priest, as was suspected, had from time to time flirted with dissident elements, the moment for such subtleties had passed, and Menahem felt that such a powerful competitor for the national leadership was better out of the way. But Eleazar also wanted to be the leader, and now he kidnapped Menahem and tortured him to death. However one assesses the relative merits of the two leaders, and of the specific, conflicting ideologies and royal or priestly Messianisms they claimed to stand for, this event (together with the immediately preceding murder of Ananias) was disastrous for the Jews, since it started the really savage internecine strife which made their victory even more impossible than it had been before.[4]

Eleazar now promised the Roman troops their lives if they were prepared to evacuate the palace towers. But when they did so he broke his promise and slaughtered them, with the single exception of their commander, who was spared at the price of accepting circumcision.[5] A Jewish calendar seems to celebrate this day of September 66, when 'the Romans evacuated Judah and Jerusalem'.[6] The reference to Judah was somewhat exaggerated. Yet it was true that the occupying power had been overthrown not only in the city but in most of the Jewish areas of the province. Like their traditional leaders, the majority no doubt remained loyal to Roman rule, or at least passive. But the vigorous, violent minority had prevailed, and the Romans were gone.

These early successes of the rebels aroused the keenest interest in other parts of the empire, and particularly in Gaul where a nationalist movement would soon be rebelling on its own account. The communities of the Jewish Dispersion, too, became increasingly excited, though their ability to send material help scarcely improved. In Alexandria the

Greeks turned on the Jews, and heavy fighting broke out. The ex-Jewish prefect Tiberius Julius Alexander unleashed two legions upon his former co-religionists, of whom Josephus declares that fifty thousand were killed – though the figure may be exaggerated. In other cities, too, where the Greeks likewise held the upper hand, they massacred the local Jewish communities. Feeling was especially strong in Caesarea Maritima, from which many of the soldiers murdered by Eleazar in Jerusalem had come. The Caesarean Greeks attacked the Jews, and the entire community, perhaps amounting to twenty thousand, was almost wiped out within an hour. The Greeks also performed wholesale massacres at various other points along the coast and in the hinterland. A Syrian general of Agrippa II exterminated the Babylonian Jews in his kingdom's Transjordanian territories and the Jewish colony in the royal capital of Caesarea Philippi. Meanwhile the Jews, for their part, slaughtered Gentiles in Samaria, Galilee, Transjordan and coastal regions of Phoenicia and elsewhere.[7]

Since the procurator Gessius Florus had virtually lost control of Judaea, it was impossible for the governor of Syria, Cestius Gallus, whose army was so much larger, to avoid intervention any longer. Bringing one of his four legions and a contingent of six thousand men drawn from the other three, he began to advance southwards, and had little difficulty in overcoming resistance in Galilee (October). Then he moved on, under harassment, towards Jerusalem. The rebels abandoned the northern part of the city, and Gallus, encouraged by secret overtures from the high-priestly establishment,[8] attacked the Antonia fortress. But all his attempts were unsuccessful, and as winter was now approaching he called off the siege and began to withdraw towards the coast. Under severe pressure from rebels on the hill-tops, the retreat turned into a rout, and in a running engagement which became known as the battle of Beth-Horon – the name of two villages ten and twelve miles north west of Jerusalem – Gallus' force was severely mauled. Indeed, he only got through to Caesarea Maritima with the loss of all his baggage and siege-equipment, and nearly six thousand men. This serious defeat reverberated round the empire. One of its immediate results was a slaughter of Jews by the Greeks of Damascus, who now felt wholly assured of impunity from Cestius Gallus.

Beth-horon had ensured that any immediate suppression of the revolt was out of the question. Triumphantly re-entering Jerusalem in November 66, the Jews, with their usual backward gaze, compared their success to the victories won at this very same place by Joshua over five Canaanite kings, and then again by Judas Maccabaeus over the Seleucids. Pro-Roman sentiments became impossible to voice, and the princes of the Herodian house who had their homes in Jerusalem fled for their lives to Caesarea Maritima. From there they went on to Greece, which Nero was visiting, and endeavoured to explain to him that everything that had happened was due to the misconduct, not of the Jews, but of the procurator Gessius Florus.[9]

Meanwhile in Jerusalem an independent secessionist government was formed. Very soon it was issuing its own coins. Along with pious Jewish designs, they display proud nationalistic inscriptions: 'Shekel of Israel', 'Jerusalem is Holy', and then in the following year 'the Freedom of Zion'.[10]

Although Matthias remained high priest, the real leadership of the new government was in the hands of one of his predecessors, Ananus II. Ananus was the only holder of the high priesthood who, during his tenure of that office, had openly defied the Romans: for it was he, four years earlier, who had taken the law into his own hands and executed James the Just. Now, once again, he adopted an anti-Roman stance – yet at first only a moderate one because, realizing the inevitable outcome, he wanted to avoid an open all-out revolt, and felt that somehow or other the Romans could be induced to offer terms.[11]

Eleazar, the son of Ananias, who had led the revolt in its earlier stages and brought about the murder of Menahem, was evidently no longer in a position of central authority. Indeed, he seems to have been sent away as one of the new regime's commanders in Idumaea.[12] The names of commanders posted to other regions have also been preserved. They include members of high-priestly families. An Essene, too, was dispatched to the coastal areas – an indication that even this quietist sect had been drawn into sympathy with the new nationalism. And Josephus the Pharisee, the future historian, was ordered to proceed to Galilee.[13] Our estimate of what these commanders were supposed to do has to be based on two sharply self-contradictory statements by Josephus. In his *Jewish War* he writes of preparations to resist the expected Roman invasion. But then later, in his *Life*, nervous of what his Roman readers (and masters) might think about his part in the war, he stressed the purely pacific character of his mission, which was solely designed, he said, to disarm those of his co-religionists who had become disaffected.[14] In fact, there is little doubt that these commanders were instructed to prepare for resistance to the Romans, though it was still hoped that some agreement might be reached.

This, however, was an unrealistic hope. For Nero, in Greece, had now been fully informed about the revolt. In particular, the Herodian princes who had journeyed to visit him were in an excellent position to stress the need to detach a considerable army to deal with the rebels: otherwise the Parthian frontier might become imperilled, and the rot would spread. The rising was inconvenient for Nero, who wanted all his eastern troops for an expedition he was planning to the Caucasus. Nevertheless, action had to be taken. As a first step, when Cestius Gallus was succeeded as governor of Syria by Gaius Licinius Mucianus, all responsibility for Judaean affairs was taken out of his hands. Nero also recalled to Rome the procurator of Judaea, Gessius Florus, and greatly upgraded the governorship by appointing a senator and ex-consul to the post (February 67). This man, Vespasian (Titus Flavius Vespasianus), had the reputation of an able soldier but was not distinguished enough to present a threat to the emperor, whom a series of real or alleged conspiracies had made suspicious of too eminent subordinates.

Vespasian, who was with the emperor in Greece, left almost at once to take up his governorship and command in Judaea. Proceeding to Antioch, he picked up two legions and marched down to Ptolemais Ace, where he was joined by his talented and popular son Titus, bringing a further legion with him from Alexandria. Including auxiliaries and contingents from the client monarchs of Syria and Nabataean Arabia, the invading army totalled about sixty thousand men. By the summer, Vespasian was in Galilee, but (to Titus' subsequent regret) did not press onwards to Jerusalem immediately. Instead he established a base at the Galilean capital Sepphoris and, in his capacity as provincial governor, issued coins there describing the place not only by its recently acquired name of Neronias, but also by a new name, Irenopolis, 'City of Peace'.[15] Sepphoris received this designation to celebrate Nero's recent closure of the Temple of Janus at Rome. The rite traditionally proclaimed the establishment of empire-wide, universal, peace – a peace rudely broken by the Jewish revolt.

Outside Sepphoris, the rest of Galilee, overrun by Cestius Gallus in the previous year but subsequently lost, was now in an extraordinarily confused and divided state. Josephus, who had been sent there by

Jerusalem, offers lengthy, though often contradictory, accounts of the region's predicament. On the one side was the army of the Romans and the troops of Agrippa II their ally, to whom the towns of Tiberias and Taricheae belonged. The other side consisted of various factions of more or less rebellious Jews quarrelling among themselves, amid strong undercurrents of class warfare. The contestants included, among others, the force of Josephus; the adherents of his much more ferocious enemy John of Gischala (Gush Chalav, Jish), a rich merchant and economic speculator; and the followers of Justus of Tiberias, a historian who, after playing an equivocal part in these events, later criticized Josephus, much to his alarm, for having adopted a hostile attitude towards the Romans and Agrippa II.

And it was, indeed, true that Josephus, even if he had initially wanted to avoid fighting, got involved in hostilities against Agrippa's troops, and then found himself besieged by Vespasian at Jotapata (Jefat), nine miles south of Sepphoris. After a siege of forty-seven days, concluding in a suicide-pact among his principal associates, he evaded the pact and surrendered to the Romans (June 67). When he was brought to their headquarters, Vespasian realized that he had gained an important potential collaborator: an impression confirmed by Josephus' judicious indication that the well-known oracle indicating that a lord of the world would come from Judaea clearly referred to Vespasian himself. He kept Josephus with him, and his son Titus began to take a liking to the prisoner.

Then, after a three weeks' rest with Agrippa II at his capital Caesarea Philippi, Vespasian fought and won a brisk naval battle on the Sea of Galilee, which was later singled out for special commemoration at his Triumph and on his coinage[16] (the Roman fleet was also used to smash nationalist flotillas in the Mediterranean). And finally, the Galilean campaign was rounded off by the capture of Gischala.

John, the rebel leader at Gischala, succeeded in making his escape southwards. Passing through Samaria, which was now in Roman hands and receiving scant sympathy from Josephus,[17] he made his way into Jerusalem. There, while pretending to be a friend of Ananus and his secessionist government, he secretly supported an extremist group which was in open opposition to Ananus' authority. These men called themselves Zealots,[18] a name that had earlier been used more loosely for various kinds of religious and political fanatics but now became

especially attached to this party which stood for adamant hostility both
to the Romans and the high priesthood. The Zealots were led by a certain Eleazar – not the captain of the temple, the son of Ananias, who
had played a leading part until now, but another man of the same name
(the son of Simon). He had played a distinguished part in the victory at
Beth-Horon, which had brought him extensive plunder. Eleazar the son
of Simon and his friends now proceeded to murder a Herodian prince
(Antipas) as well as the city's treasurer, and forcibly removed the high
priest Matthias from office. For his replacement, they employed a novel
(though allegedly ancient) process of drawing lots among candidates
taken from one of the most obscure priestly clans; the lot fell upon an
uneducated rustic named Phineas (Phanni), the son of Samuel (winter
67–8). Next, Eleazar and his gang seized and occupied the Temple precinct. However, Ananus mobilized six thousand men, who compelled
them to evacuate the Temple's courts and withdraw into the sanctuary.

The situation was now complicated by the arrival of numerous Idumaeans in the city. They had been called in by Eleazar's Zealots, at the
suggestion, if Josephus' hostility does not carry him away, of John of
Gischala.[19] In Idumaea itself there had been violent disturbances. One
resistance leader, a proselyte named Simon the son of Gioras, was terrorizing the Idumaean villages from Masada, and another, Niger of
Peraea (subsequently murdered by the Zealots), had twice attacked
Ascalon, though without success. But now that Idumaea was already
beginning to experience Vespasian's retribution, twenty thousand of its
inhabitants decamped and moved northwards, pouring into Jerusalem.
They had always been good military material, and now these descendants of proselytes, men whom fastidious followers of the Torah were
scarcely prepared to acknowledge as fellow-Jews, showed themselves the
most fanatical Jewish nationalists of all. Combining with the Zealots,
they conducted a systematic massacre of Jerusalem's upper and middle
classes. Those who died included both Ananus II and the leading Pharisee of the day, Simeon the son of Gamaliel I. Soon afterwards, however,
the Idumaeans quarrelled with the other groups, and many of them
returned to their homes; though others stayed behind.

These atrocities took place unhampered by Vespasian, who was
busy mopping up resistance in the coastal area and then across the
Jordan; this was probably the time when his forces destroyed Qumran,[20]
and the long story of its community came to an end. Then he started to
prepare an attack on Jerusalem itself. But at this juncture news came

that Nero was dead (June 68) and that an elderly general Galba had
been appointed in his place – the first emperor not to belong to the
house of Julius Caesar and Augustus. After a delay of six months Vespasian recognized Galba, but meanwhile he postponed his attack on
Jerusalem. For it seemed best to await further orders and developments,
and he was none too anxious to finish the war and return to Rome,
where the situation looked precarious.

But the three principal Jewish factions in Jerusalem gained no advantage from the pause, since they totally failed to achieve any unity among
themselves. The Galilean gangs of John of Gischala, according to
Josephus, were adopting peculiar methods:

Not content with looting throughout the city, they unscrupulously indulged
in effeminate practices, plaiting their hair and attiring themselves in
women's apparel, drenching themselves with perfumes and painting their
eyelids to enhance their beauty . . . Yet, while they wore women's faces, their
hands were murderous, and approaching with mincing steps they would
suddenly become warriors and whipping out their swords from under their
dyed mantles transfix whomsoever they met.[21]

Those of the Idumaeans who had decided to remain in the city found
these degenerate practices distasteful, and drove John of Gischala and
his followers into the 'middle of the city',[22] including the outer precinct
of the Temple, though John and his men could not enter the sanctuary
itself, since it was still occupied by Eleazar and his Zealots.

Rumours that Eleazar proposed to break out and burn the city down
prompted such members of the establishment as had survived, led by
the dismissed high priest Matthias, to make a united front with the
Idumaeans and call in yet another resistance leader. This was Simon
the son of Gioras, who in recent weeks, under pressure from Vespasian,
had evacuated Masada and was moving gradually northwards, proclaiming, as he went along, an egalitarian Jewish state. It was a programme, one would have felt, which was scarcely likely to commend
itself to Matthias and his friends, but the invitation they were willing to
extend to him shows the desperation to which they were reduced. In
April 69 Simon entered Jerusalem, where he received a warm welcome
from many elements in the population. But he could not force his way
into the outer precinct of the Temple, occupied by John of Gischala, and
still less into the sanctuary, held by Eleazar and the Zealots. From now
onwards fighting between all three leaders went on continuously. What-

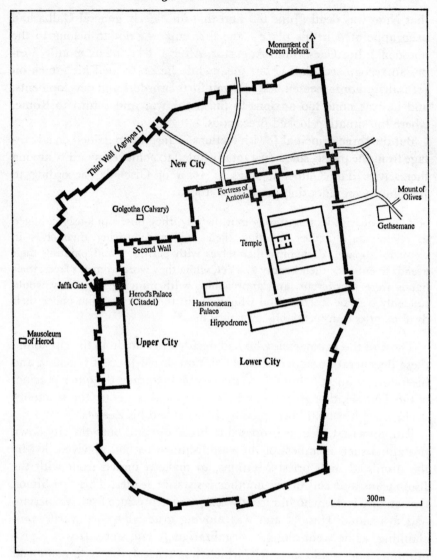

Plan of Jerusalem

ever special nuance of political and Messianic pretensions each professed, there may not, in practice, have been a very great deal to choose
between them. While Eleazar had asserted his movement's claim to the
title Zealot, perhaps John was the most cunning as well as the richest of
the three: while the high-priestly class evidently regarded Simon, in
spite of his reformist ideas, as the most efficient.[23]

Once again, the Jewish leaders were able to indulge in these internal struggles without interference from the Romans. At first, for a brief period, the succession of Galba by Otho (January 69), who appointed Vespasian's brother Sabinus as his city prefect,[24] had inspired Vespasian with sufficient confidence to revive his plan to attack Jerusalem. But then, when Otho succumbed to Aulus Vitellius (April), he abandoned the idea for a second time. For one thing, the Jews were destroying themselves, by their extraordinary disunity, quite as effectively as his whole Roman army could: Solomon Grayzel's general defence of these recurrent disunities, as demonstrating 'that there was enough intelligence and conviction and courage to question the wisdom of their leaders',[25] would have been misplaced here. Vespasian now had other and more far-reaching matters on his mind. When the dramatic changes at Rome made it clear that the effort to found a second imperial dynasty had failed, he and the governor of Syria, Gaius Licinius Mucianus, who had previously been on bad terms owing to the removal of Jewish affairs from Syrian supervision, patched up their relations and, in collusion with the prefect of Egypt, Tiberius Julius Alexander, began to intrigue against Vitellius. Their intention was to elevate Vespasian himself to the imperial throne in Vitellius' place. And meanwhile the belief asserted by Josephus that Vespasian was the man from Judaea destined by the oracle to rule the world was judiciously spread.

And so, on 1 July 69, Tiberius Julius Alexander arranged for his two Egyptian legions to salute Vespasian emperor. By mid-July, Mucianus in Syria and Vespasian's own legions in Judaea had taken similar action, and the Roman authorities in Asia Minor, as well as the commanders of the Danubian armies, soon followed. Agrippa II, who was in Rome at this time, had been obliged to recognize Vitellius, but his agents told him what was happening in the east before Vitellius himself knew, and Agrippa II hurriedly left to join Vespasian at Berytus. His sister Berenice, now aged forty, was also there. She charmed Vespasian and plied him with gifts; and during the past three years his son Titus had fallen in love with her.

Envoys came to Vespasian from King Vologases I of Parthia, offering forty thousand Parthian mounted archers to help him win the empire.[26] This dispelled finally among the Jewish rebels, if it had been necessary to do so, any hopes that they might expect Parthian aid. More than one pretender at this time was claiming to be the deceased Nero, since there was a widespread popular belief among the Jews (and Christians) that he would return, for good or ill;[27] and Vologases could easily have used these impostors against the Romans if he had wished to. But instead he chose to support Vespasian, both in his Jewish and his civil war. Before the end of the same year, 69, Vespasian's armies invaded Italy and captured Rome, where, after Vitellius had been put to death, he met with general acceptance as emperor.

It was not until late in the following summer that he himself proceeded from Alexandria to Italy. But before then terrible events had taken place in Judaea. He had left the completion of the campaign to Titus, who marched up from Egypt to Caesarea Maritima. There he assembled an army of about sixty-five thousand men, with Tiberius Julius Alexander as his chief of staff.

In Jerusalem, where three mutually hostile armies of Jewish nationalists were shattering the city, there was a totally misplaced atmosphere of confidence. It was stated in religious writings that the decisive battle between the Messianic forces and their enemies would be fought round Mount Zion.[28] Vespasian's failure to attack Jerusalem for three whole years, during all of which time the city gates had remained open in accordance with tradition, confirmed the Jewish belief that the city of God was inviolate. In 69, new coins had been issued, inscribed 'to the Redemption of Zion'.[29] However, as Passover of the following year approached, Titus marched on Jerusalem from the north – only to learn that there had been another political convulsion inside the city, reducing the number of its more or less effective Jewish groups from three to two. For John of Gischala had ejected Eleazar and his Zealots from the Temple sanctuary, forcing them to take refuge in its subterranean cellars and corridors. Simon the son of Gioras remained in charge of most of the remaining parts of the city, and at long last, in the supreme crisis, he and John agreed to act in relative harmony.

Their co-religionist Josephus, however, was still in Roman hands, and when the Roman siege of Jerusalem began in May he was often employed by Titus to move about outside the city and shout up to the people who manned the walls, reminding them, as Agrippa II had reminded them at the beginning of the revolt, of the advantages of collaboration with the Romans.[30] Although Josephus spoke with great fervour, inspired by his intense conviction that the policy of the nationalists was catastrophic, the only rewards his efforts earned were derision, execration and a hail of missiles.

The dramatic story of the siege, and of the appalling hardships suffered by the besieged Jews, is the climax and masterpiece of his *Jewish War*. In the course of a series of desperate struggles, the walls fell one after another, and late in July the Romans captured the Antonia fortress. Early in August the Temple itself was so gravely threatened that the Daily Sacrifice, which had continued for many centuries, could no longer be held: its cessation was mourned year after year as a major calamity.[31] Very soon afterwards, an even more unforgettable disaster occurred. First, Titus gave orders for the doors of the Temple to be burnt, and so the way was opened to the sanctuary itself. On the next day, some Jews who had been lurking inside the shrine rushed out, but were beaten back; as they retreated a legionary thrust a burning brand through one of the windows. The whole building burst into flames, and was destroyed. After nearly six hundred years the Temple of Zerubbabel, which had been heir to the Temple of Solomon himself, the Temple which it had been Herod the Great's pride to reconstruct, had ceased to exist. The Jewish fast-day of 9th Ab laments the catastrophe. Josephus assures us that his hero Titus had wished to spare the building, and this is possible, since he was so devoted to the Jewish princess Berenice; but we cannot be sure. In any case, if he did want to save the Temple he was unsuccessful.

Although weakened by famine, the Jews still continued to put up a savage resistance, but the final capture of Jerusalem was only a question of time. First the Lower and then the Upper City were taken – and the last days of Jerusalem were even more harrowing than those that had gone before. When the nationalists still refused to surrender, Titus allowed his troops to massacre, loot and burn. The Temple treasurer and another priest saved their lives by handing over the most holy objects of Jewish cult, including the Menorah (seven-branch candlestick) itself. Finally, before the end of September, all resistance had been brought to an end. The siege had lasted for one hundred and thirty-nine days, and the secessionist state was no more: its coins are dated from the first year of its era to this fatal fifth year, and a sixth year there was not to be.

Josephus tells how the Jews were rounded up:

Since the soldiers were now growing weary of slaughter, though numerous survivors still came to light, Titus issued orders to kill only those who were found in arms and offered resistance, and to make prisoners of all the rest. The troops, in addition to those specified in their instructions, slew the old and feeble; while those in the prime of life and serviceable they drove together into the Temple and shut them up in the court of the women. Titus appointed one of his freedmen as their guard, and his friend Fronto to adjudicate upon the lot appropriate to each. Fronto put to death all the seditious and brigands, information being given by them against each other; he selected the tallest and most handsome of the youths and reserved them for the Triumph; of the rest, those over seventeen years of age he sent in chains to the works in Egypt, while multitudes were presented by Titus to the various provinces, to be destroyed in the theatres by the sword or by wild beasts; those under seventeen were sold. During the days spent by Fronto over this scrutiny, eleven thousand of the prisoners perished from starvation, partly owing to their jailers' hatred, who denied them food, partly through their own refusal of it when offered; moreover, for so vast a multitude even grain failed.

The total number of prisoners taken throughout the entire war amounted to ninety-seven thousand, and of those who perished during the siege, from first to last, to one million one hundred thousand. Of these the greater number were of Jewish blood, but not natives of the place; for, having assembled from every part of the country for the feast of unleavened bread, they found themselves suddenly enveloped in the war, with the result that this overcrowding produced first pestilence, and later the added and more rapid scourge of famine. That the city could contain so many is clear from the count taken under Cestius.[32]

Josephus' figures, like most statistics of ancient historians, are probably exaggerated. But the losses were appallingly high (Tacitus states that the total number of the besieged was 600,000[33] – perhaps the normal population of the city was about 120,000).

For Jerusalem, when war encompassed it, was packed with inhabitants. The victims thus outnumbered those of any previous visitation, human or divine. For when all who showed themselves had been either slain or made prisoners by the Romans, the victors instituted a search for those in the mines, and, tearing up the ground, slew all whom they met. Here too were found upwards of two thousand dead, of whom some had been destroyed by their own, and some by one another's hands, but the greater number by famine. So horrible was the stench from the bodies which met the intruders, that many instantly withdrew, but others penetrated further through avarice, trampling over heaps of corpses; for many precious objects were found in these passages, and lucre legalized every expedient. Many also of the Jewish tyrants' prisoners were brought up. For even at the last they did not abandon their cruelty.[34]

John of Gischala and Simon the son of Gioras were both captured. John came up from the mines half-starved and begged for mercy. He was kept in custody for the Triumph of Vespasian and Titus at Rome. Surprisingly enough, however, he was not sentenced to death, but was condemned to life imprisonment. Perhaps the reason why his life was spared was because he had given himself up so soon after the city had fallen; and the Romans hoped that others would do the same. It was not until later that Simon too emerged from a subterranean passage – thus enabling the Romans to locate the hiding-places of many other rebels who were lurking in these tunnels and cellars. He appeared wearing a purple mantle and white tunic, and demanded to see the local commander. He too was to figure in the Roman Triumph, but after it, unlike John, he was executed. This fate may have been owed to his more prolonged resistance, but the Romans also viewed Simon with particular disfavour because of his communistic aims. Later they took special pains to hunt out and execute all who claimed a connexion with the house of David – considering that every one of them was a potential rebel and Messiah. But the Jewish princes of Adiabene (Assyria), since their country lay within Parthian territory, were allowed to survive and taken to Rome as hostages.

While thirty thousand prisoners of war were being sold by auction, Titus held a victory review, and then retired for a holiday to Agrippa II's capital, Caesarea Philippi. There, in the presence of that Jewish king, 2500 of his captured co-religionists were slaughtered in gladiatorial games, in honour of the birthday of Titus' younger brother Domitian. At Berytus, on the birthday of their father Vespasian (17 November), there were further games at which even larger numbers were immolated. Meanwhile at Antioch, the Roman capital of Syria, when a fire spread through the city the blame fell on the Jews, and a pogrom was narrowly averted. At Zeugma on the Euphrates, envoys from King Vologases I of Parthia brought Titus a golden crown. Then he proceeded to Alexandria, and back to Rome to join his father, of whom he was now the heir and almost the colleague.

And so in June 71 Vespasian and Titus celebrated a Triumph over the Jews; and their Roman procession, with the sacred objects of the defeated people carried along in the parade, can be seen to this day on the reliefs of the Arch of Titus beside the Forum.[35] Another arch, bearing a grandiose inscription, was erected to Titus in the Circus Maximus,[36] but it was destroyed in the fourteenth or fifteenth century. On the imperial coinage, too, the victory was celebrated more extensively than any previous war the Romans had ever fought. The festive occasion came at the right moment – to distract the attention of the public from the shame of Rome's recent civil wars.

However, when these coins were issued, and when the Triumph was celebrated, the Jewish revolt was not yet over. At Masada, the Dead Sea fortress which Eleazar the son of Ananias had seized at the beginning of the revolt, a determined group continued to hold out for months and years, until AD 73. They were led by Eleazar the son of Jair, a descendant of Judas the Galilean who had resisted the initial creation of the province in AD 6.[37] But Roman armies descended upon the place, and there followed a long siege, which has been dramatically illuminated by recent excavations. These discoveries, described by Yigael Yadin in his book *Masada*, include not only the large camp of the besieging Roman general, Flavius Silva, and various constructions added to Herod's palace by the rebels, but also many pathetic personal remnants – skeletons, skulls, a young woman's plaited hair, fragments of fabrics and baskets, pots and pans and leather sandals. These are all that remained after the mass suicides of the defenders which brought the siege, and the First Jewish Revolt, to their inevitable, horrible end. After the fall of Masada, some hundreds of extremists fled to Egypt. The local Jews did their best to resist them; but Vespasian ordered the destruction of the Jewish Temple at Leontopolis, much to the anger and distress of anonymous Jewish writers.[38] There was also trouble in Cyrenaica. The former high priest Ishmael, the son of Phiabi, had evidently taken refuge there; and when the disturbances were put down he was executed.

Rome had now learnt the lesson that a procurator of knightly rank was not a sufficiently senior governor for Judaea. Consequently the new practice, initiated with the governorship of Vespasian, of appointing a senator was continued; though henceforward they were ex-praetors, not ex-consuls like himself. Moreover Vespasian, now that he was emperor, concluded – as Claudius had unfortunately failed to conclude before him – that the garrison of anti-Jewish soldiers from Caesarea Maritima and Sebaste (Samaria) was unsuitable, and he replaced them by a Roman legion. Caesarea Maritima was converted into a Roman settlement or colony; and eight hundred ex-soldiers were planted at Emmaus (Qalonia), a few miles from Jerusalem. Moreover, as rewards for the loyalty of the Hellenized urban middle classes in the revolt, Vespasian established new pagan communities at Neapolis (Nablus) in Samaria and Joppa (Jaffa) on the coast.

Damage to the land had been severe, partly owing to the scorched earth policy of the rebels themselves.[39] All soil in the province became public domain, which was available for purchase or lease. As for Jerusalem, it was a wreck of its former self. Half the buildings had been destroyed, and only a small part of the wall was still standing; a mere forty thousand inhabitants remained. The city had to wait until the nineteenth century to become the largest Jewish centre in the country once again. The Temple had gone, and resumption of its worship was forbidden. Furthermore, the high priesthood itself was abolished, and so was the Council: the historic role of these bodies as intermediaries between Rome and the Jews was no longer needed. And so the year AD 70 marked the end of the nation's life in Israel until its restoration in 1948. The Jews of Palestine did not lose all their privileges, but henceforward they possessed, in their own land, only the same degree of autonomy that their co-religionists possessed in the Dispersion.

These privileges of the Dispersion were not affected by the revolt; with the exception of one vitally important sanction which hit them and Jerusalem alike. This was a decree that the tax which had formerly been paid to the Temple by Jews in Judaea and everywhere else in the world should henceforward be diverted to the Roman exchequer, under the administration of a special board or treasury known as the *fiscus Iudaicus*. Jews could take some slight comfort from the fact that the mere existence of such a tax, wholly exceptional in the Roman empire by reason of its lack of any local or domiciliary basis, implied continued recognition of themselves as a separate unity. Yet such fiscal discrimination was highly ominous for the future. Worst of all, the tax was devoted to the upkeep of the Temple of Capitoline Jupiter at Rome. This deliberate diversion of the funds to a specifically pagan purpose, and the most offensive purpose, moreover, that could be found, seemed to strike a note of malicious vengeance for all the trouble the rebellious Jews had caused. Furthermore, the tax was a severer imposition than their old Temple tax because its liability was extended to women, and because age limits, upper and lower alike, were either abolished or tightened.

13

Jewish Survival: the Menace of the Gospels

After 70 the flame of Judaism was still kept burning in Judaea, but no longer in ruined Jerusalem. Its survival was mainly due to the efforts of an elderly merchant and judge, the Pharisee Johanan ben Zakkai. He had apparently gone over to Vespasian, in circumstances glorified by legend, before the end of the siege of Jerusalem; and then he obtained permission to proceed to Jamnia on the coast and establish a settlement of refugees, which became an immensely distinguished Jewish centre and school. At this juncture the Pharisees who taught in the Jamnia academy began to be known more widely as rabbis, a term (properly a vocative) meaning 'Lord' or 'master' or 'my superior' – not a priest with sacramental powers, but a searcher, interpreter, preserver and expounder of the Law. Responding to unprecedented challenges and tensions, the rabbis of Jamnia, the new Tannaim (teachers), made it possible for Jewry to continue its millennial task of self-perpetuation.

Johanan was one of those moderate Pharisees, disciples of Hillel, who believed in collaboration with the Romans. Like Josephus, he was credited with a prophecy that Vespasian would become the world-ruler.[1] He was said to have confided this view to a certain 'Antoninus' – probably Antonius Julianus, the Roman financial agent in Judaea, who may have written a treatise about the Jews.[2] Johanan had been filled with evil forebodings of disaster for many years,[3] and, like Hanina at an earlier stage, he regarded the attempted forcible secession from Rome as a wholly wrong step to have taken, not only because the results had proved so catastrophic but on grounds of religious principle as well: 'Israel threw off the yoke of Heaven and made for themselves a king of flesh and blood.'[4]

Even allowing for the excessively eulogistic tone which the rabbinic tradition accorded to its heroes, Johanan seems to have been firm, liberal, learned, determined and humble. To many, he knew, the bringing down of the Jewish centre to the plain seemed a profound humiliation. But in reply he quoted the Second Isaiah: 'rise up, captive Jerusalem, shake off the dust!'[5] True, eventual return to Jerusalem was an article of faith, prayed for daily,[6] and many hoped constantly for the reconstruction of the Temple and for the restoration of its worship. But Johanan, who saw that this was impracticable, sought to explain that sins could be as effectively atoned for by prayer as by Temple sacrifice[7] – and equally effective, as the prophet Hosea had declared, was lovingkindness, and its expression in acts of charity.[8]

This was also the spirit of the *Book (or Revelation) of Baruch*, which was completed in its final form at this time, though Baruch himself, the friend and secretary of Jeremiah, had lived six centuries earlier. This work (preserved in Syriac) was in part an answer to those who held that the recent disaster called the goodness of God into question.[9] Superficially disguising the Roman captors under the name of Babylonians and Chaldaeans, the writer preaches that, although the Jews are destined to triumph by God's will in the end, it is necessary in the meantime to remain obedient to the secular authorities and to refrain from nationalistic outbreaks. The New Jerusalem will come in the end; but it will not be like the old one, for the House of God is not the Temple but the universe.[10]

When Titus had tried to come to terms with the besieged rebels, they were already, according to Josephus, beginning to say the same.[11] And thereafter, in fact, the new centre at Jamnia made the Temple unnecessary for Jewish survival. To have stated this explicitly would have caused shock and horror. Yet Jamnia's succession to Jerusalem was accepted with general acquiescence – except, no doubt, among such Sadducees as survived, since the new order meant their eclipse. Having formerly controlled the Temple, they could scarcely exist without it: henceforward, by a sharp reversal of roles, they were looked back upon as fringe heretics, no better than Samaritans. The Pharisees were now in charge, and it was at Pharisaic Jamnia that the foundations of Judaism, as we know it today, was laid.

The recent disaster was regarded as a repetition of the fall of Israel and Judah in centuries gone by; for the Pharisees imposed the view that the entire history of Judaism was an uninterrupted series of persecutions and martyrdoms, imposed by God's will as a result of Jewish failures. Yet, as Johanan's most eminent pupil Joshua ben Hananiah declared, 'to mourn overmuch is impossible, because we do not lay on the community a hardship which the majority cannot endure'.[12] Normal life must continue. In the eyes of these moderate Pharisees who controlled Jamnia – though no doubt their view was not echoed everywhere – the time for resistance movements and Messianic uprisings, and hopes of an immediate day of judgment, had passed.

Jamnia, at first, did not possess a shred of political authority, and could do nothing to revive the measure of autonomy which the country had enjoyed before. Yet the informal Council established there by Johanan soon began to acquire certain unofficial powers. This Council was to become widely known as the Sanhedrin, and its president was described by the title of Rabban. It performed a variety of religious and even quasi-political duties, and was gradually recognized by the Romans as exercising control over the religious affairs of Judaea, and even of the Dispersion as well. The degree to which this rabbinic influence predominated among the Jews of the empire's Hellenized cities is still greatly disputed. But at any rate it was not at all long before they, as well as the Jewish communities of the Parthian empire, began to resume the dispatch of funds to Jerusalem. The former Temple tax, now that the Temple was no more, had to be paid to the pagan *fiscus Judaicus* at Rome. But in addition, voluntarily, they sent their contributions to Judaea, and these funds were particularly devoted, in these new times, to the defrayal of rabbinical schools sponsored by the synagogues.

After the political overthrow, the study of the Law in these schools and synagogues became ever keener and more intense. Johanan and his colleagues and disciples committed to writing a great deal of traditional material that had hitherto been communicated orally, expanding the rules of interpretation laid down by Hillel from seven to thirteen. The Mishnah itself was not completed for another hundred years, but the word, meaning 'the Repetition' or 'the Instruction', was already coming into use to describe the collections of material made by the individual scholars who were developing and elaborating the rabbinic lore, and establishing a fixed Canon and text of the ancient scriptures.

The material destruction of the revolt was to a large extent repaired – rather more quickly than might have been expected. But the devastations of the central area meant that henceforward Galilee, rather than the ancient core of Israel, was destined to become the centre of Jewish population, and it was there in particular that synagogues and schools began to multiply.

In high favour at Rome because of their loyalty during the revolt, Agrippa II and his sister Berenice received fresh accessions of territory.[13] The king's coinage, taking on a much more pronouncedly Roman tinge than it had possessed before the rebellion, displayed Vespasian and his two sons Titus and Domitian and depicted the figure of Victory to celebrate the defeat of Agrippa's own co-religionists.[14] When Titus went to Rome for his Triumph (71), Berenice went too as his mistress. But the liaison was ill-regarded in Roman official circles, and gave a pretext for so many subversive comments[15] that he sent her away in the following year. She visited Rome once again with Agrippa in 75. But neither then nor four years later, after Titus had become emperor, was she able to re-establish her former position by his side.

After the fall of Jerusalem Josephus settled in Rome. There, successfully rebutting charges of complicity in the revolt of the Cyrenaican Jews, he was rewarded for his change of side by Roman citizenship and a pension.[16] It was at Rome, between 75 and 79, that he completed his history of the *Jewish War*. The work had originally been written in Aramaic, for the Jews of the Parthian empire and the east:[17] and this is an adaptation, written in Greek, for the populations of the eastern provinces of the Roman empire. The purpose of the *Jewish War* is to indicate the magnitude and significance of the recent revolt, and to demonstrate to all readers the total impossibility that it could ever have succeeded. This, Josephus states, should be a consolation to the vanquished, and should also show clearly the hopelessness of attempting any similar uprising in the future.[18] Although the historian disclaims bias, he is sure that God has been, and is, on the Roman side.[19] Consequently the blame for the disaster is placed fairly and squarely on the nationalist, extremist factions among the Jews. Because of their actions, 'out of all the cities under Roman rule, it was the lot of ours to attain to the highest felicity and to fall into the lowest depths of calamity'.[20]

The first one and a half of the seven 'books' of the *Jewish War* are introductory, offering a sketch of Jewish history from the Maccabaean rising up to AD 66, and leaning heavily, for the Herodian period, on Herod's minister and historian Nicolaus of Damascus.[21] Then follows an account of the First Revolt itself, based largely on Josephus' own notes and memories, probably supplemented by the *Commentaries* of Vespasian and Titus. Josephus was also backed by the approval, patronage and assistance of Agrippa II, himself in Rome in 75: this was a delicate point, since at one time Josephus had been fighting against his generals. The result is a startling achievement. Because of Josephus' own personal participation in these events and his gift for portraying them in a highly dramatic fashion, he rises, despite himself, above his constant efforts to vindicate his conduct and justify his betrayal of the nationalist cause, and produces one of the greatest historical masterpieces of ancient times.

The Revolt exercised a decisive and fatal effect upon the already bad relations between the Jews and the circumcised Judaeo-Christians in Judaea. According to tradition, when hostilities started in 66 the entire Christian church of Jerusalem, led by its chief Simeon the son of Cleophas, Jesus' relation, proceeded upon a single, organized flight to the Gentile city of Pella in Transjordan, formerly known as Rabbah or Amman (now Fahl). This is probably too simple a picture, designed by subsequent Christians, first to make it clear to the Romans that their co-religionists had not sided with the Jews, and secondly to explain the later eclipse and disappearance of the Judaeo-Christian church.[22] As for the first point, the truth can no longer be discovered. But the Judaeo-Christians of Jerusalem stood much closer to the Zealots than to the high priests, who had recently executed their leader James the Just; and it may well be that many of these Judaeo-Christians had, in fact, sided with the rebels, so that their subsequent need to conceal what had happened was considerable. So it was with considerable fervour that later Christians denied any such association with the revolt, declaring, with hindsight, that the fall of Jerusalem (though they themselves may have been among its sufferers!) was the divine penalty paid by the Jews for their killing of Jesus.[23]

Nor, in any case, did the eclipse of the Judaeo-Christian church occur anything like so early as these traditions about the period of the Revolt might suggest. Its records are lost – since the Epistles and Gospels, the books of their Christian rivals, effectively superseded them. Yet it may be concluded, with some probability, that there was no single departure of Judaeo-Christians to Pella, but a gradual, unorganized exodus from Jerusalem and elsewhere to Transjordan: and probably also to Caesarea Maritima, which emerged before long as the strongest Christian church in the country. Simeon the son of Cleophas remained the leader of the Judaeo-Christian community, and it continued to exist until well on into the following century.

There remained the numerous Christian communities in other parts of the empire, the uncircumcised, Hellenized Christians to whom Paul had devoted his missionary activity. In his lifetime, it did not seem that his endeavours to make these Gentiles the nucleus of the church had been crowned by any marked success. But with the suppression of the Jews by the Romans, the whole scene had been transformed. Now was the time to establish the cult of Jesus as an independent entity, disowning discredited Judaism and the Judaeo-Christianity that was its appendage, and laying a claim to the support and sympathy of the Romans.

It was in order to meet these aims, during the two decades beginning from the eve or outbreak of conclusion of the revolt, that four different Christian communities of the Greek east produced the four Greek Gospels which ensured the ultimate triumph of Christianity.[24] They are works therefore which, even if they only enlighten us to a limited extent about what had happened during the lifetime of Jesus, bring us very much closer to the feelings and events of the years AD 66–90. The centres at which the Gospels were produced, despite numerous conjectures, remain unidentifiable. So do their four authors. In Jewish as in Greek and Latin literature, countless works of unknown authorship had borne the 'pseudepigraphic' names of more famous men of the past, and so it is here. The supposed authors of the Gospel are Matthew and John, 'apostles of Jesus', Mark, 'disciple and interpreter of Peter', and Luke, 'beloved physician' imprisoned with Paul.[25] But on chronological, geographic and cultural grounds alike, none of these attributions is generally accepted.

In their narratives of Jesus' life, the Gospels differ startlingly one from another (as well as from numerous additional 'Gospels' which do not appear in the New Testament because they were later declared spurious[26]). Such divergences are hardly surprising because, like so many earlier Jewish narratives, these works were not primarily designed to reconstruct history. They were intended to demonstrate, by the use of eulogistic and miraculous material, that Jesus was a supernatural figure, and to stimulate faith in that conviction.

The relation of the Gospels to Judaism is paradoxical. On the one hand these early Christians were convinced that the Jews had made the greatest mistake of all time in failing to recognize Jesus as the Messiah. Yet at the same time the Gospels, like the Pauline Epistles, insist, with a complex elaborateness which a non-Jew may find almost incredible, upon the huge list of Old Testament prophecies fulfilled by every detail of Jesus' life.[27] His biography, as was rightly said, had been written long before his birth. He is repeatedly identified as the new Elijah, or Jeremiah or some other of the prophets.[28] Moreover, although this is underestimated or ignored in many a church sermon, ninety per cent of his reported teaching was Jewish – taken from the Greek Septuagint, which in consequence fell out of favour with the Jews from now onwards. 'Loving one's enemy as oneself' was certainly a distinctive feature. Yet, for the rest, 'Do as you would be done by' had already been a precept of Hillel; 'love your neighbour as yourself' is close to *Leviticus*;[29] 'he that is poor and of a contrite spirit' (or 'a man down-trodden and distressed') is the man for whom one of the compilers of *Isaiah* declares that the Lord has special regard.[30] Much of this teaching and much, above all, of the Sermon on the Mount reputedly delivered by Jesus was shared with a slightly earlier Jewish work *The Two Ways*, later incorporated in a Christian work which may have emanated from Alexandria, the *Didache* or *Teaching of the Twelve Apostles*. Indeed, on occasion, the Gospels go to great lengths to demonstrate the Jewishness of Jesus. The Miracle of the Phoenician Woman provides a vivid and indeed brutal example. She is pagan, and when she implores him to heal her sick daughter, he replies: 'it is not fair to take the children's bread and throw it to the dogs'.[31] He relents later; but the message unmistakably conveys the superiority of the Jews.

And yet, despite this insistence on the Judaism of Jesus, all four Gospels are at the same time markedly, indeed violently, anti-Jewish. Since they were written at a time when feelings throughout the empire were inflamed against the Jews because of their recent revolt, the hostility allegedly shown to Jesus by Jewish groups – Pharisees, scribes and

Sadducees alike – is emphasized over and over again; the Herodians, too, are treated as enemies, because the current relations between Agrippa II and his sister Berenice were such a public scandal. But above all, although Jesus died a Roman and not a Jewish death, it is the Jews, rather than Pilate, who are insistently and repeatedly blamed for his trial and execution.

The Epistles of Paul, of which the earliest seems to have preceded the first Gospel by nearly two decades, had conveyed the same message. But when we come to the 'biographical' elements in Jesus' life, the resemblance between Gospels and Pauline Epistles totally disappears. The Epistles had shown an astonishing, total, ignorance of every single fact of Jesus' life before the Last Supper. The Gospels, on the other hand, working backwards from those last days but presenting their material in what purports to be chronological order, supply the deficiency with an ample wealth of sayings, miracles and incidents. Any idea that John the Baptist called himself the Messiah is unanimously minimized (although it is admitted that such thoughts had existed at the time[32]). For, in the eyes of the writers of the Gospels, it was Jesus who had been the Messiah.

Yet on the whole these works, other than *John*, are much less concerned to go into the details of his Messianic redemptive function than to present him as a Jewish preacher who worked miracles. For example, they leave it uncertain whether he should be regarded as having himself claimed or accepted the Messiahship, or the ambivalent title of Son of Man. This ambiguity about his Messianic role was partly due to an ever-present desire, on the part of the authors, not to discredit Jesus in the eyes of the Romans, who possessed a strong conviction that the numerous Jews who got hailed, or hailed themselves, as the Messiah were potentially subversive. Furthermore, in the story of the 'Tribute Penny', Jesus is specifically indicated to have counselled obedience to the Roman authorities:

A number of Pharisees and men of Herod's party were sent to trap him with a question. They came and said . . . 'Are we or are we not permitted to pay taxes to the Roman emperor? Shall we pay or not?' He saw how crafty their question was, and said, 'Why are you trying to catch me out? Fetch me a silver piece, and let me look at it.' They brought one, and he said to them, 'Whose head is this, and whose inscription?' 'Caesar's (the emperor's)' they replied. Then Jesus said, 'Pay Caesar what is due to Caesar, and pay God what is due to God.' And they heard him with astonishment.[33]

Whether such an incident ever occurred it is impossible to say – since the writer's desire to please the Romans is so manifest. In the tense days during and after the revolt, the Christians had to show that they were in no way seditious, and their best way to offer this demonstration was to prove that there had been nothing seditious about their founder. The story of the 'Tribute Penny' has been interpreted in the most varied and sometimes perverse fashions, and it has even been suggested that what Jesus really said was the exact opposite to what the Gospels claim. What in fact he said on the subject, if anything, is quite unknown and unknowable. But what the Gospels said more than a generation after his time, in the light of the Jewish revolt, is clear enough: they asserted that Jesus, unlike the rebellious Jews, had been loyal to the Romans.

The earliest Gospel is now generally agreed to be *Mark* – though it was somewhat ignored by the early church, because of its brevity. To *Mark*, Jesus is not virgin-born: when the Baptist baptized him, he was initiated as the Son of God, and from then onwards he behaved like an old-fashioned prophet, exhorting the people to await the kingdom of God. *Mark* is interested primarily in the mighty deeds of Jesus, and only secondarily in his teaching. Speculation concerning the sources, literary or oral, behind this or any other Gospel is unavailing. Traditions there were – none of the writers of the Gospels is likely to have invented all or most of his material on his own account. But how many years back they went it is impossible to determine.

Our first surviving testimony, then, to the life of Jesus is *Mark*, which thus, despite its obscure authorship and provenance, emerges before our eyes as one of the most striking and surprising literary works of all time. Some believe that this Gospel was written in the 60s AD, when the revolt was immediately imminent. However, its author ascribes to Jesus certain words which seem to refer to a slightly later date:

When you see 'the abomination of desolation'[34] usurping a place which is not his (let the reader understand), then those who are in Judaea must take to the hills . . . For those days will bring distress such has never been until now since the beginning of the world which God created – and will never be again. If the Lord had not cut short that time of troubles, no living thing could survive. However, for the sake of his own whom he has chosen, he has cut short the time.[35]

Though certainty is unattainable, and the possibility of later additions to an original text cannot be excluded, this apocalyptic utterance seems extremely likely to refer to the destruction of Jerusalem in AD 70: either after it had happened, or at the very earliest, in immediate anticipation of the event. It is not impossible, also, that the 'rending of the Temple's curtain' at the time of the crucifixion[36] is an allusion to the destruction of the shrine in 70.

Unlike later New Testament works written in less precarious times, *Mark* is careful not to suggest that Jesus himself had any intention of destroying the Temple – an act which (unless performed in the stress of war by the Roman army) would have constituted a grave breach of public order. The work also pays a striking compliment to the Romans by testifying that the first human being to discern the divinity of Jesus was not an apostle at all, but a Roman centurion.[37] Mark's attacks on the Jews, on the other hand, are numerous and savage, both in con- nexion with Jesus' career from its very outset, and in relation to his arrest and death.[38] The Judaeo-Christians, too, come under indirect attack. For that must be why the apostles, even apart from Judas' betrayal, are presented as spiritually insensitive, ambitious, greedy and cowardly (the later *Epistle of Barnabas* even calls them 'ruffians of the deepest dye'). And for the same reason Jesus is declared to have rejected blood-relationship: 'whoever does the will of God, he is my brother, my sister, my mother'.[39] This seems to be intended as a reflection on the Judaeo-Christian church, which was still led by a member of Jesus' own family.

Matthew and *Luke* were written after *Mark*, at some period during the last three decades of the first century AD, perhaps between 75 and 90. The writers of these two Gospels possessed access to several categories of material which *Mark* had not used. Out of *Mark*'s 661 verses, *Matthew* reproduces the substance of rather more than 600. Of the various guesses concerning the place of origin of this work, perhaps the sug- gestions envisaging Antioch and Alexandria are the most plausible. *Matthew* was preferred to *Mark* in ancient times because of the superior- ity of its style, and the wealth and beauty of its additional material. (This includes the crucial passage for the Primacy of Peter[40] – perhaps a reflection of rivalries in the early church – which was cited in support of Roman Catholic claims from the third century onwards.) *Matthew* is the most Jewish of all the Gospels, placing the greatest emphasis on the fulfilment of Old Testament prophecies in Jesus' career and death. The writer has a Jewish audience in mind. Fully endorsing the religious authority of the Law, he specifically presents Jesus as the new Moses. The twelve apostles are not only the heirs to the twelve patriarchs, but 'will sit as judges of the twelve tribes of Israel';[41] and the Resurrection after three days and nights was prefigured by Jonah's three days and nights in the sea-monster's belly.[42] Referring, unlike *Mark*, to the Virgin birth, *Matthew* cites a prophecy in *Isaiah*, though it is seemingly not very relevant.[43]

It is therefore strange, and apparently contradictory, that this is also the Gospel which lays exceptional and unique stress on the crime the Jews had committed in killing Jesus Christ. For according to Matthew: ' "What harm has he done?" Pilate asked; but they shouted all the louder, "Crucify him!" Pilate . . . . took water and washed his hands in full view of the people, saying, "My hands are clean of this man's blood; see to that yourselves." And with one voice the people cried, "His blood be on us, and on our children." '[44]

This passage, written to reassure the Greco-Roman world that the Christians could not possibly have played any part in the recent Jewish revolt, was fully in keeping with the assertion of the Jews, of which it is believed that *Matthew* was fully aware, that it was they who had executed Jesus, and that they had been right to do so: so far from showing backwardness in accepting their responsibility (at least until much later times), they saw Jesus as a blasphemer who thoroughly deserved his fate at their hands. Yet the words of the Gospel have had terrible, ineffaceable consequences for them throughout the centuries. At the time when *Matthew* was written, hostility between Jews and Christians was uninterruptedly rising – particularly in western Asia Minor, where men of both religions were numerous. The Rabbi Ishmael forbade his nephew Eliezer to be healed of a snake-bite in the name of Jesus.[45] And by the turn of the century, the synagogues no longer afforded Christians their protection.

Matthew strongly develops the Christian thesis that the destruction of the Temple in 70 was divine punishment upon the Jews for the crucifixion. 'You snakes, you vipers' brood, how can you escape being condemned to hell . . . O Jerusalem, Jerusalem, the city that murders the prophets and stones the messengers sent to her! . . . Look, Look! There is your temple, forsaken and laid waste by God!'[46] And when Jesus is arrested, and one of his companions cuts off the ear of the high priest's servant, the moral is pointed: 'All who take the sword die by the sword.'[47] Obedience to the Romans, that is to say, is the only possible course. But towards others, even allowing for oriental hyperbole, uncompromising hostility is the only possible course: 'You must not think that I have come to bring peace to the earth; I have not come to bring peace, but a sword. I have come to set a man against his father, a daughter against her mother, a son's wife against her mother-in-law; and a man will find his enemies under his own roof.'[48] This spurning of blood-relationships was an attack on the Judaeo-Christians, like the censure of *Mark* but more forcibly expressed; the text was later used by triumphant Christianity to justify the persecution of heretics. But the sword proclaimed by *Matthew* was, above all, destined for the Jews who had killed Jesus.

The split between the two faiths is almost complete; and its implications are deduced in *Matthew*'s Parable of the Last Judgment. According to this, the Son of Man, returning in his glory, will separate men into two groups, as a shepherd separates the sheep from the goats; and then the righteous will enter eternal life, whereas the evil, those who rejected his Messiahship, will 'go from his sight to the eternal fire that is ready for the devil and his angels'.[49] Here is a sharp and unrelenting division of mankind into black and white, a division which has encouraged churches and sects to be content with incomprehension and intolerance.

Whether *Luke* was written before or after *Matthew* is uncertain. Its language and material have been held to support both conclusions, but there are three indications which perhaps favour the later date. First, this Gospel does not reproduce as much of *Mark* as *Matthew* does. Secondly, its writer openly describes an apostle of Jesus named Simon as a Zealot: in other Gospels, this had been decently concealed by the citation of a Hebrew equivalent (in its Greek form Kananaios).[50] But now the passions aroused by the revolt of 66–70 had subsided sufficiently to allow the inflammable word Zealot to be used. Thirdly, *Luke* makes a more determined attempt than *Matthew*, and a much more determined attempt than *Mark*, to explain the unexpected delay in the coming of the Kingdom of God, which the early Christians had believed to be imminent. *Luke* admits the existence of this belief, but allegorizes and spiritualizes it by attributing to Jesus the assurance that 'the kingdom of God is (already) within, or among, you (or within your grasp)'.[51]

Luke seems rather too late to support the tradition that its writer was a companion of Paul. Reports that he was a doctor, too, are unverifiable. The assertion that he came from Antioch, however, is not impossible.[52] In any case, he was writing for Gentiles, and his Gospel is more Hellenistic in character than the others – and composed in better Greek. The skilful writing makes it understandable that Ernest Renan should have described *Luke* as the most beautiful book in the world. On the other hand its somewhat vague and impressionistic methods fail to justify Sir William Ramsay's further conclusion that its author was one of the finest of all ancient *historians*. For example, *Luke*'s account of the census at the time of Jesus' birth is impossible because, as Roman historians generally agree, Quirinius, the governor of Syria supposed to have conducted the operation, could not have been governor at the time.[53] Moreover, *Luke*'s entire story of the birth, infancy and genealogy of Jesus, and of his appearances after death, is so entirely different from *Matthew*'s that quite divergent traditions must be assumed to have been current – neither of them with a primary concern for historical fact.

The author of *Luke*, with his strongly Gentile preoccupations, stresses the universality of Jesus' work of salvation, and its penetration to all orders of society. In the Parable of the Wedding Feast, the master ordered his servant to 'go out onto the highways and along the hedgerows and make people come in';[54] and the text was later used by Augustine to justify forcible measures against Christian 'heretic' minorities. *Luke*'s account of Jesus' trial is a substantial transformation of both *Mark* and *Matthew*, depicting a contest between Pilate and the Jews, and specifying in damaging detail (though without regard for known Jewish procedures) the alleged nature of the Jewish onslaughts upon Jesus, which are placed in sharp contrast with Pilate's assertion 'I find no case for this man to answer.'[55]

The *Acts of the Apostles*, written at the same period and perhaps by the same man as *Luke*, carry the story forward – in the form, very often, of miracle and myth – from the Resurrection to the time when Paul arrived in Rome. Although the work gives no convincing indication of Paul's teaching as described in the *Epistles*, it represents the full retrospective glorification of his Hellenizing mission which, after enjoying only moderate success in his lifetime, had now come into the ascendancy owing to the eclipse of the Jews after their revolt.

And so the Judaeo-Christians – too reminiscent of this disgraced Jewry – are disowned by the writer of *Acts*, or rather their very existence is ignored, by denying that in the years following the crucifixion this leading element in the Christian movement played any appreciable part. True, at one point the *Acts* openly admit its role, and the rift which divided it from Paul's Hellenizers. Yet, only a page or two previously, we had been told that 'the whole body of believers was united in heart and soul'.[56] For it is desired to play down any such conflicts, in favour of the all-important aim of demonstrating that nothing could stop the spread of Christianity. It was destined to be universal, with Paul seen in retrospect as the great protagonist of its Dispersion: that is why one of the earliest wonders of the *Acts* is the festival of Pentecost (Shabuoth), in which a multitude of people from all the known countries of the world are heard miraculously making themselves comprehensible, for all their difference of tongues, about 'the great things God has done'.[57]

Grudging to the Judaeo-Christians, *Acts* is hostile to the Jews. Like the Gospels, it is very eager to show that the early Christians had never shared Jewish disloyalty towards Rome. Indeed, the book contains the implication that the Romans could be permitted under the providence of God to become the instruments for the furtherance of His aims in many of their dominions. We are also assured that it was never the Romans who persecuted the Christians, but only the Jews. Their stoning of Stephen is emphasized, and Paul's arrest is timed to illustrate the ferocity of the Jewish attack; for he was arrested at a time when he was being particularly punctilious about the Law. The Jews on the other hand, when Paul was arrested as on many other occasions, are seen trying their best to embroil their Christian rivals with the Roman authorities. Meanwhile, the Jewish responsibility for the crucifixion of Jesus is emphasized over and over again.[58]

Yet the *Acts* modify the anti-Jewish charges in detail, for they do not wish the Pharisees to be the special target of their attacks. This was partly because of Paul's Pharisee origins, but there was also the consideration that in these post-revolt days, when the Pharisees had come to dominate Judaism, too critical an attitude towards them would impede the likelihood of securing Christian converts from the Jewish ranks. So the Pharisee leader Gamaliel I is represented as not unsympathetic to the apostles, and at a Council meeting after Paul's arrest the Pharisees are shown to have defended him against attacks from the

Sadducees. It is the latter who are branded as the chief aggressors; and the tetrarch Antipas, too, is named as one of the enemies of Jesus,[59] perhaps (once again) because the Herodians were discredited in the time of *Luke* by the allegedly incestuous conduct of Agrippa II and Berenice.

John is entirely different both from the other three Gospels and from *Acts*. Its writer had probably read *Mark*, and perhaps *Matthew* and *Luke* as well. Yet his material exhibits enormous differences from theirs, and he presents it not, as they do, as a sort of miraculous biography, but rather as an intense religious drama. The date of *John* is quite impossible to determine. Formerly regarded as considerably later than the other Gospels, it now seems, to certain scholars, as early as any of them. But the criteria for dating are evasive. So is the identity of the author, his place of origin, and the character and date of the sources he employed. For his approach is perplexingly vague and cryptic. It is he, more than the other Gospel writers, who presents a number of close analogies to the disbanded sect of Qumran. His debt to Greco-Jewish thinkers such as Philo, notably in respect of his philosophical doctrine of 'the Word' (Logos), is less easy to demonstrate, though they draw, in different fashions, on a somewhat similar range of ideas.[60]

Jesus, according to *John*, was scarcely an incarnate mortal at all, but a pre-existent being, openly claimed to be celestial and divine. *John*'s account of Jesus' death, and particularly of his resurrection, differ fundamentally from those in the other Gospels. The Parable of Lazarus, the man who was raised from the dead after four days, may be a symbolical forecast of the final resurrection of the just. However, salvation should not be regarded as something that is only coming *in the future*, for Jesus is made to declare that 'anyone who gives heed to what I say and puts his trust in him that sent me . . . has hold of eternal life, and does not come up for judgement, but has *already* passed from death to life.'[61]

And yet, in spite of this strong mystic element, *John* seems acutely aware of the political aspect of Jesus' career. His account of the trial presents a variety of novel touches, which have been sometimes regarded as carrying greater historical conviction than the accounts in the other Gospels. While asserting that Jesus constantly claimed the Messiahship, *John* ascribes to him the sentiment, reassuring to the Roman authorities, that 'my kingdom does not belong to this world.

If it did, my followers would be fighting to save me from arrest by the Jews.'[62]

John goes further even than *Matthew* in exculpating Pilate for Jesus' death and blaming it on the Jews. The writer feels strongly that the time has come for a complete break. Interpreting the world, like so many contemporaries of many faiths, as the scene of a dualistic fight between good and evil, light and darkness, he envisages Jesus as telling the Jews that they are the sons of evil and darkness:

Your father is the devil and you choose to carry out your father's desires. He was a murderer from the beginning, and is not rooted in the truth; there is no truth in him. When he tells a lie, he is speaking his own language; for he is a liar and the father of lies. But I speak the truth, and therefore you do not believe me.[63]

Even allowing for the habitual overstatements of near eastern literatures, it would scarcely seem that the rift could be more complete. And yet a further masterpiece of the New Testament, the *Epistle to the Hebrews*, is still able to take a very different view. *Hebrews*, which seems to belong to the final years of the first century AD, was composed for unknown readers by an unknown man, probably an Alexandrian Jew; he was acquainted with the works of Philo, and his Greek is almost classical in style. This writer is very far from rejecting Judaism. Indeed, he concentrates on showing that Jesus had been a high priest in the Jewish tradition – in the tradition, particularly, of Melchizedek, the priest-king who had welcomed Abraham to Jerusalem.[64] The intention of *Hebrews* is that he should outrank the priesthood of Aaron, to whom the Qumran sect, for example, had shown such devotion. For the author of this work, providing a reasoned, elaborate argument in favour of the supersession and repudiation of the old Temple, is eager to show that all three Messianic aspects of Qumran doctrine, the prophetic, the Davidic, and the high-priestly, are united in Jesus; though he may be compared to Melchizedek, this is only to enable Jesus to be placed above him, and above all the other sacred figures of Jewish history and legend.

For his blood will cleanse our conscience from the deadness of our former ways and fit us for the service of the living God. And therefore he is the mediator of a new Covenant, or testament, under which, now that there has been a death to bring deliverance from sins committed under the former covenant, those whom God has called may receive the promise of the eternal inheritance . . . According to the Law, it might almost be said, everything is cleansed by blood, and without the shedding of blood there is no forgiveness . . . So now, my friends, the blood of Jesus makes us free to enter boldly into the sanctuary by the new, living way which he has opened for us through the curtain, the way of his flesh.[65]

Such were the most influential criticisms of the Jewish faith that were ever written; and it was they, in the end, which played the leading part in its replacement by another faith, within its midst.

Meanwhile, however, contemporary Jewish propaganda was also vigorous. For it was during these same years that Josephus, who was still at Rome, decided that the time had come to follow up his *Jewish War* by performing a second vitally important task of enlightenment, by his *Archaeologia*, known to us as the *Jewish Antiquities*. To the deadly onslaughts on Judaism from the Christians he does not specifically refer, unless passages relating to them have been suppressed in the course of time. But what concerns Josephus is another grave result of the revolt, and that is the obliteration of the traditional Roman sympathy, or even neutrality, towards the Jews as a whole. Certainly, the revolt had quickened interest in them as a people, but it had also quickened suspicion and dislike; even the light-hearted poet Martial, writing under the Flavian dynasty founded by Vespasian, delivers himself of a wide variety of sneers.[66] It is the purpose of the *Jewish Antiquities* to emphasize the glory of the Jews and of their history.

The work was not finished until Vespasian (69–79) and his son Titus (79–81) were both long since dead and Titus' brother Domitian (81–96) was on the throne. Domitian's reign was a precarious time for writers, many of whom preferred to stay silent. Josephus was fortunate to remain in favour. Nevertheless, writing no longer under imperial patronage, but for a private patron – the learned Alexandria-trained grammarian Marcus Mettius Epaphroditus – he devoted himself, during these years, not so much to praising the Romans as to intensifying his praise of the Jews. It was a sort of compensation for his betrayal of their cause during the revolt, a betrayal for which so many of them loathed and detested him. And so, in 93–4, he published this twenty-book history of the Jews, from the Creation right up to the time mmediately preceding the rebellion.

For the epochs before the Maccabaean wars, he used the Old

Testament – with one or two modifications of passages that might seem to imply denigration of the Hebrews, or oblique criticism of the Romans.[67] Then, for the period from the Maccabees onwards – dealt with at much greater length than in the earlier *Jewish War* – he once again drew upon the writings of Herod the Great's chief minister Nicolaus of Damascus. Since Herod's great-grandson Agrippa II had died shortly before the publication of the new work, Josephus felt freer than before to write critically, in certain respects, both about Agrippa II (whose alleged incest with Berenice receives a mention) and about Herod.[68] But there are also many other revisions of which the underlying purpose, if any, escapes us.

Thereafter Josephus had intended to write two further works: *The Essence of God* and *The Laws of the Jews*. But when they were already partly drafted, progress was sharply, and as it turned out permanently, interrupted by the publication of a *History of the Jewish War* by his old enemy Justus of Tiberias. This work, now lost, perhaps formed part of a *History of the Jews* from Moses to Agrippa II, which has likewise not survived. Justus, who had enjoyed the patronage of Berenice and was employed by Agrippa II as a secretary, severely censured Josephus' conduct in Galilee during the first year of the revolt (AD 66), and accused him of bellicose acts against the Romans and Agrippa.[69] Such a charge was perilous in the last years of the suspicious Domitian, and Josephus felt it imperative to refute the allegation. And so he replied in what was termed his *Life*, but is instead, throughout the course of seventy-two of its seventy-six sections, a re-description of the Galilean campaign of more than a quarter of a century earlier. In his attempts to contradict Justus, Josephus stressed the essentially pacific nature of the command that he had held, and his many impassioned pleas for peace and submission. He also made the most of Justus' own suspect behaviour in the revolt, which had made it necessary for him to flee to Agrippa in order to escape punishment from Vespasian. The publication of the *Life* may have accompanied a second edition of the *Jewish Antiquities*.[70]

Then finally, not long afterwards, Josephus wrote a vivid defence of Judaism against its enemies, attacking the ignorant or malicious mis-statements of anti-Jewish writers at many periods from the third century BC down to Apion, who had led the Alexandrian delegation to Rome under Caligula and had subsequently, if we can believe the delighted comments of Josephus, died a very disagreeable death.[71] The work's title, as we know it, is *Against Apion*. But it may originally have been called *Concerning the Antiquities of the Jews*, and was probably prompted not by the writings of these long-dead critics whom Josephus discreetly selects as the targets of his refutations, but by recent and current pagan reactions to his own *Jewish Antiquities*. If this is so, *Against Apion* is a sequel to the *Jewish Antiquities* just as the *Life* had been a sequel to the *Jewish War*. In this essay *Against Apion*, which is of great value as an extant example of Jewish apologias to the Greek world, Josephus firmly asserts the superiority of Jewish religion over paganism – and indeed the superiority of the entire Jewish tradition, for which he claims the advantage of more venerable antiquity:

We have given practical proof of our reverence for our own Scriptures. For, although such long ages have now passed, no one has ventured either to add, or to remove, or to alter a syllable; and it is an instinct with every Jew, from the day of his birth, to regard them as the decrees of God, to abide by them, and, if need be, cheerfully to die for them. Time and again ere now the sight has been witnessed of prisoners enduring tortures and death in every form in the theatre, rather than utter a single word against the laws and the allied documents. What Greek would endure as much for the same cause? Even to save the entire collection of his nation's writing from destruction he would not face the smallest personal injury.[72]

My first thought is one of intense astonishment at the current opinion that, in the study of primeval history, the Greeks alone deserve serious attention, that the truth should be sought from them, and that neither we nor any others in the world are to be trusted. In my view the very reverse of this is the case, if, that is to say, we are not to take idle prejudices as our guide, but to extract the truth from the facts themselves. For in the Greek world everything will be found to be modern and dating, so to speak, from yesterday or the day before: I refer to the foundation of their cities, the invention of the arts, and the compilation of a code of laws; but the most recent, or nearly the most recent, of all their attainments is care in historical composition.[73]

According to the biographer Suetonius, this same reign of Domitian witnessed troubles for the Jewish community at Rome. This arose in connexion with their assessments for the tax that Vespasian had levied on all Jews after the destruction of the Temple, in place of the Temple tax. 'I recall,' he says, 'being present in my youth when the person of a man ninety years old was examined before the financial agent and a very crowded court, to see whether he was circumcised.' Whatever the exact interpretation of this incident, it was obviously a manifestation of a new and tougher policy towards evaders of the tax. Moreover, in his preceding words Suetonius indicates a further aspect of this toughness: 'Besides other taxes, that on the Jews (under the *fiscus Iudaicus*) was levied with the utmost rigour, and those were prosecuted who without publicly acknowledging that faith yet lived as Jews, as well as those who concealed their origin and did not pay the tribute levied upon their people.'[74] What Domitian had done, evidently, was to tighten up the tax by making sure that Jewish proselytes did not evade it. Very probably they had not received any explicit exemption by Vespasian but his agent had been lax in enforcing their liability. And it may well be that Jews in Italy who happened to be Roman citizens, whether or not officially exempted by Vespasian, were likewise drawn into the net by Domitian.

Shortly afterwards, further blows fell on the Jews in Rome, as on many others during the reign of terror which had characterized Domitian's rule since AD 88–9, when leading Romans had been struck down for alleged attempts to revolt. According to the historian Dio Cassius, many people who had drifted into the practices of the Jews now found themselves condemned for 'godlessness' or 'atheism' (*atheotes*) (AD 95).[75] This may seem to us a strange charge to be brought against such a highly religious people as the Jews. Yet it was a charge which, in Roman eyes, could very well be brought against those who refused to sacrifice to the emperor: the Jewish practice of sacrificing *for* him, as Caligula had pointed out, was not the same thing. Dio Cassius specifies that it was not so much long-standing Jews as those who had 'drifted into their practices' who came under attack, so that the principal targets of the campaign were evidently proselytes and Judaizers or sympathizers with Judaism (*sebomenoi*). This, then, was a recrudescence of the measures which earlier Roman emperors had adopted against Jewish proselytism, and which Republican administrations had taken before that: with the probable difference that in the grimmer atmosphere of Domitian's last years more strenuous endeavours were made to track the offenders down.

His punitive action came sharply into the public eye because its victims included two of the most eminent personages in the empire. One was his cousin Flavius Clemens, consul in this very year, and the other was the wife of Clemens, Flavia Domitilla, who was Domitian's niece. They were the parents of his heirs, since about five years earlier he had appointed two of their children as his successors. It is likely that Clemens and Domitilla were Judaizers rather than full Jews.

Nevertheless, the connexion of such imperial figures with Judaism is an impressive sign of the influence that the religion was able, at certain times, to exert. However, Clemens was now executed, and Domitilla was sent into exile. One has the impression that their Jewish tendencies were the pretext rather than the real reason for their downfall. Domitian was pathologically nervous, eager to strike down potential rivals on all sides, and Clemens and Domitilla were particularly vulnerable owing to the position of their sons. Their religious peculiarity gave Domitian the excuse he needed, and opened up the terrifying prospect of an epoch in which Jews might be persecuted just for being Jews.

The Jews of Judaea likewise felt Domitian's heavy hand. In *c*. 80 the aged Johanan ben Zakkai had resigned the leadership of the Jewish centre at Jamnia, because he felt it better that the leader should be a descendant of Hillel – a hereditary chief whom the Roman authorities would respect. He was accordingly succeeded by the young Gamaliel II, grandson of the Gamaliel I who was the teacher of Paul and had supposedly interceded for the apostles.

Gamaliel II, less learned and tolerant than his predecessor, had his troubles, including deposition by his fellow-Jews in *c*. 90.[76] Yet he resumed office and continued in it for several decades, and it was probably in his day that the president of the Jamnia academy, who led the Jewish community, was first known as Nasi (prince, or spiritual leader). Many basic norms of religious scholarship were established, and Gamaliel II imposed a strict discipline upon the Jews.[77] As was appropriate, however, for one who retained his family's extensive lands, and bathed (so it was said) in a bath-house containing a statue of Aphrodite (Venus),[78] he adopted a flexible, diplomatic policy towards the Gentiles. A supporter of the classical, rhetorical form of education and of Greek learning, he kept a school in which five hundred boys studied the Torah and five hundred studied Greek.[79] And he apparently went to Syria on some mission which may have resulted in his obtaining fuller Roman recognition of his Jewish leadership.[80]

However Domitian had apparently continued, and probably intensified, Vespasian's policy of tracking down and liquidating those who claimed to be descended from David.[81] In about 95, Gamaliel II and three other Pharisee leaders found it necessary to make a hurried winter visit to Rome.[82] The reason for their visit is unknown, but it was presumably concerned with repercussions arising from the fall of Clemens and Domitilla. It may well be that Domitian, having moved against Jewish proselytes and Judaizers, was now planning repressive action against the Jewish community as a whole. But, if so, this persecution never materialized, for in 96 a former agent of the exiled Domitilla, Stephanus, faced with an accusation of misappropriating funds, took revenge on the fate of his mistress by stabbing Domitian in the groin. Stephanus himself lost his life: but the emperor, too, was dead.

Reports that Clemens and Domitilla had been Christians, and that it was the Christians rather than the Jews whom Domitian singled out for persecution,[83] do not appear to be well-founded. They are the reflections of a situation in which the Christians wanted to take the palm of martyrdom from the Jews, because relations between the two communities throughout the empire, already bad, were rapidly worsening. For example, in retaliation for the Christian attitude such as was displayed in the *Gospels* and *Acts*, Gamaliel II ordered the inclusion in the Eighteen Benedictions of the Jews, part of the synagogue liturgy, of an anathema directed against Judaeo-Christians: 'May the Nazarenes and the heretics be suddenly destroyed and removed from the Book of Life.'

This may also have been at the time when a mysterious Christian book, known as the *Revelation of St John the Divine*, was first published. Written (in Greek of poor quality), for the churches of western Asia Minor, it sets out to be an apocalyptic sequel to the biblical prophets. Yet it launches savage attacks on the Jews. This, for example, is the message which Jesus is alleged to have sent to his followers in Smyrna (Izmir): 'I know how hard-pressed you are, and poor; and yet you are rich; I know how you are slandered by those who claim to be Jews but are not – they are Satan's synagogue.'[84] However, Jews were not the only enemies of the Christians, because *Revelation* also identifies a martyr (named Antipas) at 'Satan's seat' at Pergamum, which was perhaps the altar of the imperial cult in that city.[85] But most striking of all are the signs that the particular Christian who wrote this work, presumably like many of his Christian and Jewish contemporaries, did not by any means share the desire for accommodation with the Romans. On the contrary Rome, not specified by name but only thinly disguised, is denounced with extreme and repeated savagery as

'Babylon the great, the mother of whores and of every obscenity on earth' – drunk with the blood of God's people and with the blood of those who had borne their testimony to Jesus.[86] However, this Babylonian or rather Roman enemy is going to be overwhelmed, in her turn, with every imaginable horror, with the sun turned black as a funeral pall and the moon all red as blood.[87] And one of the appeals launched by the writer of *Revelation* is this: 'release the four angels held bound at the river Euphrates!' For once again, as in days gone by, there are the highest hopes, undaunted by the disappointment of the Jews in the revolt, that this retribution will come from easterners: with a clear reference – as far as anything is clear in this enigmatic work – to the rulers of the Parthian empire.[88]

The Messiah who will come to preside over the holocaust, and deliver the world from the present domination of Satan, is a terrible and ferocious figure, bearing little relation to the Gospels' picture of an incarnate Jesus:

Then I saw heaven wide open, and there before me was a white horse; and its rider's name was Faithful and True, for he is just in judgment and just in war. His eyes flamed like fire, and on his head were many diadems. Written upon him was a name known to none but himself, and he was robed in a garment drenched in blood. He was called the Word of God, and the armies of heaven followed him on white horses, clothed in fine linen, clean and shining. From his mouth there went a sharp sword with which to smite the nations; for it is he who shall rule them with an iron rod, and tread the winepress of the wrath and retribution of God, the sovereign Lord.[89]

There were beginning to be many Christianities. Yet, above all else, Christianity itself was truly coming to be recognized, by the Roman authorities and others, not only as a separate entity from Jewry, but also – with brief intermissions such as the reign of Domitian – as the more dangerous enemy of the two: so that, in spite of Domitian, an alliance between Rome and Judaism against the Christians must have seemed, to men such as Gamaliel II, not inconceivable.

However, within Jewry as well as Christianity there were sharp differences of attitude. For example, Jewish writings of this time dwell on the forthcoming end of the world with the same gusto as *Revelation*. Now the new Pharisaic leadership initiated by Johanan ben Zakkai was opposed to this kind of apocalyptic longing – just as Jewish authorities had so often deprecated it in the past. Johanan was opposed to such speculations, first because they looked politically subversive, and secondly because (as *Revelation* showed) they aroused such a keen interest in Christians. So the rabbis encouraged the corrective view that, even though there would be a Wrath to come, its circumstances had not been revealed to man. The Zealots and Qumran sectaries and others who would have taken a different view had been obliterated. Yet even Johanan, in extreme old age and on his death-bed (*c.* 80–5), relented and confessed to a belief in the ultimate Messiah, whom he identified as the returning king Hezekiah of Judah, victor over the Assyrian Sennacherib eight centuries earlier.[90]

Moreover, on the fringes of the rabbinical movement there were composed, at about the same time or slightly later, two important works which concentrated profoundly and fiercely on the imminent end of all things, imbuing revived Messianic declarations with a new fervour derived from the recent overthrow of the revolt. The first of these compositions was the *Ezra Apocalypse* or *II Esdras*, which has not survived in its (probably Aramaic) original or (except for a few verses) in the Greek translation, but is extant in Latin and oriental versions. Apart from two chapters at the beginning and end, the book was apparently written in about the nineties AD; its author was a Jew who remains unidentifiable.[91] The theme is a revelation disclosed to Ezra, one of the greatest of those who had presided over the return of the Jews from Persian captivity five or six centuries earlier. The writer is deeply perplexed by the inexplicable recent triumph of Babylon, meaning Rome, over the Jerusalem that has been destroyed. However, Ezra is shown a vision of a many-limbed eagle, adapted from a beast described by *Daniel* but reinterpreted here (without saying so) to mean Rome. The eagle is destroyed by a lion, identified with the Messiah who, after hideous upheavals and a temporary earthly kingdom of four hundred years, will complete the elimination of the Gentiles, bringing deliverance, resurrection, and a heavenly, incorruptible Jerusalem.[92] The author of *II Esdras* is no anti-legalist, yet his attack on Rome, and probably on Domitian specifically, got his work disowned by the rabbis: though it circulated very widely in the Dispersion.

Shortly afterwards (perhaps in its final form not until the early second century AD) came a second such work, *The Syrian Apocalypse of Baruch* or *II Baruch*, a Syriac writing translated from Hebrew or Aramaic through a Greek intermediary. Baruch, the scribe of Jeremiah, in

whose name an earlier book (his *Revelation*) had appeared in the aftermath of the Revolt, is vouchsafed God's announcement of the fall of
Jerusalem; and once again the unaccountable prosperity of the unrighteous is explained. Once again there will be frightful calamities,
and a temporary earthly kingdom followed by the kingdom of heaven.
Baruch also sees a vision of a vine destroying a mountain and cedar
forest (the Gentiles); and he is told that the ultimate resurrection will
constitute a revival of the original physical form of the earth. *II Baruch*
possesses many similarities to *II Esdras*, but its tone is less gloomy, and
it looks like an attempt to correct the over-pessimism of the earlier
work.

14

Rebellions in the East

The hostile or discontented attitude of certain Jews was apparently causing the Roman authorities concern; and Domitian's successor Nerva, during his brief reign (96–8), decided to remove certain abuses relating to the Jewish tax (*fiscus Judaicus*). His measure was celebrated by the principal brass denomination (*sestertius*) of the Roman coinage, on which a palm-tree, symbol of Judaea and the Jews, is accompanied by the inscription FISCI IVDAICI CALVMNIA SVBLATA. This indicates 'the elimination of the wrongful accusations (or perversions of justice) concerning the *fiscus Judaicus*'.[1]

To be singled out for commemoration on these official coins, the reform must have been regarded by the Roman government as very important; but we cannot say what exactly the change comprised. Evidently the assessment of the tax had caused informers to proliferate, and their activities were now curbed. Possibly one of the abuses had consisted of blackmailing threats to bring men who had ceased to be Jews, or who were only Judaizers, to the notice of the tax assessors, and these were now to be protected from such threats – in other words, the *fiscus Judaicus* was in future limited to Jews self-confessed. If this is a correct interpretation, Nerva's measure was in keeping with a series of steps he reportedly took – as part of a general elimination of the reign of terror – to relieve the Jews from sanctions imposed by Domitian. For he was also said to have put an end to accusations for 'impiety' (such as

231

the atheism charges of recent years), and to have recalled persons unjustly banished.[2]

Nevertheless, animosity against the Jews was strong – and it had no doubt contributed to the abuses which Nerva felt called upon to remove. These feelings of hostility were never shown more startlingly than in the *Histories* which the greatest of all Roman historians, Tacitus, completed during the first decade of the reign of Trajan (AD 98–117). The work, as a whole, dealt first with the Civil Wars of 69, and then with the history of the Flavian dynasty of Vespasian, Titus and Domitian (though this subsequent portion is lost). The account of Titus' campaign of 70, leading up to the siege of Jerusalem, is prefaced by an extensive excursus about the Jews, which includes the following passage:

Whatever their origin, these observances are sanctioned by their antiquity. The other practices of the Jews are sinister and revolting, and have entrenched themselves by their very wickedness. Wretches of the most abandoned kind, who had no use for the religion of their fathers, took to contributing dues and free-will offerings to swell the Jewish exchequer; and other reasons for their increasing wealth may be found in their stubborn loyalty and ready benevolence towards brother Jews. But the rest of the world they confront with the hatred reserved for enemies. They will not feed or intermarry with Gentiles. Though a most lascivious people, the Jews avoid sexual intercourse with women of alien race. Among themselves nothing is barred. They have introduced the practice of circumcision to show that they are different from others.

Proselytes to Jewry adopt the same practices, and the very first lesson they learn is to despise the gods, shed all feelings of patriotism, and consider parents, children and brothers as readily expendable. However, the Jews see to it that their numbers increase. It is a deadly sin to kill an unwanted child, and they think that eternal life is granted to those who die in battle or execution – hence their eagerness to have children, and their contempt for death. Rather than cremate their dead, they prefer to bury them in imitation of the Egyptian fashion, and they have the same concern and beliefs about the world below. But their conception of heavenly things is quite different. The Egyptians worship a variety of animals and half-human, half-bestial forms, whereas the Jewish religion is a purely spiritual monotheism. They hold it to be impious to make idols of perishable materials in the likeness of man: for them, the Most High and Eternal cannot be portrayed by human hands and will never pass away.

For this reason they erect no images in their cities, still less in their temples. Their kings are not so flattered, the Roman emperors not so honoured. However, their priests used to perform their chants to the flute and drums, crowned with ivy, and a golden vine was discovered in the Temple; and this has led some to imagine that the god thus worshipped was Prince Liber [Bacchus, Dionysus], the conqueror of the East. But the two cults are diametrically opposed. Liber founded a festive and happy cult: the Jewish belief is paradoxical and degraded.[3]

The reign of Trajan, in which this strangely ill-informed account saw the light of day, was a time which brought trouble both to Christians and Jews. With regard to the Christians, at some time during the first three years of the second century AD we learn that Simeon the son of Cleophas, who for many years past had been head of the Judaeo-Christian church, was executed by the governor of Judaea, Tiberius Claudius Atticus Herodes. Simeon was stated by Hegesippus, a Christian author writing later in the century, to have been denounced by 'heretics', of unspecified beliefs, 'as a descendant of David and a Christian'.[4] Vespasian and Domitian had looked unfavourably upon Judaean Jews who claimed to belong to the house of David, and Simeon, as a relation of Jesus, was liable to persecution under this heading. But why this charge was now brought against him after his very long tenure of office we cannot tell; perhaps he or his flock had displayed some of the hostility to the Romans recently published in *Revelation*. The Judaeo-Christian church of the circumcised was not finally extinguished by the execution of its leader, and indeed Eusebius points out that it was still numerically far from insignificant.[5] Yet from about this time onwards it ceased to play any important role in events.

An eminent Gentile Christian was also executed under Trajan. This was Ignatius, bishop of Antioch, who was sent to Rome for execution and met his death in *c.* 110. Ignatius still shows little awareness of most of the material in the Gospels, which had not yet formed strong roots. But he deserves to be described as the first significant Christian churchman. He supported an efficient centralized system of bishops, as against the more democratic institution of committee-rule by elders or presbyters. He was also indefatigable in his attempts to stamp out the disunity that prevailed within Christian communities, and one of the features which, significantly, met with his disapproval was a move to give the church at Antioch a more Jewish character. The reason why Ignatius was executed is obscure. If, officially at least, it was merely for the 'name' of Christian, that is to say because he was a self-confessed member of this sect, this was a new and general threat – such as had begun to menace the Jews, too, under Domitian, but owing to his death had never materialized against them. Presumably it was the Christians, and the Christians only, who seemed so inexplicably and obstinately hostile to the institutions of the empire – without even the Jewish excuse of ancestral custom – that they deserved to forfeit all sympathy, and qualified for capital punishment.

It was also significant for the future to note how keenly Ignatius welcomed his fate. For he seems to have shared, with fervent intensity, the enthusiasm for martyrdom which the Christians had taken over from the Jews, and had adapted to their own concept of loyalty to Jesus. 'I am God's wheat,' Ignatius cried, 'ground fine by the lions' teeth to become purest bread for Christ!'[6] The Romans might well have found this enthusiasm ominous, since its widespread extension in the years to come gradually helped to transform the Christians, first into a far more intractable minority than the Jews, and finally into a majority which eclipsed and took over the Jewish claims to universalism.

Whatever the precise causes of the executions of Simeon and Ignatius, the deaths of these leaders, at the hands of the Roman authorities, introduced a new era. It was probably at this period, and in this atmosphere, that the *First Letter of Peter* was composed or completed by a Christian – not Peter, who had been dead for decades. *I Peter* was a general homily on the Christian faith addressed to the communities of Asia Minor from 'Babylon', which is Rome.[7] This little work, differing from *Revelation* which had been written for the same region, contains a strong plea for obedience to the authorities and a warning suggestion, heard perhaps for the first time, that it was now within the bounds of possibility for Christians to incur Roman punishment because they were Christians: a punishment which they should be prepared to suffer with joy.[8]

This attitude, and the related question in what circumstances the Christians should be penalized, greatly exercised the Roman man of letters Pliny the younger (Gaius Plinius Caecilius Secundus), when Trajan appointed him to the governorship of Bithynia-Pontus (*c.* 110–12), within the very area to which *I Peter* was addressed in the same period. Pliny knew the Christians as people 'who chanted verses alternately among themselves in honour of Christ as if to a god'. However, as he explained to the emperor at considerable length, he remained uncertain how to treat them. He was unaware of precedents, being ignorant, for example, of the recent case of Ignatius. But it was clear to him that there was at least a possibility, nowadays, of punishing Christians simply for the 'name' – because they admitted that they were adherents of the Christian faith. Indeed, Pliny, at the time when he wrote to the emperor, had already penalized certain Christians merely on this score, executing some of the most persistent offenders because he disapproved of such obstinacy, though he disliked the opportunity this gave to anonymous informers.[9]

It was this question of principle which he referred to Trajan. The emperor's brief reply was as follows:

These people must not be hunted out; if they are brought before you and the charge against them is proved, they must be punished, but in the case of anyone who denies that he is a Christian, and makes it clear that he is not by offering prayers to our gods, he is to be pardoned as a result of his repentance, however suspect his past conduct may be. But pamphlets circulated anonymously must play no part in any accusation. They create the worst sort of precedent and are quite out of keeping with the spirit of our age.[10]

This was a pungent memorial to Roman administrative principles. But it conceded that merely to be a Christian was an offence, and showed how the Christians were becoming, or had become, an automatically undesirable category such as the Jews had never been.

Trajan's need to secure internal order in the eastern provinces was all the greater because he had immense and far-reaching plans to enlarge the empire's oriental territories. In AD 106 he at last carried out the plan, conceived by Pompey a hundred and sixty-nine years earlier, of annexing Nabataean Arabia as a Roman province. This rounded off the southern reaches of the frontier extending from the Black Sea to the Red Sea; and, incidentally, it enclosed Judaea on all sides within a narrow strip of Roman territory.

But that was very far from the limit of Trajan's ambitions. For he also proposed to put an end to the half-century-long peace which Nero had established with the Parthians: it was his intention to take the final step, so frequently planned but abandoned by earlier Roman leaders, of annexing the entire Parthian empire, which was weakened at this time by the recent rise of the powerful new Kushan kingdom in eastern Iran. Roman rule would then be extended far into the east, after the manner of Alexander the Great. Before long, the Parthian king Osroes gave Trajan the excuse he needed, when he dethroned Rome's protégé from the Armenian throne (110). Four years later, Trajan invaded and annexed Armenia, and his armies moved on into upper Mesopotamia and Adiabene (Assyria), the country whose ruling dynasty had been converted to Judaism for a time during the previous century. All these regions were made parts of the Roman empire. Then, in 115, the emperor crossed the Tigris, marched southwards along its bank, and captured Ctesiphon, while another force moved down the Euphrates. The winter of 115–16 found Trajan on the Persian Gulf. During these unparalleled operations the many populous Jewish communities of Mesopotamia and Babylonia fell into his hands.

At this point, however, savage Jewish revolts broke out within a number of the older eastern provinces of the Roman empire. Although the Romans must often have feared that this might happen, such a massive series of uprisings of the Dispersion was a phenomenon without precedent. No tangible, rational motive could be found, and there was not the slightest hope of success. Theodor Mommsen's detection of 'religious exasperation which had been glowing in secret like a volcano' is the best diagnosis that can be achieved. And these high feelings were intensified, no doubt, by unfaded memories of the destruction of Jerusalem and Jewish national autonomy in AD 70.

Some hint of the emotions that had been seething can be gathered from the recent *II Esdras* and *II Baruch*: Messianic yearnings were in the air once again. Moreover, the excitement of the Jews, all over the eastern world, was greatly accentuated by Trajan's large-scale hostilities against the Parthians, whom so many of them cherished as their protectors. Oracles and prophecies on the subject were in circulation,[11] and one of the Messianic legends prevalent in these years prophesied that the Parthians would prepare the way for the Messiah by conquering Judaea once again, as they had in 40 BC. Indeed certain eminent rabbis such as Jose ben Kisma, while preaching obedience and non-resistance,[12] nevertheless expressed the hope that the Parthians, as providential agents of God, would defeat Rome as they had when Crassus fell in 53 BC: 'there is not one coffin in Palestine out of which a Median horse will not eat hay'.[13]

Unfortunately this critical emergency in the history of Romano-Jewish relations is most poorly documented, and there are many chronological problems.[14] But apparently the initial outbreak occurred in Cyrenaica, where the large and ancient Jewish community centred upon Cyrene and Berenice had already been in revolt only thirty years previously. The trouble started with the usual strife between Jews and Greeks. The leader of the Jewish cause was a certain Andrew or 'Lukuas',[15] the latter designation either being an additional name or an indication that he came from Lycia in southern Asia Minor. Cyrenaica, owing to its geographical situation, was virtually an island, and Andrew, sensing that his hands were largely freed by the detachment of Roman units to serve in the eastern campaigns, soon transformed his movement into a general attack on the Greek city governments and Roman provincial authorities alike. Relying on the great numerical strength of the local Jews, his aim, apparently, was nothing less than the extermination of the non-Jewish inhabitants of Cyrenaica and the creation of a new Jewish national state. Terrible barbarities, which lost nothing in the telling by anti-Jewish authors,[16] were committed by his followers; and the archaeological evidence confirms that buildings and roads were laid waste, and extensive regions round Cyrene and elsewhere in the province denuded of their cultivators and reduced to ruins.[17] In the end, the revolt was savagely stamped out.

But meanwhile the fighting had spread to Egypt. Greeks and Jews in Alexandria had recently been engaged in their usual violent dissensions, with the customary result that two rival embassies were sent to the emperor (c. 110). According to a strongly hostile report, Trajan had already been won over to the Jewish side, which was allegedly supported by his wife Plotina. At all events, he was obliged to listen to an Alexandrian Greek delegate, Hermaiscus, asserting not only that the Jews were 'impious' (because of their contempt for images) but that the Roman senate was full of them[18] (an inaccurate assertion, since it has only been possible to identify three Jewish senators of this period, all descended from Herod). Scarcely helped, presumably, by Hermaiscus' forceful advocacy – if it is at all accurately reported – the Greeks failed to carry their point. In Judaea itself there was delight, because the emperor allegedly gave permission to rebuild the Temple; and this may have been why the Jews celebrated a 'Day of Trajan' as a semi-holiday.[19]

But even if this authorization by Trajan was authentic, it remained abortive. And in Egypt, too, his relatively favourable attitude towards the Jews could not possibly survive the events of 115. Not only was much of the Egyptian garrison, like the garrison of Cyrenaica, away fighting in Mesopotamian campaigns, but the huge Jewish community in Egypt was augmented by Cyrenaican refugees – including 'king' Andrew Lukuas himself. And so hostilities on an unprecedented scale broke out between the Egyptian Greeks and Jews. In many of the rural districts Jewish armies, under Andrew and others, ranged the country at will. In Alexandria, too, they burnt down the Greek temple of Nemesis; and their own Great Synagogue was also destroyed. But finally, through the initiative of the prefect Marcus Rutilius Lupus, Greek control was to some extent re-established in the city. In an edict of 13 October 115, the prefect reported the suppression of the revolt and ordered the general surrender of all arms in Alexandria. However, the trouble in the area was not finally put down until Trajan sent one of his most important generals, Quintus Marcius Turbo, accompanied by substantial military and naval forces. With his navy he had to crush a further savage outbreak in Cyprus, where the Jews under their leader Artemion had destroyed the capital Salamis and annihilated its non-Jewish inhabitants. After Roman troops had restored order, Trajan took the exasperated, unprecedented step of decreeing that no Jew should ever set foot on the island again on pain of death.

Meanwhile in the vast, rapidly annexed areas of what is now Iraq, he had run into the gravest trouble. In 116 southern Mesopotamia rose in a general revolt; at the same time the Parthian forces rallied, and attacked the Roman base-lines in northern Mesopotamia and Adiabene and Armenia. Trajan suppressed the revolt, setting up a Parthian puppet-king at Ctesiphon.[20] But meanwhile the numerous Jews of the country were gravely disquieted by the prospect of passing from Parthian control into the hands of the Romans, and felt that Trajan's troubles presented them with an opportunity of rising against him. A dangerous Jewish revolt, therefore, was expected behind the lines of the precarious Roman advance down the Two Rivers, and certain outbreaks that now took place seemed an ominous prelude.

The numerous Babylonian Jews presented one danger-point, and another suspect area was Adiabene, where the monarch, mindful of the Jewish proselytes who had been among his predecessors, saw a revolt, assisted by the Jews, as his only hope of regaining his throne. Trajan consequently instructed his leading cavalry general Lusius Quietus, a Libyan 'Moor' who may have been a negro, to expel or exterminate as many as possible of the Mesopotamian and Adiabenian Jews.

Having taken these steps with considerable ruthlessness, Lusius Quietus was then appointed governor of Judaea (117). After all the disturbances of the Dispersion, it seemed to Trajan – who had himself commanded a legion in the First Revolt – that the more compact population of Jews in their homeland must inevitably become infected, especially after the influx of refugees from Cyrenaica and Egypt; and that before long they would erupt in sympathy with their rebellious co-religionists elsewhere. Indeed, it appears probable that a rising actually began, under two brothers named Julianus and a certain Pappus;[21] the Jewish tradition speaks of a 'War of Quietus'.[22] But it was only a minor affair, since, even if the Roman garrison in Judaea had been denuded to meet the needs of the eastern campaigns, Lusius Quietus took prompt and harsh repressive steps. The rebel leaders were captured at Laodicea in Syria; whether they were executed was uncertain.[23] But the Roman leader apparently went to the length of erecting the emperor's statue on the site of the destroyed Temple.[24]

The rebels, in their various countries, had failed to secure the support of the very numerous Jews of Asia Minor and Syria; and now, though minor disturbances dragged on for a number of years, the revolts were as good as immobilized. They had been virtually useless. True, the Jews could claim that they had harassed Trajan's extended lines of communications. Indeed, when Trajan died in 117 and was succeeded by Hadrian – who had been holding the Syrian command – the new emperor decided upon the total abandonment of Trajan's new conquests (except in Arabia), drawing right back to the Euphrates once again. But the credit for Hadrian's massive withdrawal could not, with any plausibility, be claimed by the Jews, since his decision was based on wider strategic considerations relating to the estimated capabilities of the imperial army. The only cause for satisfaction the Jews could extract from these events was Hadrian's removal of Lusius Quietus from Judaea – not, it is true, because of his anti-Jewish repressions, but because he had supported Trajan's policy of annexation. And when, in the following year, Lusius was one of a number of leading Romans executed for conspiracy, the Jews saw the hand of God at work once again.

Before the revolts of the Dispersion, the moderate Pharisaic, rabbinical leadership, noting the attitude of governors such as Pliny towards the Christians, may have hoped with increased confidence that the time had come for an alliance with the Romans against Christianity.

But, if so, the immense upheavals of 115–17 had destroyed their hopes. And indeed Roman sentiment, both before and after the revolts, was still far from ready for any such alignment. For however great the distaste that might be felt for the Christians, all the old Roman prejudices against the Jews still remained actively rampant. The satirist Juvenal, writing under Trajan and Hadrian, unites with other writers of the generations before and after him (Pliny the elder, Plutarch, Epictetus) in reviving the time-worn attacks against Jewish imageless monotheism, abstinence from pork, circumcision, Sabbath observation and mendicant fortune telling.

> Some, whose lot it was to have Sabbath-fearing fathers,
> Worship nothing but the clouds and the numen of the heavens,
> And think it as great a crime to eat pork, from which their parents
> Abstained, as human flesh. They get themselves circumcised,
> And look down on Roman law, preferring instead to learn
> And honour and fear the Jewish commandments, whatever
> Was handed down by Moses in that arcane tome of his –
> Never to show the way to any but fellow-believers
> (If they ask where to get some water, find out if they're foreskinless).
> But their fathers were the culprits: they made every seventh day
> Taboo for all life's business, dedicated to idleness. . . .
> A palsied Jewess,
> Parking her haybox outside, comes round soliciting alms
> In a breathy whisper. She knows, and can interpret,
> The Laws of Jerusalem: a high priestess-under-the-trees,
> A faithful mediator of heaven on earth. She too
> Fills her palm, but more sparingly: Jews will sell you
> Whatever dreams you like for a small copper.[25]

Tacitus, too, now proceeded to give further consideration to the Jews. In his *Histories*, written during the early years of Trajan, he had treated them to an elaborate but hostile and misleading account. Now, in his *Annals*, published either shortly before or shortly after the accession of Hadrian, a good deal is said about them once again. The *Annals* covered the period of imperial history immediately preceding the theme of the *Histories*, that is to say the years from the death of Augustus (AD 14) to (approximately) the death of Nero (AD 68). The full, balanced, pattern of the work is hard to reconstruct owing to the disappearance of a substantial middle portion, from late in the reign of Tiberius to the sixth year of Claudius; and the last two years of Nero are also lost. Unfortunately, these vanished sections include periods of vital importance to Romano-Jewish relations. But enough passages on this subject survive to indicate that Tacitus, writing at about the time of the great Trajanic rebellions of the Dispersion, was still much preoccupied with the Jewish question, and dealt with it on the basis of greater knowledge than he had displayed in the *Histories*. Indeed, he clearly regarded the relationship between Romans and Jews as one of the most significant threads in the history of Roman imperialism, a theme which concerned him very deeply. In consequence, notable incidents on this subject studded the work in a series of spaced set-pieces. Nero's persecution of the Christians was one of them, and they no doubt culminated in the First Revolt, which must have formed one of the climactic events of Tacitus' lost final book.

15

The Second Revolt and After

Before returning home from the east in 117, the new emperor Hadrian visited Egypt, where a recently appointed prefect Quintus Rammius Martialis was still encountering trouble. This time it had arisen, as the emperor learnt from a case now brought before him, because the Alexandrians had staged a farcical performance ridiculing the Jews and their Cyrenaican king Andrew.[1] The prefect arrested sixty Alexandrian Greeks and beheaded a number of slaves. But the incident is mainly remarkable because this is the last time we hear of major disturbances between the Greeks and Jews of Alexandria. Apparently the endless troubles of the past centuries were at last producing revulsion or exhaustion. For the constant losses of life and property had reduced the country to partial desolation. Over a period of several decades, Jewish names vanish altogether from lists of taxpayers in Egypt, and until the later days of the empire the ancient Jewish community played no further political part.

While Hadrian was in Egypt, he took steps for a large-scale reconstruction in Cyrenaica, which had likewise been ruined by its recent Jewish rebellion. Whether he also visited Judaea in 117 is uncertain. If he did, he found a country which the disturbances of the two previous years had not affected very seriously. Moreover, although the rabbinic sources tell us nothing about this, a number of areas, during the past two decades, had achieved a considerable economic recovery

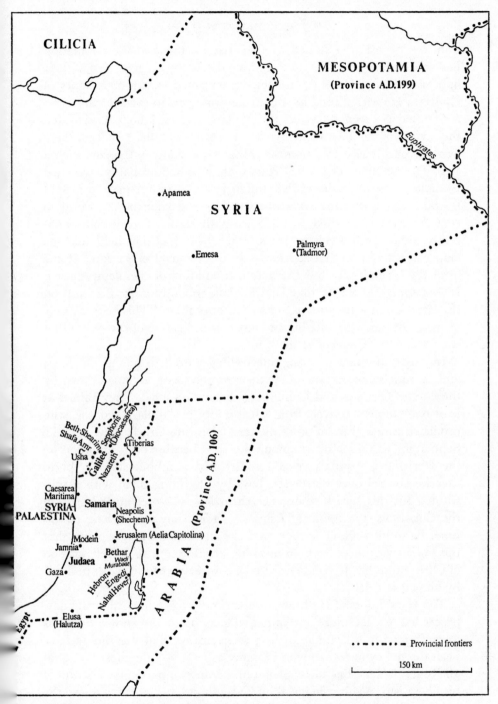

CILICIA

MESOPOTAMIA
(Province A.D.199)

Euphrates

•Apamea

SYRIA

•Emesa

Palmyra
•(Tadmor)

Beth-Shearim
Shafa Amr•
Usha

Sepphoris
(Diocaesarea)
•Tiberias
Galilee
Nazareth

(Province A.D. 106)

Caesarea
Maritima•

SYRIA-
PALAESTINA

Samaria

Neapolis
(Shechem)

Modein
Jamnia•

Jerusalem (Aelia Capitolina)

Judaea

Bethar
Wadi
Murabaat

Gaza•

Hebron•
Engedi
Nahal Hever

ARABIA

Egypt

Elusa
(Halutza)

•-•-•-•- Provincial frontiers

150 km

Syria-Palaestina and surrounding territories in the second and third
Centuries A.D.

from the devastation caused by the First Revolt; and the population had considerably risen. Encouraged, no doubt, by his execution of their oppressor Lusius Quietus, the Jews entertained rather high hopes of Hadrian. He was praised by an Alexandrian Jew in extravagant terms and hailed as a second Cyrus – the Persian monarch who had permitted the revival of the Temple nearly seven centuries earlier.[2] Indeed, there was a strong Jewish tradition that Hadrian actually authorized such a step. The eminent Joshua ben Hananiah, who had probably succeeded Gamaliel II as the leader of Palestinian Jewry at Jamnia, and professed tolerant views allowing righteous Gentiles a portion in the world to come,[3] was now granted an audience with Hadrian in person, apparently either at Antioch or Jerusalem, where tradition held that the emperor actually authorized not only the removal of Trajan's statue from the Temple site but the actual rebuilding of the Temple itself. It was added, however, that Hadrian subsequently broke his word on the latter point – because of Samaritan opposition.[4] This account may or may not be authentic, but at least it is indicative of the hopes that were lodged in Hadrian at the time.

In this atmosphere, a sanguine feeling prevailed among the Jews, and there is some evidence that their proselytizing, damped down by the fates of Clemens and Domitilla, was now resumed. They gained at least one eminent convert from Christianity in Aquila of Pontus, who produced a new translation of the scriptures into Greek. Now that the Septuagint was discredited among the Jews because of its adoption by the Christians, Aquila's version constituted a rabbinical attempt to exercise control over the Greek Jews by providing them with a substitute. But this Jewish resurgence earned a savage counterblast from the Christians, the *Epistle of Barnabas*, which may well belong to this time. Its unidentifiable author, perhaps an Alexandrian, explains that the Jewish scriptures have no meaning at all except as a prefiguration of Christ, and that Jewish beliefs to the contrary are total errors induced by an evil angel.

The Jews' hopes of Hadrian were curiously misguided, since he now proceeded to act more unsympathetically than any other emperor towards Jewish aspirations. It may seem strange that this should have been the policy of a man who in many aspects was the most liberal of all Roman rulers. But the explanation lay in two particular features of his liberalism. As his coinage abundantly shows, he had risen above the old Roman conception of the provinces as mere subject entities, with no particular individuality or pride of their own; instead, he formed an idealistic conception of all the various imperial regions as proud and worthy components of a great Roman commonwealth. But the corollary of this cosmopolitanism was that these territories should all collaborate wholeheartedly with the enlightened Roman authority which tactfully directed their progress. That is to say, any opting out, or separatism, was out of the question. Now to Hadrian, who was a most enthusiastic Hellenist, this also meant that every province should be fully integrated into the Greek culture which formed the common denominator of this happy Greco-Roman civilization throughout the eastern Mediterranean area. Such an interpretation, however, seemed to the Jews all too reminiscent of the Hellenizing keenness of Antiochus IV Epiphanes – whose temple, incidentally, Hadrian completed at Athens in AD 128.

It was evident that Palestinian Judaism was faced with a formidable problem. Its full gravity was sharply and disastrously illustrated by a measure which Hadrian now proceeded to take. This was nothing less than a total ban on circumcision. At first sight such a ban looks like a deliberate repressive measure against the Jewish religion, on a scale that had hitherto never been witnessed in the world of Rome. But Hadrian's ban must be seen in the light of Roman legal history. All bodily mutilation had long been forbidden by law, and legislation of Domitian and Nerva had specifically indicated castration, including the castration of slaves, as an offence. What Hadrian did (in addition to reinforcing the penalty on the castration of slaves) was to extend this veto to include circumcision.[5] For centuries past, the Greeks and Romans had looked on the practice as inexplicable and disgusting, and their writers were still commenting upon it unfavourably. In particular, its incompatibility with normal Greek ways had long been noted – for example it meant that Jews could not appear in the gymnasium, which was the focus of Hellenic life. Thus to Hadrian, as a Hellenist, circumcision was thoroughly unacceptable. For one thing its modification of the human body, seeing that man is the measure of all things, was offensive. But in particular, it accentuated just that very separateness which he regarded it as his bounden duty to overcome throughout the great cosmopolitan association of communities which comprised his vision of the empire.

It was for these reasons that Hadrian issued his ban on circumcision. But his action was not specifically directed against the Jews. There were others in the empire who had practised this custom, for example Phoenicians and Egyptians (probably at this time only their priests). Nevertheless the Jews were far the largest and most vociferous community affected by Hadrian's measure, and in striking at them in this way he could not fail to encounter serious opposition and disorder.[6] This did not, however, occur in the Dispersion, where the Jews were still too greatly shattered by the aftermath of their recent rebellions to revolt yet again. Instead, it was in Judaea itself, which had not been too seriously damaged by those rebellions, that trouble was destined to arise – the Second Jewish Revolt or, in Jewish eyes, the Second Roman War.

But certain further developments occurred first. As if the ban on circumcision had not been enough, Hadrian now took the unprecedented step of announcing the refoundation of Jerusalem as a Roman colony: a settlement of Roman citizens, of whom the majority were ex-soldiers. To add to the provocation, the city was to change its name and be called Aelia Capitolina. That is to say, it was to be named not only after Hadrian himself, who belonged to the family of the Aelii, but also after Capitoline Jupiter, to whom, in place of their own former Temple tax, the Jews had for the last sixty years been compelled to pay the tax of the *fiscus Judaicus*. A large amount of money was lavished upon the new Aelia Capitolina. Its east gate, known as the 'Ecce Homo' arch, still survives, and Hadrian's Temple of Zeus has recently been identified. Moreover, the town plan of the modern Jerusalem continues to reflect the main features of the Hadrianic city.

The foundation of Aelia Capitolina seems to be celebrated on an official coinage of Hadrian. As a manifestation of his concept of the Roman commonwealth, he issued a whole series of issues glorifying its provinces or principal regions by name, and illustrating them by designs which referred to their national characteristics and avoided any suggestion of their subordination to Rome. Among these mintages is a coin celebrating IVDAEA.[7] The design is an unusual one. Hadrian stands raising his right hand, while Judaea stands opposite him sacrificing at an altar; and there are also three children, of whom two carry sacrificial bowls. In this significant series the other personifications of geographical units are often flatteringly endowed with local, national attributes or costumes. Judaea, however, is not: the implication is that the less said about the Jewish character of the province the better, and that it must regard itself as fully integrated in the surrounding Greco-

Roman world. The sacrificial scene has been attributed, perhaps rightly, to the formalities accompanying the establishment of Aelia Capitolina, and the children stand for the luminous future prosperity of the province under this enlightened, internationally minded, new regime.

The Second Revolt broke out in 132, and the ancient authorities disagree whether the foundation of this blasphemous New Jerusalem was its cause or its result. Dio Cassius adopts the former view, and the Mishnah suggests the latter. But recent numismatic evidence shows that the first coins of the new colony (for such foundations minted local issues of their own) were already in circulation before 132.[8] So it must be concluded that the foundation took place before the Revolt, of which therefore, together with the ban on circumcision, it must rank as one of the prime causes.

Insufficiently versed, despite his wide learning, in the lessons of Jewish history, Hadrian evidently at first believed, like Antiochus Epiphanes before him, that the Jews of Judaea could without excessive difficulty be integrated into the general pagan world all round them. His intentions in this respect, which caused the Jewish hopes of him to be so sadly dashed, may have become apparent as early as 128, when a papyrus indicates that sporadic military operations had already been taking place.[9] Moreover, either shortly before or shortly after that date an additional legion was moved to the province: from now onwards its governors were men who had held not merely the Roman praetorship as hitherto, but the consulship as well. For the situation was now looking distinctly black. This was, of course, largely the result of Hadrian's two recent measures encroaching directly on the Jews' most cherished institutions. But it was also the culmination of a good many years of increasing unrest, not prompted by any particular or exceptional economic hardships, but dating back to the brief Judaean uprising in the last years of Trajan, and no doubt whipped up by apocalyptic and Messianic literature. Looking at the position from the Roman and Greek point of view, the traveller Pausanias naturally saw the matter in an unsympathetic light. 'In my own day,' he remarked, 'the emperor Hadrian has gone furthest to honour religion, and among all sovereigns has done most for the happiness of each of his subjects. He has never willingly gone to war. But when the Jews (who live beyond the Syrians) rebelled, he subdued them.'[10]

The Second Revolt was planned in secrecy, at a time when Hadrian was completing a great tour of the eastern provinces. During this period Jewish factory workmen engaged in making arms for the Romans deliberately started furnishing poor quality weapons, so that they would be rejected and thus made available for themselves. The emperor returned to Rome in AD 131, and it was in the following year that the rebellion broke out. Unlike the First Revolt, the Second was guided by an inspiring leader, Simeon bar Kosiba (son of Kosiba, or from a village Chezib or Chozeba). Jewish sources tell of his strength and ferocity,[11] whereas the Christian church historian Eusebius paints a more sinister picture of a Messianic leader – and a bloodthirsty bandit.[12] Simeon was also able to claim a connexion with the Maccabaean liberators of Israel, since one of his uncles, Eleazar, came from their home-town Modein.

Simeon bar Kosiba was fortunate enough to win the support of the leader of the Jewish community, the outstanding Pharisee and religious scholar of the age, Rabbi Akiba ben Joseph, successor to Joshua ben Hananiah as the country's principal Jewish leader. An ignorant shepherd by origin, Akiba had become phenomenally learned, and was one of the principal architects of the Mishnah, which was to assume its final shape at the end of the century. His exegesis, more rigorous and also more artistic than those of his predecessors, roamed over the entire spiritual domain, and 'made the whole Torah like a chain of rings'.[13] This great and influential teacher was no economic reformer, specifically accepting poverty as a desirable thing. Nevertheless, at the age of about ninety, he pronounced the opinion that Simeon bar Kosiba was the Messiah. 'When Rabbi Akiba beheld Bar Kosiba, he exclaimed, "This is the king Messiah!" . . . Rabbi Simon ben Yohai said: "Rabbi Akiba my teacher expounded the passage of the Torah 'There shall go forth a star (KWKB, Kochba) out of Jacob' as follows: There goes KWZB (Kosiba) out of Jacob."'[14] Akiba's quotation, which was from the oracle Balaam had pronounced to a legendary king of Moab,[15] caused Simeon bar Kosiba to be known as Simeon bar Kochba, Son of a Star – that is to say, the Messiah – and, according to Eusebius, to exploit the designation for all he was worth, declaring himself a luminary sent down from heaven.

Messianic ideas, recently revived by *II Esdras* and *II Baruch*, were still close to the surface at this time; and many Jews found them attractive. What particular motives, nationalistic or religious, prompted

Akiba to utter this pronouncement in his extreme old age cannot be reconstructed with any certainty. But it meant, in effect, that he intended to commit the Pharisaic Jewish leadership in Judaea to the highly uncharacteristic step of rebellion against the Romans. Akiba's influence was powerful among the Dispersion, and it was stated afterwards that he had travelled far and wide inside and outside the empire, including Parthia, to collect funds for the forthcoming Revolt. He knew Babylonia well, and perhaps hoped for assistance from the Jews of the Parthian empire. But it is difficult to believe that he really expected that help on a sufficient scale would ever become available for such a vast and hazardous enterprise. In the First Revolt the more sanguine spirits had no doubt nourished hopes of such a kind, and all that had emerged had been a measure of assistance which could not possibly make a serious imprint on events. And now once again, however hostile to Rome the Mesopotamian Jews may have felt after Trajan's repressive measures, and however much, for a time, the Parthian throne (now occupied by Vologases II) was weakened by his invasions,[16] the chances of any decisive Parthian intervention in Judaea were negligible. For although Dio Cassius, voicing fears that no doubt existed in Trajan's time, vaguely suggests that 'many outside nations were joining through eagerness for gain', as things turned out this support, such as it was, produced few or no concrete results: the contributions of the Jews in Parthia, and their co-religionists of the Dispersion in the Roman empire, proved to exercise an insignificant effect on the outcome.

Nor do we need the benefit of hindsight to make this assertion, for, except to the most unrealistic optimists, it must have been clear at the time that this would be so. However, Akiba may have been, or become, an optimist of just such a kind. Although his visit to Rome over thirty years earlier – when he was one of the companions of Gamaliel II – must have given him an opportunity to form some impression of Roman power, he was now a nonagenarian, and that is a time of life when political judgment is scarcely likely to be acute. It is a curious coincidence (if both traditions are true) that Rabbi Johanan ben Zakkai, too, had voiced a similar political miscalculation when he, likewise, was very old.

It was also said of Akiba that he showed a policy of studied liberalism to the Idumaean and Egyptian descendants of proselytes, since he saw the fatal effects that divisions would exercise upon the forthcoming revolt. That is possible, but his liberalism may have been a policy unrelated to future hostilities against Rome. What is clear, however, is that Akiba did not succeed in engaging the whole Pharisaic movement in the revolt, since when he hailed Simeon bar Kosiba as the Messiah another rabbi, Johanan ben Tortha (Toreta), offered the comment: 'Akiba, grass will grow in your jawbones, and he [the Messiah] will still not have come!'[17] Moreover a further eminent Pharisee, whose name is only preserved in the Greek pseudonym Tryphon, fled to Greece before the revolt was decided.[18] It is stated by some writers today that the Pharisees' response to the rebellion would have been keener if Jamnia, their headquarters, had not been in an area which remained throughout the ensuing events under Roman control. But the fact was, as always, that many moderate Pharisees preferred a measure of collaboration with the Romans to the likelihood of total annihilation of themselves and all they stood for and held dear.

Nevertheless the rebels possessed a much better organization, and a more powerful central authority, than their predecessors of the First Revolt. At the very outset they seem to have taken Jerusalem. The consular governor Tineius Rufus – hated for his suppression of the Parthian Jews in the Revolt of the Dispersion, and for the foundation of Aelia Capitolina – was forced to evacuate the poorly fortified city. Once in occupation of it, the Jews hastily started erecting rudimentary new defences. At the same time, perhaps at the Feast of Tabernacles (Succoth), they started issuing their own coins, which proclaimed the establishment of an independent, secessionist government. The coins name 'Simeon', that is to say Simeon bar Kosiba, as *Nasi*, President or Prince. This was a title which had been applied to the head of the community at Jamnia, but was now employed in a novel political sense, to denote the military and civil leader of the new Israel. The coins also display the name of 'Eleazar the priest', who was probably Simeon bar Kosiba's eminent uncle, Rabbi Eleazar of Modein.[19] Whether the revival of the high priesthood itself in favour of Eleazar was ever mooted is unknown, but sacrifices on the site of the Temple were surely resumed under his direction.

The designs on the coinage of this Second Revolt likewise show that its main aspiration was the re-institution of Temple worship, and no doubt the eventual rebuilding of the Temple itself. For its façade, containing the shrine of the Torah, is displayed prominently on the coins, together with a wide variety of other types relating to the Temple cult. The palm tree, which Roman emperors had already displayed to indicate the Judaean province, is now revived to denote the rebirth of independent Israel. Simeon's Messianic mission is left in no doubt by the inscription borne by certain of these coins; 'Year One of the Redemption of Israel', and subsequently the façade of the building is shown to be surmounted by a star, indicating Balaam's Messianic 'star of Jacob', with which Simeon bar Kosiba was identified.[20] Simeon's letters to his subordinates, which are among recent sensational finds in caves near the Dead Sea, refer once again to the era of national deliverance indicated on the coinage, an era which dated from AD 132 or 133.

The coins were habitually overstruck on Roman pieces; not only was this a convenient saving of metal, but it served the additional purpose of effacing impious images of human beings and animals, of which the depiction was forbidden by the Torah. For the same reason ornamental jugs found in excavations of sites occupied by Simeon bar Kosiba's supporters have the human faces carefully obliterated. Though his official correspondence oscillates between Mishnaic Hebrew, Hebraized Aramaic and Greek (with perhaps an increasing insistence on the first, as time went on) he took great care to observe religious customs and rituals in all their minutiae; his dispatches to his subordinates, for example, refer to sabbatical rest, religious tithing and the celebration of Feasts. Moreover, his followers called themselves 'Brothers', which suggests that they belonged to some form of religious order – possibly descended from the belligerent sect of Qumran, or from a surviving branch of the Essenes which, as in the First Revolt, may have abandoned its pacific tenets in the crisis. This 'League of Brothers' was apparently the backbone of Simeon's army.

Moreover, although numerous Gentiles were said to have rallied to his ranks, he refused to allow anyone who was uncircumcised to enter Jerusalem. With those who, after Hadrian's veto on circumcision, had formed the habit of taking ritual baths instead,[21] he had no sympathy whatever, and those who had concealed their circumcision by an operation (epispasm) were forced to repeat the process. Towards Christians, too, whether of the Judaeo-Christian or the Hellenizing variety, he showed ferocious hostility, which they heartily reciprocated, since the Messianic character of his movement naturally seemed to them deplorable.

The course of the revolt, briefly described by Dio Cassius, remains extremely obscure. The rebels, he says, did not dare try conclusions with the Romans in the open field, but they occupied the advantageous positions in the country and strengthened them with mines and walls, in order that they might have places of refuge whenever they should be hard pressed, and might meet together unobserved underground; and they pierced these subterranean passages from above at intervals to let in air and light.[22]

This system of interconnected fortifications, perhaps secretly prepared before the outbreak under the guise of agricultural works, does not look like a strategy calculated to win decisive victories over the Romans, especially as it was unsupported by any rebel attempts to invade Syria or other neighbouring countries. When the ultimate prognosis was so bleak, only fanatical Messianic belief can have kept enthusiasm alive.

Nevertheless, the rebels enjoyed considerable initial successes in inland and upland Judaea, of which they gained complete control. Practically all the recorded battles were in this central Judaean area. But Simeon bar Kosiba also held parts of Samaria; and although, probably, some of its population preferred to take the side of the Romans against the Jews, the Samaritans were able to assert afterwards that Hadrian had burnt their sacred writings. The rebels also made forays into Galilee. But on the whole that country failed to live up to its turbulent reputation, and the northern areas in general held aloof from the insurrectionary cause. This failure, however, was rationalized by supporters of the rebellion, supposedly under the guidance of the aged Akiba himself, who was said to have preached that salvation would come from the two tribes whose borders met beside Jerusalem, Judah and Benjamin – while the other tribes, he declared, had incurred God's disapproval.[23]

Before long, Roman counter-measures started to prove predictably effective. The governor Tineius Rufus, who had been forced to evacuate the central hill-country, regrouped his forces in a ring round the periphery of the area, and the region of the revolt was gradually encircled by an entire new system of Roman roads, with check-points everywhere. Moreover, eight legions with auxiliaries had been set in motion from many parts of the empire, and were now beginning to arrive in Judaea. To command them, Hadrian sent one of his ablest generals, Sextus Julius Severus (133), who had been governor of Britain. From his experience there, he had learnt that frontal attacks on insurgents were costly and useless. On arrival in Judaea, therefore, he adopted a policy of slow and systematic attrition by superior numbers, without risking too many of his own men.

Severus, reported Dio Cassius, 'did not venture to attack his opponents in the open at any one point, in view of their numbers and their desperation, but by intercepting small groups ... and by depriving them of food and shutting them up, he was able, rather slowly to be sure, but with comparatively little danger, to crush, exhaust and exterminate them'.

The test of a Messiah was success, and by this test Simeon bar Kosiba was failing – as many of the rabbis who lacked enthusiasm for his cause no doubt hastened to point out. A weakening of his personal position is apparent on his coinage. For whereas some issues of the second year of the revolt display the Messianic star, others without date, but apparently later in point of time, merely display an ambiguous wavy line instead. Moreover, the coins of the second year stop calling him 'President or Prince' altogether; and the inscription 'Year One of the Redemption of Israel' is replaced by 'Year Two of the Freedom of Israel', probably because it seemed desirable that the Messianic connotation of the earlier formula should be abandoned. During these internal political developments among the rebels, the pressure exercised by the Roman armies became more and more severe, and Jerusalem seems to have fallen to them in spring or summer 134. It was perhaps after this disaster, in Year Three, that a new inscription appears on the Jewish coins: 'For the Freedom of Jerusalem.'[24]

Yet the process of wearing the nationalists down remained damaging and costly. One Roman unit, perhaps a whole legion, was got rid of by a party of Pharisees, who arranged for the soldiers to be given poisoned wine.[25] There were also heavy Roman losses in battles and skirmishes; for this reason, says Dio Cassius, Hadrian in writing to the senate refrained from employing the opening phrase commonly affected by the emperors, 'If you and your children are in health, it is well; I and the legions are in health.'[26] The existence of such a dispatch suggests the presence of the emperor in person, and there is reason to suppose that he paid a visit, perhaps two visits, to Judaea shortly before his return to Rome in May 134. During his sojourn in the country, he was said to have ordered his engineer and architect Apollodorus to design a new kind of catapult for use against concentrations of men on hill-tops.

253

The emperor is also likely to have been present at the capture of Jerusalem.

In addition to his coinage commemorating the regions of his empire by their names, Hadrian, the most famous imperial traveller of all time, issued a further large series celebrating his personal visits (*adventus*) to individual territories. On each of these issues appears the standing figure of the emperor, raising the kneeling personification of the province. As in the earlier provincial series, Judaea is once again one of these personified figures; once again there are sacrificial objects (victim and cup); and once again there are children – they carry the palm-branch of the country, but otherwise national attributes are still avoided.[27] Of the war there is no mention; for the time had now come to revert to projects of reconstruction, and to Hadrian's internationalist plans for the future. Judaea does not, it is true, figure in a third great series of issues celebrating the emperor as 'Restorer' of numerous provinces; for that the situation was not yet ripe. But Hadrian could return to Rome with justified confidence that the revolt was nearly over.

The letters of Simeon's adherents in this declining period, found in caves not far from the Dead Sea – hiding-places where the Jewish leaders from Engedi, and some of its inhabitants, took refuge – tell a fragmentary but unmistakable tale of the Gentiles closing in, of rebel mobilization orders disregarded, of culpable inactivity at the still surviving rebel base at Engedi, of the requisition of wheat; there is also talk of some obscure problem relating to the Galileans.[28] Scores of skeletons and skulls bear witness to the inevitable suppression of the hide-outs. Not only in the Dead Sea caves, but in many other parts of the country also, the shattered resistance groups went underground, and hid themselves with their wives and children in deep caves and crevices, where they lived lives of horror:

It happened to one group who took refuge in a cave. One of them was told: go and fetch a corpse of one of those killed that we may eat. He went forth and found the body of his father and hid it and marked it, and buried it, then returned and said: I did not find any corpse. They said: let another go forth. One of them went out, and followed the stench of that corpse and brought it back. They ate it and the teeth of the son became blunt. He asked: whence did you bring that corpse, and was answered: from such and such corner. He asked further: what mark was on it? and was answered: such and such mark. He said: Woe to this child! He ate the flesh of his father.[29]

The end was now at hand. As his situation became desperate, Simeon bar Kosiba himself and his surviving supporters took refuge in a fortress seven miles south-east of Jerusalem named Bethar (now Bittir), two thousand feet above sea-level. There the failing cause was marred by the death of Simeon's uncle, Rabbi Eleazar of Modein. His name had long since disappeared from the coinage of the rebellion, and it must be supposed that, owing to disagreements, his priesthood had ceased to play an active part. Now his nephew, suspecting him of secret communications with the Romans, kicked him to death.[30] The miseries of the siege of Bethar are vividly preserved in the Jewish tradition. After two years the fortress fell, and the Jews blamed Samaritan treachery for its fall. When the Romans broke in, there was a general slaughter. And among those who died was Simeon bar Kosiba.

It was August AD 135 – the very day, it was said, on which the Temple had been destroyed sixty-five years earlier. The Second Revolt had inevitably gone the same way as the first. Moreover, the results in terms of human suffering were equally appalling. When Dio Cassius seeks to assess the dimensions of the disaster, he may, in terms of statistics, be exaggerating; but not too much:

Fifty of the Jews' most important outposts and nine hundred and eighty five of their most famous villages were razed to the ground. Five hundred and eighty thousand men were slain in the various raids and battles, and the number of those that perished by famine, disease and fire was past finding out . . . Many wolves and hyenas rushed howling into their cities.[31]

The prisoners of war were sold in thousands at Hebron and Gaza, where 'Hadrian's market' was spoken of for centuries[32] – a Jewish slave cost about as much as a horse. Many prisoners were transported to Egypt and died of starvation or shipwreck on the way.

Although Hadrian's coins had so recently honoured 'Judaea', the Romans now decided to eliminate this hazardous name altogether. They renamed the province 'Syria-Palaestina', thus reviving a name, not specifically associated with the Jews or their nationalism, which went back to the Philistines who had been in the land before Saul and David; in more recent times, the country had already been called Palestine informally by Josephus and others.[33] The successive governors were still to be of consular rank, and henceforward they were to have under their orders not one legion but two – one in Judaea itself as hitherto and a newly imported one in Galilee, each with its appropriate auxiliaries. As this increase in the provincial garrison clearly indicated, even the most tenuous assumption that the people of the province could henceforward be regarded as allies against the Parthians was abandoned.

The construction of Aelia Capitolina went ahead: and the old Jerusalem was finally destroyed. Furthermore, there was a far-reaching new development, of a penal and precautionary nature. Henceforward no Jew was allowed to set foot in the place, or its neighbourhood – 'not even from a distance might Jews have a view of their ancestral soil'.[34] Somewhat later, however, they were given permission to enter the city on one day a year, a Day of Mourning.[35] According to Jewish tradition, the ban was extended to the whole of the Judaean hinterland,[36] the region which had been the place of origin and main theatre of the rising. This may not formally have been the case. Nevertheless, archaeology confirms that the Jewish settlements in upland Judaea virtually disappeared – and such resettlements as can be traced belong to a considerably later time.[37]

The centre of Jewish habitation moved to the north and east of the country, and especially to Galilee, which had suffered little destruction, and was still populated to an overwhelming extent by Jews. The centre of Hebrew religious scholarship, too, was moved from Jamnia to various successive Galilean villages and towns – Usha (north-east of Mount Carmel), Shafa Amr, Beth-Shearim and then Sepphoris. Rabbis abounded in this region, and most of its towns enjoy fame from their rabbinical residents or martyrs. Galilean synagogues soon began to proliferate, though the earliest identifiable remains belong to a slightly later period. However, in Galilee as in other parts of the province, Hadrian took steps to ensure that Judaism, even of this more liberal type, should no longer hold the field alone. For the coinage of Tiberias, which had hitherto avoided giving direct offence to Jews, now displays a temple with a figure of Zeus, perhaps the Hadrianeum which was built in that city. Moreover, under Hadrian's successor Antoninus Pius (138–61), Sepphoris, renamed Diocaesarea, depicts a Temple of Zeus, Hera and Athena (the Capitoline Triad); and in Samaria, whose equivocal attitude in the revolt might have deserved a better response, a coin of Antoninus Pius at Neapolis (Shechem) shows a Temple of Zeus on Mount Gerizim itself.[38] It seems likely that Hadrian and Antoninus disfranchised the Jewish aristocracies which had previously ruled these three cities, and formed pagan administrations in them instead. However, as was already beginning to be clear in the following century, these attempts to paganize Galilee and Samaria did not, in the end, prove successful.

Jewish sources tell grim stories of the persecutions which followed the Second Revolt. These measures of retribution were organized by Tineius Rufus: now in a subordinate position, but still powerful, he had been driven out of much of the country at the outset of the rebellion, and could not be expected to feel very kindly towards the Jews. Yet apart from the ban on admission to the neighbourhood of Jerusalem there was not the general prohibition of Jewish institutions and customs to which the rabbinical authorities refer. Although life became hard, with heavy taxation and much poverty,[39] Judaism did not become a proscribed religion. It was still tolerated because of its antiquity, and because of the Romans' justified belief that such toleration would lead to less trouble for themselves in the end. The Jews were not even forced to worship the emperor. Nevertheless, there were individual executions after the revolt. Jewish records tell of Ten Martyrs, and their deaths are celebrated on Yom Kippur, the Day of Atonement.

These martyrs included Rabbi Akiba, now ninety-five years of age or more. In spite of his catastrophic political advice, his memory was cherished by his fellow rabbis and the members of their schools. So was the memory of Rabbi Eleazar of Modein, who had died during the siege of Bethar. Since it was Simeon bar Kosiba himself, his own nephew, who had killed him, Simeon's reputation was not greatly honoured. It also suffered because Messiahs were supposed to bring victory, and this he had utterly failed to do. True, there was a certain awed admiration of his bravery in the field. Yet in contrast to a modern tendency to regard him as a national hero, many rabbis blamed him for the Roman repressions which were the direct result of his rising – indeed, there was even a tradition that it was the rabbis who had killed him.[40]

The Second Revolt was the last violent outburst of the Messianic hope. Indeed, it was almost the last sign of national unrest within the entire Roman empire. Soon little remained of it, except Simeon's silver coins, invalidated by perforation and hung round the necks of young Jewish girls as charms.[41]

However, the Romans soon realized that it would be convenient to recognize a Jewish leader in Judaea once again. In spite, therefore, of

Akiba's grave lapse, they turned once again to the moderate, Pharisaic, rabbinical class which had fulfilled this role before the Revolt. Simeon II, the son of Gamaliel II, had escaped from prison and was in hiding in Babylonia, but now he returned and received Roman recognition for his reconstituted Jewish Council at Usha in Galilee. This seems to have been the time, too, when the leaders of the Jewish community in the Judaean province became officially entitled to describe themselves as Patriarchs. The term had originally been used by the Greek translators of the Septuagint, and before the Second Revolt may already have been employed unofficially for contemporary Jewish leaders, but now it passed into official parlance.

This Roman recognition, coming as it did just after open military rebellion, was a significant step, because the patriarchate became a unique office which retained the theocratic conception and attracted Jewish loyalty while also permitting a considerable degree of administrative and even, to some extent, political autonomy. Furthermore, like the 'ethnarch' created by Pompey two centuries earlier, the patriarch possessed a certain spiritual authority over all the Jews, not only in Palestine, but throughout the Roman empire. The strength of this intangible authority has been exaggerated by the rabbinical tradition, but it carried weight all the same, and so the patriarchate became a focus for the whole future of Judaism throughout the Roman world.

There was, of course, unrelieved Jewish mourning in AD 135 as there had been in 70, not only for the devastating loss of innocent human lives but for the disastrous setback to the Jewish national and economic cause. As in the years after 70, what had happened seemed an echo of the downfall of Israel and Judah many centuries ago – and once again there were rabbis ready to offer religious and theological consolation on such lines. They did not so much repress ideas of Messianism as divert them from the national to the spiritual and prophetic sphere: less was said about the earthly Jerusalem than about its heavenly counterpart. Judaism turned in upon itself and upon the Torah, and continued to develop over the centuries a hidden life upon which the outer world scarcely impinged. The attitude to Gentiles remained as ambivalent as ever: while some rabbis conceded that 'the pious of the nations of the world' were not necessarily excluded from the rewards of the hereafter, there was nevertheless a tendency to ordain that any intercourse with pagans, except in public and semi-public places, should be made impossible.[42]

As for the Christians of Palestine, the Judaeo-Christians, their circumcised state had not prevented them from incurring the hostility of Bar Kosiba, since their belief that the Messiah had already appeared was in conflict with his own claims; and while the country was under his control they had suffered severely.[43] Indeed, when Rome resumed its sway, they proved to be beyond recovery, and they were given no incentive to recover. True, since the Christians had taken no part in the revolt they were allowed, unlike Jews, to reside in Jerusalem,[44] where they maintained a church consisting largely, perhaps, of returned emigrants from Transjordan or their sons; but its leaders or bishops were henceforward of the Hellenized, uncircumcised variety.[45] The circumcised Judaeo-Christians, spiritual descendants of Paul's opponents Peter and James the Just, had finally been defeated. Lingering on in diminutive congregations at Hebron, Nazareth and elsewhere, their descendants – other than those who reverted to Judaism – split up into an astonishing diversity of sects, absorbed in angelology and esoteric revelations. Among them were the Ebionites, from the Hebrew *ebionim*, 'poor men', who rejected every Gospel except *Matthew*, and later dismissed that, too, as unsatisfactory. Other breakaway groups have left behind them strange and varied reliefs which symbolize the life-giving power of the Cross by the depiction of phalli.[46] As a historical force, however, or a significant element in the calculations of Rome, the Judaeo-Christians had ceased to exist by the middle of the second century AD. Indeed, it was not long before they were proscribed as heretical by Christians and Jews alike. Although they lingered on for centuries, Paul's version of the faith had been too much for them: when the Ebionites reviled him as an apostate, they were correctly identifying the author of the downfall of Judaean Christianity.

Antoninus Pius soon modified his predecessor Hadrian's veto on circumcision without abandoning it altogether. That is to say, he allowed Jews to circumcise their sons, but forbade them to admit converts by the rite.[47] This meant a cessation of Hadrian's interference with the Jewish community itself, but the reversal was coupled with an attack on its attempts to proselytize. While strengthening the bonds that existed within Jewry itself, the measure weakened its potentialities as a world religion by debarring it from competition with the actively proselytizing Christians.

It may not, therefore, be fortuitous that there was fresh trouble in

Syria-Palaestina under Antoninus Pius. The disturbance does not seem to have been unexpected, since not only had the garrison of the province been reinforced, but military posts were placed in a ring round Aelia Capitolina (Jerusalem), probably in order to enforce the ban debarring Jews from admission to the city. However, it is reported by the *Historia Augusta*, an unreliable but on this occasion not implausible source, that the later years of the same reign witnessed a further revolt. Whether it was in Judaea proper, or perhaps in Galilee where there were strongly pagan coinages under Antoninus, we cannot say.[48] In any case if, as seems probable, such a rebellion occurred, it was immediately crushed.

Part V

The Jews in the Later Empire

16

The Later Pagan Empire

In Galilee, where the headquarters of Jewish religious scholarship was now established at a succession of different centres, one of the Ten Martyrs, Judah ben Baba, had ordained a brilliant new generation of rabbinical teachers. One of them, Rabbi Meir 'the wonder-worker', attracted enormous audiences, and was later said to be the author of all the anonymous rulings in the Mishnah, which he allegedly based on instructions he had received from Akiba.[1] Meir's contemporaries included another pupil of Akiba, Rabbi Simon ben Yohai, who was reputedly the author of a mystical classic, the *Zohar*, and was honoured by an annual pilgrimage to his Galilean tomb. Emerging from twelve years' hiding in a cave, Simon ben Yohai went with a colleague to Rome, where Jewish scholarship, under Rabbi Theudas, had gained in stature during the previous generation; there he established personal contact with the emperor Antoninus Pius.

Nevertheless, Simon, who has already been encountered as the narrator of Akiba's acclamation of Bar Kosiba, was by no means a loyal supporter of the Roman occupying power. And he was not alone in such a view. For this was a time when a new sort of Messianic tradition was growing up. Returning to Qumran's earlier belief that there would be two Messiahs and not one, supporters of this kind of view asserted that the first of them, Messiah ben Joseph, was destined to fall in battle against the Satanic hosts, whereas the other, Messiah ben David, would bring final victory. The two patronymics were intended to take a leaf out of the book of the Christians, since Jesus' mother had been married to Joseph, who claimed descent from David. But above all this new version of Messianism was intended to explain away and justify the death and failure of Simeon bar Kosiba; he had fallen, but another would complete the sacred task.

That was the sort of spirit in which Simon ben Yohai now declared: 'When you see a Persian (Parthian) horse tied at the graveyards of Palestine, watch for the approaching steps of the Messiah.'[2] This was a hopeful prophecy of a Parthian conquest of Palestine, the sort of prophecy which Jose ben Kisma had already uttered at the time of Hadrian's persecution. Rabbis of this frame of mind saw the Parthians as instruments for the salvation of Israel, deliberately echoing the Second Isaiah who had interpreted King Cyrus of Persia in the same light. Admittedly the Parthians had given the Jews of Judaea not the slightest assistance or encouragement, in either the First or the Second Revolt. But now there seemed some reason to suppose that the situation had changed. For Antoninus Pius' adopted son and successor Marcus Aurelius (161–80) and his co-emperor Lucius Verus (161–9), in the year immediately following their succession, were compelled to face a formidable invasion from the Parthian monarch Vologases III. Armenia was overrun, the legions from Syria scattered before the enemy, and the Syrian cities turned to thoughts of disaffection. So did the thoughts of the Jews, who still remembered how, just two hundred years earlier, a Parthian invasion had heralded a welcome invasion of their own country. But this time no such hoped-for change of masters materialized. For Lucius Verus himself arrived in Syria in 163, and by that time the most eminent Roman general, Avidius Cassius (himself an east Syrian), had already reorganized its garrison. Armenia was recovered; then, in 165–6, Cassius invaded northern Mesopotamia and, like Trajan before him, made the country into a Roman protectorate. Once again the hopes of the Jews were dashed.

Ten years later, however, Cassius, who had in the meanwhile been given supreme command over all the east, revolted against the Roman government,[3] and all except two of the eastern governors joined his cause. Among those who went over to him was the governor of Syria-Palaestina – probably with the support of many leading Jews. But after three months Cassius was assassinated by a Roman officer, and in the following year Marcus Aurelius himself arrived in the east to undertake the necessary reorganization. He showed clemency to those who had sided against him, and Judaea, which was among the countries he visited, shared the benefits of this lenient policy. But Aurelius, imbued with a philosophical though less overtly Hellenic concept of Hadrian's united empire without separatist movements, formed a very poor opinion of the Jews when he came to their land, comparing them unfavourably even with the northern barbarians against whom he had been fighting for many years. 'For Aurelius,' asserts the late but excellent historian Ammianus Marcellinus, 'as he was passing through Palestine on his way to Egypt, was often disgusted with the Jews for their smelliness and rebelliousness. He is reported to have cried out, pretending to address his northern barbarian enemies: "Marcomanni, Quadi, Sarmatians! At last I have found a people more unruly than you!"'[4]

However, as he himself shows in his *Meditations*, Marcus Aurelius, in other ways one of the most enlightened emperors Rome ever produced, disapproved even more fundamentally of the Christians. What he particularly disliked about them was a feature they had borrowed from the Jews, their enthusiasm for martyrdom, which seemed to him mere wilful protest-making and self-dramatizing, and therefore wholly discreditable.[5] Moreover, in his reign (though not at his direct prompting) there had been a wave of anti-Christian feeling in Gaul and Asia Minor, where the Christians were turned upon and martyred as scapegoats for military, economic and natural disasters. By this time, as events of the time of Trajan had already foreshadowed, Christianity was well on the way to replacing Judaism, in popular estimation, as the enemy of the Roman regime and its subjects of other races.

To some Jews this may well have been a source of satisfaction. But, if so, their pleasure was damped by the fact that the Christians had also, in many parts, begun to outnumber them. And in spite of certain eminent conversions in the opposite direction, the new imbalance slowly but ineluctably increased. For example, the Jews of Egypt, weakened by their long struggles with Alexandrian Greeks, were soon reduced to insignificance by the Christians; elsewhere in north Africa, too, though their numbers were greatly increased as a result of the Second Revolt, they came under severe pressure. Meanwhile the separation between Christians and Jews had become complete and final. The most extreme reaction against Judaism was to be found in the Christian dualist 'heretic' Marcion of Sinope (Sinop) (*c*. 140). Combining devotion to the memory of Paul with knowledge of a Gospel closely resembling *Luke,*

Marcion totally rejected the entire Old Testament, as being the work of a Creator inferior to the supreme God revealed in the person of Jesus. Other Christian writers, too, regarded everything in the Old Testament purely and simply as a series of prophecies of Christ, and blamed the Jews, when they failed to accept this view, for falsifying the scriptures.

When Polycarp, bishop of Smyrna, was martyred (?*c.* 155–6), it was the Jews who were said to have caused his death, and Justin Martyr of Neapolis in Samaria, who died in *c.* 165, regarded them with hatred. Although Justin does not yet know of the final New Testament canon, and passes Paul over in silence, he has read a work called 'Memoirs of the Apostles', which probably comprised the Gospels of *Matthew, Mark* and *Luke* and provided fuel for his anti-Jewish views; and he must have known *John* too.

The central Christian churches, although internally riven by dissident movements of their own, were by this time totally divorced from the Jews.[6] The gulf between the two faiths had been steadily and rapidly widening over the years, but now in the later second century AD, when the Gospels were becoming more and more widely known, their strongly anti-Jewish tone helped to cause even the most tenuous final bridges to disappear. It was probably under Marcus Aurelius' son Commodus (180–92) that a Christian of slave origin named Callixtus (later a wealthy banker, and Pope Callixtus I) was said to have broken into a Roman synagogue and disrupted the service,[7] whereupon he was sentenced to forced labour in the mines of Sardinia. Whether the story is true or not we cannot tell, but the fact that it was told at all shows how utterly alien from the Jews the Christians had now become. And it may well have been at about this date, or just a little later, that the Jews first compiled the book which emerged subsequently as the *Toledoth Yeshu.* That work, at considerable length and in abundant detail, described Jesus as a sorcerer, the son of uncleanness. (He was also said to be a bastard, the son of a soldier called Panthera or Ben Pandera or Ben Stada.)[8] The *Toledoth Yeshu* enjoyed an enormous circulation throughout the ages, and its perusal, combined with a reading of the Gospels, explains clearly enough why the split between Judaism and Christianity was now irrevocable.

Meanwhile the Jews, as memories of the Second Revolt began to fade, enjoyed once again a considerable degree of Roman toleration. The

Jewish architect of these good relations was the patriarch Judah I ha-Nasi, 'the Prince' (AD 135–219). The son and successor of Hillel's descendant Simeon II, Judah I resided first at Beth-Shearim and then at Sepphoris-Diocaesarea. Under his guidance the patriarchate reached its highest point, and its occupants may even have possessed (subject to a Roman veto) powers of life and death; it also sent out itinerant fund-raisers on a large scale.⁹ Judah I owned great properties and maintained considerable state, surrounded by a bodyguard of Galatians or Germans. His grandeur caused satisfaction to the Jews, who felt that they had something like a national leader once again.

An able organizer and learned scholar, Judah navigated a skilful course which enabled him to be orthodox and modern at the same time. In the interests of collaboration with the Romans, he wanted to abolish the annual Day of Mourning in which visits to Jerusalem were allowed, because he was afraid it would be the occasion of inflammatory sermons; but on this matter his Council, the Sanhedrin, overruled him. Messianism, too, did not appeal to Judah I: indeed a certain Judah and Hezekiah, sons of Rabbi Hiyya, felt impelled to declare in his presence, admittedly under the influence of drink, that the Messiah would never come until the family of the hereditary patriarchs (and their counterparts in Mesopotamia) had ceased to exist.¹⁰ The confidence that Judah I inspired in the Romans is reflected in Hebrew traditions narrating his fictitious dialogues with a Roman emperor. Described as 'Antoninus', he is variously identified as Antoninus Pius and two other emperors who were called by the same name, Marcus Aurelius and Caracalla (211–17).¹¹ Moreover, at least one Antonine emperor presented a candlestick to a Palestinian synagogue.¹²

Judah I is also traditionally regarded as the principal architect of the Mishnah, that vast and marvellous repository of Jewish tradition and faith which set out to teach the oral Law without binding it directly to the text of scripture. This method of Mishnah (from *shano*, repeat, i.e. study) dated back to the time of Herod, or even earlier, and by the second century AD it had begun to be given preference over the Midrash method comprising the exposition of biblical texts. Systematization of the diverse material that finally found its way into the Mishnah, and had previously been worked over many times, had probably begun with Akiba. But later Hebrew literature assumes that the main editor was Judah I. The exact part he played in reducing the work to writing has been disputed for a thousand years, but at least he was the main editor of this written version. It may not be entirely fortuitous that one of the Roman emperors with whom Judah coincided in date was the north African Septimius Severus (193–211), under whom major steps were taken to codify the Law of Rome itself. Yet the Mishnah displays a remarkable degree of independence from the legal system of Rome, and for that matter of Parthia and Persia too – and probably from Greek systems as well, though its relation to these is much disputed.

Judah's eminence and skill ensured that the Mishnah was accorded immediate recognition. In Hebrew literature it was the most conspicuous landmark since the Torah and the Prophets; and, next to them, it was the biggest influence on the language. It is written in Mishnaic Hebrew, which is distinct from the biblical form of the Hebrew tongue. This Hebrew of the Mishnah was not an artificial language, but a vernacular employed by a considerable number of Jews of the homeland – although Aramaic was spoken by many more, and Greek by more still.[13]

Although the Mishnah is no authoritative or systematic corpus of Jewish theology, since no such thing exists, it arranged its subject matter systematically, in six sections (orders) subdivided into treatises. Though rulings and decisions are laid down, nevertheless contrary opinions, past and present, are recorded; and thus rabbinical Judaism, now established as a religion in its own right, is placed, like earlier Jewish literary works, on a historical basis – indeed even on a basis of learned antiquarianism, since half the material included was already more or less obsolete at the time of compilation. Except for one treatise, the *Aboth*, which is a guide to private conscience, there is little about ethics; and Messianism and the coming kingdom of God receive very little attention indeed.

Meanwhile, the political situation in Judaea continued to be subject to recurrent disturbances. After the murder of Commodus, followed by the violent deaths of his two successors in the following year (193), the claims of Septimius Severus were contested by the governor of Syria, Pescennius Niger. Neapolis (in Samaria) is specially mentioned as supporting him,[14] and indeed it seems possible that the Samaritans, rather than Jews, were his keenest backers. However, Niger was defeated and killed by Severus. Either before or after the decisive struggle between them, there is record of a 'Jewish and Samaritan War', for which, we are told, the emperor's son Caracalla, though only a boy, was awarded a Triumph. Severus punished the people of the Palestinian province, but later revoked their penalties.[15] In the same period a bandit named Claudius, perhaps a Jew, had been overrunning Syria and Syria-Palaestina, but finally he, too, surrendered to Severus.[16]

Parthia had supported Niger against him, and this revival of the Parthian menace must have caused Severus to harbour the usual, recurrent, and by no means unjustified suspicions of disloyalty, actual or potential, within his Syrian and Palestinian territories. In retaliation, he moved against Vologases IV of Parthia, captured Ctesiphon, and two years later (199) completed the occupation of northern Mesopotamia. Lucius Verus had overrun this country in 162–5, but now Severus formally annexed it, thus incorporating its massive Jewish communities within the Roman empire.[17]

Severus remained in the near east for the next three years. According to the *Historia Augusta* he carried the restrictions imposed by earlier rulers on Jewish proselytism one stage further by actually forbidding conversions:[18] if so, this is our first trace of an explicit ban. He was also said to have extended the same prohibition to the Christians, apparently accompanying this measure (though not the corresponding sanction against the Jews) by persecutions. These restrictions, as references by contemporary lawyers show, were regarded as coming under the heading of measures against treason and sedition.

Nevertheless, an inscription from Qeisoun (Qasioun), in Galilee which was increasingly the centre of rabbinical life, bears witness to Jewish collaboration with Severus and his family.[19] A Roman synagogue seems to have been named after him,[20] and both he and his son Caracalla specifically deferred to the religious scruples of Jewish candidates for municipal office in the cities of the empire. Furthermore, when Caracalla's famous *Constitutio Antoniniana* (212 or 213) made almost all the inhabitants of the Roman empire, other than slaves, into Roman citizens,[21] this included the Jews. But many of them had been Roman citizens already.[22] And, even if they had not, the change had no effect on their religious practices, since it was not interpreted by the Roman authorities as requiring them to perform unacceptable rites such as emperor-worship.

Caracalla's relative Elagabalus (218–22), who was not only partly Syrian like Caracalla but belonged to a hereditary priesthood of Syrian Emesa (Homs) dedicated to sun-worship, possessed a sufficiently pro-Jewish reputation (in spite of his notorious moral lapses) to be accused of undergoing circumcision and hating pork. He was also said to have announced a sweeping but embarrassing solution to the religious problem: the religions of the Jews and Samaritans and Christians alike, as well as all the most ancient cults of the Roman state, were to be transferred to the new Roman temple of his own imported sun-god El-Gabal. But all these reports are suspect,[23] and so are further stories relating to his cousin and successor Severus Alexander. When the latter emperor was allegedly mocked by the Greeks of Antioch and Alexandria as a 'Syrian president of the synagogue' (*archisynagogus*),[24] they may perhaps have been referring not to any pro-Jewish sentiments on his part but, more vaguely, to the Syrian high priesthood which ran in his family. Nevertheless Severus Alexander, while repressive to the Samaritans (who were said to have appealed to Parthia against him),[25] was said to have respected the privileges of Jews and Christians alike, and to have kept a statue of Abraham among an eclectic array of images in his private shrine.[26]

Even if this was so, the incomprehension of the Jewish religion shown by even the most intelligent Greeks remained almost as complete as it had ever been. It is true that an occasional thinker, such as Numenius of Syrian Apamea, was capable of praising the incorporeal God of the Jews, and of seeing Plato as 'Moses in Attic robes'. Yet Flavius Philostratus, who belonged to the philosophical circle patronized by Septimius Severus and his Syrian wife Julia Domna, declared that the Jews 'are separated from ourselves by a greater gulf than divides us from Susa [Shush in Persia] or Bactra [Balkh in Afghanistan] or the more distant Indies'.[27] And very much the same attitude was displayed by Dio Cassius, a Greek from Nicaea (Iznik) who completed his *Roman History* in the time of Severus Alexander. 'The Jews,' he maintained, 'are distinguished from the rest of mankind in practically every detail of life, and particularly by the fact that they do not honour any of the usual gods, but show extreme reverence for one particular god.'[28]

For after the Second Revolt, in the words of Emil Schurer, 'the Jews became more and more what they properly and essentially were: strangers in the pagan world'.[29] In the Dispersion, it is true, a more international spirit prevailed among many of them. But in Judaea itself the cosmopolitanism of an occasional patriarch or other leading figure did not make a very profound impact on his fellow-Jews. One such friend of Hellenism was the patriarch of the generation following Dio Cassius, namely Judah II Nessiah, the grandson of Judah I. But his long reign (*c.* 230–86) spanned a period of extreme difficulty. For after the death of Severus Alexander (235) the Roman empire foundered into political and economic chaos, and the populations of its provinces were ground down by taxes of appalling severity and arbitrariness. In Palestine as elsewhere – in the words of Rabbi Eleazar ben Azariah – 'earning a living became more difficult than the crossing of the Red Sea'.[30] The patriarch Judah II, in the precarious position of a buffer between Romans and Jews, had to absorb much of the popular resentment.[31] Nevertheless, he successfully asserted his administrative powers. He also moved his patriarchal capital to yet another town of Galilee, the flourishing watering-place Tiberias, where he satisfied his Hellenizing tastes and shored up his prestige by maintaining an almost royal court. In the time of Jesus, Tiberias had been shunned by Jews as artificial, unclean and half-Greek. Under Hadrian it had depicted a temple of Zeus on its coins. But now it became the capital of world Jewry.

Tiberias possessed thirteen synagogues, including one each for men from Babylon, Antioch and Tarsus. At this time the number of synagogues in other parts of Galilee, too, was increasing; and the remains of many of them are still to be seen today. The earliest that can be identified dates back to just before AD 200,[32] but most belong to the two centuries that followed. Their monumental baroque façades embody interesting adaptations of Greco-Syrian styles to the requirements of Jewish cult. Inside the synagogues, a special apse, facing towards Jerusalem, and approached through a chancel, was provided for the Scrolls of the Law; a synagogue frieze from Capernaum shows one of the wheeled Arks of the Covenant in which these scrolls were kept. But the most remarkable features of these buildings are the floor-mosaics, which, like sarcophagi,[33] completely disregard the Torah's ancient ban on human and animal representations. Indeed at one of the earliest synagogues, recently excavated at Hammath, there is even a mosaic portrait of the pagan god Apollo-Helios as a charioteer, framed in a Zodiac and supported by the four seasons.[34] This inclination towards figurative art may have been associated with importations of pagan mysticism; though the extent to which this took place remains conjectural. At all events the trend was acknowledged, gradually and reluctantly, by rabbinical relaxations of doctrine.[35]

Tiberias became not only the site of the patriarchal court and of numerous synagogues, but also the most important centre of Jewish scholarship. For it was the residence of the principal rabbis – and, since the patriarchs after Judah I were mostly not first-class scholars, it was to the rabbis, known as Amoraim (speakers, interpreters), that authority increasingly passed. Teaching in the Tiberias academy, the school of a new generation of scholars coming from Babylonia and many other countries, they prepared the way for the Palestinian (or 'Jerusalem') Talmud. After the Bible, the Talmud was the Jews' principal guide to life and object of study, comprising an entire literature in itself. It consisted first of the Mishnah and then of the Gamara, which in turn comprised first the Palestinian and then the Babylonian Talmud.

The Palestinian Talmud was only completed by the fourth or fifth century AD, its final development being hampered by militant Christianity. But its foundations had been laid under the direction of Rabbi Johanan bar Nappaha (AD 199–279), who perhaps became the first undisputed leader of the Tiberias college.[36] Though conceited about both his learning and his looks, Johanan had a reputation as a mild, sensitive individual. Unlike his brother-in-law Resh Lakish, a pious ex-highwayman (the Jewish tradition relishes these pairs and foils), he possessed Hellenizing sympathies, thus resembling the patriarch of his time, Judah II. Yet, living on as he did into a disturbed and terrible epoch of imperial history, Johanan's attitude towards Rome was not uncritical. For example, he declared governmental taxes to be an evil – though he did add that he ascribed them to the misdeeds of the Jews.[37] He also identified the Romans with the Fourth Beast of *Daniel*, dreadful and grisly, which was killed and its carcass destroyed.[38] Moreover, during some partial breakdown of the Roman provincial authority, Johanan ventured to order the destruction of all the images of pagan gods in the public baths of Tiberias: for some Jews, it was asserted, had come under suspicion of offering incense there.[39]

Meanwhile the Jews of the Dispersion, numerically increased in the aftermath of the Second Revolt, still lived on; and some of them prospered. Moreover, as Solomon Grayzel points out, 'although the Jews were no longer a nation, in the usual sense of a territorial group, they still continued to feel united. That is one of the outstanding marvels in all human history . . . The reason for this most unusual situation is that the Jewish Idea, or Judaism, was made more important than the Jewish land and national life.'[40]

Our most extensive information about the Dispersion of this time, though still tantalizingly inadequate, comes from the large Jewish community at Rome. Although the language of this community was overwhelmingly Greek rather than Hebrew (or Latin), its local academy was already recognized in the second century AD by the Palestinian rabbis. From a somewhat earlier period, perhaps rather before AD 100, date the earliest burials in the community's cemeteries, situated in underground catacombs made possible by the geological substructure of Rome.[41] The surviving wall-paintings in these catacombs, however, date from the second and more particularly the third centuries. Like Jewish sarcophagi from the same city,[42] these scenes show the disregard for the scriptural ban on figurative representations that also characterized the Galilee synagogues, though once again the degree to which this reflected the borrowing of pagan mystic ideas remains disputed.[43]

Another unresolved question relates to the extent to which these Jewish paintings, and their far more abundant and varied counterparts in the Christian catacombs at Rome, share a common Jewish source that has now vanished. For the subjects selected for the Christian pictures are curiously significant. Like other early Christian art, they show little awareness of the Gospels (other than *John*), and display an extraordinary, total, avoidance of the death of Jesus, or even of his arrest and trial. For evidently these events were still regarded by many, for all that the New Testament had said, as horrible and hideous defeats, or at least as happenings all too likely to make the pagan world despise their faith. Moreover, the painters' concern for the alleged events of Jesus' life is highly selective, directing its emphasis over and over again towards a few chosen miracles, notably the Raising of Lazarus and Feeding of the Five Thousand.[44] There is also a good deal of reference to what became known as the sacraments – the Last Supper and Baptism.

But what is most noteworthy about these Christian artists is their enormous concentration on incidents from the Old Testament, and on those of its heroes who illustrate the power of God to intervene against oppressors and deliver his people. The most popular scene of all is that of Moses striking the rock to find water: out of 233 counted scenes, no less than sixty-eight represent this miracle alone. Next, in point of frequency, comes Jonah rescued from the belly of the monster (a symbol of the Resurrection), and then Daniel's companions saved from the fiery furnace; Noah and Abraham, too, appear as harbingers of salvation. These themes have been traced back, conjecturally but plausibly, to lost Jewish paintings in catacombs, or, conceivably, in illuminated editions of the Septuagint, though no such works of anything like so early a date have survived. If either of these hypotheses is correct, then the Christian paintings provide indirect testimony to a vital lost chapter of Jewish art and history, and the inspiration which Giotto and the Renaissance derived from the Christian art goes back to the Jews.

The future of Judaism depended upon many other centres of the Jewish Dispersion even more than upon Rome. But archaeological evidence for all these centres remains sparse. There were catacombs at Venusia (Venosa) in south Italy. The Jewish necropolis of Gamart in Carthage shows figured representations, like the Jewish catacombs at Rome; and north African cemeteries, in contrast to the doctrines and attitudes of religious leaders on both sides, provide evidence of inter-burial between Jews and Christians. At Stobi (near Monastir) in Macedonia there was a synagogue at least as early as AD 165.

Across the Aegean in Asia Minor, where the large population of Jews only enters rarely into history, the three-hundred-foot-long synagogue at Sardes (Sart) is the largest yet excavated or known. Its great table was apparently flanked by two pairs of seated lions, with a spread eagle on either support. Under Septimius Severus, Apamea (Dinar) in Phrygia, a city also known as 'Cibotus' (a wooden box or chest), issued a coin which surprisingly depicts Noah, identified by name and displayed in his ark.[45] There was presumably some local legend of a flood, which lent itself to adaptation to the Bible story; and it must be supposed that, to gain this special numismatic notice, the Jewish colony at Apamea was unusually influential.

But the most significant Jewish remains of the Dispersion within the Roman empire come from its very remotest frontiers. For at the point where the province of Mesopotamia, annexed by Septimius Severus, came to an end stood the frontier-post of Dura-Europos. At first it was the Parthian empire that this fortress confronted. But then came a fundamental change: for Parthia, weakened by Severus' invasions, succumbed to the far more formidable and centralized power of the Sassanian Persians under Artaxerxes (Ardashir) I, who overthrew the last Parthian king Artabanus V (c. 223–6). Excavations of the third-century remains of Dura-Europos have revealed a synagogue which is the most impressive of all ancient survivals of this type of building. From floor to ceiling this house-synagogue was covered with three tiers of closely juxtaposed, rectangular panel paintings, dating from the years 245–55.

These pictures, which can be seen in the National Museum at Damascus, illustrate passages of the Old Testament. The artistic style displays Mesopotamian frontality and the figures wear Iranian dress, but the general method of composition may well be derived, ultimately, from Greco-Roman copybooks. As for the biblical themes, it has been suggested that, like the themes depicted in the Jewish catacombs in Rome, they may owe something to earlier illustrated Bibles, as yet unknown; but there also remains the possibility that the artists worked direct from sacred texts, using their own imagination.

The paintings reveal that the Judaism of Dura-Europus differed, in important respects, from the rabbinical schools either of Babylonia or Palestine. For here at Dura-Europus there is much greater emphasis on that alternative tradition, avoided by the rabbis, which stressed Messianism and the end of the world. It was in this spirit that the artists of the Dura-Europus synagogue depict Moses and Enoch, who were said to have ascended to heaven, and Ezra (Esdras), who was credited with apocalyptic visions.

While this synagogue was in use at Dura-Europus, a far more significant Jewish phenomenon was taking place farther south in Babylonia, that is to say in the portion of the Land of Two Rivers which was not under Roman control but belonged first to the Parthian and then the Persian empire. For in that country the Jewish communities were experiencing a great efflorescence. Between AD 200 and 500 they may have increased in numbers from one million to two; and before long their impressive educational centres eclipsed the scholarship of Palestinian Jewry itself. This transference of the centre of Judaism from the Roman to the Parthian empire is a prime example of that characteristic feature of the history of the Jews, the development of a 'reserve' area – under providential guidance, as they believe – when the previous centre is in danger. In these years the growth of the Babylonian communities enabled Judaism to survive the various disasters of the later Roman Empire.

The first place among the Babylonian Jewish communities was occupied by Nehardea on the Euphrates. During the first century AD this town had been the centre of a transitory Jewish state, and now it became known as the 'Babylonian Jerusalem'. Its academy, founded in *c.* AD 212 (?), was led by a district magistrate Mar ('my lord') Samuel, a legal expert who was also a scientist, astronomer and doctor. But his

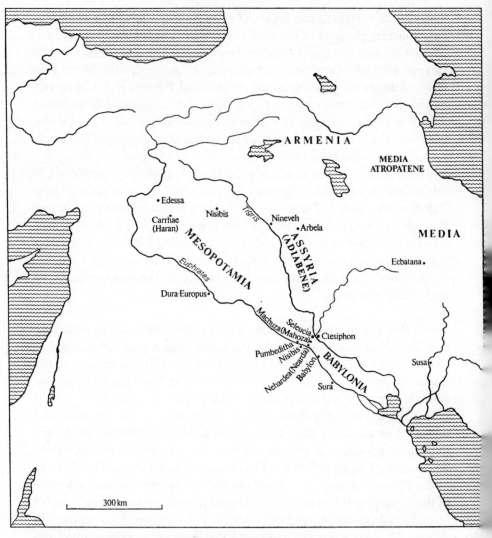

The Parthian and Persian (Sassanian) empires

school was equalled by that of Sura, established in 219 on an indentation of the Euphrates further downstream. Celebrated for its poverty and honesty, the Sura school was headed for nearly thirty years by the Babylonian Abba Arika, known as Rav ('master' or 'teacher' in the local dialect of Aramaic). The patriarch Judah II, wishing to retain the primacy of Palestine, had refused ordination to Abba Arika. Nevertheless, he returned to his native land and founded the academy at Sura, in which the old Jewish learning of Babylonia was combined with the religious scholarship of the Holy Land.

It was during the careers of Mar Samuel and Abba Arika that Parthia succumbed to the new Persian (Sassanian) power. Samuel became a staunch Persian patriot, enunciating in their favour the traditional principle 'the law of the land is law', and looking forward to the Messianic coup which would bring the Jewish nation independence from Rome. As for Abba Arika, he had been a friend of the last Parthian king Artabanus v. But when the Persians assumed control, he declared that, although the violent happenings that accompanied the change were deplorable, he would rather live under Persia than under Rome. Furthermore, men on the other side of the imperial frontier felt the same. For one thing, they were attracted by the easier taxation in Babylonia – which, in consequence, experienced a wave of immigration from Roman territory. The great Persian monarch Sapor (Shapur) I (c. 239–70), who inflicted terrible invasions and defeats upon the Romans, particularly raised the hopes of the Jews, who saw visions of the return of the lost Ten Tribes to their ancient homeland. Moreover, Sapor was reputedly familiar with Jewish customs, and was credited with complimentary comments on rabbinical sexual morals.[46]

The Jews in the Persian empire had their own official leaders, the 'Princes of the Captivity' or exilarchs (Resh Galuta), who were the counterparts of the patriarchs in Judaea itself. It is uncertain if these officials had existed in Parthian times (or even earlier) or were first created by Sapor I. On the grounds that they were reputedly descendants of the house of David, the exilarchs claimed superiority to the patriarchs, and they enjoyed a far higher position. Although the Persian monarchs reserved the right to confirm their elections, their residence at Ctesiphon resembled a whole township, and they maintained great state, ranking as vassal princes or semi-autonomous provincial governors, and affording the Jewish community a high degree of protection.

Meanwhile, within the Roman empire, the Jews were able to watch in relative tranquillity the successive persecutions of the Christians by Maximinus I (235–8), Trajanus Decius (249–51) and Valerian (253–60). Since the Christians, in imitation of the Jewish tradition, positively welcomed the glory of martyrdom, these repressive measures achieved exactly the opposite to what the Romans intended: the holy deaths of the martyrs enormously stimulated enthusiasm for Christianity. At this time, the Christians were increasingly divided between those of the west, who stressed Jesus' sonship of God, and those of the east, who emphasized God's singleness.[47] By this time, however, the Jews were entirely dissociating themselves from the Christians, even of this second and more understandable category.[48]

Moreover, when persecution led many Christians to take refuge in hermitages and monasteries, especially in Upper Egypt, this aroused no answering echo in Jewish official thought, to which the monastic solution was alien. Two centuries earlier, the Jewish leaders had extended no sympathy to semi-monastic Essenes and Qumran sectaries. And now, if a student wished to devote his life to secluded religious study – as the rabbis agreed was a desirable thing – they sought to encourage the idea that he should not withdraw to a monastery but should remain in the community and receive support from its wealthier members. Furthermore, as the Christians, following these other-worldly trends, withdrew more and more from any service to Roman society, the rabbis deliberately moved in the opposite direction, shifting away from their earlier discouragement of public life to the inculcation of a sense of responsibility – a policy which they hoped would, in Roman eyes, set them altogether apart from the deeply suspect Christians.

Valerian's attack on Christianity was intended to distract attention from military and economic disaster. In the east, he lost a number of Mesopotamian cities to Sapor I, and Dura-Europus was destroyed. Then, in 259 or 260, Rome suffered the unprecedented humiliation of learning that its emperor himself had been captured by the Persians. For once, Christians and Jews were of the same mind, for both communities delightedly believed that what had happened was a fulfilment of the scriptures: the Christians because their persecutor was gone, and the Jews because they entertained high hopes that the Persians, like the Parthians just three hundred years earlier, would liberate their homeland.[49]

Matters turned out differently, however, for when Odenathus, the hereditary chieftain of Syrian Palmyra (Tadmor), suffered a rebuff from Sapor I, it was he, and not the Persians, who assumed control of all the eastern Roman provinces, including Syria-Palaestina; and though officially the Roman commander-in-chief in the east, he became virtually an independent ruler. Then, in 262, he launched a powerful invasion of Persian Mesopotamia. In spite of violent resistance from Persia's Jewish subjects, he captured Nehardea and razed the town and its great academy to the ground, capturing the late Mar Samuel's daughters and carrying them away to Sepphoris-Diocaesarea.

After Odenathus' death (*c.* 267), his widow Zenobia asserted complete independence from Rome. Subjection to Palmyra, however, was highly unwelcome to the Jews, who had an age-long record of hostility to Syrian cities and recalled that Palmyra (in spite of its reputed foundation by Solomon) had contributed to their ruin in the First Revolt – and had done the same, centuries earlier, when the First Temple had been destroyed by Nebuchadrezzar II. 'Blessed is he,' declared Rabbi Johanan ben Nappaha, 'who will live to see the fall of Tadmor.'[50] Zenobia herself was reputed to feel sympathy towards the Jews, whose envoys visited her court. Yet Jewish guerrillas harassed her troops, and she launched retaliatory persecutions.

However, after Palmyra had ruled over Palestine for twelve years, the country fell to the armies of the Roman emperor Aurelian, and shortly afterwards he captured Palmyra itself (272). On the whole, despite every reservation about Rome, the Jews were not sorry. After all, as the more far-sighted among them were aware, it was Rome which, throughout all these years of the mid-third century, was fighting off the German invaders from the north, who had irrupted as far as Asia Minor: as Rabbi Isaac Nappaha pointed out, 'if it were not for the Romans, the Germans [if this is the meaning of the term he uses] would overrun the world'.[51]

Meanwhile the Babylonian Jews had replaced the destroyed academy at Nehardea by another noble centre of learning at Pumbeditha beside the bank of a large canal. The new foundation rapidly became a rival of Sura and, unlike it, attracted attention for its fine buildings and astute inhabitants. It is true that a proverb declared it better to live on a dung-heap in Sura than in the palaces of Pumbeditha. Nevertheless the heads (*geonim*) of both schools were informally recognized, by the Persians as well as their fellow-Jews, to possess religious authority throughout the whole territory. The Sura presidency, the senior of the two, was for forty years occupied by Abba Arika's pupil Huna (d. 297), who raised the dignity of Mesopotamian Jewry to full parity with Palestine: 'In Babylonia we consider ourselves exactly as if we were in the Holy Land.' Moreover, there was now a further centre of Jewish life and scholarship in the country, namely Machuza (Mahoza), beside the Tigris not far from Ctesiphon. In spite of the strategic importance of the town, which possessed powerful walls and a steep moat, the Persians entrusted it to the control of its Jewish inhabitants. But being descended from converts, its leading inhabitants retained worldly tastes, and were described by stricter Jews as 'candidates for hell'.

However, the Persian regime soon posed a threat to these prosperous communities. Its official religion was Zoroastrian sun-worship, inherited from the Parthians, but the Persians developed it in a much more militant form. In *c.* AD 240, however, one of the world's outstanding religious teachers, Mani, had begun to introduce the cities of the Tigris and Euphrates to another doctrine, the eternal dualist struggle between Light and Darkness. Mani held that true religion, subject to local limitations, had been taught by many prophets, and that Adam, Enoch and Jesus were all among their number: thus he sought to bring both Jews and Christians into the Manichean block.

Mani was a friend of Sapor I, but under Sapor's son Bahram (Vahahram) I (273–6) he was executed, and another of Sapor's former protégés became chief priest and judge of all the empire. This was Kartir, a tough protagonist of the state religion, and guardian of patriotic orthodoxy. All the minority religions under Parthian rule, including Jews, Manicheans and Christians alike, now began to feel his heavy persecuting hand. Even in the more beneficent earlier days of the Persian regime, the position of the Babylonian Jews had been somewhat precarious: now that precariousness was greatly accentuated. For one thing, segregation was more complete than in any Roman territories, and local office-holding impossible. This was welcomed up to a point by the exilarchs and rabbis. But it also meant that the Persian government could not always defend the Jews from its own religious leaders, the *magi*; and customs such as the lighting of candles, the ritual slaughter of clean animals and the burial of the dead caused Zoroastrians profound offence. The Jews, in consequence, to the accompaniment of excuses from the Talmud, felt it diplomatic to honour the Persian king with obeisances that they had never been willing to accord Roman emperors, introducing his statues into the synagogues and even practising the oriental custom of prostration before them.[52] Nevertheless, the regime of Kartir caused the Jewish communities to wonder if they were really so much better off under Persia than under Rome after all.

However, there were still important Jews, in Palestine as well as Babylonia, who were delighted when the Persian King Narses (Narseh) I (AD 293–302) invaded Syria and heavily defeated the Romans. Among those who welcomed this development was the eminent Rabbi Abbahu (*c.* 279–320), who hailed the victory of Narses as heralding a massive vengeance upon Rome.[53] Abbahu headed an academy at Caesarea Maritima in the Roman province of Syria-Palaestina. This city still contained a very mixed population, but its components had somewhat changed. In contrast to Palestine as a whole, where the Jews were now in a minority, Caesarea had become increasingly Jewish in character. However, it contained an even larger proportion of Samaritans, whose complete separation from Judaism was re-affirmed by the Sanhedrin at this time. And yet these were years when the Jewish community at Caesarea, for all its large size, was increasingly on the defensive, since the city also contained an unusually powerful Christian bishop, against whose increasingly hostile flock Abbahu experienced difficulty in protecting his co-religionists. Nevertheless, he eclipsed the patriarch of the day in importance, describing him as 'a small man' and often acting in his place as the Jewish spokesman to the Romans.

Narses did not fulfil Jewish hopes, because he was subsequently defeated in Armenia (296) by Galerius, one of the three co-emperors of Diocletian (284–305). But it was perhaps in order to counter Jewish disaffection, encouraged by Narses, that Diocletian, when he made sacrifices to the emperor compulsory for all peoples of the empire, specifically and uniquely exempted the Jews.[54] He also took steps to enhance the official dignity of the patriarchal office.[55] All this was in profound contrast to his oppression of the Christians, who underwent at the hands of Diocletian, Galerius and Maximinus II the gravest and most long-lasting of all their persecutions, resulting, over a period of ten years (303–13), in the loss of perhaps three thousand lives.

17

Epilogue: The Jews in the Christian Empire

During the later years of the pagan empire, the Jews had not caused the Roman authorities any serious anxiety. But the determined nature of the persecution which Diocletian and his colleagues launched against the Christians shows that, although the adherents of the Christian faith numbered only between ten to fifteen per cent of the populations of the empire, the pagan authorities had become seriously worried by their subversive menace to the traditional religion. In this they were amply justified, since after Constantine the Great (AD 306–37) had defeated and killed his pagan rival Maxentius at the battle of the Milvian Bridge (312), Christianity replaced paganism as the official religion of the Roman state. Once again Jerusalem was called Hierosolyma, instead of Aelia Capitolina. Yet this was by no means because of its sacredness to the Jews, but as a resplendent centre of Christian pilgrimage. Thereafter more and more people, all over the Roman world, quite rapidly became Christians, and the Jews were the minority in a Christian instead of a pagan empire.

Why did Christianity, instead of Judaism from which it originated, become the successor to the pagans, and the dominant faith in the western world? The two religions had so much in common. Their ethical systems, for the most part, shared the same ground. Their excellent social and philanthropic services, too, were comparable, although the services of the Christians were by now the better organized of the two,

282

since the centralized arrangements of Christian episcopacies were more efficient than the decentralized efforts of individual Jewish communities and presbyteries. The Christians also outdid the Jews in their presentation of a truly universal charity and compassion and consolation, embracing even the sinners and the destitute. True, all these features are also found in the Jewish scriptures. But they are found more vividly in the Gospels. The authors of these books possessed exceptional dramatic gifts; and so did Paul.

Yet the success of Christianity was not entirely due to the New Testament, since the interest in its contents – shown, for example, by the wall-painters of Rome's Christian catacombs – was patchy and limited. However, the themes which these artists do choose to stress are revealing, as was indicated in the last chapter. For these themes display Jesus, above all, as a miracle-worker and saviour. There had been many saviours in many religions – bringers of immortality to efface the miseries of this world. But the Christian saviour was peculiarly satisfying to the emotions, because he could be linked with an actual, allegedly historical, life upon earth, such as had never been ascribed to any of his pagan counterparts. This was what provided the irresistible drama. And to those who could face the emotional horror of his martyrdom, that Jewish conception so triumphantly assumed by the Christians, the drama was greater still. In the last resort, therefore, the reason why Christianity instead of Judaism became the religion of the western world was because that world hankered after a saviour, and the Christians could provide the most satisfying of all saviours, and recall his vivid existence among mankind. All that the Jews could say, on the other hand, was that a Messiah would come in the future, which did much less to arouse the emotions – and in any case their leadership, for the most part, only said it cautiously.

Nevertheless, any attempt to assess the reasons why Christianity and not Judaism gained this sweeping triumph requires that one further thing should be said. Historians do not like to attribute sweeping changes to the accidental peculiarities of a single individual. But if there was ever a man in history of whom this might be said, it was Constantine the Great. The vigorous but confused workings of his mind and emotions, linking and merging sun-worship with the saviourship of Jesus, played a dominant part in the extraordinary turn of events that, within a few decades, brought Christianity, the religion of quite a small minority, into a position of complete supremacy throughout the empire.

This revolutionary change confronted the patriarchs of the time, from Judah III (275–320) onwards, with appalling new problems. Judah's court and entourage were diminished to a scale far more modest than that maintained by his predecessors. But he had prepared for the new situation, in so far as he could, by organizing the dispatch to numerous parts of the Dispersion of teams of itinerant school-inspectors. They also redoubled their professional fund-raising efforts, which strained the patience and generosity of many communities.[1]

The history of Judaism is a continuous one, extending from the remotest Old Testament times to the present day, and beyond it into the indefinite future. But this is the point at which the story that has been told here must have a stop. For the Roman authorities and their Greek subjects, with whom the Jews had hitherto had to deal, had belonged to the pagan religion. When the rulers of the empire became Christian, an entirely different chapter of Jewish history opens up, with fresh themes and problems. Nevertheless, a brief epilogue may be added. In particular, it has to be recorded that this new chapter spelt disaster for the Jews – a disaster which some of them had specifically feared, well in advance, as one of the ultimate plagues announcing the end of the world. For the Christian emperors and religious leaders were far less tolerant to the Jews than the pagans had ever been.

This worsened situation was clearly announced by the Christian authors of the day – for example, Constantine's panegyrical biographer and ecclesiastical historian Eusebius. Writers such as Eusebius emphasize, time after time, the message of *Matthew* that the Jews were corporatively responsible for the death of Jesus Christ, and that all the troubles which had come upon them, or might come upon them in the future, were part-payment for that perfidiousness. 'It seems unworthy,' as Constantine wrote to the churches after the Council of Arelate (Arles), 'to calculate this most holy feast of Easter according to the customs of the Jews, who, having stained their hands with lawless crime, are naturally, in their foulness, blind in soul . . . What right opinions can they have who, after the murder of the Lord, went out of their minds, and are led, not by reason, but by uncontrolled passion?' Nor was this madness surprising, the argument continued, since the Jews who had committed this crime, seeing that they had rejected God, were likewise rejected by him: the Law had only been a temporary dispensation, and to observe it, without recognizing Christ, was nothing better than diabolical: and yet the Jews, who had spread everywhere, actually hoped to become the masters of the Roman world – a vain hope, yet they irritatingly persisted in regarding themselves as superior to everyone else.[2]

In the eyes of Christian theologians, however, this condemnation still retained a powerful element of ambivalence. For the immense debt of Christianity to Judaism could neither be escaped nor denied. By proving the verity of the Old Testament, it was pointed out, the Jews could not help being witnesses, however unwilling, to the verity of Jesus Christ who fulfilled so many of its prophecies. And Eusebius, like others, astonishingly took this doctrine a big stage further by professing that the great figures of the Old Testament had actually seen and recognized Jesus themselves!

Ever since man was first created, all who are said to have been distinguished for righteousness and the purity of their religion – the great servant Moses and his companions; before him Abraham, the very first, and his children; and all the righteous men and prophets who have since appeared – recognized him in visions seen with the pure eyes of the mind, and paid due honour to him as God's Son.[3]

In view of this interpretation there could be no question of the new Christian regime seeking to suppress the Jews by force, in the same way as it rapidly began to suppress 'heretics' within its own ranks. On the contrary, as Paul had said to the Romans, citing Isaiah: 'God brought upon them a numbness of spirit: he gave them blind eyes and deaf ears, and so it is still . . . I now ask, did their failure mean complete downfall? Far from it! Because they offended, salvation has come to the Gentiles, to stir Israel to emulation.'[4] And so the professed doctrine of the late imperial church was that the Jews must be tolerated until the Second Coming: because they had prepared the way for Jesus Christ and brought him forth, they must be protected from total extinction.

Yet the same Christian theology which taught that the Jews should still be allowed to exist also taught that, because they had killed Jesus, the sufferings which had been inflicted upon them (and might be inflicted upon them in the future) were justifiable. In particular, because of the Dispersion, they were for the first time declared permanent aliens and wanderers: because of their repudiation of Christ, they had lost their homes for ever. In other words, they must be allowed to live, but this life, in the present and future, ought to be miserable – the minimum possible existence. This was the attitude, above all, of many members of the Christian clergy, whose revolutionary ascent to power proved fiercely damaging to the Jews. The inflammatory words these clerics uttered, and the condemnatory sermons they preached, naturally intensified anti-Jewish feeling among the masses (and encouraged tradesmen to demand action against their Jewish rivals). The more responsible bishops, on the other hand, often deprecated such firebrands.

In so doing they were supporting the policy of the imperial government. Yet this policy, though avoiding extremities because pogroms were undesirable breaches of public order, was still hostile to the Jews, far more hostile than anything they had ever experienced from the Romans before. For menacing lip-service paid to the theological condemnation of Judaism was accompanied by action. Many measures were taken to lower the status of the synagogue, to segregate Jews from believing Christians, to prevent conversions to Judaism, to penalize Jewish attempts at winning back those who had been converted to Christianity,[5] and to curtail any possible rivalry to ecclesiastical domination.

Yet the policy of Constantine himself, in practice, was less wholeheartedly severe than that of his successors. A.H.M.Jones writes:

Though for theological reasons he held them in detestation and publicly vilified them ... his actual treatment of them was not oppressive. He abolished, it is true, their ancient immunity from membership of city councils, but when Christians were compelled to serve, Jews could hardly expect exemption; and he maintained the immunity of two or three persons in each city, and later extended it to all synagogue officials, thus giving them equal status with the Christian clergy. He was not, however, prepared to tolerate proselytism, and he penalised Jewish owners who circumcised their pagan or Christian slaves. And when an opportunity presented itself for launching a mission to convert the Jews, he subsidised it lavishly ... From henceforth the contemptuous toleration which the Roman government had hitherto shown towards Judaism changed slowly but steadily into hostility, culminating in drastic penal laws.[6]

This further worsening of the situation became apparent during the reign of Constantine's son Constantius II (337–61). As a consequence, under his viceroy Constantius Gallus (351–3), rebels in Palestine proclaimed a Jewish king named Patricius – a serious attempt to exploit bad relations between the Romans and Persians.[7] The next emperor Julian (361–3), in order to strike a blow against the Christians from whom he had apostatized, and in the hope of protecting his rear during a forth-

coming invasion of the Persian empire, planned to allow the reconstruction of the Temple at Jerusalem – a project and a policy which,
for all its transience, deserves a book to itself.[8] But Julian's interest in
Judaism was not based on any genuine sympathy, and in any case the
rabbis did not relish the prospect of a renewal of bloody sacrifices on the
Temple mount, presumably under the leadership of Jews other than
themselves. And so the plan came to nothing – ostensibly because work
on the substructure released inflammable gases. When Julian crossed
the eastern frontier, he failed to capture Ctesiphon and, far from doing
the Jews any good, reduced Machuza and its Jewish academy to ruins.

After his death as the result of a wound, the Roman empire, now permanently divided into eastern (Byzantine) and western halves, became
Christian once again. Despite brief liberal intermissions under Theodosius I (379–95) and Eutropius (395–9)[9] – the minister of Theodosius'
son Arcadius – the position of the Jews deteriorated once again. In 415
the hereditary patriarch Gamaliel VII, the last member of the house of
Hillel, was penalized for abusing his functions. In 425 he died, and
four years later the patriarchate was abolished and its finances annexed
by the emperor. Meanwhile the attitudes of Christian writers, including
St Ambrose (d. 397), St John Chrysostom (d. 407), St Augustine (d.
430) and St Cyril of Alexandria (d. 444), were sharply anti-Jewish.
Moreover, the Codex of the eastern emperor Theodosius II, published
in 438, systematized numerous recent restrictions upon the Jews;
although as always their basic right to remain alive was safeguarded,
and it has even been argued that the Codex slightly improved their
position.[10]

In this period the Samaritans came into the public eye once again.
Still constituting a large majority of the population of Samaria, they
had experienced a brief renaissance in the previous century under Baba
Rabba, who built many synagogues round Neapolis. Subsequently,
however, they were penalized in the various anti-Jewish laws; and now
in 451, encouraged perhaps by deep rifts in the Christian ranks, they
burst into a brief but bloody revolt. Meanwhile, official hostility against
the Jews, too, remained inexorable. When the bones of Jewish dead
were burnt in a conflagration of the Antioch synagogue, the emperor
Zeno (474–91) remarked: 'Why did they not burn the living Jews along
with the dead?'

In the Persian empire, for a time, their situation had remained much
better than in the Roman world. Rav Ashi of Sura flouted a rabbinical

ban on the sale of arms by supporting the provision of weapons to the Persians, for use against Rome.[11] Under the Persian monarch Yazdegerd I (399–420), the Jews were treated with particular tolerance; and this was the period which witnessed, under the guidance of Ashi, the compilation of the greater part of the Babylonian Talmud – the second and last part of the Gamara, which formed the continuation of the Mishnah.[12] Thereafter, however, there was a terrible change. The Persian king Yazdegerd II (*c.* 438–57) and his son Firuz (Peroz) (*c.* 459–86) became very hostile to the Jews resident in their empire, and many emigrated to Arabia and India. The academies at Sura and Pumbeditha were temporarily closed, and at the end of the reign of Firuz the exilarch Mar Huna Mari was condemned to death. His son Mar Zutra II escaped, however, and set up a little separate state for seven years.

In Italy, for a time, things took a turn for the better, after the last western emperors had been succeeded by the German king Odoacer. Moreover, his supplanter and successor Theoderic (493–518), though eager for the conversion of the Jews to Christianity, did not deny them the 'preservation of their ancient rights'. But the improvement was only transitory, since that most orthodox of Byzantine emperors Justinian I (527–65), the reconqueror of Italy, inflicted increasingly severe disabilities upon Jews and Samaritans alike – with all the greater ferocity after renewed Samaritan revolts.

One of his successors, Maurice (582–602), went so far as to coordinate his anti-Jewish measures with the Persian king Chosroes (Khosrau) II Parvez (590–628). However, these friendly relations between the two empires did not last. In the reign of Heraclius I (610–41) the army of Chosroes invaded Palestine, whereupon both the Jews (under Benjamin of Tiberias) and the Samaritans rallied to his cause – and were said to have massacred nearly 100,000 Christians. Jerusalem fell to the invader, and at this point Palestine, in the words of N.P.Kondakov, 'enters upon the troubled period which might very naturally be called the period of the Middle Ages, were it not for the fact that it has lasted to our own times'.[13]

In 629, Heraclius reoccupied Jerusalem, and the Christian clergy took a savage revenge on the Jews. The emperor ordered the baptism of every one of them throughout the empire – although, like similar decrees by many of his successors, the order was never enforced, or enforceable. However, in 636–40 Palestine and the Persian empire were conquered by the second Arab Caliph Omar, with warm support from the Jews, who subsequently flourished under Arab rule.[14] Palestine and eastern Judaism had ceased to belong to the familiar world.[15]

In the countries that remained within the Byzantine empire, the Jews pursued, on the whole, an unfavoured existence. But this was not where their main destiny lay. It lay with all those communities of the European Dispersion – for example in Italy, France, Spain and Germany, from which the earliest evidence for Jewish residents is an edict of Constantine to Colonia Agrippinensis (Cologne) in AD 321, now in the Vatican collection. These communities had been leading their own lives for many generations under the Roman empire, and still did so, achieving greater prominence under the national and regional regimes that succeeded Roman rule.[16] In the face of terrific external pressures and temptations to apostasy, they persistently survived. As Werner Keller has written:

No other people has experienced a history like that of the descendants of the People of the Book in the Dispersion. The whole world has served as backdrop for their destiny ... Only a few happy hours have intervened amidst long periods of suffering. But despite all oppression and misery, without a state or a country of their own, defenceless, powerless, and without rights, this people has survived all storms and disasters.[17]

'The Lord,' declared *Deuteronomy*, 'will disperse you among the peoples, and you will be left few in number among the nations to which the Lord will lead you.'[18] But the book of *Ezekiel*, in the early days of the Dispersion, had prophesied that the time would come when Israel would be restored to its home. He had uttered that prophecy at a time when the Assyrians and Babylonians had obliterated it. Now the national home had been ruined again, as a result of the two Jewish revolts against the Romans. And, since then, Rome's adoption of the Christian faith had made the official attitude to the Jews a great deal harsher still.

Nevertheless, continued *Ezekiel*:

Say to them, These are the words of the Lord God: I am gathering up the Israelites from their places of exile among the nations; I will assemble them from every quarter and restore them to their own soil. I will make them one single nation in the land, on the mountains of Israel ... They shall conform to my laws, they shall observe and carry out my statutes. They shall live in the land which I gave my servant Jacob, the land where your fathers lived ... I will make a Covenant with them to bring them prosperity; this Covenant shall be theirs for ever.[19]

The Dispersion has not ended, and will never end. Yet to the Jews throughout the world today, this prophecy of *Ezekiel* has now been fulfilled by the re-establishment of the state of Israel. By this fulfilment, the tribulations described in the foregoing pages have at long last received at least a measure of recompense.

Notes

The following abbreviations are used in the notes:

B.	*Babylonian Talmud*
Baron	S. Baron, *A Social and Religious History of the Jews*
BMC.	British Museum catalogues: Greek coins
BMC. Emp.	*Coins of the Roman Empire in the British Museum*
Eusebius	Eusebius, *Historia Ecclesiastica* (History of the Church)
J.	*Jerusalem (or Palestinian) Talmud*
Josephus, *AJ.*	Josephus, *Antiquitates Judaicae* (Jewish Antiquities)
Josephus, *BJ.*	Josephus, *Bellum Judaicum* (Jewish War)
Josephus, *C. Ap.*	Josephus, *Contra Apionem* (Against Apion)
M.	*Mishnah*
Meshorer	Y. Meshorer, *Jewish Coins of the Second Temple Period*
SHA.	*Scriptores Historiae Augustae*

Introduction
1 *Times Literary Supplement*, 24/3/72.
2 J. W. Parkes, *Whose Land?* (1970 ed.), p. 9.
3 A. H. M. Jones, *The Herods of Judaea* (1967 ed.), p. xii.

Part I   THE JEWS BEFORE THE ROMANS

1   Prologue: The Traditions of Israel
1   Corresponding to the ancient Israelite tribes of Judah (N.E. section), Benjamin, Dan, Ephraim (S.E. section).
2   *Num.* 20, 18.
3   *Deut.* 23, 8; *Ps.* 137, 7; *Ezek.* 25, 12; etc.
4   *Isa.* 43, 18.
5   *Gen.* 5, 24. The Catholic Catechism stated that the return of Enoch and Elijah will prelude the end of the world.
6   It has also been suggested, however, that this was a colony of Ur in northern Mesopotamia.
7   *Gen.* 17, 10–11.
8   *Gen.* 32, 28.
9   Rabban Gamaliel II, *M. Pesahim*, 10, 5.
10 *Isa.* 43, 16 f. (Exodus); *Num.* 24, 17 (Balaam).
11 *Exod.* 19, 5.
12 *Num.* 23, 9.
13 *Esther* 3, 8 (Haman to Ahasuerus: probably Xerxes I).
14 *Gen. rabba* (commentary), I, 1, 4.
15 C. H. Dodd, *The Meaning of Paul for Today*, cf. *Deut.* 11, 26, *Exod.* 21, 24.
16 Josephus, *AJ.* IV, 48.
17 *I Sam.* 8, 5.
18 *I Sam.* 10, 1.
19 *II Sam.* 7, 12 ff.
20 *Ezek.* 40, 45; 44, 15. David's other high priest was Abiathar.
21 *Lev.* 24, 16.
22 Not 'Jehovah', which is an erroneous Christian reconstruction based on the combination of the consonants YHWH with the vowels of 'Adhonai' (Lord).
23 *Jer.* 2, 28 (or 'as many blood-spattered altars').
24 *Isa.* 14, 27.
25 R. Learsi, *Israel: A History of the Jewish People*, World Publishing Company (Meridian) (1949), pp. 679 f.
26 *II Kings* 2, 11.
27 *Mal.* 4, 5.
28 *Amos* 9, 7.
29 *Hos.* 13, 2.
30 *Isa.* 2, 4 (inscribed at the entrance of the UN building); cf. 11, 6–9.

31 *Isa.* 7, 14–15; 9, 6.
32 *II Kings* 19, 35.
33 *Jer.* 12, 1.
34 *Lam.* 1, 8–9.
35 An Aramaic inscription reflects an Aramaic community at Sardis (Sart) in 455 or 394 BC – Buckler and Robinson, *Sardis*, I, p. 117, VI, p. 223.
36 *Ps.* 137, 1 and 5.
37 *Ezek.* 18, 20.
38 *Ezek.* 34, 23–4. Ezekiel's alleged tomb in Iraq was still cared for at least as late as 1966.
39 *II Sam.* 7, 16.
40 *Ezra* 4, 3.
41 Since 1623 they have claimed descent for their high priest from Aaron's uncle Uzziel.
42 Josephus, *C. Ap.* II, 165.
43 *Mal.* 2, 10.
44 See Ch. 2 and n. 17.
45 Appendix (Baraitha) to *B. Pirke Aboth*, 5.

2   *Liberation from the Greeks: the Maccabees*
1 *Gen.* 9, 27.
2 There is a disputed earlier example at Delos: and a piece of pottery from Elat (about sixth century BC) refers to a 'house of meeting'.
3 Coins of *c.* 400 BC of the Persian province of Judah copy the design of an owl from the coinage of Athens (Meshorer, p. 116, nos. 2 ff.).
4 Diodorus Siculus, XL, 3, 4.
5 Josephus, *C. Ap.* I, 179, Diogenes Laertius, preface, 9.
6 Josephus, *AJ.* XII, 11 f.
7 'Longinus', *On the Sublime*, 9, 9, is the exception.
8 *II Macc.* 3, 7 ff.
9 Josephus, *BJ.* VII, 43 ff.
10 *I Macc.* 1, 11.
11 *Dan.* 9, 27; 11, 31; 12, 31; *I Macc.* 1, 37–40.
12 *II Macc.* 6, 2.
13 *II Macc.* 7, 37.
14 *Num.* 25, 7–8.
15 *I Macc.* 8, 23–30.
16 *I Macc.* 12, 1–23; 14, 16–23.
17 *Exod.* 30, 13. (At one time the sum had been $\frac{1}{3}$ shekel: *Neh.* 10, 32.) Many contributed more.
18 *I Macc.* 10, 20.

19 *I Macc.* 15, 20–21.
20 Valerius Maximus, I, 3, 3. Cf. Livy, *Epitome*, 54.
21 Josephus, *AJ.* XIV, 249–55.
22 Josephus, *AJ.* XIV, 241 f.: John Hyrcanus I more probably than II.
23 Damocritus: Josephus, *C. Ap.* II, 91 ff.
24 Josephus, *C. Ap.* II, 80.
25 Diodorus Siculus, XXXIV, 1, 3, XL, 3, 4.
26 Josephus, *C. Ap.* I, 1; cf. *AJ.* I, 21 f.
27 *Letter to Aristeas* (A. Lesky, *History of Greek Literature*, p. 800 and n.1).
28 *Wisdom of Solomon* 19. 2: or the Egyptians had escorted them, Josephus, *BJ.* V, 383.
29 *Oxford Classical Dictionary*, 2nd ed. (1970), p. 894, s.v. 'Pseudepigraphic Literature'.
30 *Sibylline Oracles*, III, 271–2.

3   *The Divisions within Judaism in Maccabaean Times*
1 *Dan.* 11, 34.
2 *Dan.* 12, 2. For partial earlier analogies cf. *Isa.* 26, 19, and *Job* 19, 25–6. It was because of such passages that *Daniel* was not in the Hebrew canon of the prophets: he seemed too apocalyptic to the Pharisees.
3 *Dan.* 9, 25.
4 *Dan.* 7, 1–4. 'Son of Man' is the Aramaic *bar 'enash*; cf. the Hebrew *ben 'adham*.
5 *The Psalms of Solomon* call the Pharisees 'Hasidim'.
6 The earliest manner of transmitting the oral Law was said to have been by 'Midrash', exposition or running commentary on the biblical text.
7 The Pharisees took a middle path on determinism: 'all is foreseen, and free will is given' (R. Akiba, *M. Aboth*, III, 19; cf. Josephus, *BJ.* II, 163).
8 For the admission that there were 'true' and 'false' Pharisees, cf. *J. Berakoth*, IX, 6; and for complacency *B. Berakoth*, 28b.
9 For the ideal scribe, cf. *Ecclesiasticus* 38, 24–39, *M. Aboth*, I, 2. Perhaps the scribes had begun as copyists under the Persian empire.
10 According to another theory, there was at this stage both a political (Sadducee) Council and a religious body (Great Beth Din) presided over by the legendary Pharisee 'pairs' (Ch. 5, n. 4).
11 *Matt.* 23, 15.
12 The Essenes may also have derived their name from the *Hasidim*, though there are other alternative derivations. Josephus, *AJ.* XIII,

171, attributes their origin to Jonathan's reign, but they may have been earlier. See now their Temple Scroll.

13 Pliny the elder, *Natural History*, V, 15, 73.

14 Josephus, *BJ*. II, 140.

15 Philo, *Quod Omnis Probus Liber Sit*, XIII, 91.

16 Josephus, *BJ*. II, 159.

17 When Onias III had been deposed in 174 BC, *II Macc.* 4, 7.

18 Perhaps the choice of site was dictated by *Hos.* 2, 14 f.

19 V. Tcherikover, *Hellenistic Civilisation and the Jews* (1966), p. 402.

20 *Commentary on Hosea* (G. Vermes, *The Dead Sea Scrolls in English*, 1970 ed., p. 230).

21 References in M. Grant, *Herod the Great* (1971), p. 242, notes 24 ff. The enemy are riddlingly described as 'Kittim'.

22 *Hymn (Dead Sea Scrolls)* 10 (G. Vermes, op. cit., pp. 51, 172).

23 *Hymn* 4 (ibid., p. 157): this may or may not be a reference to the Suffering Servant of the Second Isaiah.

24 *Zech.* 6, 9–13.

25 *Community Rule (Manual of Discipline)*, 9 (G. Vermes, op. cit., p. 87).

26 *Commentaries on Isaiah*, I (ibid., pp. 49, 227).

27 *Community Rule*, 5–7, and 3 (ibid., pp. 79 ff., 75).

28 *Amos* 5, 27.

29 *Damascus Document*, 8 (G. Vermes, op. cit., p. 106, etc.).

30 Ibid., 8 (ibid., p. 105, etc.).

31 Eusebius, II, 17.

32 Josephus, *AJ*. XIII, 354.

33 Josephus, *AJ*. XIII, 395.

34 Meshorer, p. 118, nos. 5 ff.

35 Meshorer, p. 119, no. 12.

36 *J. Berakoth*, VII, 2; cf. *J. Nazir*, III, 5.

37 Cf. Philo, *Legatio ad Gaium*, 216, Josephus, *AJ*. XVIII, 311–13.

38 *B. Kiddushin*, 66a (but the name Jannai (Yannai) is often used loosely of a monarch in general; so the reference could be to John Hyrcanus I).

39 *B. Sotah*, 22b. Alexander Jannaeus' later coins have 'Jonathan the high priest' overstruck on 'Jehonathan the king', Meshorer, pp. 120 f., nos. 17 and 17a.

40 Queen Athaliah of Judah (841–835 BC) was exceptional.

Part II HEROD AND HIS SUCCESSORS

4 The Jews under Pompey, Caesar and the Parthians

1 When references to Josephus are given here, only one of his works will normally be indicated; unless they differ markedly.

2 Josephus, *AJ*. XIV, 41.

3 Josephus, *AJ*. XIV, 74 (referring to Jerusalem). Pompey also executed Silas, a Jewish prince of Lysias in Syria, ibid., XIV, 40.

4 Josephus, *AJ*. XIV, 196, refers this provision to Julius Caesar, but it probably originated earlier.

5 *M. Gittin*, IV, 6, 9.

6 Cicero, *Pro Flacco*, XXVIII, 66. See p. 62.

7 Ibid., XXVIII, 69 (trans. L. E. Lord).

8 Diodorus Siculus, XXXIV, 1, 3.

9 *Psalms of Solomon*, XVII, 11–14; II, 26 ff., refers to the death of Pompey in 48 BC.

10 Ibid., XVII, 45.

11 *Religious Calendar* (G. Vermes, op. cit., p. 58).

12 *War Scroll*, 11 (ibid., p. 138).

13 Caesar's attempt to launch Aristobulus II and his son against them failed, and both died.

14 Josephus, *AJ*. XIV, 228, 230, 234, 237, 240.

15 A. N. Sherwin-White, *Racial Prejudice in Imperial Rome* (1967), p. 89.

16 Josephus, *AJ*. XIV, 224.

17 R. Eleazar ben Hyrcanus 'the Great' less optimistically stressed the intrinsic undesirability of converts owing to their proneness to fall back into idolatry.

18 R. Eleazar ben Pedat (died *c*. AD 279); for references to him see Baron, index, s.v.

19 Philo, *De Specialibus Legibus*, I, 9, 52.

20 Cf. Josephus, *AJ*. XX, 41 ff.; *B. Yebamoth*, 46a.

21 Baron, p. 3.

22 Heavy burial expenses accentuated class differences, which were lessened, however, by rabbinical measures.

23 Philo, *In Flaccum*, VII, 43.

24 Though some individual Jews acquired Alexandrian citizenship.

25 Strabo in Josephus, *AJ*. XIV, 117.

26 *B. Sukkah*, 51b, etc.

27 In some parts of the Dispersion there were also centres with residential accommodation, *J. Gittin*, I, 1.

28 Dio Cassius, XXXVII, 17, speaks of their large increase, in spite of occasional measures to check conversions.

29 The *archisynagogi* were not the same as the civil rulers of the community (*archontes*), though the posts were sometimes combined. Archonships were also, evidently, sometimes honorary, since children held them.

30 E.g. in north Africa, the Mediterranean islands and Galilee (Beth-Shearim).

31 Ovid, *Ars Amatoria*, I, 75.

32 E.g. vessels inscribed *garum castum, muria casta*.

33 Meshorer, p. 122, no. 24.

34 To be delivered at Sidon, except during the sabbatical year (*Lev.* 25, 1–7).

35 This is the most likely interpretation of Josephus, *AJ.* XIV, 172.

36 Suetonius, *Divus Julius*, 84 (Rome).

37 *Lev.* 21, 17 ff.

38 Meshorer, p. 124, nos. 1 ff.

5   The Kingship of Herod the Great

1 Further references are given in M. Grant, *Herod the Great* (1971).

2 Meshorer, p. 125, no. 36; although the depiction of the Menorah was forbidden by the Talmud: sources in E. R. Goodenough, *Jewish Symbols in the Greco-Roman Period*, vol. IV, p. 71.

3 Josephus, *AJ.* XIV, 403.

4 He had come to Jerusalem as a pupil of the leading Pharisees Shemaiah and Abtalion. It was subsequently believed that there had been similar 'pairs' (Zuggoth) of Pharisaic leaders going back to 165 BC.

5 The central point of interest was now the organization of the Halakah ('Walking'), the teaching and repetition of the traditional laws. Later tradition also maintained that Hillel and Shammai laid down the great divisions (Orders) of the Mishnah.

6 *M. Aboth*, I, 10.

7 *Exod.* 28, 3; *Ecclesiasticus*, 45, 7.

8 Nittai of Arbela had been president of the Council of Elders in the second century BC.

9 The first of these 'Boethusians' was Boethus the father of the second of the two Mariammes successively married to Herod.

10 *B. Pesahim*, 57a.

11 *Exod.* 20, 4; *Deut.* 5, 8.

12 *Numbers rabba*, XIV, 1 and 3 studiously avoid reference to Herod in this connexion.

13 The plain of Batanea (En-Nukra), the hills of Trachonitis (Leja and Safa) and Auranitis (Jebel Hauran or Druz).

14 Ulatha and Panias (with the shrine of Panion).

15 E.g. inscription of Berenice Jews of *c.* 25 BC (?) thanking benefactor M. Tittius; and Jewish Cyrenaican inscription of 8 or 6 BC, now at Carpentoracte (Carpentras), thanking Dec. Valerius Dionysius for building and decorating an 'amphitheatre' (auditorium), J. & G. Roux, *Revue des études grecques*, LXII, p. 294.

16 Josephus, *AJ.* XVI, 160.

17 A contemporary Greek from Asia Minor, Strabo of Amaseia (Samsun), maintained that the Jews had first been good, under Moses, but had then fallen into superstition (XVI, 36 f., 761).

18 Josephus, *AJ.* XVI, 28.

19 Josephus, *AJ.* XVI, 36.

20 Josephus, *AJ.* XVI, 59.

21 Josephus, *AJ.* XVI, 167–70.

22 Perhaps in *c.* 7 BC the ban on associations was reimposed, and Jews were again exempted, in Rome and the provinces.

23 Josephus, *AJ.* XVI, 175.

24 This is probably the point of Philo, *In Flaccum*, 74; Josephus, *AJ.* XIX, 293. The ethnarch was temporarily suspended, or his powers decreased.

25 Mariamme I's sons were Alexander and Aristobulus (d. *c.* 6 BC); and Herod's eldest son (by Doris) was Antipater (d. 4 BC).

26 Herod had also possessed, and probably now lost, the unique privilege of reclaiming fugitive subjects from territories outside his jurisdiction.

27 Under Zamaris, with a hundred of his kinsmen: they were settled in Trachonitis to secure the safety of the pilgrim traffic: Josephus, *AJ.* XVII, 26.

28 Herod also fortified the Negev frontier: S. Applebaum, *Zion*, XXVII, 1962, pp. 3 ff.

29 Aretas IV remained in power until AD 40, and became the greatest of all Nabataean monarchs.

30 E.g. Gangra (Vezirköprü) oath of 3 BC to Augustus and his sons and kinsmen: Dessau, *Inscriptiones Latinae Selectae*, II, 8781.

31 *Dan.* 3, 12.

32 Josephus, *C. Ap.* II, 73.

33 Philo, *In Flaccum*, VII, 49.

34 *Isa.* 56, 3.

35 *M. Aboth*, 2, 7.

36 M. Grant, *Herod the Great*, p. 205, cf. Meshorer, p. 65 (but not indicated in p. 127, no. 37).

37 *Num.* 24, 17.

38 Josephus, *AJ.* XVII, 151 ('golden').

39 Meshorer, p. 130, no. 54 (uncertain date).

40 *Deut.* 32, 11, etc. Solomon had adorned his Temple with bulls and lions and eagles. Herod erected his own statues in non-Jewish centres (e.g. S'ia).

6 Principalities and Province

1 Josephus, *BJ.* II, 10–13 (trans. H. St. J. Thackeray).

2 Josephus, *AJ.* XVII, 272. Judas seized the palace at Sepphoris and its armoury. Apparently Samaria did not join the revolts.

3 Tacitus, *Histories*, V, 9.

4 Josephus, *BJ.* II, 53.

5 *Seder Olam rabba*, fin. (correcting 'Asveros' to 'Varos'); cf. Josephus, *C. Ap.* I, 34.

6 To Salome: Jamnia, Azotus, Phasaelis. To Syria: Gaza, Gadara, Hippos. Archelaus repeats Herod's coin-types of an anchor and galley (Meshorer, p. 130 ff., nos. 56–60A), in order to show he retained the ports of Caesarea Maritima and Joppa.

7 Josephus, *AJ.* XVII, 342: 'he had disobeyed his instructions to show moderation in dealing with them'.

8 *Matt.* 22, 16; *Mark*, 3, 6; 12, 13.

9 P. Z. Bedoukian, *American Numismatic Society Museum Notes*, XVII, 1971, pp. 138 ff.

10 *Assumption of Moses* (ed. R. H. Charles, 1897).

11 *Samaritan Chronicle* (*Revue des études juives*, XLV, p. 80).

12 Mention is also made of 'winter quarters' in Jerusalem, Josephus, *AJ.* XVIII, 55.

13 The attribution of Quirinius' census to an earlier date by *Luke* 2, 2 is – despite endless discussion – wrong, and cannot be vindicated by re-translation or the supposition of an earlier tour of duty.

14 Was Caesar's exemption from tax deliveries in the sabbatical year cancelled?

15 *Lev.* 25, 23.

16 *II Sam.* 24, 1 and 15.

17 The alternative ascription of Judas' revolt to Gaulanitis or Galilee is less probable.

18 According to some calculations, the Fifth Monarchy of *Daniel* was at hand.

19 *I. Macc.* 2, 26.

20 Josephus, *BJ.* VII, 254.

21 Josephus, *AJ.* XVIII, 23–4 (the other 'philosophies' are those of the Sadducees, Pharisees and Essenes). The 'Fourth Philosophy' has

often been identified with the Zealots, though it may not be capable of so specific an attribution.

22 *B. Pesahim*, 57a.

23 *B. Yoma*, 69a.

24 This is important in relation to the 'trial' of Jesus.

25 W. Dittenberger, *Orientis Graecae Inscriptiones Selectae*, 598, *Supplementum Epigraphicum Graecum*, VIII, 169; cf. *Ezekiel*, 44, 9. *John* 18, 31, recording the absence of capital jurisdiction, need not perhaps, as has been suggested, be narrowed down to refer to the eve of Passover only.

26 Tacitus, *Annals*, II, 42.

27 J. P. V. D. Balsdon, *The Emperor Gaius* (1934), p. 128.

28 Philo, *Legatio ad Gaium*, 160.

29 Tacitus, *Annals*, II, 85.

30 Josephus, *AJ*. XVII, 81–4 (Fulvia, wife of Saturninus).

31 Herod's niece Berenice and her son Agrippa I: Josephus, *AJ*. XVIII, 165.

32 Josephus, *AJ*. XVIII, 310 ff., 377 ff.

33 Josephus, *AJ*. XVIII, 174.

34 Meshorer, p. 170, nos. 221 ff.

35 Ishmael son of Phiabi, Eleazar son of Ananus I and Simon son of Camithus (of the house of Ananus).

Part III   THREATS FROM ROMANS, GREEKS AND CHRISTIANS

   7   *The Problems of Pontius Pilate*

1 Philo, *Legatio ad Gaium*, 299–305.

2 Josephus was probably well informed on this period since Tiberius' memoirs were the favourite reading of his own patron Domitian: Suetonius, *Domitian*, 20.

3 Meshorer, p. 172, no. 229 (AD 29).

4 Josephus, *AJ*. XVIII, 55–6 (trans. L. H. Feldman).

5 Tacitus, *Annals*, II, 17.

6 Josephus, *BJ*. II, 175.

7 *M. Shekalim*, 4, 2.

8 Philo, *Legatio ad Gaium*, 299.

9 Meshorer, p. 135, no. 76.

10 *Luke* 13, 32.

11 *B. Berakoth*, 61b.

12 Josephus, *AJ*. XVIII, 27. The name 'Autocratoris' did not last.

13 Meshorer, p. 133, nos. 63 ff.
14 *John* 1, 20–28.
15 Cf. *Zech.* 13, 15
16 *Luke* 3, 4; cf. *Isa.* 40, 3.
17 *Matt.* 11, 12; Josephus, *AJ.* XVIII, 116–19.
18 *Lev.* 18, 16; 20, 21. Had they been childless, however, such a remarriage would have been obligatory.
19 Josephus, *AJ.* XVIII, 118.
20 *Mark* 6, 14.
21 *John* 4, 2.
22 *Matt.* 11, 2–6; *John* 1, 29–36.
23 *Mark* 2, 18.
24 *Luke* 8, 3 (Joanna, wife of Chuza).
25 *Matt.* 14, 13.
26 For the latest discussion of the historicity of Jesus see W. H. C. Frend, *English Historical Review*, 1972, pp. 345 ff.
27 The famous alleged reference in Josephus, *AJ.* XVIII, 63–4, conflicts with his known views and is an interpolation – possibly it replaces another less satisfactory statement. The Slavonic version of Josephus, too, cannot be relied upon at all as an ancient source, cf. M. Grant, *The Ancient Historians*, pp. 400, 449 n. 56.
28 H. Conzelmann, *Jesus Christus*, in *Religion in Geschichte und Gegenwart*, 1957–65, p. 620. On the significance for Christianity, see A. J. Vidler, *Objections to Christian Belief*, pp. 49 ff.
29 Cf. *Isa.* 11, 1.
30 *Matt.* 1, 16; *Luke* 3, 24.
31 Cf. Julius Africanus in Eusebius, I, 7.
32 *Matt.* 2, 1; *Luke* 2, 5.
33 *John* 7, 41; cf. *I Sam.* 16, 1.
34 *John* 1, 46; *Mark* 1, 9.
35 *Luke* 2, 4.
36 *Num.* 6, 2.
37 The emperor Julian called his anti-Christian polemic *Against the Galileans*.
38 *Matt.* 2, 1–8; cf. M. Grant, *Herod the Great*, p. 248 n. 4.
39 *John* 6, 15.
40 R. Bultmann, *Glauben und Verstehen*, IV (1965), p. 70. See pp. 216 f.
41 *Mark* 15, 7; *Luke* 13, 1; cf. 13, 4.
42 *Mark* 15, 29.
43 *Matt.* 10, 34.
44 *John* 2, 15.
45 *Luke* 6, 15.

46 *Luke* 22, 36 and 38 and 49–50. The pagan Hierocles (third century AD) maintained that Jesus had led a band of more than nine hundred highway robbers, and a medieval Hebrew 'copy' of a lost version of Josephus raised the figure to two thousand.

47 *Mark* 12, 2.

48 *John* 18, 3.

49 Origen, *Contra Celsum*, II, 4, 5, 9, etc. The Cambridge text of the *Toledoth Yeshu* (Ch. 16 and n. 8) records both a Jewish and a Roman trial, and again attributes the execution to the Jews. The leading figures in the proceedings are 'the great elder' Marinus and Rabbi Joshua ben Perachiah and Rabbi Judah, 'the gardener'. But an alternative Jewish contention, dating back to the second century (i.e. at least equally old), maintained that Christ died of necessity, so that no one was responsible (Origen, op. cit., II, 20; Justin, *Dialogue with Tryphon*, 95, 141). See also below, n. 56.

50 The fall and death of Sejanus at Rome (AD 31) cannot safely be introduced as a cause of this collaboration, owing to the uncertainty of the date of Jesus' trial and death.

51 *John* 11, 50.

52 The informality has been stressed in an unpublished lecture by F. G. B. Millar, to whom I am grateful for showing it to me.

53 *Luke* 23, 6. It was normal for the trial to take place where the deed was done, Paulus, *Digest*, I, 18, 3.

54 Son of God: only the Father knew who the Son was, *Matt.* 11, 27; *Luke* 10, 22. A god: *John* 10, 33.

55 'Forty years before the destruction of the Temple': cf. *J. Sanhedrin*, I, 1.

56 One of the passages of the Babylonian Talmud which were subsequently censored (describing Jesus as a rabbinical student who had strayed into evil ways) refers to a man of that name, presumably the same, who after condemnation as a sorcerer was executed by stoning. The report was preserved at a Paris Disputation of 1240. Justin Martyr, *Dialogue with Trypho*, 90, quotes objections to the tradition that Jesus' death was by crucifixion.

57 Jesus was probably nailed to the cross in a sitting position with both legs slung together sideways, and the nails pierced his wrists not his palms (unless he was tied to the crossbar): cf. the bones of a crucified man named Johanan found on a hill north of Golgotha in 1968, with both heel-bones transfixed by iron spikes.

58 *John* 19, 32 ff. (probably *speculatores* of the governor's praetorian guard). Crucifixion, originally a non-Jewish custom (it was employed in Persia), had been adopted in Palestine, even by Jewish

courts, since the second century BC, e.g. for political offences and robbery.

59 Josephus, *AJ*. XVIII, 119.
60 *Deut.* 18, 15 and 18.
61 *Acts* 5, 34; cf. *M. Sotah*, IX, 15 (described as 'Rabban', great master).
62 *Acts* 5, 38–9.
63 The earliest reports appear to be those in *I Cor.* 15, 3–8.
64 *Mark* 6, 16.
65 *Hos.* 6, 2.
66 *John* 20, 25 (cf. 9); *Matt.* 28, 16–20.
67 R. Abbahu (*c.* AD 279–330) denied that Enoch provided corroboration of the ascension of Jesus. There were also Jewish theological protests at the incompatibility between bodily resurrection and ascension to heaven.
68 Same day: the later *Epistle to Barnabas* (Ch. 10, n. 56), 15. Fortieth day: *Mark* 16, 19; *Luke* 24, 51; *Acts* 1, 1–11.
69 *Acts* 2, 1 ff.
70 The theory that his name 'Barjona' (*Matt.* 16, 17) represents not Son of Jonah but an Akkadian (Babylonian) word for terrorist is much disputed.
71 *Gal.* 2, 11 (Peter and Paul at Antioch); *Acts* 9, 32 (Peter's journey).
72 *I Cor.* 1, 12 (Cephas (Rock) = Peter).
73 Dositheus: Pseudo-Clement of Rome, *Homilies*, II, 24, *Recognitions*, II, 8; Origen, *Contra Celsum*, I, 57, VI, 15. Simon: *Acts* 8, 9 ff.: perhaps he was one of the originators of the Gnostics (professing esoteric knowledge and dualism, cf. M. Grant, *The Climax of Rome*, pp. 197 ff.).
74 *Acts* 6, 1.
75 *Acts* 7, 47; cf. 6, 14.
76 *I Kings* 8, 27; *Isa.* 66, 1; *Ps.* 11, 4.
77 Josephus, *AJ*. XVIII, 95, 123.
78 *Phil.* 3, 5.
79 This is the likely meaning of *Acts* 21, 39.
80 *Acts* 22, 28, probably means that Paul was born a Roman citizen.
81 *Acts* 7, 58.
82 *I Cor.* 15, 9; *Gal.* 1, 13; cf. *Acts* 8, 3.
83 In *II Cor.* 5, 6, the cryptic words 'after the flesh' are omitted in the New English Bible.
84 *Gal.* 1, 17–18.

8 *The Peril from Caligula and the Greeks*

1 Josephus, *AJ.* XVIII, 145.
2 Josephus, *C. Ap.* I, 70.
3 Philo, *In Flaccum*, II, 9.
4 Philo, *In Flaccum*, VIII, 57.
5 Meshorer, p. 138, no. 85.
6 Meshorer, p. 141, no. 94.
7 Meshorer, p. 138, no. 86. Agrippa I named his daughter Drusilla (II) after Caligula's deified sister.
8 S. Perowne, *The Later Herods* (1958), p. 69.
9 Philo, *De Vita Mosis*: cf. the few extant fragments of his *Apology for the Jews*, probably identical with his *Hypothetica*.
10 Philo, *Legum Allegoriae*, II, 102; *De Ebrietate*, XXIX, 111; but the story is told 'straight' in *De Vita Mosis*, I, 180.
11 Philo, *Quis Rerum Divinarum Heres*, 98: 'the land' just means 'wisdom'.
12 Philo, *In Flaccum*, VII, 45 ff. – anticipating the Balfour Declaration of 1917 by its stress on Jerusalem combined with safeguards for the rights of the Dispersion.
13 Philo, *De Abrahamo*, XIX, 98; *De Opificio Mundi*, LXI, 171–2.
14 Philo, *De Opificio Mundi*, loc. cit.
15 The complete shape of Philo's works on the Jews in Caligula's reign is impossible to reconstruct from Eusebius, II, 5, 1 ('five books').
16 It is less likely that 'Marullus' (Josephus, *AJ.* XVIII, 237) is a corruption of 'Marcellus'.
17 Philo, *Legatio ad Gaium*, 353–67.
18 Josephus, *AJ.* XVIII, 377.
19 Philo, *Legatio ad Gaium*, 216.
20 Josephus, *BJ.* II, 197.
21 Tacitus, *Histories*, V, 9.
22 Josephus, *AJ.* XIX, 81.
23 Josephus' account of Philo's banquet for Caligula (*AJ.* XVIII, 289–97) is a fiction somewhat reminiscent of *Esther* 7, 1–7.
24 In *BJ.* II, 203 (unlike *AJ.* XVIII, 307), he says that Caligula only 'threatened' Petronius with death.
25 *Megillath Taanith* (Scroll of Fasts) XXXI, 22 (H. Lichtenstein, *Hebrew Union College Annual*, VIII/IX, 1931–2, p. 300).

9 *The Kingship of Agrippa I and After*

1 Josephus, *AJ.* XIX, 236 ff. Dio, LX, 8, 2.
2 *Acta Isidori*: H. A. Musurillo, *Acts of the Pagan Martyrs* (*Acta Alexandrinorum*) (1954 and 1961), pp. 23 ff., 123.
3 Josephus, *AJ.* XIX, 278 f.

4 F. G. Kenyon and H. I. Bell, *Greek Papyri in the British Museum*, no. 1912 (trans. A. H. M. Jones). The *gymnasiarches* and *cosmetes* are both officials of the gymnasium. For Balbillus, see Ch. 11, n. 11. Josephus' significantly distorted version is in *AJ*. XIX, 280–5.

5 Josephus, *AJ*. XIX, 287.

6 Philo, *Legatio ad Gaium*, 373.

7 Josephus, *AJ*. XIX, 279, 288.

8 Meshorer, p. 139, nos. 89 ff.

9 Josephus, *AJ*. XIX, 335.

10 Meshorer, p. 139, no. 90, etc.: cf. the semi-official title *amicus principis* in Rome.

11 Meshorer, p. 140, no. 93; cf. Josephus, *AJ*. XIX, 275.

12 Josephus, *AJ*. XIX, 300–11.

13 Meshorer, p. 138, no. 88.

14 Josephus, *AJ*. XIX, 331.

15 *Deut.* 17, 15.

16 *M. Sotah*, VII, 8.

17 Josephus, *AJ*. XIX, 313–16.

18 Short tenures were not due to unwillingness to serve owing to the restrictions imposed on high priests, since ex-high priests were almost equally restricted, *M. Horayoth*, III, 4.

19 He was replaced by Elionaeus the son of Cantheras in 44, Josephus, *AJ*. XIX, 342.

20 *Acts* 11, 26.

21 *Acts* 26, 28; *I Pet.* 4, 16.

22 *M. Sanhedrin*, 7, 3.

23 *Acts* 12, 2.

24 *Acts* 12, 17. It has been conjectured that he may have gone to Alexandria – about whose Christian community there is a very strange silence in the narrative.

25 The relatives of Jesus became known as the 'Desposynoi'. The *Gospel of Thomas* attributed the pre-eminence of James to Jesus' command.

26 E. M. Hamrick, *Bulletin of American Schools of Oriental Research in Jerusalem and Baghdad*, CXCII, 1968, pp. 21 ff. Additional defences were necessitated by the increased range of ballistas, cf. Josephus, *BJ*. V, 270.

27 Josephus, *AJ*. XIX, 341.

28 Meshorer, p. 139, nos. 89 (the temple still needs to be explained) and 90.

29 Josephus, *C. Ap.* I, 70.

30 *Acts* 12, 23.

31 Josephus, *AJ*. XIX, 328, stresses his huge expenditure.

32 Josephus, *AJ*. XIX, 362.

33 Josephus, *AJ*. XX, 97–8. The Theudas of *Acts* 5, 36, is quite wrongly dated – or possibly a different person.

34 Josephus, *AJ*. XX, 16, 103.

35 Philo dedicated his *De Providentia* (complete in an Armenian version) to Ti. Julius Alexander, and Pseudo-Aristotle, *De Mundo*, was also dedicated to him.

36 Berenice had been married to Ti. Julius Alexander's brother Mark, who was now dead.

37 Josephus, *BJ*. II, 220.

38 *Acts* 11, 28: Egyptian papyri show the high price of wheat.

39 *Genesis rabba*, XLVI, 10, Josephus, *AJ*. XX, 46. Some see in this dispute echoes of the differences between Hillel and Shammai, or between Stephen (and Paul) on the one hand and James (and Peter) on the other.

40 Tacitus, *Annals*, XII, 54, 3, seems to be wrong in limiting Cumanus sphere to Galilee.

41 Josephus, *AJ*. XX, 135.

42 Called Marcus Agrippa on coins: Meshorer, p. 142, no. 100.

43 *Acts* 18, 2.

44 Dio Cassius, LX, 6, 3.

45 Suetonius, *Claudius*, 25, 4.

46 Tertullian, *Apologeticus*, 3, 5.

10   Paul's Bid to Change the Jews

1 *Gal.* 2, 1–14; *Rom.* 11, 25, etc.

2 *Gal.* 2, 8.

3 *Phil.* 3, 5 f. Cf. *Acts* 21, 20; 6, 7.

4 *Rom.* 1, 16; 2, 9 f; 3, 1.

5 *Gal.* 1, 21; *Acts* 9, 20.

6 *Acts* 11, 22–4.

7 *Acts* 15, 4–21; cf. *Gal.* 2, 2. Some regard the Council as fictitious, or a conflation of two (or more than two) conferences.

8 *Acts* 4, 32.

9 *Gal.* 2, 9. The apostle John (son of Zebedee) is also mentioned – in the course of a momentary reconciliation.

10 *Gal.* 1, 11.

11 *Rom.* 3, 29.

12 *Rom.* 11, 11.

13 Josephus, *BJ*. II, 224.

14 *M. Sotah*, IX, 9, Josephus, *BJ*. II, 253. With him was a certain
   Alexander, *BJ*. II, 235.
15 Cf. Josephus, *AJ*. XX, 135. The Jews named one of their beacon
   stations (for signalling to the Dispersion) after Agrippina.
16 H. A. Musurillo, *Acts of the Pagan Martyrs (Acta Alexandrinorum)*, p. 123.
   This is an alternative to attributing the event to AD 41; cf. Ch. 9, n. 2.
17 Paul apparently never crossed into Parthian territory. Jesus'
   correspondence with King Abgar the Black of Edessa (Urfa)
   (Eusebius, I, 13), and the dispatch of his disciple Thaddaeus to
   Edessa, are fictitious.
18 W. Dittenberger, *Sylloge Inscriptionum Graecarum*, II, 3rd ed., no. 801.
19 *Acts* 18, 12–17.
20 *Acts* 19, 24.
21 *Eph.* 2, 14 f.
22 The 'heretic' Marcion, who made the first known collection of the
   Epistles in *c.* AD 140, treated *Galatians* as the key to Paul's thought.
   Some, however, regard it as post-Pauline.
23 *I Cor.* 11, 17–34 (if not interpolated), may be the earliest reference to
   this. The passage has also been held to suggest that Holy Week was
   commemorated before the Gospels were ever written.
24 *I Thess.* 2, 15 f. (after AD 70).
25 *I Thess.* 3, 11.
26 *Phil.* 2, 6.
27 *Gal.* 3, 13.
28 Omitted from *Acts* 9, 5, in the New English Bible.
29 A. D. Nock, *St. Paul* (1938), pp. 73 f.
30 *I Cor.* 2, 8.
31 *Ezek.* 9, 31: understood as a prophecy of the sign of the cross by the
   early Christians. In the Greek and Latin alphabets the letter
   assumed the T-form, and Christ's cross is depicted in this shape
   in early Christian art, cf. *Epistle to Barnabas*, 9.
32 Meshorer, p. 128, nos. 41 ff.
33 Cf. M. Grant, *Herod the Great*, p. 71.
34 *Deut.* 21, 23; cf. *Gal.* 3, 10.
35 *Zech.* 12, 10.
36 *I Thess.* 4, 14; *I Cor.* 5, 7.
37 *I Cor.* 15, 8. The New Testament never actually describes the
   Resurrection.
38 *Rom.* 1, 4.
39 *I Thess.*, loc. cit.; cf. *I Cor.* 15, 51.
40 *I Cor.* 15, 12 ff. But *Phil.* 2, 9, writes of the Ascension without
   mentioning the Resurrection.

41 *II Thess.* 2, 1 ff.

42 *Rom.* 12, 19; 13, 2.

43 *I Cor.* 10, 16.

44 A. D. Nock, *St. Paul*, pp. 54 f. The thanksgiving was originally incorporated in the Common Meal, and only later separated.

45 *I Cor.* 10, 1–4; cf. *Exod.* 16, 15 and 35; and 17, 6.

46 *Rom.* 6, 4.

47 *Jer.* 31, 31–4.

48 *I Cor.* 5, 7; 7, 23.

49 *I Cor.* 15, 17; *II Cor.* 5, 13–17.

50 *I Pet.* 2, 21.

51 *Rom.* 5, 12–21: cf. C. H. Dodd, *The Meaning of Paul for Today*, 1958 ed., pp. 57–8.

52 *Rom.* 2, 25; cf. *Phil.* 3, 2.

53 *Gal.* 3, 13.

54 *Gal.* 3, 23 ff.

55 *Gen.* 15, 6.

56 *Rom.* 3, 28; the *Epistle of James* 11, 24 (of uncertain authorship), later replaces faith by works. The *Epistle of Barnabas* (a later treatise on the use of the Old Testament, regarded as scriptural at Alexandria) 10, 9, declares that the Jews' literal interpretation of the Law was a misunderstanding.

57 *Gal.* 2, 15 f. and 21.

58 *I Thess.* 2, 14–16.

59 *Rom.* 13, 1–6.

60 Antony's daughter by Octavia, Antonia (minor), was Claudius' mother.

61 Meshorer, p. 174, no. 233; cf. *BMC. Emp.* I, p. 179, no. 104.

62 *Numismatic Chronicle*, 1950, pp. 284 ff.

63 Meshorer, p. 174, no. 232.

64 Josephus, *AJ.* XX, 145–7 (after Agrippa II's death!), cf. Juvenal, *Satires*, VI, 156–60.

65 Josephus, *BJ.* II, 254–6 (trans. H. St J. Thackeray). See p. 90.

66 Josephus, *AJ.* XX, 163; not in *BJ.* II, 256.

67 Josephus, *BJ.* II, 259.

68 *Acts* 21, 38; Josephus, *BJ.* II, 261 f., *AJ.* XX, 170.

69 *Acts* 21, 29.

70 *Acts* 22, 30; 23, 3.

71 This is the most probable interpretation of *Acts*, 24, 27.

72 Josephus, *BJ.* II, 267.

73 Josephus, *AJ.* XX, 182.

74 Jesus son of Phiabi under Herod the Great, and an earlier Ishmael I son of Phiabi in *c.* AD 15.

75 *M. Sotah*, IX, 15.

76 Though the priests were not allowed to come to the threshing floors to collect it themselves, *B. Kiddushin*, 6b.

77 Josephus, *AJ*. XX, 180–1 (trans. L. H. Feldman).

78 Tacitus, *Histories*, V, 9; *Annals*, XII, 54.

79 *Acts* 25, 3.

80 *Acts* 25, 12; i.e. Nero.

81 *Acts* 26, 22 f.

82 *Acts* 26, 25–32.

83 *Acts* 28, 30. Probably he had been handed over to the *princeps castrorum* of the praetorian guard, cf. 28, 16.

84 Clement, *First Letter to the Corinthians* (*c.* AD 95), 5; possibly deduced from *Rom.* 15, 24 and 28.

85 Summed up by Eusebius, II, 25. The supposed Tomb of St Peter beneath St Peter's Basilica goes back to *c.* AD 160–70. *John* 13, 36 and 21, 18 contains 'prophecies' of Peter's martyrdom.

86 I Clement, op. cit., 4–5, cites 'jealousy' as the cause of Paul's tribulations (and mentions his death).

Part IV   THE WARS AGAINST THE ROMANS

11   The Prelude to the First Revolt

1 Meshorer, p. 141, no. 95, cf. p. 86, and H. Seyrig, *Revue numismatique*, 1964, pp. 55–65. Josephus, *AJ*. XX, 211, dates Neronias rather too late.

2 Agrippa II must also have been pleased when his cousin once removed, Tigranes VI, was made king of Armenia by the Romans in *c.* AD 60 (though his reign was very brief). Agrippa II's cousin Aristobulus had been given a strip of Lesser Armenia in *c.* 57, and his territory was now enlarged.

3 Josephus, *AJ*. XX, 199.

4 Josephus, *AJ*. XX, 200; less accurate account by Hegesippus (*c.* AD 160) in Eusebius, II, 23.

5 Origen, *Contra Celsum*, I, 47 (attributing this view to Josephus); Eusebius, loc. cit.

6 Hegesippus in Eusebius, III, 11 ('Clopas').

7 Eusebius, IV, 5.

8 Josephus, *AJ*. XX, 201 f.

9 Seneca, *Epistulae Morales ad Lucilium*, 95, 4–7; and in Augustine, *City of God*, VI, 11.

10 Petronius, fragment 97(B); cf. Persius, *Satires*, V, 181.

11 Balbillus: identity discussed by D. Magie, *Roman Rule in Asia Minor*, II, p. 1399, n. 5. Chaeremon: Josephus, *C. Ap.* I, 288 ff.
12 Josephus, *AJ.* XX, 195.
13 Josephus, *Vita*, 16.
14 Josephus, *AJ.* XX, 184, gives too late a date – if Pallas (d. 62) was still alive.
15 Josephus, *AJ.* XX, 205.
16 Josephus, *BJ.* II, 272 ff., *AJ.* XX, 204.
17 *B. Yoma*, 18a. He was connected by marriage to the house of Boethus, *AJ.* XX, 213.
18 Josephus, *AJ.* XX, 215.
19 Josephus, *AJ.* XX, 218.
20 Tacitus, *Annals*, XV, 44 (trans. M. Grant).
21 Suetonius, *Nero*, 16, 2.
22 *I Pet.* 4, 2; *Jas.* 3, 6 and 5, 3.
23 Tertullian, *Apologeticus*, 13.
24 Josephus, *Vita*, 14.
25 *Lev.* 14, 4 f.
26 Josephus, *BJ.* II, 292.
27 Josephus, *BJ.* II, 356–7, 361–2 (trans. H. St J. Thackeray).
28 Josephus, *BJ.* II, 388–9 (trans. H. St J. Thackeray).
29 S. Perowne, *The Later Herods*, p. 125.
30 G. Vermes, *The Dead Sea Scrolls in English*, 1970 ed., pp. 250–2.
31 Tacitus, *Histories*, V, 1; Josephus, *BJ.* III, 68 (Malchus II, AD 40–71).
32 Baron, II, p. 115; cf. *M. Aboth*, III, 2.

12   The First Revolt

1 Josephus, *BJ.* II, 427.
2 Josephus, *BJ.* II, 434.
3 Josephus, *BJ.* II, 312.
4 Josephus, *BJ.* II, 448.
5 Josephus, *BJ.* II, 454.
6 *Megillath Taanith*, XXXIII, p. 302 (see Ch. 8, n. 25).
7 Jews were massacred at Ptolemais Ace, Tyre, Ascalon and Caesarea Philippi, and in Batanea; Gentiles at Sebaste, Gaza, Anthedon, Gaba, in Decapolis and Gaulanitis, and at Ptolemais Ace and in the territory of Tyre.
8 Josephus, *BJ.* II, 523.
9 Josephus, *BJ.* II, 558.
10 Meshorer, pp. 154–8, nos. 1 ff. The designs include a chalice, *lulab* (bunch of twigs) and *ethrog* (citron).

11 Josephus, *BJ.* II, 562–3, 648–51.

12 Amending 'Neus' in Josephus, *BJ.* II, 566, to 'Ananias'.

13 Gamala in Gaulanitis was also part of his sphere (ibid., 568).

14 Josephus, *Vita*, 29.

15 H. Seyrig, *Numismatic Chronicle*, 1955, pp. 157 ff.

16 Battle: *BJ.* III, 522 ff. Triumph: *BJ.* VII, 147. Coinage with
   VICTORIA NAVALIS (probably interpretable in this way, pace H. St
   J. Hart, *Journal of Theological Studies*, 1952, p. 188, n. 2): *BMC.
   Emp.* II, p. 129, no. 597, etc.

17 Josephus, *BJ.* III, 308.

18 Josephus, *BJ.* IV, 161.

19 Josephus, *BJ.* IV, 216 ff.

20 On the site were found Roman arrowheads, and eighty-three coins
   of the second year of the revolt but only five of the third.

21 Josephus, *BJ.* IV, 563 (trans. H. St J. Thackeray).

22 Tacitus, *Histories*, V, 12.

23 Some have seen a new coin inscription of year 4, 'To the
   Redemption of Zion' (Meshorer, p. 157, no. 161), as an indication
   of his social programme.

24 Plutarch, *Otho*, 5.

25 S. Grayzel, *A History of the Jews*, p. 91.

26 Tacitus, *Histories*, IV, 51.

27 *Sibylline Oracles*, IV, 130 ff., V, 137 ff.; and apparently *Rev.* 13, 3
   (cf. 17, 8 and 11).

28 *II Esd. (Apocalypse of Ezra)*, 13, 6 ff.

29 Meshorer, p. 157, no. 161.

30 Josephus, *BJ.* V, 362 ff.

31 *M. Taanith*, IV, 6.

32 Josephus, *BJ.* VI, 414–22 (trans. H. St J. Thackeray).

33 Tacitus, *Histories*, V, 13.

34 Josephus, *BJ.* VI, 428–32 (trans. H. St J. Thackeray).

35 For the future destiny of these objects see M. Grant, *The Roman
   Forum*, p. 169. The Jews of Rome held a demonstration at the Arch
   of Titus on 30 October 1947 – the day after the United Nations
   voted to re-establish the state of Israel.

36 Dessau, *Inscriptiones Latinae Selectae*, 264.

37 Josephus, *BJ.* VII, 253. Eleazar ben Jair had been an associate of
   Menahem, and had escaped after his murder.

38 *Sibylline Oracles*, V, 507–10.

39 E.g. at Jericho: Pliny the elder, *Natural History*, XI, 111–23.

13   Jewish Survival: the Menace of the Gospels

1 *Aboth de' R. Nathan*, 4.

2 If the personages in Josephus, *BJ*. VI, 238, and Minucius Felix, *Octavius*, 33, 4, are identifiable.

3 *B. Yoma*, 39b.

4 *Tosefta, Baba Kamma*, VII, 5. (For the Tosefta, see Ch. 16, n. 9.)

5 *Isa.* 52, 2.

6 14th and 17th of the Eighteen Benedictions (Shemoneh Esreh).

7 *Lev.* 17, 7, gave some support for the view, later held by Maimonides, that sacrifice was a survival from the idolatrous past.

8 *Aboth de' R. Nathan*, 4, etc.

9 *Baruch*, 3, 5; 14, 19.

10 *Baruch*, 4, 18–21; 4, 2–5; 3, 24.

11 Josephus, *BJ*. V, 458.

12 B. Joshua ben Hananiah founded a branch academy at Peqi'in (El Boukeia), and Johanan's other pupil Eleazar ben Hyrcanus at Lydda (Lod).

13 Cf. E. M. Smallwood, *Oxford Classical Dictionary*, 2nd ed., p. 30. The whereabouts and extent of the new territory are unknown.

14 Meshorer, p. 144, nos. 109 ff., p. 147, nos. 120, 121.

15 Dio, LXV, 15.5. She is the heroine of Racine's *Bérénice*.

16 Josephus, *BJ*. VII, 448; *Vita*, 424 f.

17 Josephus, *BJ*. I, 6.

18 Josephus, *BJ*. III, 108.

19 Josephus, *BJ*. I, 1–2; VII, 341 ff.

20 Josephus, *BJ*. I, 11.

21 Josephus refers to Herod's memoirs (*AJ*. XV, 174), but he may only have known them at second hand.

22 Later, the Aelia Capitolina church felt able to claim that it was the lineal descendant of the suspended Jerusalem church.

23 Eusebius, II, 6; cf. III, 5 and 7.

24 The view that the Gospels are translations from the Aramaic (cf. Papias about sayings allegedly compiled by Matthew: Eusebius, III, 39) is not generally accepted.

25 For these authorships (and sources) see R. M. Grant, *Historical Introduction to the New Testament* (1963), pp. 105–60.

26 Eusebius, III, 25.

27 Cf. *Oxford Cyclopedic Concordance*, pp. 53, 235 f.

28 *Mark* 6, 15 and 8, 28; *Matt.* 16, 14. His name also invited comparisons with Joshua.

29 *Lev.* 19, 34.

30 *Isa.* 66, 2.

31 *Mark* 7, 23.
32 *Luke* 3, 15.
33 *Mark* 12, 13–17.
34 *Dan.* 11, 31.
35 *Mark* 13, 14 and 18–20.
36 *Mark* 15, 38.
37 *Mark* 15, 39.
38 *Mark* 2, 6 and 16; 3, 16; 14, 55–64; 15, 10.
39 *Mark* 3, 31–5.
40 *Matt.* 16, 19.
41 *Matt.* 19, 28; cf. 23, 1–3.
42 *Matt.* 12, 40.
43 *Matt.* 1, 23; cf. *Isa.* 7, 14.
44 *Matt.* 27, 23–5.
45 *Tosefta Hullin*, II, 22 f. (For the Tosefta, see Ch. 16, n. 9.)
46 *Matt.* 23, 33 and 37 (various readings). The murder of Zechariah son of Berachiah (ibid., 35) perhaps refers to an event of AD 60.
47 *Matt.* 26, 52.
48 *Matt.* 10, 34–6.
49 *Matt.* 25, 41.
50 *Matt.* 10, 4; *Mark* 3, 18; *Luke* 6, 15.
51 *Luke* 17, 21; cf. 19, 11.
52 Eusebius, III, 4.
53 *Luke* 2, 2; cf. Ch. 6, n. 13.
54 *Luke* 14, 23.
55 *Luke* 23, 4.
56 *Acts* 4, 32; cf. 6, 1.
57 *Acts* 2, 11.
58 *Acts* 2, 36; 3, 15; 5, 30; 10, 39; 13, 29.
59 *Acts* 4, 27.
60 *John*'s prologue asserts that the cosmological 'Logos' (used by the Stoics to indicate the intelligible law of the universe, and adapted in Greco-Jewish literature to signify the divine wisdom: cf. Philo, *Quis Rerum Divinarum Heres*, 205 f., etc.), was incarnate in Christ, as the unique son of God.
61 *John* 5, 24.
62 *John* 18, 36.
63 *John* 8, 44–5.
64 *Heb.* 5, 5–11; 7, 14–16.
65 *Heb.* 9, 15–22; 10, 19–20.
66 Martial, *Epigrams*, IV, 4, 7; VII, 55, 7–8; VII, 82, 6; XII, 57, 13; etc.

67 Anti-Jewish material omitted, e.g. Golden Calf story (*Exod.* 32, 4–35). Potentially anti-Roman material toned down: Nebuchadnezzar's dream (*Dan.* 2, 44; cf. Josephus, *AJ.* X, 203 ff.). But *AJ.* IV, 125, hints at a belief in the eventual downfall of Roman power.

68 E.g. *AJ.* XVI, 151–9; cf. XX, 145.

69 Josephus, *Vita*, 340.

70 Josephus, *AJ.* XX, 259 and 267, are separate endings: the latter gives the date, AD 94.

71 Josephus, *C. Ap.* II, 143.

72 Josephus, *C. Ap.* I, 42–4 (trans. H. St J. Thackeray).

73 Josephus, *C. Ap.* I, 6–7 (trans. H. St J. Thackeray).

74 Suetonius, *Domitian*, 12, 2 (trans. J. C. Rolfe).

75 Dio Cassius, LXVII, 14, 2.

76 On 'That Day' of Testimonies (Eduioth), when many doubts were cleared up, and the Mishnah foreshadowed.

77 *M. Berakoth*, II, 5–8.

78 *M. Abodah Zarah*, III, 4.

79 *B. Sotah*, 49b, ascribes the school to Gamaliel's 'close association with the government'.

80 *M. Eduyoth*, VII, 7.

81 Hegesippus in Eusebius, III, 19 f.; cf. 12.

82 *Exodus rabba*, XXX, 9.

83 Eusebius, III, 18.

84 *Rev.* 2, 9.

85 *Rev.* 2, 13.

86 *Rev.* 17, 5–6, etc.

87 *Rev.* 6, 12.

88 *Rev.* 9, 14; 7, 2; 17, 12.

89 *Rev.* 19, 11–15.

90 *B. Berakoth*, 28b.

91 *II Esd.*, Chs. 3–14 = *IV Esd.* in the Vulgate (fourth-century Latin Bible ascribed to St Jerome). Chs. 1–2 and 15–16 are of separate (Christian) origin.

92 *II Esd.* 12, 2; 13, 1–58; 14, 16; cf. *Dan.* 7, 4, etc.

14   Rebellions in the East

1 *BMC. Emp.* III, p. 15, no. 88. Private prosecutors were required to swear that they were not proceeding *calumniae casa*.

2 Dio, LXVIII, 1, 2; Eusebius, III, 20.

3 Tacitus, *Histories*, V, 5 (trans. K. Wellesley).

4 Eusebius, III, 32.

5 Eusebius, III, 35.

6 Ignatius, *Epistle to the Romans*, 4.

7 *I Pet.* 5, 13.

8 *I Pet.* 2, 13; 4, 14–16.

9 Pliny the younger, *Letters*, X, 96, 1 and 3–5.

10 Trajan, ibid., X, 97 (trans. B. Radice).

11 E.g. G. Manteuffel, *Mélanges Maspero*, II, 1934–7, pp. 119 ff.

12 *B. Abodah Zarah*, 18a.

13 *B. Sanhedrin*, 98a.

14 Sources in R. Syme, *Tacitus* (1948), p. 239, n. 7.

15 Dio Cassius, LXVIII, 32, Eusebius, IV, 2 (Lukuas).

16 Dio Cassius, LXVIII, 32, 1–3.

17 *L'année épigraphique*, 1928, nos. 1–2; 1929, no. 9.

18 *Acta Hermaisci*: H. A. Musurillo, *Acts of the Pagan Martyrs (Acta Alexandrinorum)*, pp. 44 ff., 161 ff.

19 *Megillath Taanith* (12 Adar). But see also n. 23 below.

20 *BMC. Emp.* III, p. 223, no. 1045 (Parthamaspates).

21 Sources in E. M. Smallwood, *Historia*, XI, 1962, pp. 500 ff.

22 *M. Sotah*, IX, 14.

23 Was 12 Adar declared a semi-holiday (n. 19 above) because their execution was averted by the death of Trajan? Or were they among the 'slain of Lydda'? *B. Resahim*, 50a, etc.

24 Hippolytus, *In Gaium* (Achelis, *Hippolyts kleinere exegetische und homilitische Schriften*, pp. 197, 244).

25 Juvenal, *Satires*, XIV, 96–106; VI, 542–7 (trans. P. Green).

15   The Second Revolt and After

1 *Acta Pauli*: H. A. Musurillo, *Acts of the Pagan Martyrs (Acta Alexandrinorum)*, pp. 57, 181 ff.

2 *Sibylline Oracles*, V, 46, 492 ff.

3 *B. Sanhedrin*, 105a.

4 'Rot his bones!' says *Genesis rabba*, lxxviii, 1.

5 *SHA. Hadrian*, 14, 2; cf. Dio Cassius, XLVIII, 8, 11. Sulla had banned mutilation in the *Lex Cornelia de sicariis et veneficiis*.

6 *SHA. Hadrian*, op. cit., regards this as the prime cause of the Second Revolt.

7 *BMC. Emp.* III, p. 512, no. 1757.

8 Dio Cassius, LXIX, 12, *M. Taanith*, IV, 6, *BMC. Palestine*, p. 82, nos. 1 f.

9 *Catalogue of the Greek Papyri in the John Rylands Library, Manchester*, no. 189.

10 Pausanias, I, 5, 5 (trans. P. Levi).

11 *Lamentations rabba*, II, 2.

12 Eusebius, IV, 6.

13 *Aboth de' R. Nathan*, 18.

14 *J. Taanith*, IV, 8: cf. Y. Yadin, *Bar Kochba*, pp. 18 f.; F. M. Abel, *Histoire de la Palestine*, II, p. 87, n. 1.

15 *Num*. 24, 17.

16 The reign of Vologases II (or according to another numbering III) was interrupted at this period by Mithridates IV in the east, and then by an unknown usurper in *c*. 140 (?).

17 *Lamentations rabba*, II, 2, cf. Y. Yadin, op. cit., p. 255.

18 Justin, *Dialogue with Trypho*, I, 3.

19 Meshorer, p. 159, nos. 167 ff., 166.

20 Meshorer, p. 160, no. 170 (palm-tree), p. 162, no. 179 (star, year 2).

21 *B. Yebamoth*, 46a, 71a.

22 Dio Cassius, LXIX, 12 (trans. E. Cary).

23 L. Ginzberg, *Legends of the Jews*, VI, p. 408.

24 Meshorer, p. 165, no. 301 (wavy line), p. 162, no. 182 (freedom of Israel), p. 164, no. 194 (freedom of Jerusalem).

25 Julius Africanus in Eusebius, *Chronicle*; perhaps the Legio XXII Deiotariana, which disappeared from the army list after the war.

26 Dio Cassius, LXIX, 14; cf. Fronto, *De Bello Parthico* (ed. Naber), p. 218.

27 *BMC. Emp*. III, p. 493, no. 1658.

28 Wadi Murabaat (1952), Cave of Letters near Nahal Hever (1961–2): Y. Yadin, *Bar Kochba* (1971), pp. 124 ff.

29 *Lamentations rabba*, I, 16, 45.

30 Ibid.

31 Dio Cassius, loc. cit.

32 *Chronicon Paschale*, I, 474.

33 Josephus, *AJ*. XX, 259.

34 Eusebius, IV, 6 (Tertullian, *Adversus Judaeos*, 13, says they could see it from afar).

35 Jerome, *Ad Zephaniam*, I, 25.

36 *J. Taanith*, IV, 6.

37 Sources in Baron, II, pp. 123, 377, n. 38.

38 *BMC. Palestine*, p. 8, no. 23 (Tiberias), p. xii (Sepphoris), p. 49, no. 25 (Neapolis).

39 Appian, *Syriaca*, VII, 50; cf. *M. Nedarim*, IX, 10, etc.

40 *B. Sanhedrin*, 93b.

41 Meshorer, pp. 99 f.; cf. *J. Maaser Sheni*, I, 2, on the invalidated silver coins of Bar Kosiba.

42 *M. Abodah Zarah*, 2, 1; 5, 5, implies less strictness.

43 Eusebius, *Chronicle*, s.v. Hadrian, year 17; Orosius, VII, 12.

44 Orosius, loc. cit.
45 Eusebius, IV, 6; id., *Chronicle*, s.v. year 18.
46 *Crucible of Christianity* (Thames and Hudson, 1969), pp. 268 f.
47 *Digest*, XLVIII, 8, 11.
48 *SHA. Antoninus Pius*, 5, 5.

Part V THE JEWS IN THE LATER EMPIRE

16 The Later Pagan Empire
1 *B. Sanhedrin*, 86a (R. Johanan bar Nappaha).
2 *Song of Songs rabba*, VIII, 9, cf. Baron, II, p. 96 and n. 8.
3 Dio Cassius, LXXII, 22 ff.
4 Ammianus Marcellinus, XXII, 5, 5. However, Marcus Aurelius and Commodus passed laws admitting the Jews to guardianship over non-Jews, and to other offices.
5 *Meditations*, XI, 3 (not to be rejected as a gloss).
6 Irenaeus of Smyrna, bishop of Lugdunum (Lyon) (*c.* 185), devoted his vast work *Adversus Haereses* to an attempt to extirpate deviations.
7 Hippolytus, *Philosophumena*; cf. H. J. Leon, *The Jews in Ancient Rome*, p. 43.
8 *Toledoth Yeshu*; see now W. Horbury in E. Bammel (ed.), *The Trial of Jesus* (1970), pp. 103 ff.; and see above, Ch. 7, n. 49. Illegitimacy of Jesus: Origen, *Contra Celsum*, I, 32; *B. Shabbath*, 104b; *B. Sanhedrin*, 67a.
9 Powers of life and death: W. Horbury, op. cit., pp. 108, 111. Fund-raising: a famous pioneer was R. Hiyya bar Abba (*J. Hagiga*, I, 7), who was also a learned, but unpopular, travelling lecturer, and one of the chief compilers of the *Tosefta* or *Baraitha* (comprising supplements to the Mishnah).
10 Judah I overruled: *J. Yebamoth*, VI, 6. Judah and Hezekiah: *B. Sanhedrin*, 38a. It is uncertain if their father R. Hiyya was the same as R. Hiyya bar Abba (see last note).
11 Sources in Baron, II, p. 400, n. 19, cf. p. 187.
12 *J. Megillah*, III, 2.
13 A list of epitaphs at Beth-Shearim included 175 Greek and 32 Hebrew or Aramaic inscriptions.
14 *BMC. Palestine*, p. xlii: an alleged coin of Pescennius Niger at Aelia Capitolina is a forgery.
15 *SHA. Severus*, 9, 5 (Neapolis); ibid., 16, 7 and 17, 1 (penalties).
16 Dio Cassius, LXXV, 2, 4.

17 However, in the latter half of the second century the kings of Edessa, within this area, were converted to Christianity.

18 *SHA. Severus*, 17, 1.

19 F. M. Abel, *Histoire de la Palestine*, II, p. 152 and n. 3.

20 David Qimbi's *Commentary on Genesis*, I, 31; cf. Baron, p. 400, n. 19.

21 Dio Cassius, LXXVIII, 9, 4 f.

22 Only fifteen per cent of the double or triple names of Jews recorded at Rome are 'Aurelii', i.e. enfranchised under Caracalla's act.

23 *SHA. Antoninus Elagabalus*, 3, 5. R. Syme, *Ammianus and the Historia Augusta* (1968), pp. 61 ff., sees in this an echo of events of *c.* AD 395.

24 *SHA. Alexander*, 28, 7.

25 Samaritan chronicles cited (and doubted) by F. M. Abel, op. cit., p. 182.

26 *SHA. Alexander*, 22, 4; 29, 2; the latter doubted by R. Syme, op. cit., p. 138.

27 Flavius Philostratus, *Vita Apollonii*, V, 33.

28 Dio Cassius, XXXVII, 17.

29 E. Schurer, *History of the Jewish People in the Time of Jesus* (ed. N. N. Glatzer), 1961, p. 308.

30 The *fiscus Judaicus* had gradually been replaced by irregular exactions, often levied suddenly. R. Jannai was consequently obliged to abolish the sabbatical year, *B. Sanhedrin*, 26a.

31 *Genesis rabba*, LXXX, 1.

32 E.g. at Chorazin, Capernaum, Kefr Bir'im.

33 E.g. at Beth-Shearim, N. Avigad, *Eretz-Israel*, V, plates 12, 17, 20. Ark of the Covenant: Custodia di Terra Sancta; *Crucible of Christianity*, p. 80.

34 A. Boethius and J. B. Ward-Perkins, *Etruscan and Roman Architecture* (1970), p. 575, n. 9.

35 *J. Abodah Zarah*, IV, 1; for official permission by R. Abun early in the fourth century, cf. W. F. Albright, *The Archaeology of Palestine* (1949), p. 172.

36 Unless this was achieved by his teacher R. Hanina ben Hama after Judah 1's death: sources in Baron, p. 403, n. 30.

37 *Genesis rabba*, LXXVI, 6.

38 *Dan.* 7, 7 and 11.

39 *J. Abodah Zarah*, 43d.

40 S. Grayzel, *A History of the Jews*, 2nd ed., 1968, p. 180.

41 Monteverde, Via Labicana, Villa Torlonia, Vigna Randanini, Vigna Cimarra, S. Sebastiano, Via Appia Pignatelli. There are also catacombs from the second to the fourth centuries at Beth-Shearim (N. Avigad, *Israel Exploration Journal*, 1955, pp. 205–39; 1957, pp. 73–92, 239–55).

42 E.g. a sarcophagus cover in the Museo Nazionale delle Terme at Rome shows a Menorah in a shield held by two geniuses; three naked boys and figures of the seasons are also depicted (*Crucible of Christianity*, p. 63).

43 There was a Jewish animal painter called Eudoxius. The Tomb of Vincentius shows a partly Jewish, partly pagan sect admitting neophytes from every sect to its mystic ceremonies.

44 Raising of Lazarus: only in *John* 11, 43 ff. Five Thousand: all Gospels.

45 *BMC. Phrygia*, p. 101, no. 182.

46 B. *Abodah Zarah*, 76b, cf. Baron, II, p. 397, n. 7.

47 The split approached its climax when Pope (St) Stephen (254–6) claimed the subordination of all churches to Rome, against Firmilian who asserted that every bishop is the successor of the apostles. The removal of the imperial capital from Rome to Mediolanum (Milan) by Gallienus (260–8) and Maximian (286–305) gave greater independence to the Roman bishopric.

48 However, Judah II's brother Hillel was consulted on Biblical matters by Origen (d. 254–5), head of the institute of advanced Christian studies at Alexandria.

49 The Jews lost very heavy casualties defending Caesarea Mazaca (Kayseri) in Cappadocia in *c*. 260; but see Baron, II, p. 397, n. 7.

50 Johanan: *J. Taanith*, IV, 5; cf. *J. Yebamoth*, I, 3. Temples: *Lamentations rabba*, II, 2, 4. See also Baron, p. 407, n. 43 (sources: cf. p. 211), W. Keller, *Diaspora* (1971), p. 87.

51 Cf. Baron, p. 238.

52 Statue at Nehardea: *B. Rosh ha-Shanah*, 24b; prostration: *B. Shabbath*, 73a.

53 Baron, p. 397, n. 8.

54 *J. Abodah Zarah*, V, 4.

55 Diocletian also added Petra and two other towns, and the greater part of the Sinai peninsula, to the Palestine province.

17   Epilogue: The Jews in the Christian Empire

1 Baron, pp. 194 f., 403, n. 28.

2 Cf. J. Juster, *Les juifs dans l'empire romain*, II (1914), p. 230 n.; in general, see pp. 226–39.

3 Eusebius, I, 2.

4 *Rom.* 11, 11.

5 E.g. Joseph, a former fund-raiser of the patriarch Judah IV.

6 A. H. M. Jones, *Constantine and the Conversion of Europe*, 1972 ed., pp. 207 f., 162.

7 In 358 the province was divided into two parts, Palaestina and Palaestina Salutaris (capital Elusa (Halutza) in Idumaea). At about this time the young patriarch Hillel II renounced the patriarchate's greatest power, the right to fix ritual months and years everywhere.

8 Ammianus Marcellinus, XXIII, 1, 2–3; for the other ancient sources, see Juster, op. cit., p. 247, n. 3.

9 For Theodosius I, see now R. Syme, *Ammianus and the Historia Augusta*, pp. 62 ff., stressing the role of the patriarch Gamaliel VI. For Eutropius, F. M. Abel, *Histoire de la Palestine*, II, pp. 317 f. In 399 Arcadius reorganized Palestine into three provinces, with capitals at Caesarea Maritima, Scythopolis and Petra.

10 The measures of Theodosius II are collected by Juster, op. cit.

11 *B. Abodah Zarah*, 16a.

12 The Babylonian Talmud was completed under Rabina bar Huna (488–99). For censored passages relating to Jesus, see Ch. 7, n. 56.

13 N. P. Kondakov, *An Archaeological Journey through Syria and Palestine* (1904, in Russian), pp. 173 f.

14 The exilarch Bustanai, whom the Persians had deprived of his office and forced to flee, welcomed the Arabs in Babylonia in 636.

15 It was not, however, until after the death of Saadia ben Joseph, head of the Sura academy from 928 until 942, that Babylonian Jewry lost its cultural leadership and its link with the west. Sura was then closed; and Pumbeditha was closed in 1040, when its last head was executed.

16 The tenth century AD has been described as the Golden Age of the Dispersion.

17 W. Keller, *Diaspora* (1971), p. xx.

18 *Deut.* 4, 27.

19 *Ezek.* 37, 21–6.

Some Books

I DISCUSSIONS OF THE ANCIENT SOURCES

(a) Josephus†

FARMER, W. R., *Maccabees, Zealots and Josephus*, New York 1956.
FELDMAN, L. H., *Studies in Judaica: Scholarship on Philo and Josephus 1937–1962*, New York 1963.
FINLEY, M. I. (ed.), *Josephus*, New York 1965.
GLATZER, N. N. (ed.), *Josephus, Jerusalem and Rome*, New York 1960.
JACKSON, F. J. FOAKES, *Josephus and the Jews*, London 1930.
LAQUEUR, R., *Der judische Historiker Flavius Josephus*, Giessen 1920, reprint 1970.
MONTEFIORE, H. W., *Josephus and the New Testament*, London 1962.
SHUTT, R. J. H., *Studies in Josephus*, London 1961.
THACKERAY, H. ST J., *Josephus: the Man and the Historian*, 1929, reprint New York 1967.
THACKERAY, H. ST J., MARCUS, R., WIKGREN, A. & FELDMAN, L. H., *Works of Josephus* (Loeb ed.), London and Cambridge, Mass. 1926–65.
WILLIAMSON, G. A., *The World of Josephus*, London 1964.

(b) Other Jewish writings

BENOIT, P., MILIK, J. T., DE VAUX, R., *Les grottes de Muraba'at* (Discoveries in the Judaean Desert, II), Oxford 1961.

* For Christian sources, see also section IV.
† For his works, see above, Chapter 13.

BOX, H. (ed.), *Philonis Alexandrini In Flaccum*, Leiden 1939.

BROCKINGTON, L. H., *A Critical Introduction to the Apocrypha*, London 1961.

Cambridge History of the Bible, I, Cambridge 1970.

CROSS, F. M., *The Ancient Library of Qumran*, revised ed. 1961.

DANBY, H., *The Mishnah*, Oxford 1933.

EPSTEIN, I. (ed.), *The Babylonian Talmud in English*, 36 vols., London 1935-53.

FELDMAN, L. H., see section (a).

FREEDMAN, H. & SIMON, M., *Midrash Rabbah*, 10 vols., London 1939.

GOODENOUGH, E. R., *An Introduction to Philo Judaeus*, revised ed., 1962.

HERFORD, R. T., *Talmud and Apocrypha*, London 1933.

New English Bible: with Apocrypha, Oxford and Cambridge 1970.*

PFEIFFER, C. F., *The Dead Sea Scrolls and the Bible*, Grand Rapids 1969.

RUSSELL, D. S., *The Jews from Alexander to Herod* (Part III, *The Literature*), Oxford 1967.

SCHUBERT, K., *The Dead Sea Community*, London 1959.

SMALLWOOD, E. M., *Philonis Alexandrini Legatio ad Gaium*, Leiden 1961.

STRACK, H. L., *Introduction to the Talmud and Midrash*, London 1963.

TCHERIKOVER, V. & FUKS, A., *Corpus Papyrorum Iudaicarum*, 3 vols., Cambridge, Mass. 1957-64.

TRACY, S., *Philo Judaeus and the Roman Principate*, Williamsport 1933.

VERMES, G., *The Dead Sea Scrolls in English*, revised ed., London 1970 (with bibliography).

WAXMAN, M., *History of Jewish Literature*, 3rd ed., New York 1960.

(c) Other writings

GRANT, M. *The Ancient Historians*, London and New York 1970.

MILLAR, F. G. B., *A Study of Cassius Dio*, Oxford 1964.

MUSURILLO, H. A. (ed.), *The Acts of the Pagan Martyrs (Acta Alexandrinorum)*, Oxford 1954, 1961.

REINACH, T. (ed.), *Textes d'auteurs grecs et romains relatifs au judaisme*, 1895, reprint Hildesheim 1963.

WACHOLDER, B. Z., *Nicolaus of Damascus*, Berkeley and Los Angeles 1962.

WALLACE-HADRILL, D. S., *Eusebius of Caesarea*, London 1960.

WALSER, G., *Rom, das Reich und die fremden Völker in der Geschichtsschreibung der frühen Kaiserzeit*, Baden Baden 1951.

(d) Archaeology and Art

ALBRIGHT, W. F., *From the Stone Age to Christianity*, 2nd ed., Baltimore 1957.

* Biblical quotations in this book are mostly taken from this version.

AVI-YONAH, M., *Oriental Art in Roman Palestine*, Rome 1961.
FINEGAN, J., *Light from the Ancient Past: the Archaeological Background of the Hebrew-Christian Religion*, 2 vols., 2nd ed., Princeton 1959.
GOODENOUGH, E. R., *Jewish Symbols in the Graeco-Roman Period*, 11 vols., New York 1953-64.
HILL, G. F., *British Museum Catalogue of Greek Coins, Palestine*, London 1914.
KRAEHLING, C. H., *The Excavations at Dura-Europos, Final Report, VIII, 1: The Synagogue*, 1956.
LEON, H. J., *The Jews of Ancient Rome*, Philadelphia 1960.

(e) Coins
MATTINGLY, H., *et al.*, *Coins of the Roman Empire in the British Museum*, London 1923-.
MESHORER, Y., *Jewish Coins of the Second Temple Period*, Tel Aviv 1967.
REIFENBERG, A., *Israel's History in Coins*, London 1953.

II THE JEWISH BACKGROUND

ABEL, F.-M., *Histoire de la Palestine*, 2 vols., Paris 1952.
AVI-YONAH, M. (ed.), *A History of the Holy Land*, London 1969.
BARON, S., *A Social and Religious History of the Jews*, vols. I and II, 2nd ed., New York 1952.
BEVAN, E. R., *Jerusalem under the High Priests*, London 1904.
BEVAN, E. R. & SINGER, C. (ed.), *The Legacy of Israel*, Oxford, reprint 1969.
BOX, A. H., *Judaism in the Greek Period*, Oxford 1932.
BRIGHT, J., *A History of Israel*, London 1960.
BUCHLER, A., *Types of Jewish Palestinian Piety from 70 B.C.E. to 70 C.E.*, Oxford 1926, reprint 1969.
DENTON, R. C. (ed.), *The Idea of History in the Ancient Near East*, New Haven 1955.
DIMONT, M. A., *Jews, God and History*, New York 1962.
EPSTEIN, I., *Judaism*, London 1959.
FINKELSTEIN, L., *The Pharisees*, 1939.
FORSTER, W., *Palestinian Judaism in New Testament Times*, Edinburgh 1964.
GASTER, M., *The Samaritans*, London 1925.
GILBERT, M., *Jewish History Atlas*, London 1969.
GRAYZEL, S., *A History of the Jews*, rev. ed., New York 1968.
HENGEL, M., *Die Zeloten*, Leiden 1961.
HENGEL, M., *Judentum und Hellenismus*, Tübingen 1969.

HERFORD, R. T., *The Pharisees*, new ed., Boston 1962.

KLAUSNER, J., *Die Messianische Idee in Israel*, 3rd ed., Tel Aviv 1950.

LEARSI, R., *Israel*, Cleveland 1949, reprint 1966.

MOORE, G. F., *Judaism in the First Centuries of the Christian Era*, 3 vols., Cambridge, Mass. 1927–30.

NEUSNER, J., *The Rabbinic Traditions about the Pharisees before 70 AD.*, 3 vols., Leiden 1971.

New Atlas of the Bible, London 1968.

OLMSTEAD, A. T., *History of Palestine and Syria to the Maccabean Conquest*, New York 1931.

PARKES, J. W., *A History of the Jewish People*, revised ed., London 1964.

PFEIFFER, C. F., *Between the Testaments*, Grand Rapids 1959.

ROTH, C., *A Short History of the Jewish People*, London 1953.

ROWLEY, H. H., *The Faith of Israel*, London 1956.

RUSSELL, D. S., *Between the Testaments*, London 1960.

SCHLATTER, D. A., *Die Geschichte Israels von Alexander dem Grossen bis Hadrian*, 3rd ed., Stuttgart 1926, reprint 1971.

SCHURER, E., *Geschichte des judischen Volkes in Zeitalter Jesu Christi*, 3 vols., Leipzig, 1888–92 (abridged by N. N. Glatzer, *A History of the Jewish Peoples in the Time of Jesus*, New York 1961).

SIMON, M., *Jewish Sects at the Time of Jesus*, Philadelphia 1967.

SMITH, G. A., *The Historical Geography of the Holy Land*, 25th ed., reprint London 1966.

SNAITH, N. N., *The Jews from Cyrus to Herod*, Wallington 1949.

TOYNBEE, A. (ed.), *The Crucible of Christianity* (Chapters 2, 3), London 1969.

ZEITLIN, S., *The Rise and Fall of the Judaean State*, Philadelphia 1962.

III THE RELATIONS OF THE JEWS WITH THE ROMANS AND THE GREEKS*

ASKOWITH, D., *The Toleration and Persecution of the Jews in the Roman Empire under Julius Caesar and Augustus*, New York 1915.

BELL, H. I., *Jews and Christians in Egypt*, London 1924.

BEYER, H. W. & LIETZMANN, H., *Die Judische Katacombe der Villa Torlonia in Rom*, Leipzig 1930.

BICKERMANN, E., *The Maccabees*, New York 1947.

BRECCIA, E., *Juifs et Chrétiens de l'ancienne Alexandrie*, 1927.

DIX, G., *Jew and Greek*, London 1953.

FUCHS, H., *Der geistige Widerstand gegen Rom*, Berlin 1964.

FUCHS, L., *Die Juden Ägyptens in ptolemäischer und römischer Zeit*, Vienna 1924.

* See also the historical works in the last section.

GINSBURG, M. S., *Rome et la Judée*, Paris 1928.

GLOVER, T. R., *The Conflict of Religions in the Early Empire*, London 1920.

GOODENOUGH, E. R., *Jewish Symbols in the Graeco-Roman Period*, 11 vols., New York 1953–64.

GRANT, M., *Herod the Great*, London and New York, 1971.

GUTERMAN, S. L., *Religious Toleration and Persecution in Ancient Rome*, London 1951.

HENGEL, M., *Judentum und Hellenismus*, Tübingen 1969.

HESS, M., *Rom und Jerusalem*, Vienna 1935.

JONES, A. H. M., *The Cities of the Eastern Roman Provinces*, 2nd ed. (revised by M. Avi-Yonah), Oxford 1971.

JONES, A. H. M., *The Herods of Judaea*, revised ed., Oxford 1967.

JUSTER, J., *Les juifs dans l'empire romain*, Paris 1914.

KELLER, W., *Diaspora*, London 1971.

LEON, H. J., *The Jews of Ancient Rome*, Philadelphia 1960.

LIEBERMAN, S., *Hellenism in Jewish Palestine*, New York 1950.

MOMIGLIANO, A., *Ricerche sull' organizzazione della Giudea sotto il dominio romano 63 a. C.-70 d.C.*, Bologna 1934, reprint Amsterdam 1967.

PEROWNE, S., *The Later Herods*, London 1958.

PEROWNE, S., *The Life and Times of Herod the Great*, London 1956.

PIN, B., *Jérusalem contre Rome*, Paris 1938.

POLIAKOV, L., *Histoire de l'antisémitisme*, 2 vols., Paris 1955, 1961.

RADIN, M., *The Jews among the Greeks and Romans*, Philadelphia 1915.

ROSTOVTZEFF, M. I., *A Social and Economic History of the Hellenistic World*, 3 vols., Oxford 1941.

SCHALIT, A., *König Herodes*, Berlin 1969.

SHARF, A., *Byzantine Jewry from Justinian to the Fourth Crusade*, London 1971.

SHERWIN-WHITE, A. N., *Racial Prejudice in Imperial Rome*, Cambridge 1967.

SMALLWOOD, E. M., *The Jews under Roman Rule*, projected.*

STAUFFER, E., *Jerusalem und Rom im Zeitalter Jesu Christi*, Berne 1957.

TARN, W. W. & GRIFFITH, G. T., *Hellenistic Civilisation*, 3rd ed., London 1952, reprint 1966.

TCHERIKOVER, V., *Hellenistic Civilisation and the Jews*, Philadelphia 1966.

WILLRICH, H., *Das Haus des Herodes zwischen Jerusalem und Rom*, Heidelberg 1929.

WILLRICH, H., *Juden und Griechen*, Göttingen 1895.

YADIN, Y., *Bar Kochba*, London 1971.

YADIN, Y., *Masada*, London 1966.

* Dr Smallwood has also contributed numerous very important articles (which will no doubt be listed in her forthcoming book).

BAECK, L., *Paulus, Die Pharisäer und das Neue Testament*, Frankfurt am Main 1961.

BAMMEL, E. (ed.), *The Trial of Jesus*, London 1970.

BEAUJEU, J., *L'incendie de Rome en 64 et les chrétiens*, Brussels 1960.

BIENERT, W. (ed.), *Das Christentum und die Juden*, Cologne 1966.

BLAIKLOCK, E. M., *The Century of the New Testament*, London 1962.

BORNKAMM, G., *Das Ende des Gesetzes: Paulusstudien*, in *Gesammelte Aufsätze*, I, 3rd ed., Munich 1961.

BRANDON, S. G. F., *Jesus and the Zealots*, Manchester 1967.

BRANDON, S. G. F., *The Fall of Jerusalem and the Christian Church*, 2nd ed., London 1957.

BRANDON, S. G. F., *The Trial of Jesus of Nazareth*, London 1968.

BULTMANN, R., *History of the Synoptic Tradition*, New York 1963.

CARMICHAEL, J., *The Death of Jesus*, London 1963.

CHADWICK, H., *The Early Church*, London 1967.

DAVIES, J. G., *The Early Christian Church*, London 1965.

DODD, C. H., *The Meaning of Paul for Today*, revised ed., London 1958.

FINKER, A., *The Pharisees and the Teacher of Nazareth*, Leiden 1964.

FREND, W. H. C., *Martyrdom and Persecution in the Early Church*, Oxford 1965.

GOODSPEED, E. J. & GRANT, R. M., *A History of Early Christian Literature*, Chicago 1966.

GRANT, F. C., *Ancient Judaism and the New Testament*, 2nd ed., Edinburgh and London 1960.

GRANT, R. M., *A Historical Introduction to the New Testament*, London 1963.

HOSKYNS, E. & DAVEY, N., *The Riddle of the New Testament*, London 1958.

ISAAC, J., *L'antisémitisme a-t-il des racines chrétiennes?*, Vienna 1960.

JEREMIAS, J., *Jerusalem in the Time of Jesus*, revised ed., London 1969.

KLAUSNER, J., *From Jesus to Paul*, London 1942.

LOEWE, H., *Render unto Caesar: Religious and Political Loyalty in Palestine*, Cambridge 1940.

MANCINI, I., *Archaeological Discoveries relative to the Judaeo-Christians*, Jerusalem 1970.

MARTINO, C. M., *Il problema storico della Resurrezione negli studi recenti*, Rome 1959.

MILBURN, R. L. P., *Early Christian Interpretations of History*, London 1954.

NOCK, A. D., *Early Gentile Christianity and its Hellenistic Background*, revised ed., New York, 1964.

NOCK, A. D., *St. Paul*, London 1938.

REICKE, B., *The New Testament Era*, London 1969.

ROBERTSON, A., *The Origins of Christianity*, London 1953.

ROBINSON, J. M., *A New Quest of the Historical Jesus*, London 1959.

SCHOEPS, H. J., *Barocke Juden, Christen, Judenchristen*, Berne and Munich 1965

SHERWIN-WHITE, A. N., *Roman Society and Roman Law in the New Testament*, Oxford 1963.

SIMON, M., *Verus Israel. etude sur les relations entre chrétiens et juifs dans l'empire romain 135–425*, Paris 1948.

STYGER, P., *Juden und Christen im alten Rom*, Berlin 1934.

TOYNBEE, A. (ed.), *The Crucible of Christianity*, London 1969.

WALKER, T., *Jewish Views of Jesus*, London 1931.

WILDE, R., *The Treatment of the Jews in the Greek Christian Writers of the first three centuries A.D.*, Ann Arbor 1949.

WINTER, P., *On the Trial of Jesus*, Berlin 1961.

1 THE HASMONAEANS (MACCABEES)

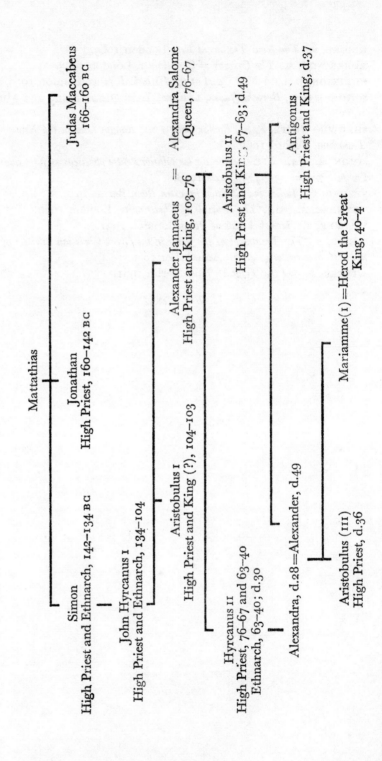

Mattathias

Judas Maccabeus
166–160 BC

Jonathan
High Priest, 160–142 BC

Simon
High Priest and Ethnarch, 142–134 BC

John Hyrcanus I
High Priest and Ethnarch, 134–104

Aristobulus I
High Priest and King (?), 104–103

Alexander Jannaeus = Alexandra Salome
High Priest and King, 103–76   Queen, 76–67

Hyrcanus II
High Priest, 76–67 and 63–40
Ethnarch, 63–40; d.30

Aristobulus II
High Priest and King, 67–63; d.49

Alexandra, d.28=Alexander, d.49

Antigonus
High Priest and King, d.37

Mariamme(I) =Herod the Great
King, 40–4

Aristobulus (III)
High Priest, d.36

2 THE FAMILY OF HEROD THE GREAT

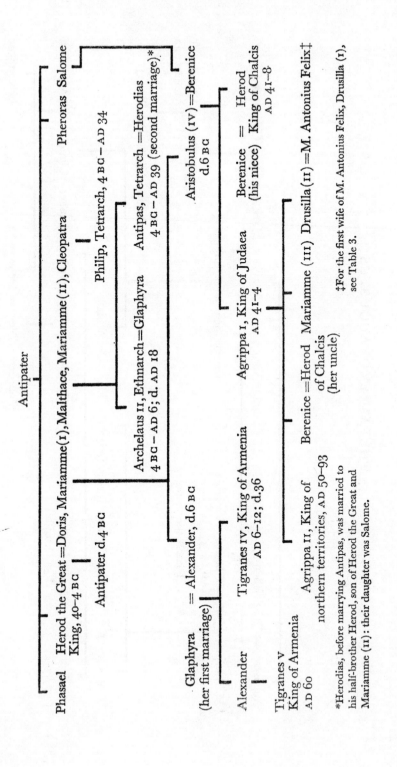

Antipater

Phasael Herod the Great =Doris, Mariamme(I),Malthace, Mariamme(II), Cleopatra Pheroras Salome
King, 40–4 BC

Antipater d.4 BC

Philip, Tetrarch, 4 BC – AD 34

Archelaus II, Ethnarch=Glaphyra   Antipas, Tetrarch =Herodias
4 BC – AD 6; d. AD 18   4 BC – AD 39 (second marriage).*

Aristobulus (IV) =Berenice
d.6 BC

Glaphyra   = Alexander, d.6 BC
(her first marriage)

Tigranes IV, King of Armenia   Agrippa I, King of Judaea   Berenice =Herod   Mariamme (III) =M. Antonius Felix‡
AD 6–12; d.36   AD 41–4   of Chalcis
                                                                    (her uncle)

Berenice = Herod   Drusilla(II) =M. Antonius Felix‡
(his niece)   King of Chalcis
              AD 41–8

Alexander

Tigranes V
King of Armenia
AD 60

Agrippa II, King of
northern territories, AD 50–93

*Herodias, before marrying Antipas, was married to
his half-brother Herod, son of Herod the Great and
Mariamme (II): their daughter was Salome.

‡For the first wife of M. Antonius Felix, Drusilla (I),
see Table 3.

3 THE FAMILY OF AUGUSTUS

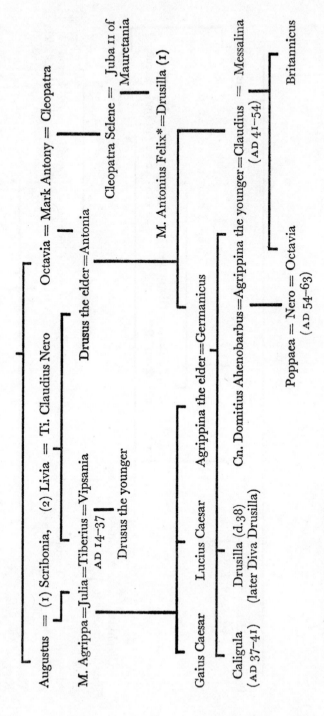

Augustus = (1) Scribonia, (2) Livia = Ti. Claudius Nero

M. Agrippa = Julia = Tiberius = Vipsania
AD 14–37

Drusus the younger

Gaius Caesar   Lucius Caesar

Caligula
(AD 37–41)

Drusilla (d.38)
(later Diva Drusilla)

Octavia = Mark Antony = Cleopatra

Drusus the elder = Antonia

Cleopatra Selene = Juba II of
Mauretania

M. Antonius Felix* = Drusilla (I)

Agrippina the elder = Germanicus

Cn. Domitius Ahenobarbus = Agrippina the younger = Claudius = Messalina
(AD 41–54)

Poppaea = Nero = Octavia
(AD 54–63)

Britannicus

*For the second wife of M. Antonius Felix, Drusilla (II),
see Table 2.

Index

Index*

* The following abbreviations are used for Roman first names (praenomina): A: Aulus. C: Gaius. Cn: Gnaeus. Dec: Decimus. L: Lucius. M: Marcus. P: Publius. Q: Quintus. T: Titus. Ti: Tiberius.